**SPRINGER PUBLISHING**

MW01155100

GET THE MOST FROM YOUR BOOK

SPRINGER PUBLISHING
CONNECT™

VOUCHER CODE:

KTG2DATV

Online Access

Your print purchase of *Foundations of School Counseling* includes **online access via Springer Publishing Connect**™ to increase accessibility, portability, and searchability.

Insert the code at http://connect.springerpub.com/content/book/978-0-8261-8753-6 today!

Having trouble? Contact our customer service department at cs@springerpub.com

Instructor Resource Access for Adopters

Let us do some of the heavy lifting to create an engaging classroom experience with a variety of instructor resources included in most textbooks SUCH AS:

INSTRUCTOR'S MANUAL

POWERPOINTS

TEST BANK

Visit **https://connect.springerpub.com/** and look for the **"Show Supplementary"** button on your **book homepage** to see what is available to instructors! First time using Springer Publishing Connect?

Email **textbook@springerpub.com** to create an account and start unlocking valuable resources.

Foundations of
School Counseling

Cher N. Edwards, PhD, LPCC, is a professor of counselor education and doctoral programs at Seattle Pacific University and currently serves as the director of clinical training. She is a past president of the Washington School Counseling Association, the Ohio Association for Multicultural Counseling and Development, and the founding president of Washington Counselors for Social Justice. She is a recipient of the O'Hana Award for Social Justice Advocacy presented by Counselors for Social Justice, a division of the American Counseling Association.

Mary Amanda Graham, PhD, NCC, LMHCA, ESA, has been in the field of counselor education for 15 years. Her career has spanned two universities. She was at Indiana University of Pennsylvania and is currently at Seattle University. She was promoted to full professor at Seattle University, where she has been a faculty member for 14 years. Dr. Graham is currently the program director of the School Counseling Program in the College of Education at Seattle University. She is a certified school counselor in Washington and has practiced at the K–12 level, as well as internationally. Dr. Graham is also a practicing licensed mental health professional in Washington State with a focus on children and adolescents. Dr. Graham is passionate about school counseling, diversity, equity, and inclusion. She is focused on providing practical applications for school counselors in the field as they emerge as systemic change agents.

Foundations of School Counseling

Innovation in Professional Practice

Cher N. Edwards, PhD, LPCC

Mary Amanda Graham, PhD, NCC, LMHCA, ESA

Editors

SPRINGER PUBLISHING

Springer Publishing Company, LLC
11 West 42nd Street, New York, NY 10036
www.springerpub.com
connect.springerpub.com/

Acquisitions Editor: Rhonda Dearborn
Compositor: S4Carlisle Publishing Services

ISBN: 978-0-8261-8752-9
ebook ISBN: 978-0-8261-8753-6
DOI: 10.1891/9780826187536

SUPPLEMENTS:

A robust set of instructor resources designed to supplement this text is located at http://connect.springerpub.com/content/book/978-0-8261-8753-6. Qualifying instructors may request access by emailing textbook@springerpub.com.

Instructor's Manual: 978-0-8261-8374-3
Test Bank: 978-0-8261-8375-0 (Also available on Respondus®.)
PowerPoints: 978-0-8261-8376-7

22 23 24 25 / 5 4 3 2 1

Library of Congress Cataloging-in-Publication Data is available.

Contact sales@springerpub.com to receive discount rates on bulk purchases.

Publisher's Note: **New and used products purchased from third-party sellers are not guaranteed for quality, authenticity, or access to any included digital components.**

Printed in the United States of America by Gasch Printing.

I dedicate this work to my children and to my parents, who have all taught me in different ways to always strive to make a positive difference in the lives of others, and to my many colleagues and students, who give me hope and confidence in the future of the counseling profession.

—Dr. Cher N. Edwards

I dedicate this work with much appreciation, love, and admiration to my two beautiful children, Hannah and Noah Gauntz, who support all of my endeavors and work.

—Dr. Mary Amanda Graham

Contents

PART II: DIFFERENTIATING ASPIRATIONAL FROM ACTUALITY: THE IMPACT OF THE AMERICAN SCHOOL COUNSELOR ASSOCIATION ON THE SCHOOL COUNSELING PROFESSION

Contributors

LaTraci D. Aldridge, PhD (she/her)   School Counselor, Memphis-Shelby County Schools, Memphis, Tennessee

Jenna M. Alvarez, PhD, LSC, LPC (she/her)   Assistant Professor-Educator and School Counseling Program Coordinator, Department of Human Services, College of Education, Criminal Justice, and Human Services, University of Cincinnati, Cincinnati, Ohio

Kyle L. Bellinger, MEd, LPC (he/him)   Doctoral Candidate, Department of Counseling, Indiana University of Pennsylvania, Indiana, Pennsylvania

Melanie Bikis (she/her)   Master's Candidate, Lewis and Clark College, Portland, Oregon

Hannah Brinser, MEd, LPC, NCC (she/her)   Doctoral Student, Counselor Education, Idaho State University, Pocatello, Idaho; School Counselor, Holy Spirit Catholic School, Pocatello, Idaho

Erika Cameron, PhD (she/her)   Provost and Vice President of Academic Affairs, Palo Alto University, Palo Alto, California

Constance B. Certion, EdD (she/her)   Counseling Services Manager, Memphis-Shelby County Schools, Memphis, Tennessee

Nancy Chae, PhD, LCPC, NCC, NCSC, ACS (she/her)   Assistant Professor, Department of Counseling, Montclair State University, Montclair, New Jersey

Courtney Conachan (she/her)   Master's Candidate, Lewis and Clark College, Portland, Oregon

Janet Contreras-Guevara (she/her)   Graduate Student, College of Education, Seattle University, Seattle, Washington

Calvin C. Craig IV, MA, LSC (he/him)   School Counselor, North Carolina Public Schools, Rolesville, North Carolina

Kimberly J. Desmond, PhD, LPC, NCC (she/her)   Chairperson, Department of Counseling, Indiana University of Pennsylvania, Indiana, Pennsylvania

Stephanie Eberts, PhD, LPC (she/her)   Assistant Professor, Counselor Education Program, Louisiana State University, Baton Rouge, Louisiana

Jacqueline Eddy (she/her)   Doctoral Student, School Psychology; Department of Counselor Education, School Psychology, and Human Services, University of Nevada, Las Vegas, Las Vegas, Nevada

Elizabeth Galvan (she/her)   Graduate Student, College of Education, Seattle University, Seattle, Washington

Lee Nathan Gardner, PhD (he/him) Whitworth University, Spokane, Washington

Eva M. Gibson, EdD (she/her) Assistant Professor, Psychological Science and Counseling, Austin Peavy State University, Clarksville, Tennessee

Arie Greenleaf, PhD (he/him) Professor, School Counseling, Seattle University, Seattle, Washington

Julie Hartline, EdD (she/her) Associate Director of Professional Development, Hatching Results, LLC, Atlantic Beach, Florida

Trish Hatch, PhD (she/her) President and CEO, Hatching Results, LLC, San Diego, California

Shelby Hawkinson (she/they) Master's Candidate, Lewis and Clark College, Portland, Oregon

Nita Hill, MEd (she/her) Elementary Counselor, Puyallup School District, Puyallup, Washington

Laura I. Hodges, PhD, LPC-S (TX)(AL), NCC, ACS (she/her) Associate Professor, Department of Counseling, Rehabilitation and Interpreter Training, Troy University Montgomery, Montgomery, Alabama

Rebecca Hruska (she/her) Graduate Student, Counselor Education, Gonzaga University, Spokane, Washington

Constance Johnson, MS (she/her) School Counselor, Charles County Public Schools, Waldorf, Maryland

Lisa Koenecke, MS, NCC, IICDP, LGBTBE (she/her) Counselor Educator, Lakeland University, Sheboygan, Wisconsin

Lashaun Limbrick, PhD, NCC, NCSC (he/him) Department Chair, Counseling, School Counselor, Desert Pines High School, Las Vegas, Nevada

Sandra Logan-McKibben, PhD, NCC, NCSC, BC-TMH, ACS (she/her) Clinical Assistant Professor and School Counseling Program Director, Isabelle Farrington College of Education & Human Development, Fairfield, Connecticut

Rafe McCullough, PhD (he/him) Associate Professor, Lewis and Clark College, Portland, Oregon

Kathy McDonald, PhD, LPC (OK), NCC (she/her) Associate Professor, Department of Behavioral Sciences, Southeastern Oklahoma State University, Durant, Oklahoma

Stephanie A. McHugh, EdD, NCC (she/her) Vice Provost, Commonwealth Charter Academy, Harrisburg, Pennsylvania

Michelle McMillan (she/they) Master's Candidate, Lewis and Clark College, Portland, Oregon

Taylor Milner (she/her) Doctoral Student, School Psychology; Department of Counselor Education, School Psychology, and Human Services, University of Nevada, Las Vegas, Las Vegas, Nevada

David Moran, PhD (he/him) Assistant Professor, School of Professional Counseling, Lindsey Wilson College, Columbia, Kentucky

Heidi L. Morton, PhD, NCC (she/her) Assistant Professor, School of Education and Department of Psychology, University of Puget Sound, Tacoma, Washington

Lisa Linnea Nelson (she/her) Master's Candidate, Lewis and Clark College, Portland, Oregon

Robert Pincus, PhD, LSC (he/him) Assistant Professor, Department of Counselor Education and Family Studies, Liberty University, Lynchburg, Virginia

Jessica Porter, MEd, LSC (she/her) ELL School Counselor, grades 7–12, Aiken New Tech High School, Cincinnati, Ohio

Lucy L. Purgason, PhD, LSC, ACS, NCC (she/her) Oregon State University–Cascades, Bend, Oregon

Megan Reinikka (she/her) Graduate Student, College of Education, Seattle University, Seattle, Washington

Amanda Rosenfeld, MEd (she/her) School Counselor, Tacoma, Washington

Sam Runckel (he/him) Master's Candidate, Lewis and Clark College, Portland, Oregon

Marsha Rutledge, PhD (she/her) Assistant Professor, Department of Education and Counseling, Longwood University, Farmville, Virginia

Emily Sallee, PhD (she/her) Assistant Professor, Department of Counseling, University of Montana, Missoula, Montana

Jordan Shannon, PhD, NCC (he/him) Assistant Professor, Department of Counselor Education, Seattle Pacific University, Seattle, Washington

Angela I. Sheely-Moore, PhD (she/her) Associate Professor, Department of Counseling, Montclair State University, Montclair, New Jersey

Amy Hayes Siler, MEd (she/her) Doctoral Candidate, Indiana University of Pennsylvania; Counselor, Department of Counseling, Community College of Allegheny County, Pittsburgh, Pennsylvania

Samuel Song, PhD (he/him) Professor, Department of Counselor Education, School Psychology, and Human Services, University of Nevada, Las Vegas, Las Vegas, Nevada

Sam Steen, PhD (he/him) Associate Professor and Academic Program Coordinator, Counseling Program, George Mason University, Fairfax, Virginia

Jennifer Susko, MEd (she/her) Elementary School Counselor, Atlanta Public Schools, Atlanta, Georgia

Adriana M. Wissel, PhD (she/her) Associate Professor, Counselor Education, Gonzaga University, Spokane, Washington

Voices From the Field Participants

Roberto "Aggie" Aguilar (he/him)   Milwaukie High School, Milwaukie, Oregon

Aléx Bassi (they/them)   Jackson Middle School, Portland, Oregon

Kyle L. Bellinger, MEd, LPC (he/him)   Doctoral Candidate, Department of Counseling, Indiana University of Pennsylvania, Indiana, Pennsylvania

Hannah Brinser, MEd, LPC, NCC (she/her)   Doctoral Student, Counselor Education, Idaho State University, Pocatello, Idaho; School Counselor, Holy Spirit Catholic School, Pocatello, Idaho

Constance B. Certion, EdD (she/her)   Counseling Services Manager, Memphis-Shelby County Schools, Memphis, Tennessee

Calvin C. Craig IV, MA, LSC (he/him)   School Counselor, North Carolina Public Schools, Rolesville, North Carolina

Nicole Dock (she/her)   School Counselor, Kent, Washington

Nita Hill, MEd (she/her)   Elementary Counselor, Puyallup School District, Puyallup, Washington

Constance Johnson, MS (she/her)   School Counselor, Charles County Public Schools, Waldorf, Maryland

Lashaun Limbrick, PhD, NCC, NCSC (he/him)   Department Chair, Counseling, School Counselor, Desert Pines High School, Las Vegas, Nevada

Taylor Meyer, MEd (they/them)   High School Counselor, Tacoma School District, Tacoma, Washington

Kaley Mitchell, PhD (she/her)   School Counselor, Everett, Washington

Jessica Porter, MEd, LSC (she/her)   ELL School Counselor grades 7–12, Aiken New Tech High School, Cincinnati, Ohio

Bonnie Robbins (she/her)   School Counselor, Whittier Middle School, Portland, Maine; Adjunct Professor, University of Southern Maine, Portland, Maine

Marwan Stanford (he/him)   School Counselor and Department Chair, Clearwater High School, Clearwater, Florida

Jennifer Susko, MEd (she/her)   Elementary School Counselor, Atlanta Public Schools, Atlanta, Georgia

Alaine Williamson (she/her)   Elementary School Counselor, Baton Rouge, Louisiana

Felipe R. Zañartu (he/him)   California School Counselor, San Diego, California

Foreword

One consistent complaint in school counselor education over the last 25 years has been a persistent gap between theory and practice. While great theoretical advancements and empirical studies are essential to the profession, they are not always based in the realities of contemporary school counselor practice. Similarly, the dismissal or unfamiliarity of data-informed practice threatens efficacy and results in practice that may be at the whim or preference of the practitioner.

This gap is exacerbated by counseling curriculum standards not necessarily tailored to the reality of school counseling and by instruction and supervision by faculty who may have never worked in a school.

I believe this text is responsive to those problems.

Dr. Edwards and Dr. Graham blend important Council for Accreditation of Counseling and Related Educational Programs (CACREP) and American School Counselor Association (ASCA) content, contemporary research, and voices from the field in substantive ways. They have walked the walk—been school counselors—and hence recognize that the school counselor role is complex, diverse, and appropriately responsive to both research findings and school culture/context.

The authors make cultural context and social justice a core part of the text, not an afterthought or a disconnected agenda. Not only is cultural competence one of the eight core areas of identity for counselors (e.g., CACREP curricular standards), it also is ubiquitous and part of the fabric of school counseling. Both authors have walked the walk here, too—leading organizations and trainings around social justice and diversity.

All the key notes are hit in this text. The ASCA National Model delivers the framework (who we are), while extensive information about interventions and direct service (what we do) enhances school counselor readiness. What we do also is provided in an extensive resource depository. This foundational knowledge is enhanced with writing that speaks to the passion that brings many into the profession—social justice. Rather than a political briefing on the topic, the authors cite specific examples in the field to illustrate the critical need and what school counselors can do to make a difference. Finally, although positively utilitarian and helpful, the text does not leave out indirect services and broader school counselor challenges that will emerge.

The content is contemporary practice and transformative.

Patrick Akos, PhD
Professor
University of Tennessee

Preface

WHY WE WROTE THIS BOOK

As coeditors, we have a combined total of over 40 years of experience as school counselor educators. During our time training school counselors at various institutions, graduates often share that they experienced a gap between what was taught in their program and their reality as practicing school counselors. Students have reported that they struggle to understand the application of standards, policies, and interventions and desire to see a strong connection between theory and practice.

In response, we have sought to create a text that honors the voices of academics, practitioners, and, usually missing from training, the voices of the K–12 students who we seek to serve. Counselor educators contribute a data-driven foundation that includes years of experience in the field and research related to best practices. Current school counselors speak to how the work of school counselors often looks and feels in practice. K–12 students share how the interventions of school counselors have impacted their lives.

In addition to ensuring intentionality with the voices present in this text, we focused on inclusion of issues that we feel are important to the profession. You'll notice an entire chapter on LGBTQIA+ issues—a group that is often assigned a few pages within a chapter focused on diversity in schools. Additionally, we have ensured that issues related to culturally relevant school counseling interventions and social justice advocacy are not only a stand-alone chapter of import but also woven in a very present way throughout each chapter of the text. Current issues that have impacted the field of education, such as antiracism and virtual counseling, are present in this text to acknowledge issues that have impacted and will continue to impact our work as school counselors.

FEATURES AND BENEFITS

We've included features in this text to provide exceptional support to faculty and students. Chapters include case studies and discussion questions to prompt students to apply covered content. The practical application portion of each text will allow the instructors to provide guidance for future practicum and internship students regarding how to apply what they have learned. The supplemental instructor's materials include an Instructor's Manual and PowerPoints, which can be used as is or edited to include additional content per faculty discretion, and a Test Bank that includes multiple choice, true or false, and short answer questions and may be used for formative or evaluative purposes. Links to online resources to augment chapter content are included in the manual to allow students to begin building a toolbox of useful resources available for use within the program and as new professionals. All materials are intended to save time and energy for course instructors!

As researchers and counselors, we are passionate about school counseling, diversity, equity, inclusion, and systemic change. We recognized the need for a comprehensive school counseling text that addresses the theories that inform the work of school counselors as well as the need for concrete and tangible guidance that can be readily applied in practice. We wanted to honor the voices of traditionally unrecognized authors in the text to include a large representation of women, BIPOC community members, and those who identify within the LGBQIA+ community, as well as K–12 students.

HOW THE BOOK IS ORGANIZED

The text is organized into five sections. The first section serves as an introduction to the school counseling profession. Based on our belief system that school counselors have an ethical and professional responsibility to serve as social justice advocates, antiracists, and equity agents for student success, our text begins in a way that is different from most. The first chapter addresses issues related to culturally relevant school counseling interventions and a call for school counselors to be agents of change. We chose this as our first chapter to give context for the social justice and multicultural focus within each chapter. Chapters addressing strengths-based practice and the history and future trends of the profession round out the first section of this text.

Part II of the text addresses the hot topic of differentiating aspirational practice from what school counselors report as the reality of their work in schools. This chapter acknowledges the importance of ongoing advocacy for American School Counselor Association (ASCA) guidelines related to best practice recommendations, a focus on prevention, and lower caseloads, while at the same time recognizing that the ASCA National Model that most programs use to train future school counselors does not always equate to the experience of recent graduates. For example, we are taught that there are inappropriate duties identified by ASCA—what school counselors should *not* be doing in the schools, and then—you guessed it—we're presented with "other duties as assigned" in our employment contracts. We believe that we need to better prepare students for the current environment of K–12 schools while arming them with the skills required to advocate for change and better alignment with the ASCA model. This section addresses the *ASCA National Model*, *Mindsets & Behaviors*, and *Data-Driven Services*.

Part III of the text addresses the nuts and bolts of school counseling interventions—the basics of school counseling direct services, including individual, group, classroom guidance, and crisis intervention. These chapters are intended to provide students with a solid foundation related to how these services look in the schools, how they differ from community mental health practice, and how they can be used to—you guessed it—advocate for systemic change and support all students' success through equity and inclusion.

Part IV moves the discussion from practice to an awareness of power and privilege as we call on our future colleagues (that's what students are!) to use their positions to be leaders for student success. This section includes chapters focused on creating safer schools for LGBTQIA+ students and engaging students with Individualized Education Plans (IEPs) and 504s, as well as the impact of families and the home environment on student success and mandated reporting.

The last section of the text focuses on a key component of effective school counseling—collaboration. Chapters provide best practice recommendations for family engagement, collaborating with school staff, building a comprehensive school counseling program (CSCP), and online delivery of school counseling interventions.

Each chapter begins with a K–12 student testimony to engage the reader to better understand how the chapter topic impacts the lives of the students that we serve. This section is followed by an introduction and chapter content. It concludes with a section from a practicing school counselor who shares their experience and recommendations related to how to apply the chapter content into practice, followed by a case study that serves to launch a discussion to encourage course engagement and application.

We hope you find this text to be a useful resource and a guide that will serve students well as they enter their training program, complete their practicum and internship training, and graduate to become our colleagues. We wish you the very best on this journey!

Cher N. Edwards, PhD, LPCC
Mary Amanda Graham, PhD, NCC, LMHCA, ESA

 A robust set of instructor resources designed to supplement this text is located at http://connect.springerpub.com/content/book/978-0-8261-8753-6. Qualifying instructors may request access by emailing textbook@springerpub.com.

Acknowledgments

We would like to acknowledge the many colleagues who have mentored us and continue to walk alongside us on the journey of preparing others for a profession that we love, our students who teach us through their diverse experiences and perspectives, and the many supportive individuals at Springer Publishing who advocated for and supported this text.

Instructor Resources

 A robust set of instructor resources designed to supplement this text is located at http://connect.springerpub.com/content/book/978-0-8261-8753-6. Qualifying instructors may request access by emailing textbook@springerpub.com.

Available resources include:

- Instructor's Manual
- Test Bank
- Chapter-Based PowerPoint Presentations

PART I

Introduction and Foundation of Professional School Counseling

CHAPTER 1

School Counselors as Antiracist and Social Justice Advocates

MARSHA RUTLEDGE, ERIKA CAMERON, AND JENNIFER SUSKO

LEARNING OBJECTIVES

After reading this chapter, students will be able to:

- Explain the history of anti-racism in educational settings.
- Evaluate the impact racism has on Black children's academic, personal/social, and career success.
- Create and understand the role of school counselors in leading and working from an antiracist framework.
- Apply responsibilities and actions of school counselors to address racism and bias in schools.

STUDENT VOICE

Student "S" provided the following testimonial about their experience with a school counselor:

"Things have definitely shifted over the past year. As a Black student in a predominantly White, rural environment a lot of things have changed. The way we view and interact with each other, the way we joke and play, and even how our parents allow us to socialize outside of school, all due to political or racial differences. I have not seen many acts of blatant racism at my school, but this year a White, hybrid student brought a Black doll with a noose around its head to school and carried it around the halls. This student faced little to no consequences, and I have even seen him roaming the halls a few times since I went back to school. This made racism more real for me, as I had never seen it firsthand."

INTRODUCTION: HISTORY OF ANTI-BLACK RACISM IN EDUCATIONAL SETTINGS

The educational system that exists today has a long and rich history regarding the education of Black students. Many historians, researchers, and Black individuals would say that the system was built on a racist foundation. It is a system not designed to see Black children succeed. Subsequently, Black children have been met with various challenges throughout their educational lives, resulting in negative consequences and outcomes that continue to permeate their way of life and how they are viewed in society today. The obstacles found in education are a direct result of racism and have brought about racialized trauma for many students and families. However, despite the challenges, Black children have survived the racial trauma generated by opportunity gaps. Educators who work specifically with this demographic must be aware of the historical context of the effects that racism has had on Black students' performance (National Child Traumatic Stress Network, Justice Consortium, Schools Committee, and Culture Consortium, 2017). According to Bettina Love, author of *We Want to Do More Than Survive*, "Education is one of the primary tools used to maintain White supremacy and anti-immigrant hate. Teachers entering the field of education must know this history, acknowledge this history, and understand why it matters in the present-day context of education, White rage, and dark suffering" (2019, p. 23). This quote, although intended for teachers, applies to school counselors as well. To effectively work with Black students, school counselors must be critically conscious and have cultural humility (Francis & Mason, 2022) as well as be culturally competent, sustaining, and responsive (Grothaus et al., 2020; Holcomb-McCoy, 2022). *Cultural competence* is defined as having the awareness, knowledge, and skills to work with diverse populations effectively (Matthews et al., 2018; Sue et al., 2019; Tummala-Narra et al., 2017). The American School Counselor Association ([ASCA], 2016) suggests that cultural competence is an ethical responsibility of school counselors (ASCA, 2016, B.3.i). Cultural competence is displayed by implementing culturally responsive school counseling programs. The ASCA's position on cultural diversity is that "school counselors demonstrate cultural responsiveness by collaborating with stakeholders to create a school and community climate that embraces cultural diversity and helps to promote academic, career, and social/emotional success for all students" (ASCA, 2015, para. 1). School counselors may lack cultural responsiveness due to their own biases and prejudices (West-Olatunji et al., 2011). Self-awareness is an imperative foundation of the multicultural and social justice framework used by counselors when working with diverse clients. To begin to do the work of dismantling systemic racism within their schools, school counselors must first understand the historical context of racism in education and then explore thoughts and emotions that surface surrounding that knowledge. Understanding the historical context allows blame to be placed on the system for education-related barriers rather than on the students, which has been a recurring issue. School counselors are tasked with identifying and addressing barriers that consistently perpetuate racial divides and hinder student success (Hines et al., 2020; Leibowitz-Nelson et al., 2020). Cultural competence is a minimum requirement for ethical school counseling as school counselors should also work toward becoming antiracist. Antiracist school counseling occurs when school counselors go beyond identifying barriers facing marginalized students to working to eradicate racist systems (ASCA, 2021a; Holcomb-McCoy, 2022; Stickl Haugen et al., 2021). School counselors are ethically obligated as antiracists to serve all students. This chapter discusses the impact of the Black Lives Matter (BLM) movement on school counseling as it pertains to Black students. School counselors must have the ability to use transferable skills when working with other marginalized populations as these concepts and strategies pertain to all students from all marginalized communities.

Historical Racism

Systemic racism in education can be traced back to the 1800s when segregation maintained separate educational experiences based on skin color. This separation extended beyond the classroom, to communities religious institutions, places of employment, and throughout society. Separation was enforced through policies, procedures, and laws (e.g., *Plessy v. Ferguson*, 1986) that maintained a "separate but equal" doctrine of racial segregation. This landmark case (*Plessy v. Ferguson*, 1986) permitted states to segregate based on race, including, but not limited to, restaurants, water fountains, transportation, and schools. Although the separate but equal doctrine (e.g., *Plessy v. Ferguson*, 1986) focused on transportation, it ultimately ended up creating an educational system of segregated schools where Black students were forced into education systems that lacked sufficient facilities and resources. Despite the legal intentions of equality, these facilities desperately failed (Figure 1.1). According to Love (2019, p. 28), separate but equal was a "tactic to maintain White superiority."

Brown v. Board of Education

In 1954, *Brown v. Board of Education* overturned the separate but equal doctrine. The Supreme Court ruled that this precept was unconstitutional and the Court legally required schools' integration. There were many benefits to this legislation; perhaps the most notable is the potential for Black students to gain access to resources and improved education (American Psychological Association [APA], 2012; McNeill & Rowley, 2019). The results of this case were thought to improve educational opportunities for Black students; however, many note the consequences of integration.

Although *Brown v. Board of Education* was intended to better educational outcomes for Black students, many would argue that the results were not as positive as initially thought. Love shares that "Black schools were proud institutions that provided Black communities with cohesion and leadership" (2019, p. 28). After the *Brown v. Board of Education* ruling, there was ambiguity in interpreting the legislation and enacting it, thus allowing school districts to delay integration (McNeill & Rowley, 2019). Many systems refused to integrate or made it extremely difficult for Black students to enroll and attend. The most familiar stories are those of The Little Rock Nine and Ruby Bridges. In Little Rock, Arkansas in 1957, nine Black students were denied entrance to Central High School. Their admittance into the building required the assistance of over 1,000 army troops. Despite the federal aid, they were still met with routine verbal and physical abuse.

FIGURE 1.1 Separate but not equal.

Source: 1904 caricature of White"and Jim Crow rail cars by John T. McCutcheon. (Image: John T. McCutcheon/Public domain.)

In 1960, 5 years after *Brown v. Board*, New Orleans, Louisiana, began its desegregation plan, which was met with significant opposition and attempts to thwart efforts. For example, the state required an entrance exam for admission to the state's historically White institutions. Due to the lack of preparation provided to Black students, only six Black children passed, one being Ruby Bridges. At 6 years old, Bridges was the first Black student to integrate into a White elementary school. Due to the violent protesters, she was escorted to school by U.S. Marshalls and was met with racial slurs, derogatory chants, and more (Michals, 2015). White parents unenrolled their students and White teachers refused to teach in protest of the integration law. As a result, for the entire school year, Ruby sat in a classroom by herself with one teacher from Massachusetts who agreed to be her instructor.

Another consequence of desegregation was the treatment of Black students in integrated schools. As schools merged, Black teachers were not accepted into the White schools, resulting in Black students being taught by mostly White faculty. In turn, there was a decline in the number of qualified Black educators. Some Black community members believe that there would not have been a push to integrate if there had been equality within the segregated systems. However, in an attempt to push back on integration, segregation and inequities continued in what is known as "White flight," which resulted in unequal learning institutions that continue today (Love, 2019; McNeill & Rowley, 2019). Despite the movement toward the progress of fully integrated schools and better educational opportunities for Black students, responses such as White flight confirm that racism still exists and permeates educational institutions. Whether overt or covert, authors term it as *new racism* (Kohli et al., 2017).

Racism Today

Racism and bias can harm and impede students from reaching their full potential (Gershenson & Papageorge, 2018; Leath et al., 2019; Trent et al., 2019). *New racism* is defined as the replacement of "overt and blatant discriminatory policies and practices of the past with covert and more subtle beliefs and behaviors, reflecting the persistent and pervasive nature of racism" (Kohli et al., 2017, pp. 184–185). The American Academy of Pediatrics ([AAP], 2019) has reported that racism has been associated with birth disparities (mortality rate and birth weight) and mental health issues in youth. Exposure to stress hormones as a result of chronic stress due to racism results in inflammatory reactions leading to chronic disease (Trent et al., 2019). Additionally, the impact of racism and bias in PK–12 education is associated with (a) gaps in achievement, opportunity, and attainment; (b) disproportionate rates of discipline and suspension for students of color; (c) lower attendance rates; (d) self-destructive behavior such as acting out, withdrawal, and nonparticipation in class activities; (e) gatekeeping of underrepresented students for access to and placement in rigorous curricula such as Advanced Placement and International Baccalaureate; and (f) lower participation of underrepresented groups in higher education (ASCA, 2020). The National Center for Education Statistics (NCES) report, *Condition of Education 2020*, confirms that systemic racism is seen through various school policies, procedures, and initiatives that have negatively impacted Black students. Biased educators, whitewashed curriculum, and programmatic representation failures (e.g., overrepresentation in special education services and underrepresentation in gifted programs) point to the struggle of Black students in public education (Hussar et al., 2020). Additionally, Cai (2020) offered the following highlights from a report by the National School Boards Association:

- The poverty rate is still the highest for Black students.
- A lack of internet access at home has become a barrier to learning or Black students.
- A high percentage of Black students attend high-poverty schools.
- More Black students with disabilities receive services for emotional disturbances.

- The disproportion between Black students and Black teachers has not improved.
- The achievement gap between Black and White students has not been closed.
- School dropout rate remains high among Black students.
- Graduation rates and college enrollment rates remain low for Black students.

ACHIEVEMENT AND OPPORTUNITY GAPS

One concept that focuses on systemic racism is the achievement/opportunity gaps between White students and students of color. Achievement gaps are educational disparities identified between racial and ethnic minorities and their White peers. Many social and justice advocates prefer the term *opportunity gaps* as it better captures the reasons behind the disparity (Hall Mark, 2013). Achievement gaps imply that there is something inherently wrong with the student, whereas opportunity gaps put the onus on the system that results in the disparity (Pitre, 2014). Opportunity gaps reflect the barriers that Black, indigenous, and people of color (BIPOC) students encounter, resulting in a lack of opportunities (Flores, 2018; Wiener, 2007). As stated by The Glossary of Education Reform, the conceptualization of achievement versus opportunity is that *"opportunity gap* refers to inputs—the unequal or inequitable distribution of resources and opportunities—whereas *achievement gap* refers to outputs—the unequal or inequitable distribution of educational results and benefits"' (Great Schools Partnership, n.d.).

Underrepresentation

As of the 2017–2018 data, reported by the Office for Civil Rights (OCR), there remain stark differences in advanced academic programs between BIPOC and White students (U.S. Department of Education [U.S. DOE], n.d.). Table 1.1 compares data related to advanced placement, gifted identification, International Baccalaureate programs, and advanced math placements (Table 1.1).

Standardized Testing

Standardized testing has long been viewed as biased against BIPOC students and further perpetuates an academic, college, and career readiness divide, resulting in social and economic consequences. According to the National Education Association "standardized tests have been instruments of racism and a biased system" (Rosales & Walker, 2021, para. 4) by compromising equity efforts and educational quality (National Center for Fair and Open Testing, n.d.).

One well-known test, the Scholastic Aptitude Test (SAT), has been the center of significant controversy regarding not only accessibility to testing but also inaccurate assessment of BIPOC students' college readiness. The College Board in 2019 reported that of the high school graduates who took the current SAT during high school, 12% of that population was Black, as opposed to 43% White, with 20% of the Black students and

TABLE 1.1 Underrepresentation by Race/Ethnicity

RACE/ETHNICITY	ADVANCED PLACEMENT	GIFTED	INTERNATIONAL BACCALAUREATE	ADVANCED MATH
Black	9.3%	8.2%	14.4%	13.3%
White	52.4%	58.4%	43.7%	52.9%

Source: U.S. Department of Education, Office for Civil Rights, Civil Rights Data Collection, 2017–18. http://ocrdata.ed.gov.

57% of White students meeting both English and math benchmarks. According to several studies, evidence supports the lack of validity of using these scores for college admission decisions for Black students (Freedle, 2003; Santelices & Wilson, 2010).

Lack of Access

There remain heavily racial/ethnic minority–populated schools in the educational system for which the evidence supports the challenges such as lack of "highly qualified" diverse educators, lack of representation of BIPOC educators, lack of resources, and lack of culturally responsive curriculum. The teacher shortage is a genuine concern in PK–12, primarily for high-poverty schools that typically have a higher concentration of BIPOC students. According to The Condition of Education 2020 (Hussar et al., 2020), in 2017–2018, only 7% of public-school teachers and 11% of public-school principals were Black. Yet, more than 15% of Black students attended public schools. In 2019, the Economic Policy Institute reported the difference in teacher qualifications in low-poverty versus high-poverty schools and found that teachers in high-poverty schools had fewer certifications, less experience, and less comprehensive education as compared to low-poverty schools (García & Weiss, 2019). Unfortunately, 45% of Black students attended high-poverty schools, compared with 8% of White students (Hussar et al., 2020). Although these statistics, along with the increasing teacher shortage, are cause for concern, the definition of *highly qualified* is not as alarming as it may seem. Cultural competency has become an integral part of the educational curriculum taught to preservice teachers and counselors. Therefore, you may find that students graduating may have more exposure to and knowledge about working with diverse student bodies. If so, the concern isn't necessarily the lack of "highly qualified," but rather the lack of diverse teachers overall. The barrier for new educators is the experience within their first few years of teaching and the burnout that results. These teachers often find themselves in underfunded and underperforming schools with the pressure of high expectations in terms of student outcomes. Often teachers of color may have entered the teaching profession through alternate routes and, according to the U.S. Department of Education, find themselves working in poorer districts with higher numbers of students of color (U.S. Department of Education [U.S. DOE], 2016).

In addition to the lack of diverse teachers, you also find a shortage of diverse school counselors. According to data from 2019, of the degrees awarded in School Counseling and Guidance Services, 57.5% were awarded to White graduates as compared to 16.7% to Hispanic graduates and 12.6% to Black graduates. The counseling profession overall continues to be dominated by a White female presence with stark differences in racial-ethnic employment rates (DATA USA, n.d.).

An additional concern is not only the lack of counselors but also the limited access to school counselors (American Civil Liberties Union [ACLU], n.d.; National Office for School Counselor Advocacy, 2012; The Education Trust [Ed Trust], 2019). Although there is a critical shortage of mental health professionals in schools, data indicate that the deficiency increases for heavily minority-populated and low-poverty schools. Data collected by organizations, such as the ASCA, Reachhigher, and The Education Trust confirm the high ratios between school counselors and students. Across the nation, there are at least 38 states where BIPOC students have less access to school counselors and counseling services (Ed Trust, 2019). Comprehensive school counseling programs have benefited students by improving attendance, decreasing disciplinary incidents, and increasing graduation rates. However, lowering ratios is currently an advocacy initiative for ASCA and many state school counseling associations.

Lastly, and maybe most importantly, racist views and beliefs from educators expected to serve *all* children contribute to the disparity in achievement (APA, 2012). There are numerous accounts of racist acts against BIPOC children. These instances highlight the negative consequences that impact the ability of BIPOC students to be successful in the classroom. When students are already faced with other existing barriers, teacher perception, engagement, and strategies compound those effects. This results in students becoming disengaged, developing a dislike for schools, demonstrating a lack of academic progress, and exhibiting behavioral issues (Leath et al., 2019).

Overrepresentation

Impacted by self-segregated or forced segregated school communities, failed *Brown vs. Board of Education* integration initiatives, and systemic racism, BIPOC students are underrepresented academically in advanced level courses and gifted identification and overrepresented in areas such as special education (Farkas, 2020; Gentry et al., 2019; Grindal et al., 2019; Morgan, 2020; National Association for Gifted Children, n.d.). This is an excerpt from the Committee on Minority Representation in Special Education et al. (2002),

> Schooling independently contributes to the incidence of special needs or giftedness among students in different racial/ethnic groups through the opportunities it provides. Schools with higher concentrations of low-income, minority children are less likely to have experienced, well-trained teachers. (p. 4)

As a result, you find that BIPOC students, specifically, are stereotypically labeled with disabilities, which may impact future academic and career opportunities. Research suggests that in school systems where there are predominately White teachers and students, the majority of Black students are in special education (Ladner & Hammons, 2001). According to the *42nd Annual Report to Congress*, which was published in 2021, approximately 12.4% of the Black population was serviced under the Individuals with Disabilities Act (IDEA) versus 8% of the White population (U.S. DOE, 2021b).

Overrepresentation is also evident as related to disciplinary actions and school suspensions. Many studies highlight the disproportionate use of harsher disciplinary procedures for BIPOC students. For example, OCR reported that "in 2017–18, Black students received one or more in-school suspensions (31.4%) and one or more out-of-school suspensions (38.2%) at rates that were more than twice their share of total student enrollment (15.1%)" (U.S. DOEDOE, 2021a, p. 16). Suspensions impact attendance and class time, depriving students of valuable learning opportunities. According to OCR data, Black students lost 103 days per 100 students enrolled, 82 more days than the 21 days their White peers lost due to out-of-school suspensions, perpetuating the negative cycle resulting from systemic racism (Losen & Martinez, 2020). Therefore, educators should consider and address the trauma that results from historical and current racist school environments.

RACIALIZED TRAUMA

Racial trauma is the mental and emotional impact of racism (Mental Health America, n.d.; Williams et al., 2019). Black students face racism both in society and in the educational system. The consequences are salient, impacting self-concept, health and well-being, and life trajectories (Svetaz et al., 2018). In schools, racism is evident in physical violence, constant alienation, discrimination, and microaggressions (Henderson & Lunsford, 2016). Research acknowledges a link between racism and posttraumatic stress symptoms and suggests that racial trauma leads to cognitive, emotional, and behavioral challenges that negatively impact academic performance (Comas-Díaz et al., 2019; Jernigan-Noesi & Peeples, 2019). Exhibit 1.1 highlights inadequate responses to trauma that educators should recognize. As a result of systemic racism, these responses help feed what is called the school-to-prison pipeline.

EXHIBIT 1.1 Responses to Trauma

- **Increase aggression**—Street gangs, domestic violence, defiant behavior, and appearing tough and impenetrable are ways of coping with danger by attempting to control our physical and social environment
- **Increase vigilance and suspicion**—Suspicion of social institutions (schools, agencies, government), avoiding eye contact, only trusting persons within our social and family relationship networks
- **Increase sensitivity to threat**—Defensive postures, avoiding new situations, heightened sensitivity to being disrespected and shamed, and avoid taking risks
- **Increase psychological and physiological symptoms**—Unresolved traumas increase chronic stress and decrease immune system functioning, shift brains to limbic system dominance, increase risks for depression and anxiety disorders, and disrupt child development and quality of emotional attachment in family and social relationships
- **Increase alcohol and drug usage**—Drugs and alcohol are initially useful (real and perceived) in managing the pain and danger of unresolved traumas but become their own disease processes when dependency occurs
- **Narrowing sense of time**—Persons living in a chronic state of danger do not develop a sense of future, do not have long-term goals, and frequently view dying as an expected outcome

Source: Smith, W. H. (2010). *The impact of racial trauma on African Americans* (p. 5). African American Men and Boys Advisory Board. The Heinz Endowments. https://www.heinz.org/userfiles/impactofracialtraumaonafricanamericans.pdf. Reprinted with permission.

School-to-Prison Pipeline

The school-to-prison pipeline is the process by which students are pushed out of educational systems into the correctional system (ACLU, n.d.; Elias, 2013; Heitzeg, 2009). This process results from disciplinary policies and procedures used in school systems that connect students to law enforcement officials at an early age. Zero-tolerance policies and the use of police officers in schools have exacerbated this issue for BIPOC students (Dutil, 2020). These policies are harsh punishments used for any infraction, regardless of severity. With a police presence in schools, offenses that were historically dealt with inside the school are now referred to law enforcement, which begins the criminalization of youth. It is estimated that as of 2015–2016, over 1.7 million students were found to be in schools with law enforcement presence but without school counselors (Whitaker et al., 2019). Federal data confirms the negative impact that these procedures have on Black students. According to data collected by the U.S. DOE 2015–2016 Civil Rights Data Collection (CRDC), "Black students had an arrest rate of 28 per 10,000, which was three times that of White students" (Whitaker et al., 2019, p. 24). These arrests support the increased incarceration rate of BIPOC youth. School divisions have chosen more punitive measures rather than supportive measures that could be implemented through school counseling professionals (Welfare et al., 2021).

BLACK LIVES MATTER MOVEMENT

In response to tense political climates, police murders of Black citizens, and other incidents of racial tension, the Black community rallied together in support of many advocacy efforts to improve outcomes for Black people. One such effort was the Black Lives Matter (BLM) movement. The BLM movement was started by Alicia Garza, Patrisse Cullors, and Opal Tometi in 2013 in response to the acquittal of George Zimmerman, the individual tried for the murder of Trayvon Martin, a young Black male in Florida. Initially, the hashtag #BlackLivesMatter was a platform used to bring awareness to racism across the country (blacklivesmatter.com, n.d.). It has later become a worldwide movement with many BLM chapters in various localities across the United States.

Black Lives Matter at School is a supportive presence in the educational world. Although the Black Lives Matter and Black Lives Matter at School organizations are not affiliatedr, they both work toward the common goal of supporting the Black community. According to organizers, "The Black Lives Matter at School Movement is the story of resistance to racist curriculums, educational practices, and policies" (Jones & Hagopian, 2020, p. 1). It is a national coalition organizing for racial justice in education. The movement began in 2016 in Seattle with a single protest at John Muir Elementary School, which included faculty wearing BLM t-shirts. This statement was met with resistance from White supremacists in the form of a bomb threat. This one day of action and the response fueled further events that turned into a week of reaction and now a national movement (Jones & Hagopian, 2020).

The first week of February became the Black Lives Matter at School Week (Jones & Hagopian, 2020), which is a week of action dedicated to advocating for the following goals:

- End zero-tolerance discipline in school, and implement restorative justice.
- Hire more Black teachers.
- Mandate Black history and ethnic studies in PK–12 curriculum.
- Fund counselors not police officers.

This week is promoted with classroom lessons, community events, and organized rallies that support schools' engagement in "critical reflection, honest conversation, and impactful action" (NEA, 2022, para. 1) regarding the education of Black students. Black Lives Matter at School, similar to the BLM movement, has been catapulted in its recognition and efforts due to continuous adult and child murders at the hands of law enforcement. Consequently, you have "#sayhername" and "#saytheirnames" social media campaigns that recognize and raise awareness of these Black victims. Movements such as BLM and Black Lives Matter at School are intentional about identifying, honoring, and speaking the names of the Black victims so that the reason behind the advocacy efforts is not lost. The educational system is not exempt from the racial tension behind these movements. Black Lives Matter at School "incites new urgency and radical possibilities for advancing abolitionist practice and uprooting institutional racism" (blacklivesmatteratschool.com).

As a part of the week of action, teachers are provided with a free curriculum that includes various lessons that they can use in their classrooms. According to the organization, these resources are provided at no cost, and sharing is encouraged. The resources are used to "challenge racism and oppression and provide students with the vocabulary and tools needed to take action" (Black Lives Matter At School, n.d.). Lesson topics include intersectional Black identities, institutional racism, African diasporic histories and philosophies, and contributions and struggles of Black people to the nation and the world. Exhibit 1.2 includes the 13 guiding principles used as teaching points during the week.

Despite the goals of social justice advocacy and antiracism, the Black Lives Matter at School movement has been met with significant criticism and opposition. A quick search of BLM at schools provides numerous examples of administrators, college professors, and parents who criticize the effort, citing that it causes "fear and anger" in students. Districts such as Washoe County School District banned BLM topics from classrooms,

EXHIBIT 1.2 Thirteen Guiding Principles

1. **Restorative Justice**
We are committed to collectively, lovingly, and courageously working vigorously for freedom and justice for Black people and, by extension, all people. As we forge our path, we intentionally build and nurture a beloved community that is bonded together through a beautiful struggle that is restorative, not depleting.

2. **Empathy**
We are committed to practicing empathy; we engage comrades with the intent to learn about and connect with their contexts.

3. **Loving Engagement**
We are committed to embodying and practicing justice, liberation, and peace in our engagements with one another.

4. **Diversity**
We are committed to acknowledging, respecting, and celebrating difference(s) and commonalities.

5. **Globalism**
We see ourselves as part of the global Black family, and we are aware of the different ways we are impacted or privileged as Black folk who exist in different parts of the world.

6. **Queer Affirming**
We are committed to fostering a queer-affirming network. When we gather, we do so with the intention of freeing ourselves from the tight grip of heteronormative thinking or, rather, the belief that all in the world are heterosexual unless s/he or they disclose otherwise.

7. **Trans Affirming**
We are committed to embracing and making space for trans siblings to participate and lead. We are committed to being self-reflexive and doing the work required to dismantle cis-gender privilege and uplift Black trans folk, especially Black trans women who continue to be disproportionately impacted by trans-antagonistic violence.

8. **Collective Value**
We are guided by the fact all Black lives matter, regardless of actual or perceived sexual identity, gender identity, gender expression, economic status, ability, disability, religious beliefs or disbeliefs, immigration status or location.

9. **Intergenerational**
We are committed to fostering an intergenerational and communal network free from ageism. We believe that all people, regardless of age, show up with capacity to lead and learn.

10. **Black Families**
We are committed to making our spaces family friendly and enable parents to fully participate with their children. We are committed to dismantling the patriarchal practice that requires mothers to work "double shifts" that require them to mother in private even as they participate in justice work.

11. **Black Villages**
We are committed to disrupting the Western-prescribed nuclear family structure requirement by supporting each other as extended families and "villages" that collectively care for one another, and especially "our" children to the degree that mothers, parents and children are comfortable.

(continued)

EXHIBIT 1.2 Thirteen Guiding Principles (*continued*)

12. **Unapologetically Black**

    We are unapologetically Black in our positioning. In affirming that Black Lives Matter, we need not qualify our position. To love and desire freedom and justice for ourselves is a necessary prerequisite for wanting the same for others.

13. **Black Women**

    We are committed to building a Black women affirming space free from sexism, misogyny, and male-centeredness.

Source: Jones, D., & Hagopian, J. (2020). *Black lives matter at school: An uprising for education justice* (pp. 12 and 13). Haymarket Books. Reprinted with permission.

insisting that the issues were political and improper for school. However, organizers continue to advocate for an educational system where antiracist pedagogy is evident and systemic racism is eradicated. Yet, the question remains, "Will Black lives ever truly matter in the education system?" Hagopian, coauthor of Black Lives Matter at School: *An Uprising for Educational Justice*, answers with "whether we will someday see a school system worthy of Black students lies in the hearts of educators, students, parents, and antiracist organizers everywhere who tire of inequality and rise up to strike the blow for freedom" (p. 24).

ROLE OF THE SCHOOL COUNSELOR IN ANTIRACISM WORK

The ASCA in its Antiracist Practices Position Statement suggests that school counselors should be culturally competent, antiracist, and implement comprehensive school counseling programs that include advocacy efforts to change racist policies, procedures, practices, guidelines, and laws that create and maintain barriers to student success (ASCA, 2021a). They further assert that the school counselor's role is to improve outcomes for *all* students by implementing a comprehensive school counseling program. A comprehensive school counseling program, if implemented correctly, is vital to a student's academic, personal and social, and career development leading to the ability to become contributing members of society (ASCA, 2019). In this fight for social justice, school counselors should lead and collaborate with other educational professionals to advocate for minoritized students working toward systemic change. School counselors can lead the charge by ensuring that in addition to discussions about reimagining schools, academic processes, and in-class experiences, educators can also begin dismantling inequities and systemic policies and procedures that have negatively affected BIPOC students (Rutledge, 2020). According to Atkins and Oglesby (2018, Introduction, para. 4), "If you are not actively seeking to interrupt racism, you are contributing to its perpetuation." Therefore, the call to action for school counselors is for antiracist work that results in the changing of antiracist policies and ideas (ASCA, 2020). Unfortunately, many school counselors continue to operate their comprehensive school counseling programs in ways that harm BIPOC students. As stated earlier, for school counselors to do the work of dismantling systemic racism within schools, school counselors must explore their thoughts and emotions, and advocate to eliminate system barriers for BIPOC students. While that is not an easy task, school counselors can start by engaging in multiculturally competent and socially just school counseling practices.

Multicultural and Social Justice School Counseling

School counselors' privilege, authority, power, and identity can influence the counseling relationships with the students that they serve. A White school counselor may create a systemic hierarchy in counseling with BIPOC students, and the counselor's authority and power are increased because they are adults. To increase school counselors' multicultural sensitivity in working with students and their caregivers, this section uses the Multicultural and Social Justice Counseling Competencies (MSJCC) Model (Ratts et al., 2015) (see electronic resources) to offer school counselors a framework to use to implement multicultural and social justice competencies into their comprehensive school counseling program, practices, and interventions. According to the authors, the model illustrates the complex connection between the constructs and competencies of the framework (Ratts et al., 2015). The model depicts four quadrants that are used to identify the intersections of identities in the counseling relationship while also examining issues of power, privilege, and oppression and how they impact the counseling relationship. In the center of the model are four developmental domains that guide a school counselor to multicultural and social justice competence. They are (1) counselor self-awareness, (2) client worldview, (3) counseling relationship, and (4) counseling and advocacy interventions. Lastly, surrounding the model are aspirational competencies that guide the process. It is believed that one's attitudes and beliefs will increase their knowledge and thus improve their skills, and lastly call them to action. The following sections will provide an overview of each domain of the MSJCC model and practical ways school counselors can engage in their development to be more multiculturally competent and socially just.

Counselor Self-Awareness

In the first domain, MSJCC calls for school counselors to develop self-awareness so that they are able to understand their attitudes and beliefs, develop knowledge and skills, and act based on their beliefs and worldview. This level of self-awareness often results in discomfort and even defensiveness for some school counselors who are resistant to or unfamiliar with advocacy work. Awareness involves understanding one's own view as well as the worldview of the student, which may differ from one's own. From a multicultural view, school counselors' awareness of the cultural differences between the student and counselor is often highlighted more than their cultural similarities (Bryan et al., 2004). Although having similar cultural identities can help school counselors understand subtle and unique cultural perspectives, similarities can also camouflage counselors' biases, stereotypes, and assumptions (Hird et al., 2004). School counselors' unconscious biases and stereotypes may discount the obstacles the student is facing. For example, a school counselor might assume that a Black male student who is failing a class did something to cause his low academic performance versus a personal, familial, community, or systemic barrier that may be impeding the student's academic performance.

To proactively fight against implicit biases and stereotypes, school counselors must actively and continually engage the outlined the ASCA Mindsets for school counselors. They are as follows:

- Every student can learn, and every student can succeed.
- Every student should have access to and opportunity for a high-quality education.
- Every student should graduate from high school prepared for postsecondary opportunities.
- Every student should have access to a comprehensive school counseling program.
- Comprehensive school counseling programs promote and enhance student academic, career, and social/emotional outcomes.

Student Worldviews

The ASCA Mindsets and Behaviors standards "promote academic achievement, college and career readiness and social/emotional learning, which have the long-term effect of preventing and overcoming racism and bias" (ASCA, 2020, p. 3). To encourage a socially just mindset in students so that they are able to address and deal with racism and bias, school counselors can use the ASCA Mindsets and Behaviors to prepare students to (a) be able to combat racism and bias they may witness and (b) overcome racism, bias, and oppression they may experience. To do so, school counselors need to

- encourage the student's belief in development of the whole self, including a healthy balance of mental, social/emotional, and physical well-being;
- encourage the student's self-confidence in their ability to succeed; and
- encourage the student's sense of belonging in the school environment.

School Counseling Relationship

While the self-awareness of school counselors is imperative for understanding and identifying "one's cultural values, beliefs, and biases" (Ratts et al., 2016), the insight can also help the school counselor to understand their student's worldview and what barriers may be preventing them from academic, social-emotional, and career success. This understanding of their students will also aid in supporting the student's identity development. By school counselors recognizing and attending to the "shared and unshared identities; privileged and marginalized statuses; values, beliefs and biases; and culture" (Ratts et al., 2016, para. 9) between them and their students, they will assist students to engage in a positive counseling relationship. In schools, students see school counselors as authority figures. Because of the traditional cultural values and respect for hierarchical relationships within schools, students and school counselors may not engage in an equal counseling relationship between the student and counselor. In addition, high schoolers may want to be exercising their ability to make their own decisions and may base their thoughts and emotions on what they want or what their peers say rather than what their counselors say. Because school counselors and students perceive the positive therapeutic alliance differently (Bachelor, 2013), school counselors unconsciously harm the student and counseling relationship if they are not aware of these relational dynamics. For example, a student may be called in to see the school counselor about a schedule change. The student, Black female, might come to the school counselor's office with a great deal of anxiety or distrust based on racial biases and African Americans' history of oppression in the United States. If the school counselor doesn't understand the sociopolitical events and their impact on the student, they may misinterpret the student's anxiety and mistrust as rude or disrespectful behavior toward adults.

School Counseling and Advocacy Interventions

One of the roles of school counselors is to be advocates. School counselor advocacy is to "work with and/or on behalf of their clients/students who [a]re struggling with systemic barriers" (Toporek & Daniels, 2018, p. 1). When school counselors aim to dismantle harmful systems, they must be equipped to look through a trauma-informed lens and specifically consider race-based trauma to determine its impact on mental health and academic success of BIPOC students. To assist counselors with evaluating and implementing culturally relevant and ethical advocacy, the American Counseling Association (ACA) developed the ACA Advocacy Competencies (Lewis et al., 2003). The ACA Advocacy Competencies outline the skills, knowledge, and behavior used to identify and address student barriers (Toporek & Daniels, 2018). The ACA Advocacy Competencies model (see web resources) consists of levels of client/student involvement, advocacy intervention, and the intersection of six advocacy domains (Client/Student Empowerment, Client/Student Advocacy, Community Collaboration, Systems Advocacy, Public Information, Social/Political Advocacy). Additionally, according to the ASCA National Model, school counselors are recognized as leaders in reform efforts as they advocate for student academic success (ASCA, 2019). The National Model states,

> school counselors' advocacy efforts are aimed at a) eliminating barriers impeding students' development; b) creating opportunities to learn for all students; c) ensuring access to a quality school curriculum; d) collaborating with others within and outside the school to help students meet their needs, and e) promoting positive, systemic change in schools (Trusty & Brown, 2005, p. 259).

School counselors' advocacy for BIPOC and other marginalized students requires school counselors to lead, collaborate, and create systemic change. School counselors often advocate for students and their families, underrepresented student groups, campus practices, district policy evaluation, enhanced community resources, legislative changes, and the school counseling profession (Trusty & Brown, 2005). For example, school counselors can be instrumental in advocating for the educational attainment of many students, especially Black males. The underachievement of Black males historically has been a recurring theme in the literature (Education Trust, 2003; The College Board, 2010). School counselors can focus their counseling efforts on working individually and in groups with Black males, work with teachers to support the academic needs of the student, advocate for community resources and interventions to support Black males who may experience home and food insecurities, and work with school administration to examine policies and procedures that may be systemic barriers to Black male academic achievement. With the right attitude and beliefs, knowledge and skills, school counselors are able to deploy appropriate interventions and better advocate for their students.

ABOLITIONIST EDUCATION AND SCHOOL COUNSELING

The efforts to address racism and bias in schools have a long-standing history in education, but in light of the events in 2021, national attention has been given to schools and districts to examine their support and promotion of diversity, equity, inclusion (DEI), and access. In 2021, the ASCA released the 2020 State of the Profession (ASCA, 2021b). It was reported that one-third (36%) of school counselors stated that their schools or districts required DEI training for all school faculty. Unfortunately, it also reported that one third of the schools and districts took no action to address DEI or access. Furthermore, school counselors reported that only about 42% of them monitor student behavior to identify racist behavior or speech, and only 22% of school counselors have identified and advocated to revise or remove policies that disproportionately affect students of color. Finally, 30% of the school counselors responded that incorporating antiracism practices/pedagogy/curriculum was a challenge, and 25% said it was a challenge to address school/district policies that result in institutional discrimination. Despite the ASCA Ethical Standards and the National Model explicitly stating it is the school counselor's role to advocate for change and support *all* students, school counselors have unfortunately helped to perpetuate systems of oppression in PK–12 education. There are instances where school counselors have tracked BIPOC students in lower academic coursework, offered poor postsecondary career planning, and set lower expectations for students of color.

Because the school counseling profession needs to move beyond just recognizing these issues, it is important for school counselors to monitor and expand personal multicultural and social justice advocacy awareness, knowledge, and skills to be effective, culturally competent school counselors. School counselors need to engage in abolitionist education and school counseling by understanding how prejudice, privilege, and various forms of oppression based on ethnicity, racial identity, age, economic status, abilities/ disabilities, language, immigration status, sexual orientation, gender, gender identity expression, family type, religious/spiritual identity, appearance, and living situations (e.g., foster care, homelessness, incarceration) affect students and stakeholders.

According to Love (2019), education reform needs to happen in the United States in order for Black students to succeed. Abolitionist education and teaching "comes from a critical race lens and applies methods like protest, boycotting, and calling out other teachers who are racist, homophobic, or Islamophobic" (Stoltzfus, 2019, para. 4). Abolitionist school counselors will know how to talk about racism and homophobia in their counseling sessions and classroom lessons. In addition, school counselors will be called to action and organize marches and boycotts to stand up against systemic racism. In conjunction with the ASCA ethical standards, this means school counselors are ethically obligated to have a grasp of the historical context of oppression. They cannot understand how prejudice, privilege, and oppression based on these various identities impact the mental health and well-being of students if they do not know what happened historically and why that matters. Adhering to this standard requires school counselors to inform and educate themselves on accurate history that is not whitewashed so that they can equip themselves with the most beneficial response to give students who, for example, may say things like "build that wall." In that case, school counselors should help walk that student through a critical thought process and perspective broadening by asking, "But who was on this land first? Does it belong to us/you?" They are not imposing beliefs on them, but rather are guiding them to open their minds and see things through a different lens, as well as teaching them real, true history they might not otherwise be exposed to, which is what school counselors should be doing as educators and which is ultimately good for their mental health as well. Additionally, building a coalition is important for school counselors responding to resistance to antiracism efforts. It's impossible to sustain this work alone. Consult and collaborate with other counselors doing this work and plan together. White counselors, learn what it means to leverage your privilege. The leadership required of us as White counselors may look like passing on opportunities offered to us to have BIPOC to lead instead. To demonstrate how school counselors can lead abolitionist education, we have provided an example of a core curriculum lesson below.

VOICES FROM THE FIELD

Name: Jennifer Susko (she/her)

Where You Practice: Georgia

Professional Job Title: School Counselor

Bio: Jennifer Susko has been a school counselor for 10 years at the high school and elementary levels. She uses culturally relevant teaching and critical race theory as lenses to design comprehensive, data-driven school counseling programs that include antibias, antiracist activities and interventions to increase equity in schools. Jennifer believes that the work to end racial injustice is integral to the work we do as ethical school counselors.

My antiracism story began with Rodney King's brutal, televised police beating. I was in fourth grade when I saw the riots in LA on the news. I knew then that I had an enduring love for my Black friends, the Black people I studied about from freedom and liberation movements, and those I knew from sports and entertainment deeply. I knew about racism, but it was not until I saw the community in Los Angeles rise up like they did that I felt the intense heartache of how current racism still was. Feeling a strong call to action but not knowing exactly what I was talking about, I wrote a letter to Georgia's governor to fix this injustice.

While I am grateful to have started learning antiracism young, the unfortunate part is that I did not have the BLM movement or others helping my school counselors guide my learning. As such, I got a lot wrong over the years because I had to be self-taught. No educators were helping me understand the complex issues of race and racism. From what I see today, the BLM movement has encouraged and motivated more school counselors to develop themselves professionally in antiracism to adhere to our ethics. This is vital for all students so that they are supported through positive racial identity development and so that they learn the language and tools necessary to dismantle White supremacy and stand up against racism. For Black students, though, antiracist school counselors can assist with navigation of racist educational environments and ensuring student safety and mental health as the school counselors work simultaneously to effect changes that abolish the systemic barriers that result in the racist setting.

Ever since BLM began, I have drawn connections from the movement to our ethical standards as school counselors so that I can show the link between my practice and some of the movement principles. The ASCA standard B3b says we are to ". . . stay up to date on current research and to maintain professional competence in current school counseling issues and topics." Sometimes we focus on staying on top of the research that interests us. But the movement helped illuminate how that is not all we have to do in terms of staying up to date. We know that students will have strong emotions surrounding issues like contentious elections and racism in our current landscape. We know kids will be significantly impacted by it, which makes it a current school counseling issue and topic. We need to maintain professional competence in handling it. But if we don't know how to maintain or create an inclusive, safe climate for students of all identities in our school, particularly when talking with them about racism, then we must prioritize our time to read up on how to do that competently at the same level as other important issues and topics we already grasp completely. The inclusive environment piece is vital to Black student well-being and is addressed in ASCA standard: A10a. "School counselors: a. Strive to contribute to a safe, respectful, nondiscriminatory school environment in which all members of the school community demonstrate respect and civility."

With BLM bringing antiracism to the forefront of students' awareness, I strive to know the best practices for helping students dialogue about and process feelings around racism. This is a life skill, and if we are going to help them achieve their maximum potential, it is our responsibility to teach them how to engage in their system of government and talk about current issues like BLM diplomatically and in a way that's least harmful for them, since it will come up in their daily lives. If we feel weak in this area, then we must get up to date by diving into learning the hard history of anti-Black racism that we don't know and researching the dynamics and impact of power, privilege, and oppression to guide our practice as ethical professionals.

SUMMARY AND CONCLUSION

Black children have been met with various challenges throughout their educational lives, resulting in negative consequences and outcomes that continue to permeate their way of life and how they are viewed in society today. The obstacles found in education are a direct result of racism and have brought about racialized trauma for many students and families. For school counselors to begin to do the work of dismantling systemic racism within their schools, they must first understand the historical context of racism in education and then explore thoughts and emotions that surface surrounding that knowledge. The BLM movement brought a much needed and heightened awareness to how we all should play a role in antiracism. School counselors can start the work of dismantling systemic racism by engaging in multiculturally competent and socially just school counseling practices. School counselors need to engage in abolitionist education and school counseling by understanding how prejudice, privilege, and various forms of oppression based on ethnicity, racial identity, age, economic status, abilities/disabilities, language, immigration status, sexual orientation, gender, gender identity expression, family type, religious/spiritual identity, appearance and living situations (e.g., foster care, homelessness, incarceration) affect students and stakeholders.

CASE STUDY

Imagine that you are working as a school counselor in an elementary school. Over the summer, you are called into your principal's office to discuss a phone call she received from the father of a student who will be on your caseload next school year. The father saw some of your social media posts indicating that you are an antiracist school counselor. He has also read some articles and texts on Critical Race Theory. Since he is ardently opposed to any discussion of race or racism in schools and finds your posts offensive, he tells the principal he does not want his daughter working with you in an individual setting under any circumstances. Your principal tells you that she will document this in your human resource file as an example of your performance being negatively impacted by what you posted on social media about antiracism.

DISCUSSION QUESTIONS

1. As a school counselor, how would you respond?
2. What supportive resources might benefit the school counselor's response to the principal?
3. What is the school counselor's role in advocacy?
4. What aspects of the Ethical Standards or the ASCA National Model are applicable in responding to the situation?

PRACTICAL APPLICATION

- Form an advocacy and antiracist group with fellow counselors and colleagues to facilitate safe spaces for discussion.
- Create and disseminate DEI needs assessments to collect data from students, teachers, parents, and community members.
- Join a curriculum workgroup to assist in decolonization of curriculum and materials.
- Focus on grants to build and strengthen services and support for BIPOC students and faculty.
- At every meeting, group, or systemic interaction, ask who is missing at the table?

KEY REFERENCES

Only key references appear in the print edition. The full reference list appears in the digital product on Springer Publishing Connect: connect.springerpub.com/content/book/978-0-8261-8753-6/part/part01/chapter/ch01

American School Counselor Association. (2020, August). *ASCA standards in practice: Eliminating racism and bias in schools: The school counselor's role.* https://www.schoolcounselor.org/getmedia/542b085a -7eda-48ba-906e-24cd3f08a03f/SIP-Racism-Bias.pdf

American School Counselor Association. (2021a). *The school counselor and anti-racist practices.* https://www.schoolcounselor.org/Standards-Positions/Position-Statements/ASCA-Position-Statements/The -School-Counselor-and-Anti-Racist-Practices#:~:text=ASCA%20Position,career%20and%20social% 2Femotional%20development

Atkins, R., & Oglesby, A. (2018). *Interrupting racism: Equity and social justice in school counseling.* Routledge. https://doi.org/10.4324/9781351258920

Black Lives Matter At School. (n.d.). *Curriculum.* https://www.blacklivesmatteratschool.com/ curriculum.html

Francis, D., & Mason E. (2022). Proactively addressing racial incidents in schools: Two perspectives. In C. Holcomb-McCoy (Ed.), *Antiracist counseling in schools and communities* (pp. 57–80). American Counseling Association.

Love, B. L. (2019). *We want to do more than survive: Abolitionist teaching and the pursuit of educational freedom.* Beacon Press.

Trusty, J., & Brown, D. (2005). Advocacy competencies for professional school counselors. *Professional School Counseling,* 259–265. https://www.schoolcounselor-ca.org/files/Advocacy/Advocacy%20 Competencies%20for%20School%20Counselors.pdf

CHAPTER 2

Strengths-Based Practice for School Counselors

LUCY L. PURGASON AND CALVIN C. CRAIG IV

LEARNING OBJECTIVES

After reading this chapter, students will be able to:

- Identify the concepts associated with the social justice, equity, and strengths-based frameworks of community cultural wealth, relational-cultural theory, multicultural and social justice counseling competencies leadership framework, and youth participatory action research.

- Explain how school counselors can deliver strengths-based tiered interventions as foundational to a culturally responsive comprehensive school counseling program.

- Describe the professional advocacy roles of school counselors and the importance of marketing the school counseling program with supportive data.

- Recognize why developing school-family-community partnerships are critical to the advocacy role of the school counselor.

- Discuss how social media has become an ecological context for students that can contribute to or take away from student resiliency.

STUDENT VOICE

The student highlighted in this section is a White female attending high school in the southeastern United States. A young woman who knows what she wants out of life, she aspires to attend college and law school. She is a student athlete involved in numerous clubs and works a part-time job to ensure that she is a competitive college applicant. An important context for her high school experience is that it began during the COVID-19 pandemic. Switching from in-person learning to virtual learning to hybrid learning, she has not had a traditional high school experience. A personable teenager who has a thriving social and academic life, she expresses that her classmates, as well as herself, are experiencing constant moments of sadness as it relates to the COVID-19 pandemic. While her school has a mental health and suicide awareness curriculum that is presented to students each year, she feels this is ineffective because students experience this as being told what to do rather than engaging students in dialogue about these concerns.

Desiring an opportunity to discuss these topics with someone at school, she connects with her school counselor weekly during her lunch period to talk about grades, college options, family and friend issues, coping strategies, and the troubling posts she comes across on social media. Her daily responsibilities include going to school, completing assignments, studying for classes, participating on the volleyball team, and working a part-time job. Whereas she enjoys her friendships and positive adult relationships built with teachers and staff, she struggles to manage the level of class work that is assigned, bullies in school and on social media platforms, and the pressure to engage in activities that would compromise her morals and values.

Growing up in a rural area with the nearest major city 2 hours away, she takes it upon herself to research current events and vocalize her support of marginalized communities. Although her opinions in school and social media are not always popular among her fellow classmates in their small town, she acknowledges her privilege as a White person in America and strives to use that privilege to advocate for others who do not.

During the summer of 2020 she recalls students creating social media posts and expressing confusion on distinguishing the facts of the murder of George Floyd, Black Lives Matters protestors, and COVID-19. There was not a safe place in school to process these events other than the counselor's office when students returned from summer break. With only two counselors serving a population of over 900 students, connecting with each student needing support would be challenging. The student expressed her desire for conversations in class with teachers who might bring in trustworthy sources for discussion; however, teachers expressed hesitancy bringing up these issues for fear that the conversations would turn political.

INTRODUCTION TO STRENGTH-BASED PRACTICE

As this chapter is being written, much is happening in the world that underscores the need for school counselors and their role in meeting the academic, college and career, and social-emotional needs of PK–12 students. We are amid a global pandemic responsible for killing over 5.5 million people worldwide (Johns Hopkins University, 2021) intersecting with the preexisting virus of racism spreading its toxicity and lethality over generations. School counselors witnessed students and families navigating multiple online learning platforms, negotiating competing schedules, and dealing with financial and health-related stressors. The COVID-19 pandemic in its complexity, however, showed educators worldwide the importance of meeting students where they are. Whereas some students flourished in a strictly online environment, other students struggled with not being able to socialize or get one-on-one instruction as needed. Isolation was a contributing factor to the mental health challenges some students faced. As a result, the mental health needs of students and other educational stakeholders became more apparent. In a national survey of school counselors, participants indicated students and families required greater emotional support during this time (Savitz-Romer et al., 2020).

Responding to student crisis and trauma is becoming an increasing part of the school counselor's job because of both human-made (e.g., racism, mass school shootings, drug and alcohol abuse) disasters and those resulting from the interactions of humans and their environment (e.g., climate change, natural disasters). With the evolution of the school counseling profession from a vocational resource to a more multifaceted role in the school, stakeholders can sometimes find themselves unsure of what services school counselors can bring to their student population. Stakeholder knowledge of the school counseling role is crucial because traumatic events outside of school can have a direct impact on student functioning in the classroom. As professionals working in schools, school counselors have unprecedented access to students and families and therefore provide frontline response and preventive care to safeguard the lives of students. The likelihood that a student will experience a form of historical or isolated trauma is high (Benjet et al., 2016); therefore, embracing a trauma-informed approach is critical. School counselors are poised to provide mental health support and trained to implement targeted and tiered interventions (Zyromski et al., 2021). Serving on the front lines of identifying students with the most need, using evidence-based and practice-informed interventions to support students, and connecting with collaborative and referral sources within the community is paramount (Rumsey & Milsom, 2019; Zyromski et al., 2021). In this way, school counselors support student resilience within key developmental periods potentially changing students' short-term and long-term academic, college/career, and social-emotional trajectories (Center on the Developing Child, 2021).

It is important to remember that students, and the communities they represent, already possess a great deal of strength and resilience. By excavating resources predicated from successfully navigating prior challenges (including those imposed by unequitable opportunity structures), school counselors unearth valuable student assets to build upon when assisting students through current stressors. Strengths-based school counselors help students identify strengths, leverage resources, and use individual and collective assets in the promotion of student goals and outcomes (Galassi & Akos, 2007). This is particularly important for students who may not see themselves, and members of their community, reflected and represented in other aspects of the school environment or who may experience the personal biases of educators that may negate or ignore their lived experiences. Working in collaboration with community members, parents, teachers, and administrators, school counselors create avenues for learning about the specific needs of students and families and can use existing strengths to meet these needs. Within this chapter we will be identifying key frameworks, models, and research paradigms that school counselors can use in support of a strengths-based approach. These frameworks include community cultural wealth (CCW; Yosso, 2005), relational-cultural theory (RCT; Jordan et al., 1991), the multicultural and social justice counseling competencies leadership framework (Ratts & Greenleaf, 2018), and youth participatory action research (YPAR).

STRENGTH-BASED FRAMEWORKS

CCW, a social capital concept focusing on the strengths of students of color, brings a culturally responsive lens to multitiered system of supports (MTSS) interventions identified in the school counseling literature (Purgason et al., 2020). CCW originated in LatCrit (Latinx critical race theory) but has been applied to the experiences of students across ethnic and cultural identities. In contrast to the cultural deficit perspective, which focuses on how students from underrepresented groups may lack access to cultural capital, CCW acknowledges the cultural strengths students bring to the school community. CCW includes six types of cultural assets, that is, aspirational, familial, social, linguistic, navigational, and resistant capital (Yosso, 2005). *Aspirational capital* refers to the hopes and dreams for the future possessed by students and their families. *Familial capital* encompasses the cultural knowledge transmitted between members of a family facilitating connection to family and community. *Social capital* includes the networks of relationships that strengthen and provide support for students. The ability to speak and translate multiple languages and the connection to cultural identity maintained through language is reflected in *linguistic capital*. *Navigational capital* refers to the ways students have learned to traverse systems not designed with them in mind. Finally, *resistant capital* are the strategies that students use to persevere through challenges imposed by inequitable opportunity structures. CCW challenges the deficit notions embedded within the PK–12 education pipeline and can be accessed by students of color as a protective factor against racism experienced in the school environment (Acevedo & Solorzano, 2021).

RCT is a counseling approach emerging from the 1970s in response to psychological theories rooted in individuation and separation as an ideal goal and indicator of wellness, ignoring the experiences and values of women and other historically marginalized groups (Jordan, 2018). RCT is a social justice– and strengths-focused perspective, recognizing that deep connection requires embracing vulnerability and demonstrating courage to engage with others authentically. In addition, recognition of power and privilege are prioritized and acknowledged for the ways this influences the development and maintenance of relationships. These areas are important considerations in a school setting, where historically, certain students have been advantaged due to privileges afforded by their affiliation with aspects of the dominant culture. Although few applications of RCT to the school setting exist, scholarship highlighting school-based interventions inspired by RCT are forthcoming (Grant et al., 2021).

Privilege and marginalization are core concepts of the multicultural and social justice counseling competencies (MCSJCC; Ratts et al., 2016). Revised in 2015, the MCSJCC highlight the need for counselors to identify and reflect on self-possessed areas of privilege and marginalization due to the intersectionality of identities and how this may impact the development of a counseling relationship. For example, a person's privilege can conflict with other identities of which they are a part, such as race, gender, sexual orientation, class, abilities/disabilities, and others. Furthermore, it increases awareness about the ways that counselors must attune to the personal-social-cultural identities of students and incorporate these identities when customizing counseling interventions. Ratts and Greenleaf (2018) used these competencies as the basis for a school counseling leadership framework, emphasizing the role of school counselors in addressing and dismantling systemic inequities within the school setting. As part of this framework, attention is given to six ecosystemic levels influencing students: intrapersonal (e.g., individual characteristics), interpersonal (e.g., relationships), institutional (e.g., school context), community (e.g., societal norms), public policy (e.g., laws), and global/international (e.g., world events) (Ratts & Greenleaf, 2018).

YPAR is a research method that actively engages students in the research process and gives voice to their experiences, ideas, and intuition to create equity-driven changes toward disempowering structures (Ozer et al., 2020). Students are involved as co-researchers through multiple stages of the research process, including identifying the research questions, selecting the research design, collecting and analyzing data, and sharing the findings. It is important to remember that student voices are not a monolith—they are a collective, each with unique and distinct nuances, identities, perspectives, and experiences that represent the diversity present in today's schools.

Deficit-Based Practice Versus Strengths-Based Practice

Historically, a deficit-based approach has often permeated the ways in which educators address students with identified needs. Students experiencing barriers as a result of social influencers of health and education (SIHE; National Center for School Mental Health, 2020) such as lack of safe housing, food insecurity, exposure to adverse childhood experiences, and experiencing discrimination were labeled "at risk." The focus of interventions was placed on the individual student, bringing emphasis to areas identified as lacking often without a consideration for how environmental and systemic factors were the cause of challenges experienced. Protective factors and areas of resilience students possess could often be overlooked in this process, especially times when students exhibited personal agency to overcome restricting and limiting beliefs about their abilities. As students navigate developmental milestones along their journey in PK–12 education, they are engaging in identity development and are increasingly exposed to and able to understand stereotypes. During these formative years, students may feel that their identification with certain communities is associated with accompanying stereotypes, causing internal conflict. Bryan et al. (2020) underscore that "focusing exclusively on risk factors can leave families, schools, and communities feeling stigmatized or unfairly judged" (p. 6). Operating from a deficit perspective that focuses on struggles perpetuates these labels.

Several protective factors contributing to student resilience have been identified in the literature. Protective factors are strengths or qualities that contribute to positive development and well-being (Child Welfare Information Gateway, 2020). The Centers for Disease Control and Prevention (CDC; 2021) has a four-level social-ecological prevention model: individual, relationship, community, and societal factors. Individual protective factors include things such as access to support, stress management, and problem-solving skills. Relational factors include peer and family relationships and school engagement. Community and societal factors encompass the availability of basic needs and services. This perspective acknowledges the multiple spheres of influence impacting students at any given time and has been incorporated within the school counseling literature (McMahon et al., 2014; Ratts & Greenleaf, 2018). A consideration of these levels allows school counselors to understand students holistically and to identify areas where students are most impacted and areas where students possess strengths. The National Center on Safe Supportive Learning Environments (2021) identifies three key protective factors schools can activate to support students. The first is the establishment of supportive relationships. Next, educators should set high expectations for student achievement. Finally, students should have access to experiences that allow them to contribute to the learning process.

The American School Counselor Association (ASCA) School Counselor Professional Standards & Competencies (2019) include several mindsets and behaviors school counselors should possess in order to address student needs through a strengths-based approach. The mindsets reflect beliefs regarding the rights of every student to access a high-quality education including a school counseling program (M1, M4), ability for every student to achieve success (M1), and the leadership role necessary for school counselors (M6), particularly when collaborating with school and community stakeholders. Included in the behavior section of this document are standards school counselors should implement in the delivery of a comprehensive school counseling program (CSCP) divided into three categories: professional foundation, direct and indirect student services, and planning/assessment. Notably, the professional foundation standards address the need for school counselors to understand "the impact of cultural, social, and environmental influences on student success and opportunities" (ASCA, 2019; B-PF 6, p. 2) and serve as advocates and change makers through the implementation of a CSCP (B-PF 8, B-PF 9). Correspondingly, ASCA has articulated a set of student mindsets that are based on research of the importance of noncognitive factors in student success (ASCA, 2021a). Noncognitive factors associated with academic performance are categorized as academic behaviors, perseverance, mindsets, learning strategies, and social skills, and include skills and beliefs such as organizational skills, self-discipline, belief in ability to grow, goal setting, and relationship skills (University of Chicago Consortium on School Research, n.d.). The *ASCA Student Standards* include six student mindsets and 30 behavior standards divided into learning strategies, self-management skills, and social skills. Recent updates to the *ASCA Student Standards* include a consideration for incorporating greater attention to behaviors associated with promoting diversity and multicultural understanding (ASCA, 2021b).

STRENGTHS-BASED INTERVENTIONS

A common theme of the profession is the need for school counselors to create opportunities to hear from students about their experiences within their school, home, and community and to integrate these perspectives when designing and implementing school counseling interventions to address the complex realities of students' lives. First and foremost, school counselors must establish relationships with students in which they feel comfortable talking with them about their concerns. Visibility of the school counselor within the school is essential. Unlike teachers who spend most of their day in direct contact with the same group(s) of students, school counselors must often find unique and creative ways to build connections with students (especially in schools where the ratio can be upward of 1:500). These student–school counselor relationships are critical because the ability to identify appropriate school counseling interventions will be restricted if student voices are omitted from conversations about how school counselors can support students and address needs (Williams et al., 2015).

In a qualitative study published in *Professional School Counseling*, Williams and colleagues (2015) interviewed 24 middle school students from low-income backgrounds to gain their perspectives on ways school counselors could enhance their academic achievement. Based on these interviews, three main themes were identified: (1) build meaningful relationships with students; (2) build on the cultural wealth of students; and (3) provide mental health services in schools. Two types of CCW were explicitly referenced in this article: aspirational and social capital. Students identified that school counselors can help access aspirational capital by providing early opportunities for students to explore their values and interests, establish goals, and learn how education can support goal attainment (Williams et al., 2015). Students themselves highlight the criticality of school counselors in activating and highlighting student strengths and using these to tailor and customize interventions. For example, social capital can be leveraged when "counselors can use our strengths and the supports available in our families and communities to help us overcome our problems" (Williams et al., 2015, p. 160).

SCHOOL COUNSELING CURRICULUM

School counseling curriculum is in many ways the developmental and preventive heart of the school counseling program. School counselors can craft a curriculum that intentionally reflects student experiences and identities and helps students understand more about themselves—in terms of who they are as learners, who they are as individuals, and how they uniquely come together to contribute to a larger community. An important opportunity exists for students to strengthen their identity and sense of self, as a positive ethnic identity is associated with many positive academic and social-emotional outcomes. In addition, curriculum lessons targeting identity-related concepts can build empathy and understanding among students from different cultural and ethnic backgrounds. For some students, the only diversity they encounter is at school. Educating and exposing students to the experiences of students from various backgrounds promotes cultural understanding and empathy and engages students in learning about power and privilege that is crucial in developing students' ability to engage in advocacy and allyship.

School counseling curriculum lessons are an intentional, targeted, and efficient way to reach the entire student population. Effect sizes achieved through the delivery of school counseling curriculum lessons are comparable to other responsive counseling services (Whiston et al., 2011). Furthermore, systematic and schoolwide implementation permits school counselors to use data to determine the impact of the lessons on identified school counseling goals. Customizing the school counseling curriculum to reflect the specific needs of the school, along with reflecting the identities of the school community and the experiences they have faced, is an important way to incorporate a strengths-based and antiracist approach. For example, Dena Simmons, former assistant director at the Yale Center for Emotional Intelligence, emphasizes that "students need the skills to navigate unjust realities" (Madda, 2019). She offers several suggestions that are beneficial to school counselors, including providing curriculum for students to reflect on identity and equity to build self-awareness, develop responsible decision-making skills through community-based projects (e.g., YPAR), and explore different expectations for self-management and the impact of implicit bias (Madda, 2019).

Ratts and Greenleaf (2018) underscore in the MCSJCC leadership framework that school counselor leadership involves understanding the six spheres of influence on students and how to respond within each sphere. Social media is now an ecological context that heavily influences students' lives, impacting students interpersonally through ways their friendships are developed and maintained. It has impact at the institutional and community levels as well, as the values, beliefs, and events happening within the larger macro-context are communicated and processed over social media. Students from historically marginalized communities are confronted with individuals posting on social media views that perpetuate systemic oppression and encounter tensions regarding how or when to respond. According to the PEW Research Center (Anderson & Jiang, 2018), 45% of adolescents report feeling overwhelmed by the drama on social media. Social media use has been implicated in the rise of bullying and harassment online and has been linked to negative indicators of well-being, such as increased anxiety and depression. However, social media also provides unique avenues and platforms for students to maximize cultural assets and engage in advocacy and social justice efforts. As students are growing up with social media, it is vital to assist them in regulating their emotions that are a result of these encounters and to learn to balance their social media use.

Culturally responsive computing (Scott et al., 2015) is a framework that addresses the transformational role that technology can play in promoting social change. It is inherently a strengths-focused versus deficit approach, focusing on empowerment and the harnessing of cultural strengths. Hashtag activism is a way to harness resistance capital for students to connect with others united around a common cause or concern. The website of *Learning for Justice*, learningforjustice.org, includes a middle school lesson plan designed to present students with information about hashtag activism and identify ways that hashtags can be used in social justice work (2017). Included in the lesson plan are examples of hashtag campaigns such as #blacklivesmatter, #blackgirlmagic, #transisbeautiful, and #latinxcellence. The objectives of the lesson involve students analyzing and evaluating the campaigns and extending these ideas to issues relevant to their lives.

Classroom curriculum lessons can be organized in units, with school counselors presenting material to individual classrooms across the school. An alternative is for school counselors to identify students who may benefit from additional regular interaction with the school counselor and create a specific course. For example, Ian Levy, former school counselor and current school counselor educator, created a hip-hop lyricism course for 10th–12th graders at his high school in New York City. The aim of the course was to increase coping skills and to provide a platform for students of color to experience empowerment and increase comfort in accessing counseling services (Levy, 2019). The class ran like a counseling group and met every other day for 50 minutes for the entire school year. The content of the course was codeveloped and cotaught with students. The course content included students creating a mix tape highlighting emotional themes of their lives. By composing lyrics, students were able to write about their stress, gain insight into their emotional experiences, and release emotions. Students evidenced aspects of aspirational and resistance capital in lyrics detailing an awareness of the skills they possessed and refused to be limited by others' preconceived notions. In addition, they used these spaces to process their emotions and articulate their perspectives on the killing of unarmed Black teenagers including Trayvon Martin, Mike Brown, and Jordan Davis. Levy acknowledged the criticality of school counselors establishing a culturally responsive classroom environment and embodied this by creating a space for students to explore systems of oppression (both inside and outside of school). Hip-hop and spoken word therapy (HHSWT; Levy, 2012) utilizes counseling interventions responsive to urban and youth culture, providing a conduit to express complex emotions and process experiences through a medium and platform historically connected to articulating the experiences and voices of youth missing or exploited within the dominant culture (Levy, 2019).

STRENGTH-BASED PRACTICAL APPLICATION

Giving students the opportunity to be a part of the learning process is a great way to help foster engagement. Some students are involved in clubs and athletics, but there are numerous students who are not involved in any activities. Reasons include lack of transportation, self-esteem issues, and other unique obstacles, leaving some students feeling a lack of belonging. School counselors can remedy this by including students in the teaching of curriculum lessons, having them co-lead small groups, as well as actively asking what positive changes they would like to see in the school counseling program.

School counselors may need to be prompted to consider how they can incorporate cultural strengths when designing curriculum lessons. Currently, the ASCA lesson plan template provides no space to consider how the lesson can be tailored more specifically to address cultural assets and incorporate aspects of CCW. Collaborating with teachers on lesson planning can provide an opportunity to capitalize on student strengths. For example, an elementary school counselor partnered with the English as a second language (ESL) teacher to design a curriculum lesson that incorporated the linguistic strengths of emerging bilingual newcomer students, incorporating key concepts in both English and students' first language. Another school counselor in a rural, low-income community in the southeastern United States involved teachers and students in a needs assessment to identify college- and career-related needs. She then partnered with teachers to implement lessons across common core curriculum areas. Students were provided an opportunity to design a research-based project on a postsecondary option and present their research project to other students, school staff, and community members. In addition, older students took on the responsibility of presenting information in classroom curriculum lessons to students in younger grades, providing an opportunity to demonstrate leadership skills and involve themselves as mentors and role models. In this community with a high percentage of first-generation college students, this school counselor helped draw on students' social capital by involving family and community members in the student-led presentations as guests. Navigational capital was maximized by providing students an opportunity to learn from one another and for older students to mentor younger students about information obtained from the projects. Lastly, the school counselor helped increase students' motivation and efficacy for postsecondary pathways by harnessing the aspirational capital students had for their future goals.

The success of this curriculum was due in large part to the school counselor narrowing in on college and career readiness as a topic area based on feedback from an administered student needs assessment. In addition to needs assessments, school climate assessments provide valuable data that can guide school counselors. School climate assessments often contain questions about relationships between students based on identity group membership, perceptions of safety at school, experiences of identity-based bullying, and other aspects of the school environment that contribute to students' sense of belongingness. Using information from school climate assessments, school counselors can understand areas of need, identify topics to address these areas, and use pre- and postassessment data to evaluate intervention efficacy. Minute meetings are a great way for counselors to gather information about their caseload that goes beyond demographic information. Minute meetings are a series of questions that can be done face-to-face, on paper, or via an online form.

Example of minute meeting questions:

Do you have a trusted adult on campus? Do you have friends here at school? Is there anything you would like to talk to your school counselor about?

STRENGTH-BASED INDIVIDUAL COUNSELING

Students are experiencing high rates of anxiety and depression because of numerous eco-systemic factors, many of which are outside the control and direct influence of the students themselves. For example, it is likely that students from marginalized groups will experience microaggressions in the school environment by another student or school staff member. The experience of this type of interaction can have devastating consequences on self-esteem, self-confidence, and a sense of belongingness in the school environment. Furthermore, the everyday experiences of microaggressions may intersect with more ubiquitous and ongoing harassment through targeted identity-based bullying. Students themselves report that they would benefit from school counselors providing mental health counseling interventions (Williams et al., 2015).

Haskins and Appling (2017) introduced an empowerment and social justice–based counseling approach integrating RCT and reality therapy. Although not specific to the school environment, the counseling strategies described can be used by school counselors to address student concerns arising from within and outside the school setting. For our review, we will focus on the RCT components of the approach and consider how this can be used when working with students in individual counseling from a strengths-based perspective. Haskins and Appling (2017) identified a four-part counseling process: exploring the problem, developing a relationship, identifying counseling goals, and moving to action. The first phase includes the school counselor examining relational images (i.e., schemas for relationships based on prior experiences) and how these impact students' relationship development. Many students have not had positive experiences with adults in school, often having adults be dismissive or punitive in their interactions. Students may initially express distrust toward the school counselor, fearing they will receive the same power-over dynamics experienced in other adult relationships.

Adding to this complexity is, that for students from communities experiencing marginalization, the exposure to barriers and the historical lack of acknowledgment of inequities experienced in the school environment may contribute to hesitancy to talk with school counselors about personal concerns. Currently, 76% of school counselors are White (ASCA, 2020). Having a counselor from a different gender, race, or cultural background can be associated with initial hesitancy to bring out identity-related concerns. Furthermore, talking to someone outside the family about challenges often goes against family and cultural values. Within an RCT approach, the school counselor can acknowledge these differences and broach with the student how this may impact the development of a counseling relationship. Awareness of identity intersectionality and how the identities of the school counselor and student may dynamically experience privilege and oppression based on the quadrants within the MCSJCC is important when establishing the relationship. Acknowledging disempowering practices within the larger sociocultural context can help students by "shifting them from a deficit perspective to a strengths viewpoint that focuses on the unique qualities that they bring to the relationship" (Haskins & Appling, 2017, p. 92).

The third phase of this counseling approach includes identifying relational goals. Awareness of student's struggles and the resiliency shown when working toward their goals creates an opportunity for school counselors to celebrate students' progress toward goal attainment. Students have often articulated the difference that having one adult in the school that's "in their corner" made in their academic trajectory. A supportive relationship with the school counselor can model for students the possibility of developing other supportive relationships at school. By considering the different ecosystemic levels, school counselors can also highlight areas of strength or where things are going well. For example, if students are challenged in maintaining friendships within the interpersonal level, they may have strengths related to advocating for causes they care about at the public policy level. In this way, the final phase of the counseling process can help support students' relational resilience through a consideration of ways to enhance student's sense of self, connection to their ethnic identity, and access to supportive friend and family relationships (Haskins & Appling, 2017).

STRENGTH-BASED GROUP COUNSELING

Unfortunately, students do not always feel that the school counselor is someone they can turn to when they face challenges. For example, in Dr. Ken Jackson's research with LGBTQ college students (2017), participants shared that they didn't experience their high school counselor as someone they would go to for social-emotional issues. Participants reported feeling isolated in the school environment and identified the lack of a Gay Straight Alliance as an opportunity to provide support and connection. Students can benefit from an opportunity to connect with peers experiencing similar stressors. Group counseling is an important avenue for students to gain support from one another and draw on each other's strengths. While groups go through various stages to establish norms and protocols, the group experience can yield positive results for participants, such as access to social capital, an opportunity to connect with others sharing similar experiences, and a platform to hear the diverse perspectives of others.

MULTICULTURAL COMPETENCIES AND SOCIAL JUSTICE ADVOCACY

Implementing the frameworks described in this chapter requires a commitment to engaging in culturally responsive practice, ongoing self-reflection, and personal/professional development. Ratts and Greenleaf (2018) define multicultural and social justice school counseling leadership as "leadership interventions that consider the cultural values, beliefs, and worldviews of culturally diverse students and that address systemic inequities and barriers impacting students' academic, social/emotional, and career development" (p. 2). School counselor advocacy involves interacting across ecological levels to support students (McMahon et al., 2014), communicating with stakeholders inside and outside the building. Unfortunately, school staff, including administrators and teachers, do not always possess a detailed understanding of the school counselor's role (Havlik et al., 2019). Communicating with stakeholders may involve professional advocacy to educate stakeholders about the benefits of school counseling and describing interventions delivered as part of a CSCP. This type of advocacy may be critical to eliminating responsibilities associated with the position that are not in the direct service of students (Havlik et al., 2019).

Conversely, communication with school staff may involve advocacy on behalf of students. For example, Hipolito-Delgado and colleagues (2021) interviewed students about their experiences during distance learning due to COVID-19. Based on student comments, they suggested that school counselors could serve as communication brokers between students and teachers to advocate for how the challenges students experience outside the school environment impact their learning. Providing teachers with this important context is a way that school counselors can help build stakeholder empathy for the student experience, increasing understanding about the multiple roles students take on beyond learner, such as caregiver and financial contributor to their family (Hipolito-Delgado et al., 2021). Furthermore, the authors called for school counselors to "take a strengths-based approach and challenge educators' assumptions about students, particularly related to internet access, study space, and deficit perspectives on families" (Hipolito-Delgado et al., 2021, p. 8).

As a school counselor, you may possess varying levels of familiarity with the cultural assets of students in your school. For school counselors with less knowledge of student cultural wealth, advocacy may involve identifying individuals in the school setting possessing greater knowledge of students' cultural assets and consulting and collaborating with these individuals. Considerations in developing these collaborations is outlined in the next section. For school counselors with greater knowledge of cultural wealth represented in the student population, implementing professional development opportunities for school staff is a way to advocate for students and families. For example, CCW is not a concept that is currently widespread in PK–12 education. School counselors might consider educating stakeholders about CCW through professional development. In addition, professional development designed to elucidate ways the school system may inhibit student connections to personal-social-cultural identities and perpetuate deficit-based thinking is an important area for school counselor leadership. The second author is a Black man who grew up with an individualized education plan (IEP) and speech impediment and experienced what it felt like to be marginalized as a PK–12 student. These experiences led to an ongoing desire to advocate and educate stakeholders to serve students through an equitable lens. Researching and hosting professional development presentations, including those on topics such as working with students in poverty as it relates to college and career readiness, as well as how racial battle fatigue can impact how students learn in a PK–12 setting. Even when presenting data, citations, and testimonies to support awareness of problems, resistance from stakeholders may exist. While everyone may not be onboard to implement equity initiatives, energy can be focused on those who are ready to do the work. With buy-in from stakeholders who support creating solutions to the student experience, a seed of advocacy can be planted that will grow in various districts around the state.

Joining or creating an equity team at your school can help bridge the gap between educators and the student experience. There are students who lack involvement in sports or clubs on their campus but who have a strong interest in social issues and equity. This platform would give them the opportunity to interact with staff members such as administrators, creating a sense of belonging, purpose, and facilitating student advocacy. Presenting at the school, local, state, and national level are great ways to educate others about what equity can look like in the classroom. Offering teachers, administrators, and staff realistic ways students can be supported through equitable interventions can combine theory with practice. Researching evidence-based approaches as well as analyzing data specific to the demographics that teachers are working with will bring a custom-made experience unique to the culture of the school or district.

Assessment of school policies that may placing students at risk or creating additional barriers is critical. Working with stakeholders outside the school may be necessary to advocate for students, especially if barriers exist in the school setting (e.g., limiting stakeholder beliefs, unsupportive administrators) that pose challenges (Beck et al., 2018). For example, to advocate for LGBT+ students, Beck and colleagues (2018) presented an ecologically informed advocacy framework with examples of how school counselors can advocate across environmental contexts. Examples included engaging in personal self-reflection at the microsystem level, developing an advocacy message shared within the school and to all stakeholders at the mesosystem level, and building partnerships with LGBT-focused community groups at the exosystem level (Beck et al., 2018).

BUILDING ON STUDENT STRENGTH: A SYSTEMS APPROACH

School counselor advocacy involves the development and maintenance of partnerships within the school and community. The power of school-family-community partnerships in meeting the needs of students and communities is well established. ASCA acknowledges the importance of being "mindful of school and community perceptions of the treatment of underrepresented groups and understand the importance of collaborating with school and community groups to help all students succeed" (ASCA, 2018, p. 1). Bryan et al. (2020) outline four principles that guide partnership development: democratic collaboration, empowerment, social justice, and strengths focus. The principles are framed within a consideration of protective factors and developmental assets that highlight strengths of families, schools, and communities.

One middle school in the Pacific Northwest embodied these tenets in the creation of a school-family-community night. The school had traditionally been a predominantly White school, with a burgeoning community of Latinx families enrolling. Previous school administrators had ignored ways to incorporate the numerous assets families and students possess that would strengthen the school environment and contribute to the school community. A new principal began inviting conversations with families and collaborated with parents and community partners to develop a school-community-family night. Parents who were also small business owners participated in an employment fair. Parents also initiated a tamale fundraiser. Information sessions informed by parent and community feedback were provided in Spanish, with interpretation available for English speakers. In addition, the school leadership worked with parents to establish a Latinx Parent Teacher Association.

Part of the success of these initiatives was due to the intentional desire on the part of school staff to increase their awareness and knowledge of community and cultural values and to self-reflect on assumptions and biases held. Bryan et al. (2020) underscore that "partnerships must focus on reducing the power inequities and cultural barriers between school staff and family members. School counselors and other school staff must embrace strengths-based, equity-focused, and culturally appropriate traditional and non-traditional types of involvement" (p. 10). In the above example, the school counselor created a summer opportunity for school staff to volunteer at an enrichment program for migrant students held at a local Catholic church in the morning and enroll in Spanish language classes in the afternoon. A goal was to facilitate greater cultural awareness and knowledge on the part of school staff. Partnerships with the local university were also important, as college undergraduate and graduate students served as volunteers for the event and also as mentors for the newly established equity and diversity club.

Similarly, Elisabeth Arriero, a school counseling intern at the time, created a career and college readiness program for Latinx high school students using community asset mapping. She interviewed students enrolled in the ESL program to better understand their experiences at school and solicit insights on what content should be covered (Arriero & Griffin, 2019). Elisabeth used this information to create the ¡Adelante! program, customized with student input, involving several collaborations with the university professor/ supervisor, school administration, data manager, ESL teacher, and school social worker. The goals of the program not only included increasing students' postsecondary knowledge but also included the promotion of ethnic pride and connection to the heritage culture. As such, guest speakers from the Latinx community were invited to present on needs identified by the students, including representatives from Latinx community college and university organizations, individuals from faith-based groups, and Latinx college students. All meetings were conducted in Spanish, with students delivering presentations at the commencement of each meeting.

Hallmarks of this collaboration included communicating with parents and families across a variety of platforms including social media, customizing program content to reflect student interests and concerns, and identifying existing community resources to support students and families. In addition, Elisabeth created a space in the program meetings for students to take on leadership roles, an important component of school counselor advocacy. Identifying opportunities for stakeholders, including students, to occupy leadership positions within the school can take many forms. School counseling advisory boards are another platform to use to capture the voices of students, families, and community members, and membership on the board can reflect the voices and perspectives of the entire school population.

Another important avenue for school counselor collaboration is to work alongside students to identify initiatives and implement changes within the school. Coleman (2020), a school counselor in a rural community in the Appalachian region, engaged middle school students through YPAR. Sixth-grade student researchers collected information through a photovoice project documenting their experiences during their first month of middle school. Using the information collected, students developed a transition plan for rising sixth-graders that focused on building community and establishing relationships.

VOICES FROM THE FIELD

Name: Calvin C. Craig IV, MA (he/him)

Where You Practice: North Carolina

Professional Job Title: School Counselor

Bio: Calvin C. Craig IV is a school counselor in Rolesville, North Carolina. After obtaining a bachelors in business degree from Fayetteville State University and working in sales, he decided to switch career fields and enrolled in graduate school at Appalachian State University to become a school counselor. Since becoming a school counselor, Calvin has presented at the North Carolina School Counselor Conference and written publications about equity and strategic programming within schools. A proud millennial, Calvin uses culturally relevant content that reflects the culture and climate that students are currently living in to help promote social and emotional regulation, coping skills, as well as college and career readiness.

As a school counselor, no one day is the same. You never know what your day will consist of from moment to moment. Within my role, I find myself doing academic check-ins with students on my case load, monitoring student academic progress, auditing transcripts, conducting suicide assessments, facilitating parent–teacher conferences, participating in department meetings to gather student concerns, and serving as a member of various school initiatives with staff and stakeholders. The majority of my work in this profession has been at the high school level. While working with high schoolers, I have had the unique opportunity to support students as they are laying down the foundation of their adult life. With an estimated caseload of 1:450, I am far from the ASCA recommendation of 1:250; therefore, I must be intentional about how I get face time with students while being mindful of instructional time.

Creating relationships with stakeholders and being able to sell your school counseling curriculum as a valuable resource to students is a critical skill that has helped me become effective in this work. There is a stigma about the relevance of the school counseling profession.

As a result, school counselors must work toward changing the image of school counselors and helping to rectify any less than positive past experiences. The best way to gain the trust and confidence in your students and stakeholders is to take a grassroots approach—have specific data that reflects how programming, interventions, and the overall school counseling program can influence positive growth in the lives of students. For example, asking to pull a student from a class during instruction might be considered offensive. However, taking the time to visit department meetings, presenting at staff meetings, or using whatever platform makes the most sense to get to speak with teachers at the school about reasons that you may have to pull students at inconvenient times of the day will help to relieve any feelings of frustration or uncertainty that teachers may feel. When making these connections, we must maintain confidentiality; however, explaining the process of why students may be pulled versus pulling them with no prior insight into your working with students will help to clarify any unreadiness.

What I love about being a school counselor is the ability to connect, assist students with overcoming hardships, and see them grow into the best versions of themselves. With academics being the primary focus in a school setting, students do not always think to take care of their emotional and social well-being. Being there to serve as a friendly reminder that they are not only students but a whole person is an honor. Being a part of their matriculation gives countless opportunities to serve as a positive influence. For some students, the level of care and compassion we show is the only act of love they may encounter daily; therefore, we must strive to be consistent and considerate forces every day. During my first year as a school counselor, a student came into my office asking for a schedule change. I politely denied his request. As we were talking, however, I asked him how his summer was. His response was that just a few weeks prior to the start of school he was shot. He was grazed by a bullet and purposely covered his forehead with his hair so he would not be reminded of the scar. I was the first person at school he told about the incident. From that moment, this student became a frequent visitor. While our relationship started with assisting him as he dealt with this traumatic incident and other family issues, we were able to further the relationship throughout the remainder of his high school experience by discussing resiliency, college and career readiness, and overcoming stereotypes set by society that can bring feelings of insecurity. Seeing him graduate knowing the hardships he faced was one of the proudest moments of my life. My desire for whoever is reading this is that you will one day be able to see the impact that you have made in the positive choices of your students as well.

Working with students, it is natural to feel overwhelmed or even defeated; however, there is a quote by one of my favorite rappers, the late Nispsey Hussle, that has helped me overcome these feelings of not being good enough. "The game is going to test you. Never fold! Stay ten toes down. It's not on you, it's in you and what's in you they can never take away" (London, 2019). This quote reminds me that even when the going gets tough, we are qualified and able to overcome hardships. You are more than able!

SUMMARY AND CONCLUSION

School counselors can consider ways in which they can incorporate identification of strengths throughout each of the three-tiered MTSS levels of intervention and provide opportunities to connect identified strengths to student opportunities to showcase these strengths at school. Within student advising and planning, school counselors can consider questions to include on forms that would access information about student assets. Careful customization and creation of a school counseling curriculum responsive to and inclusive of the needs and experiences of students is a way to ensure that all students in the building have access to content designed to promote protective factors. Using pre- and postassessments as a part of school counseling curriculum lessons can identify students needing additional support through individual and group counseling. Individual and group counseling interventions can be attuned to developmental assets that students and communities possess and incorporate ways to capitalize on these resources. Building culturally responsive partnerships with families and communities is instrumental in student advocacy and when designing interventions.

On a final note, we would be remiss to talk about strengths-based counseling without considering ways school counselors can create opportunities to infuse joy and celebration within the school environment. On average, students spend at least 8 hours daily at school. They will see their classmates, teachers, and staff more than some members of their own family. Highs and lows students may face during their home life can impact how they function in school. Building a school culture where students feel as if they are seen and valued can strengthen the resiliency of those who do not have support at home and enhance resiliency for those who do. School counselors can increase student belongingness by creating student spaces that affirm and celebrate student identities, presenting programming to students connected to their interests, and creating opportunities to celebrate student successes. In times of crisis, school counselors rise to the occasion to help students balance anxiety and fear with the need to have fun, socialize with their friends, and play. As we work to actively build student resilience, we also create opportunities to expand students' capacity for connection with one another and the larger school community.

CASE STUDY: A STRENGTHS-BASED APPROACH WITH JAMIE

Jamie, a 15-year-old Black student, is returning to school after being suspended for fighting. In April 2020, during the start of the COVID-19 shutdown, Jamie lost her mother due to suicide. She confronted another student for comments that were made on social media regarding her mother and how she died. The school district in which the student lives does not have policies or protocol about online bullying occurring off school grounds; therefore, Jamie was the only party punished. Prior to the suspension, Jamie had minor write ups for her "attitude." Prior to the passing of her mother, she was an honor roll student who had never been in disciplinary issues. On Jamie's first day back, she is tasked with writing a current event in class. The student expresses a desire to write about the murder of Breonna Taylor. When the student shares the idea with the history teacher, the teacher refuses the topic telling the student they need to "get over it." This student is the only student of color in the class and one of 60 Black students out of a total student population of 900. Upset by the teacher's comment, the student appears at the office of the school counselor for support.

DISCUSSION QUESTIONS

1. What should the school counselor do?
2. How would you support the student?
3. How would you navigate a conversation with the teacher about why the student is upset?
4. How do you advocate on a student's behalf to stakeholders while maintaining confidentiality?

OPERATIONALIZING STRENGTH-BASED PERSPECTIVES

From a deficit perspective, it is easy to bring up all of Jamie's struggles and speak to how resources could help. It is crucial to include her in a plan of action and express what she feels comfortable sharing. When responding, it is important to highlight her strengths. For example, her desire to dedicate her class assignment to the death of Breonna Taylor shows that she is passionate about advocating for social causes as well as her ability to support others in their time of need. Using this as a positive reframe when working with her will assist in self-esteem and counteract any negative thoughts she may have about herself or that she perceives from others. From this conversation it would be appropriate to discuss with her what change she would like to see in the school and what outlets are offered to help her be a part of that change if she so chooses. This will give her an opportunity to harness her leadership skills while being involved in work that she is interested in completing.

When speaking with teachers and other stakeholders, it is important to be mindful of confidentiality. Unless a student specifically asks to be mentioned in a conversation with their teacher, the conversation should be framed in a way that all students who share similar struggles can be supported without being singled out. Having a general understanding of the assignment that Jamie and her classmates were assigned is a great segue into asking specific questions about what kinds of topics are allowed and what topics are not. Additionally, asking about the spectrum of topics students decided to write about is a way to gain data while respectfully inquiring about what makes some topics unacceptable. It is understandable if students ask questions about current events, even if it is not applicable to a specific class. Hesitancy for teachers to host platforms to discuss events may be a natural feeling, as teachers may have varying levels of comfort and training in leading these discussions. Advocating for staff collaboration on supporting staff in leading dialogue with students and researching professional development opportunities to assist with this matter is a great start. From there schools can develop a systemic and customized approach that is relevant to the school's culture and value system. Jamie has missed numerous days of instruction due to her mother's passing and the suspension. Advocacy for Jamie may involve examining schoolwide data on suspensions and write ups. It is important to also ensure that the school's approach is aligned with district/county policies. Advocating for this change at the school level as well as the county/district level is instrumental in striving for systemic change. Using data to back up your suggestion can help in the advocacy process.

PRACTICAL APPLICATION

- When teachers refer students for counseling services, ask them to identify two to three strengths the student possess prior to your meeting with them.
- Along with the feelings chart, create a strength-based check-in chart and ask students to self-identify two to three strengths they have.
- Always begin every meeting as the school counselor (teacher, student, parent, caregiver) with identifying multiple areas of the meeting recipient's strengths.

KEY REFERENCES

Only key references appear in the print edition. The full reference list appears in the digital product on Springer Publishing Connect: connect.springerpub.com/content/book/978-0-8261-8753-6/part/part01/chapter/ch02

Arriero, E., & Griffin, D. (2019). Adelante: A community asset mapping approach to increase college and career readiness for rural Latinx high school students. *Professional School Counseling, 22*(2), 1–9. https://doi.org/10.1177/2156759X18800279

Bryan, J., Williams, J. M., & Griffin, D. (2020). Fostering educational resilience in urban schools: Through equity-focused school-family-community partnerships. *Professional School Counseling, 23*(1 part. 2), 1–14. https://doi.org/10.1177/2156759X19899179

Haskins, N. H., & Appling, B. (2017). Relational-cultural theory & reality therapy: A culturally responsive integrative framework. *Journal of Counseling & Development, 95*, 87–99. https://doi.org/10.1002/jcad.12120

Jordan, J. V. (2018). *Relational-cultural therapy* (2nd ed.). American Psychological Association.

Levy, I. P. (2019). Hip-hop and spoken word therapy in urban school counseling. *Professional School Counseling, 22*(1b). https://doi.org/10.1177/2156759X19834436.

Purgason, L. L., Honer, R., & Gaul, I. (2020). Capitalizing on cultural assets: Community cultural wealth and immigrant-origin students. *Professional School Counseling, 24*(1), 1–11. https://doi.org/10.1177/2156759X20973651

Ratts, M. J., & Greenleaf, A. T. (2018). Multicultural and social justice counseling competencies: A leadership framework for professional school counselors. *Professional School Counseling, 21*(1b), 1–9. https://doi.org/10.1177/2156759X18773582

CHAPTER 3

History of the Profession and Future Trends

JENNA M. ALVAREZ, SANDRA LOGAN-McKIBBEN, JESSICA PORTER, AND MARY AMANDA GRAHAM

LEARNING OBJECTIVES

After reading this chapter, students will be able to:

- Summarize the history of the school counseling profession, including critical events that have shaped the field.
- Identify professional counseling organizations that support the work and role of school counselors.
- Discuss current trends relevant to the school counseling profession and their impact on roles and responsibilities.
- Employ strategies for building a comprehensive school counseling program.

STUDENT VOICE

Student "X," a ninth-grade urban school student, provided the following testimonial about her experience with a school counselor:

"A school counselor is there to talk through anything with you. Whether it is about things going on at home, how I feel about school and the other students I am surrounded by in the school building, choices I have for my future and how I can achieve them, and sometimes my counselor is just someone in the building that I can chat with about something other than schoolwork and my academic abilities. I love that I have a safe place to go to when I am feeling overwhelmed or don't know how to handle a situation. Sometimes I don't know exactly why I am feeling the way I am feeling, and I always leave my counselor's office feeling in control of my emotions and myself as a person. My counselor always makes me feel seen in moments when I feel like just another student in the building, and it has boosted my confidence. Overall, my counselor has helped me realize that my voice as a Black student holds value, that I am not just another kid who will end up in the system or who has to deal with the stories from our community and the national news alone. She is someone who has made me feel like we can talk about our hurt and worry and that it is valid. Outside of that, I know she has helped me know when I need to reach out for help.

The beginning of the school year has been scary not having busing in the way that we used to, so she has helped me navigate bus routes and create a plan for getting to and from school. It's really little things most of the time. I tell my friends some of the things that we talk about and the coping strategies we can use to calm ourselves down when we are frustrated and overwhelmed, so I feel like she has not only helped me, but also my friends."

INTRODUCTION

As with any profession, counselors' roles, responsibilities, and focus areas will evolve as technological and societal needs change. All school personnel play an important part of students' schooling experience. These roles shape the future generations. School counselors hold an important place in supporting the success of all PK–12 students across the domains of academic, career, and social-emotional development. This chapter begins by providing foundational knowledge about the school counseling profession and its historical pathway. Key events in the United States have shaped the profession in recent years, leading to identification of the current trends affecting school counselors. Advancements in technology, increasing responsibilities, and future directions will be discussed.

THE EMERGENCE OF SCHOOL COUNSELING: FROM THE 1920s UNTIL TODAY

School counseling has changed since its inception into our school systems as vocational guidance (Cinotti, 2014). Throughout this chapter, we will provide an overview and discussion of the evolution of the school counseling profession from the emergence of school counseling, around the 1920s, to where the profession currently stands. The goal is to highlight some of the historical events that have influenced our profession and shaped our current school counseling practices. Thus, it is also important for us to discuss the current and future trends related to school counseling. The role of the school counselor has shifted from a career-driven, college-bound, *guidance* model to a profession that also focuses on mental health needs (Cinotti, 2014). School counseling still focuses on academics and college-career building, but it has a larger focus on students' social-emotional learning (SEL). Over the last few decades, as a profession, counseling places more emphasis on supporting the student as a whole. We will explore the evolution of school counseling in three primary stages: foundational, transitional, and transformational.

FOUNDATIONAL

The profession of school counseling as we currently know it was not known by this name until the 1980s. However, throughout history, our profession emerged through vocational guidance and the evolution of the U.S. educational system. Indeed, we see the first glimpses of school counseling work in secondary schools through vocational guidance in the early 1900s (Gysbers, n.d.-a). Additionally, Erford (2019) noted that the roots of school counseling started at the very end of the 19th century, with much of the work carrying into the very early years of the 20th century. Later, in the transitional section, we discuss events that occurred within the 20th century. The foundational section is intended to focus on the events that paved the way for our profession.

It is important to discuss the impact of vocational guidance on the profession of school counseling. Concerns for a streamlined standard of practice for vocational guidance surfaced between the 1920s and 1930s (Gysbers & Henderson, 2001). There were many individuals who were instrumental in giving a voice to vocational counseling. Many consider Frank Parsons to be a founding father of vocational guidance. Another foundational individual to the vocational movement is Meyer Bloomfield, who authored vocational guidance, worked at the Vocational Bureau, and conducted lectures related to vocational guidance at Harvard University, Columbia University, Colorado State College, and University of California (Gysbers & Henderson, 2001; Hershenson, 2006; Zytowski, 2001). Additionally, Pauline Agassie Shaw set the foundation for Parsons' ideas around vocational counseling and provided the funding needed to open the bureau (Hershenson, 2006). Furthermore, Frank Parsons wrote a proposal for a Vocational Bureau that would address the educational career needs of youth, and later, in 1908, the bureau itself opened in Boston (Zytowski, 2001). Prior to writing the proposal and the opening of the bureau, Parsons would provide educational lessons to high school students on choosing a career (Zytowski, 2001). In 1909, the Vocational Bureau responded to the need for teachers in Boston elementary and secondary schools to have vocational counseling skills by training approximately 117 teachers to support students' career needs (Zytowski, 2001). Jesse Davis was also influential because he brought guidance into the school systems in Michigan (Zytowski, 2001). All these individuals helped to shape the current focus of college and career readiness in our American schools.

The Role of the School Counselor: Early Days

When we look back on the early days of school counseling specific to our evolution to address social justice and advocacy, Gysbers (n.d.-b) noted that our first social justice issues as school counselors in the 1900s centered around child labor laws. The use of children in the workforce occurred during the Industrial Revolution. At the time, there were no regulations regarding age requirements for entering the workforce or how many hours children were allowed to work. Reform related to how children were used in the workforce started to occur around the early 1900s when The National Child Labor Committee was created in 1904. In 1916, movements by worker unions and legislation started a shift in child labor (Hansan, 2011). In addition to child labor laws setting the groundwork for future school counseling advocacy work, the profession was shaped in the 1920s due to a focus on mental hygiene (Erford, 2019). *Mental hygiene* was the term used in the 1920s to address the mental health needs of students; we now widely refer to this as mental health. During this time, there were studies that focused on children's overall mental hygiene (Erford, 2019; Gysbers, n.d.-a), which caused school counseling to take on a more clinical model of operation, with less focus being placed on economics (Gysbers, n.d.-a). Child labor laws, vocational guidance, and emphasis on mental hygiene were pivotal points that have shaped our current profession, which focuses on academics, college-career, and SEL.

The 1930s brought various job titles associated with guidance personnel. Some of those titles included vice principal, teacher counselor, student counselor, and vocational counselor (Gysbers, n.d.-b). The structure of pupil personnel services was established within this system. The role of the guidance counselor was housed within pupil personnel services along with other key school personnel that supported students within various roles (Gysbers & Henderson, 2001). For example, other pupil personnel services positions included nurses and social workers. The goal was to provide expectations for the work of school counselors. This provided a structure of professional duties housed within pupil personnel services (Gysbers. n.d.-a). While a day-to-day professional role was continuing to develop in the 1950s, our professional identity through our professional organization started to emerge. Next, we will explore the impact of professional organizations on our profession.

Professional Organizational History

Another foundational event occurred when the American School Counselor Association (ASCA) formally became a part of the American Personnel and Guidance Association (APGA), which is currently known as the American Counseling Association (ACA; ACA, n.d.). Erford (2019) highlighted the development of ASCA in 1952. Then, a year later in 1953, the association joined as a division under the umbrella of ACA. Until 2018, ASCA was considered a division of ACA, although they acted as separate organizations for decades. ASCA and ACA formally separated in 2018; at that time, ASCA was recognized as an independent association (Wong, 2018). It is important to highlight the association's history as it is foundational to how school counseling continues to establish and promote a professional identity. It also sheds light on how the profession has changed throughout the decades. Furthermore, it demonstrates how school counseling continues to evolve through the years. In the next section, we will discuss some core transitional pivots within our profession.

Federal Funding and the National Defense Act

Prior to the National Defense Education Act (NDEA) in 1958, the federal government had not provided funding for our public schools. Notably, between 1917 and the early 1950s, most of the federal funding focused on vocational education (Harden, 1981). However, a major turning point related to funding was associated with pressures related to space exploration (Cinotti, 2014). After the Soviet Union's launch of Sputnik in 1957, the U.S. federal government financially invested in education in public schools (United States Senate, 1957). Harden (1981) noted that during this time, many Americans, focused their dissatisfaction on lagging behind the Soviet Union. With the attention on our schools, an opportunity to provide funding came when key individuals, Senator Lister Hill and Representative Carl Elliott, decided to take a different approach to help secure funds needed to make changes within our schools (Harden, 1981; United States Senate, 1957). Between the pressure to compete with the Soviet Union's launching of Sputnik and Congress feeling pressure to support American schools in a new way, the NDEA of 1958 was passed. It is important to first understand the details of the NDEA and how it has influenced the history of school counseling.

The NDEA focused on providing major financial support within 10 areas of the act, called titles (Harden, 1981). Major points of focus for the history of school counseling include *Title V: Counseling Programs and Training of School Counselors*. The primary goal was to support high school students who were considered gifted in becoming college-bound. Additionally, Title V provided the necessary staff training to provide college and career readiness services to high school students. Beyond school counseling support, the NDEA provided higher education loans to support the efforts of school counselors in preparing high school students for postsecondary education. The NDEA still included a focus on vocational education programs, but it also placed an emphasis on math, science, and foreign language programs. The NDEA created a blueprint for how federal funds were distributed and used for multiple areas of public education that previously did not receive federal attention (United States Senate, 1957). In the next section, we explore how our profession continues to develop into the 1960s, 1970s, and beyond.

The Evolution of School Counseling Post-Sputnik

The NDEA paved the way for the profession of school counseling because it provided federal funding for training. Within this act, we see the first partnership between higher education institutions and the government related to providing aid for institutions to develop school counseling training programs. Additionally, through amendments to the NDEA, changes were made to include elementary schools, community colleges, and technical schools. By 1965, the Elementary and Secondary Education Act (ESEA) was passed to help equalize education and address the needs of students with disabilities, students of low socioeconomic status (SES), and English language learners (ELL). Later within this chapter, we discuss how ESEA impacted our profession.

The biggest impact of Sputnik, as we have discussed, was the passage of the NDEA. However, school counseling did not immediately take off in 1958. In fact, during the 1958–1959 academic year, almost all U.S. high school students lacked access to a school counselor or a school counseling program (Flattau et al., 2006). In 1965, it was reported that about 83% of high schools included a school counselor and a school counseling program (U.S. Congress Senate Committee on Labor and Public Welfare Subcommittee on Education, 1967, as cited in Flattau et al., 2006). After the launch of Sputnik in 1957 and the passage of the NDEA in 1958, the number of school counselors within high schools tripled by 1966 (U.S. Department of Health, Education, and Welfare Office of Education Bureau of Elementary and Secondary Education, 1969, as cited in Flattau et al., 2006).

During this time period, the school counselor ratio was set to be one school counselor to 300 students. As the profession continued to be established, the ratio climbed from one counselor to 960 students. Later, the ratio was reduced to one counselor for 450 students (Flattau et al. 2006). In the next section, we will discuss the impact the 20th century had on the profession of school counseling.

TRANSITIONAL

We associate the transitional period with the shift in the professional title of *guidance counselor* to *school counselor*. While the debate over the title and role confusion continues well into the 21st century, we consider the title shift as a transitional period within the profession that led the way for school counseling programming and state-adopted models of school counseling in the 1970s and 1980s. Prior to the title shift, in the 1960s, school counseling started to emerge in elementary schools. In this section, we discuss the impact that the professional title has on our profession. Additionally, we will dive deeper into the impact of the Education Trust and the development of the national standards.

Shift From Guidance to School Counselor

A substantial change in the profession could be noted as the job title shifted from *guidance* counselor to *school* counselor. We were formally referred to as *guidance* counselors, as the work was centered around giving advice and clerical- and administrative-based tasks (Erford, 2019). This is a vast difference from the current role of the school counselor, which is collaborative in nature, data informed, and focused on the best interest of the students through a social justice lens. Erford (2019) noted that during the 1980s, the title of *guidance* counselor started to lose its appeal and was no longer considered the acceptable job title. The transition to the formal title of school counselor was becoming more widely adopted around this time. Gysbers (n.d.-b) noted that in 2001, the term *guidance counselor* was replaced with *school counselor* in federal legislation.

Despite the shifts in terminology by legislation and much of our profession, *guidance* counselor is still being used to refer to the professional work conducted by school counselors. This is problematic as it creates identity confusion for key stakeholders and the public as to what our role is as school counselors. While some might not believe interchanging the terms *guidance* and *school* are problematic, Zyromski and colleagues (2019) explained, "A professional's title may become detached or misaligned from their actual roles and responsibilities" (p. 2). Logan-McKibben and Alvarez (2022) noted the professional identity transitions can be found in the ASCA's current vision and mission statements that reflect the roles and responsibilities of school counselors who embrace social justice and advocacy.

Our title must accurately match the work we do through our comprehensive school counseling program (CSCP). The work is systemic, multilayered, and multifaceted (Gysbers, n.d.-b; Zyromski et al., 2019). Zyromski and colleagues created a survey using a combination of the *ASCA School Counselor Professional Standards and Competencies* (2019a) and the Council for the Accreditation of Counseling and Related Educational Programs (2016) standards. To test the impact of professional titles, two versions of the survey, one using the title *school counselor* and the other using the title *guidance counselor*, were distributed to practicing school counselors (Zyromski et al., 2019). The results of the study indicated that participants who received the survey containing guidance counselor throughout the document were less likely to believe that they could perform the 25 duties listed within the document. However, those who received the version containing the title of school counselor were found more likely to score higher (Zyromski et al., 2019).

While it is important to understand the impact of title within the profession, it is also important to recognize the public and historic events that have shaped and influenced the work of school counselors. Baker and colleagues (2021) decided to replicate the previous study (Zyromski et al., 2019) to determine the public's perception of school counselors versus *guidance* counselors. Like the original study, the researchers found that the general public associated competence with title; higher scores when the title school counselor was used and lower scores when replaced with the term *guidance* counselor (Baker et al., 2021). In addition to the influence of title, school counseling during both the 20th and 21st centuries continued to evolve as a profession.

School Counseling: 20th Century

A critical piece of history that led to our national standards in 1997 and later the development of the first ASCA National Model in the 20th century was the lack of infrastructure and standards that guided the work of vocational counselors. Thus, the work of school counselors could be done by teachers or other individuals who may not have had the formal training needed for the professional (Gysbers & Henderson, 2001). The NDEA started in the late 1950s and was funded through 1968 (Erford, 2019; Flattau et al., 2006). From this act, we saw the birth of the ESEA, which included continued funding opportunities for school counseling. Through ESEA, elementary schools, junior colleges, and technology institutes were added through amendments of NDEA (Flattau et al., 2006). The ESEA has been extensively revised since it was originally established (United States Code, 2010). The Education Trust Fund Act (1995) detailed how local schools could use these funds. The money available through the National Education Trust Fund was designated for use related to the education of students. This could include things such as updated school buildings or teacher wage increases. In 1997, the *National Standards of School Counseling Programs* was developed by Campbell and Dahir (1997) in partnership with the ASCA. As we have mentioned throughout this chapter, a theme for our profession has been the desire to establish a framework or operational system that allowed school counselors to have a professional identity and standard of practice.

The Goals 2000 Educate America Act was passed with the hope of bringing educational reform to address systemic issues in education. Specifically, the act focused on improving the quality of education, increasing graduation rates, and creating a shared vision for education in American schools. Similar to the profession of school counseling in which we are called to support all students, the Goals 2000: Educate America Act sought to support all students in having equal opportunities through access to a quality education. The act included specific goals to decrease high school dropout rates and to ensure that students have adequate nutrition and partake in physical activity. Additional goals included a focus on teachers having access to professional development that would prepare them to educate students in the 21st century. This included specific professional development opportunities regarding students from diverse backgrounds, addressing not only academics but also social and other health needs of students. While the act did not explicitly address school counseling, it did address school safety, the social needs of students, social skill development, and training school staff on working with students who are at risk.

TRANSFORMATIONAL

The 21st century is most notably a period of school counseling where we have seen the profession grow into its current identity. Yet, as Sears and Granello (2002) noted, school counselors were still struggling with their professional identity, which highlights an ongoing theme of professional identity that has occurred for several decades. However, within this century, we see the profession of school counseling continue to grow through the ASCA's release of the first National Model in 2003, with the fourth edition being released in 2019. Prior to the initial release of the model in 2003, we saw federal legislation acknowledge the terminology of school counselor as our professional title in 2001. The Education Trust is still a focus within this century as role definition has continued to evolve.

School Counseling: 21st Century

School counseling in the 21st century is still evolving, growing, and developing. This section focuses on notable developments that have occurred during the 21st century. First, school counselors experienced the national framework for comprehensive school counseling services (ASCA, 2003). Through the years, the ASCA framework has provided accountability and credibility to the profession.

In March 2020, we saw school counseling shift into a virtual model of delivery with the emergency shutdown of U.S. schools due to the COVID-19 global pandemic. During the ongoing pandemic, continued police brutality and the death of George Floyd sparked an outcry for police reform, antiracist practices within our educational systems, and a movement for antiracist school counseling (Mason et al., 2021). The sections below dive deeper into the history and development of the ASCA National Model, virtual school counseling, and the emergence of multicultural competencies. In the Future Directions section, we explore in more detail the role of school counselors as social justice advocates and as antiracist school counselors.

ASCA National Model

Efforts to create the first National Model started in 2001 as the ASCA brought together a professional group of individuals that included counselor educators, practicing school counselors, and other key stakeholders (ASCA, 2012). The goal was to create a system that could continue to help shape the profession to provide services for all students and continue to bridge gaps in professional identity by creating a standard of practice (ASCA, 2012). To continue to shape and encourage a standard of school counseling practice that was comprehensive in nature, the ASCA created the Recognized ASCA Model Program (RAMP) after initially creating the National Model (ASCA, 2012).

A few short years later, in 2005, the ASCA released the second edition of the National Model with the goal of adding theory-based applications (Gysbers, n.d.-a). The third edition of the ASCA National Model was released in 2012, 7 years after the second edition was released, and focused heavily on leadership, advocacy, collaboration, and systemic change. Another seven years later, the fourth and current edition was release in 2019. The ASCA National Model, fourth edition, while similar to the third edition, was streamlined in terms of being more user-friendly and using widely understood language. Notable changes in the fourth edition include the words assess, manage, deliver, and define (ASCA, 2019b). In the third edition, the term *assess* was formerly known as *accountability*, *manage* was *management*, *deliver* was *delivery*, and *define* was called *foundation* (ASCA, 2012).

Virtual School Counseling

It is vital that when we speak of the history of our profession and its future direction, we talk about the impacts of technology and the state of virtual school counseling. Sears and Granello (2002) mentioned that integration of technology is critical to our profession through our CSCPs. Over the last 21 years, technology has continued to shape school counseling in various ways. Sears and Granello noted that they cannot imagine school counselors not using technology to shape how they deliver content to students. The statement holds a lot of truth related to the most notable technological impact that came in 2020 when the worldwide pandemic closed American schools for several months. School counselors were facing new challenges regarding how to support students not only academically, but also socially and emotionally, while being fully remote. In addition, the 2020–2021 academic school year brought a new hybrid school counseling programming approach, as some schools were doing a combination of online and in-person learning to address health and safety concerns associated with the pandemic (Pincus et al., 2020).

Logan-McKibben and Alvarez (2022) noted that while virtual school counseling has gained momentum due to the pandemic, there is currently no widely accepted and adopted virtual school counseling definition or model. However, with the pandemic, several resources did emerge to help support school counselors in the transition back to a multiplatform style of learning, including in-person, hybrid, or fully remote. For example, the ASCA (2020a) released grade level–specific virtual school counseling toolkits. The elementary version includes links to on-demand SEL content, such as Second-Step and Mind Yeti, as a way for school counselors to cultivate learning experiences for students in virtual platforms. Additional online materials include academically focused content that supports students using videoconference platforms. The middle school virtual toolkit provides lessons focused on SEL through Nearpod (ASCA, 2020b), which is an interactive platform that allows counselors and educators to create more interactive content and allows students to provide real-time feedback (Nearpod, n.d.). Just like the elementary version, the middle school virtual toolkit includes contents related to academic development as well as college and career development. As the pandemic has forever shaped our education system, it has also influenced how we use technology to not only address students' needs, but also to interact with students. We are hopeful that the postpandemic period will bring more models and frameworks to help support school counselors develop virtual school counseling materials and practices.

During the 2020–2021 academic year, school counselors not only had to learn how to deliver content virtually, but they also had to learn how to advocate for all students while being in a virtual setting. Hipolito-Delgado and colleagues (2021) explored the experiences of students engaging in remote learning during the COVID-19 pandemic and found that students noted struggling with the adjustment to online learning, access to the appropriate technology, and working through health, family, and financial stressors brought on by the pandemic. School counselors are trained to be active collaborators and communicators within our school systems; thus, we are positioned to support students through the challenges related to communicating during remote learning. Hipolito-Delgado and colleagues recommended that school counselors take a strengths-based approach to actively advocate for students with teachers and administrators in addressing inequity barriers with distance learning during a pandemic. Within their study, they noted that many students did not feel they were supported by their school counselors. Throughout the history of our profession, inequities in education for students are present. School counselors must continue to advocate, within this century and beyond, for the needs of all students.

The Emergence of Multicultural Competencies

In 2021, ASCA adopted *The School Counselor and Anti-Racist Practices* position statement. Creating such a position statement came from ongoing advocacy efforts by school counselors and school counselor educators. This section will focus on the work that led up to the ASCA position statements and other declarations that address working with students with disabilities (SWDs) and lesbian, gay, bisexual, transgender and questioning (LGBTQ+) students. We expand on our social justice efforts as a profession later in this chapter.

In 1992, the first Multicultural Counseling Competencies (MCC) were created by Sue, Arredondo, and McDavis and was intended for all specialty areas of counseling, including school counseling. In 2015, the Multicultural and Social Justice Counselor Competencies (MSJCC) were established as an updated version of the original competencies to reflect the importance of social justice within our multicultural work (MSJCC Revisions Committee, 2015). Sue and colleagues (1992) released a call to the profession in relation to the MCC standards outlining the importance of standards related to multicultural competence within our profession. While the ASCA (2021) calls for the importance of antiracist practices, to date school counselors do not have multicultural competencies standards that are focused on their working within schools, a system that is historically rooted in racism. Our ASCA ethical standards (2016) call us to be change agents, advocates, and leaders within our schools to ensure all students have access to high-quality education. However, some school counselors might need additional support or training to continue to develop in their multicultural and social justice competence. In the Future Directions in School Counseling section, we highlight where the profession is heading and share important resources to aide in antiracist school counseling practice and social justice advocacy (Lewis et al., 2002; Ratts et al., 2010; Trusty & Brown, 2005).

TRENDS IN THE SCHOOL COUNSELING PROFESSION

As with any profession, the roles and responsibilities evolve with the everchanging landscape of our society and technological developments. The role of school counselors has, as it should, evolved into that of leader, social justice advocate, and systems change agent (ASCA, 2019a). Zyromski and colleagues (2019) highlighted the importance of making the transition in title as well, from *guidance counselor* to *school counselor*, to ensure that there is appropriate alignment of expectations that are parallel to the evolution in responsibilities. School counselors must be positioned to address and lead in the areas of virtual school counseling, SEL, college and career readiness, multicultural competency, social justice advocacy, and antiracism work. Over the past six decades, the school counseling profession has evolved; school counselors are uniquely trained to support students' development and successes in personal/social, academics, and career domains (ASCA, 2019b; Savitz-Romer, 2019).

It is easy to understand that technology has improved our lives significantly in many ways. As with any advancement, there are pros and cons. While technology has increased school counselors' ability to connect and communicate with key stakeholders, it has also increased expectations regarding availability, challenging the boundaries that are necessary for work–life balance. Society has impacted the profession as well, challenging school counselors to be fierce advocates for diversity, equity, and inclusion; to promote opportunities for academic success and advancement nd college and career readiness; and to support student's social-emotional development and overall mental health. The role of the school counselor is critical in incorporating all of these aspects of student development and success into school operations. We will now discuss some of these trends and advancements in the school counseling profession.

Social-Emotional Learning and Development

SEL has gained recent attention in the research and practice of school counseling (DePaoli et al., 2017). The ASCA has contended for many years that we, as school counselors, address the three domains of academic, career, and social/emotional development. In recent years, there has been focus brought to the domain of social and emotional learning. SEL is described as the ability to acquire and apply the knowledge, skills, and attitudes toward thinking, feeling, effective communication, and well-being to self and others. Educators and key stakeholders are recognizing the importance of addressing the whole child, which includes their interpersonal development. The Collaborative for Social-Emotional Learning, otherwise known as Collaborative for Academic, Social, and Emotional Learning (n.d.), is a fundamental force related to SEL and development, with a focus on five key areas of competence for all students: *self-awareness, self-management, social awareness, relationship skills,* and *responsible decision-making.*

Social Justice Advocacy and Culturally Sustaining School Counseling

School counselors are advocates for all students, especially those who are marginalized. The ASCA Professional Standards (2018) expect school counselors to demonstrate leadership behaviors that promote advocacy and systemic change. As a school counselor, you *are* a leader and an advocate that promotes social justice, including antiracism, for students and the school environment.

As, emerging school counselors, you may be wondering specifically what antiracist school counseling practices entail. The ASCA's (2021) position statement, *The School Counselor and Anti-Racist Practices,* outline the responsibilities of the school counselor within the areas of awareness/reflection, knowledge/skills, and action and advocacy. Additionally, you should review the following two position statements, *The School Counselor and Cultural Diversity* and *The School Counselor and Equity for All Students,* to gain a better understanding of what cultural diversity and equity is within a school system and in your role as school counselor.

One step that trainees and practicing school counselors alike can take is to form book clubs to better understand and connect with their professional development. *Interrupting Racism: Equity and Social Justice in School Counseling* by Atkins and Oglesby (2019) is an excellent book to facilitate professional dialogue about how school counselors are to engage in this critical work on behalf of their students and families. Another book that is reflective in building your competency as a social justice advocate is *Culturally Sustaining School Counseling* by Grothaus and colleagues (2020). Additionally, your graduate coursework ideally includes learning experiences and assignments that promote your development and ability to identify and disrupt systems of oppression, as recommended by Mason et al. (2021).

College and Career Readiness

School counselors are equipped and expected to provide services that support the college and career readiness (CCR) of all students. There is a continuum of development and services for students within this domain. At the elementary level, school counselors should focus on experiences that promote career awareness, whereas middle school can focus on career exploration, and career preparation will occur during high school. There have been a number of federal initiatives focused on promoting CCR, including Reach Higher, an initiative sponsored by former first lady Michelle Obama, and initiatives that seek to identify and support science, technology, engineering, and mathematics careers for women and minorities (The White House, n.d.). *Career and College Readiness Counseling in P–12 Schools* by Curry and Milsom (2017) is an excellent resource for thoroughly understanding what this area of our role looks like and for specific direction on curriculum and other activities that are developmentally appropriate, by grade level.

FUTURE DIRECTIONS IN SCHOOL COUNSELING

The profession of school counseling is primed to evolve to best meet the needs of students, families, schools, and communities. Along with the trends previously discussed, the areas of professional identity development, training programs, roles in student mental health, and virtual school counseling seem to be at the forefront of shifts in our profession.

Professional Identity Development and Reform

Identity development is an important part of professional training. There has been long-standing debate as to whether school counselors identify themselves as a counselor or as an educator, or a hybrid of the two, and with which identity being recognized as the primary. Levy and Lemberger-Truelove (2021) contend that the role ambiguity that has plagued the profession for many decades could be mitigated by revising the public narrative to understand school counselors as educators who are informed by counseling. Moreover, they suggest that such a shift could sharpen school counselors' practice, which may contribute to improved outcomes, individually for students and systemically for schools. From an opposing perspective, Lambie et al. (2019) purport it is critical to reexamine the role of school counselor and the integration of mental health. This ensures students can receive the appropriate mental health services in schools. The conflict over identity is likely to continue to be an area of contention in coming years and will directly influence how school counselors' responsibilities are shaped.

Regardless of professional identity, Savitz-Romer (2019) asserts that the following four principles are necessary in promoting school counseling reform: building the counseling community, creating a coalition, making room for diversity, and expanding the research base. By advocating, collaborating, and educating with key stakeholders, school counselors do have the ability to impact change and promote successful outcomes for students.

School Counselor Preparation

A critical aspect that is a major contributor to a counselor's professional identity development is their counselor preparation program. As one would expect, not all counselor preparation programs are created equal. That is not necessarily a bad thing, as each program has its own unique attributes and benefits. Yet, it is important that there is a foundational standard for what emerging school counselors' knowledge and behaviors are expected to be. Thus, the professional standards set forth by the Council for the Accreditation of Counseling and Related Educational Programs (CACREP) and the Council for Accreditation of Educator Preparation's (CAEP) Specialized Professional Association (SPA), integrated with standards set forth by the ASCA, create the baseline for the consistent and global training of school counselors.

Virtual School Counseling

Given the advancements in technology and improved accessibility, virtual school counseling is expected to flourish in coming years (Pincus et al., 2020). Whether online learning is taking place as an option for student learning or in response to community needs, school counselors will need to develop the competencies to effectively deliver virtual school counseling services and programming to continue to meet the needs of their studentbody. We encourage counselors to review the ASCA's position statement on virtual school counseling to better understand the counselor's responsibilities (ASCA, 2017). Considerations are needed for how to navigate ethical dilemmas, issues of confidentiality, and relevant school/district/state policies. This area of our profession is still in its infancy and will have many years to develop to full implementation and best practice.

School Counselors and Student Mental Health

Lambie and colleagues (2019) promote the idea that school counselors are a critical part of addressing the increasing student mental health needs, even though the ASCA clarifies in their position statement on student mental health that school counselors provide short-term counseling interventions and referrals to community organizations for long-term care and support (ASCA, 2020). Nonetheless, school counselors would be remiss if they did not understand the intersectionality that exists between student success and mental health. School counselors are well-positioned to support student success, including basic needs, academic development, career development, and social-emotional needs. As the profession evolves, it is possible that the role of school counselors will also continue to evolve in the expectation that school counselors support student mental health initiatives, whether through direct or indirect services.

VOICES FROM THE FIELD

Name: Jessica Porter, MEd, Certified School Counselor (she/her)

Where You Practice: Cincinnati, Ohio; Cincinnati Public Schools

Professional Job Title: ELL School Counselor, Grades 7–12

Bio: Jessica received her Masters from the University of Cincinnati and has served as a school counselor since 2020. She works with students learning English as their second (or third) language, many of whom have experienced a disruption in their education in their home country. Her mission is to serve her students in the areas of academic readiness, social/emotional well-being, and postsecondary planning through culturally responsive practices. Prior to her role as a school counselor, Jessica was an intervention specialist working with students in grades 6–9 in both Columbus, Ohio, and Cincinnati, Ohio.

Starting my career in 2020 at the height of a global pandemic, racial injustices reported nationally, and globally, on every media platform, and the inequity highlighted in Black, Indigenous, People of Color (BIPOC) communities indoctrinated a need for social justice advocacy work by school counselors across the nation. Continuing the school year through 2021, the pandemic did not slow, the injustice did not halt, the natural disasters that swept the nation roared, the political upheaval continued to swell, and the civil unrest and collapse of democratic government in a foreign country solidified the need for school counselors to step in and act. These events in our world directly affect our students, not just those who come from, or are currently part of, those communities. These crises infiltrate our buildings and make students feel unsafe, unseen, burdened, sad, and scared. As school counselors, we can be mindful of the injustices toward our black and brown, out-of-state, refugee, asylum-seeking, undocumented, underrepresented, and socially disadvantaged communities and students who live in and around our school buildings, but the act of being mindful is not enough. This is where we step in. We act, we advocate, we listen, we educate—we become part of the systemic shift.

This is a huge responsibility and one that can feel impossible if we do not start where we see our students currently needing us as change agents. In the school counseling field, we know the importance behind meeting students where they are at. We utilize needs assessments and other evidence-based assessments to know where to start. This year, however, was not a school year that could wait for assessments to learn more about what students are needing from their school communities and counselors. I work at a public school in a large metropolitan Midwest city. We service around 36,000 students (Preschool–12th grade) across 66 schools in a 91 square mile (about twice the area of Manhattan) radius. According to the 2019 Report Card, 80.4% of students in our district are economically disadvantaged (Ohio Department of Education, 2020). Working with students in families who experience economic disadvantages means our support systems need to be at work constantly and consistently. This year, transportation disadvantages have been a source for advocacy work exceedingly early in the year. To provide some perspective, several of the schools within the district work with our local transportation authority, Metro. Metro created extra bus routes in order for students to have access to busing that mimics the access the yellow bus inherently provides. Two weeks before the start of the school year, the close working relationship between the district and local transportation authority dwindled, and Metro canceled those extra routes. The extra bus routes that were in place to ensure students had the transportation they needed were cut off. The result of this meant students were now responsible for their own bus routes while ensuring their own physical safety. Students and families were now expected to find a bus route that would get them to school on time and safely. Transportation to and from school was now not privately accessible to thousands of students, as young as 12 years old.

Before students have entered buildings for the school year, school counselors step in. ASCA Ethical Standards (2014) explicitly state our responsibilities to students and families when handling issues of inequity and access to safety in any aspect of their education.

A.1. Supporting Student Development
g. Are knowledgeable of laws, regulations and policies affecting students and families and strive to protect and inform students and families regarding their rights.
h. Provide effective, responsive interventions to address student needs.

A.10. Underserved and At-Risk Populations

c. Identify resources needed to optimize education.

f. Advocate for the equal right and access to free, appropriate public education for all youth, in which students are not stigmatized or isolated based on their housing status, disability, foster care, special education status, mental health or any other exceptionality or special need.

My classroom lessons have strayed from excitedly sharing who I am as a person, how much I am looking forward to getting to know them as people, where my office is, the supports I am here for, and how I can help them. Instead, they have shifted toward addressing personal safety, how to look up a bus route, how to read a map, how to plan out mornings and evenings to arrive to school on time and get homework done while getting enough sleep. I have spent countless hours on the phone with families, many of whom do not speak English, helping them understand how to support their student in getting to school. I have gathered information such as phone numbers, email addresses, and contacts for families to reach out to for answers to their questions. Additionally, our counseling program wrote a script for families to recite when making phone calls to address the inequity that no safe and reliable transportation to and from school highlights so clearly.

The school counselor's role has shifted significantly in the last 100 years and will continue to do so. As our world changes and grows, so will our students. With that, our responsibility to them will shift. Sometimes, our students' needs may include supporting students in building confidence, improving grades, forming healthy boundaries and habits. Other years, it will look like holding space for them when they are grieving, feeling isolated, oppressed, unloved, and unseen. Unfortunately, we will also experience times in which we will be called to stand up for basic rights our students and families have which should be met without our interference but are not. In whatever ways our students and families need us, we show up not only because it is our duty to do so, but because we are the voice for those whose voices are drowned out.

SUMMARY AND CONCLUSION

With human beings continually evolving and adapting to their environment, the profession of school counseling is expected to do the same. Growth comes from learning from the historical underpinnings and deciding how to proceed from them to advance the profession. Whether it be refining and solidifying your professional identity, developing skills in providing effective virtual school counseling services, or cultivating skills that support students' mental health needs, school counselors are a part of an exciting profession that has the potential to impact the lives of children and adolescents, as well as the community at large.

CASE STUDY

The school counselor met with a 15-year-old female student who was having trouble engaging appropriately with some of her peers. Whether in the classroom, in the cafeteria, on the bus, or in the hallways, the student did not feel as if she could coexist with her peers. She would come to the school counselor's office to request schedule changes, skip classes that were not able to be changed, and was generally disengaged while in class, while also avoiding her teachers' attempts to get her back on track.

The student had no prior reported discipline history and had a record of decent attendance and grades in the A to B range consistently since elementary school. Following her individualized education plan (IEP), she attended one period daily with her intervention specialist to receive extra instructional and academic supports.

When speaking with the student, the school counselor inquires further about why the student does not feel able to interact with others. The student explains that they talk too much, are too loud, and are incredibly disrespectful. While the school counselor attempts to learn more about what each of those annoyances look and feel like, the student opens up about the recent fight between two seventh-grade students at a nearby school, resulting in one of them being killed. She mentioned that while she did not know them herself, she hated that other people were making fun of the situation. There were comments being made on the bus about how her peers would do the same if they were in the situation the two seventh graders were in. It made her uncomfortable, and she was not understanding how her own peers could reflect on that situation and deem such violence as necessary and acceptable. The school counselor asked if the same students who she was having a challenging time interacting with were the same students who were making the comments. With hesitation, the student confirmed.

The next day, the school counselor started to connect with as many students as possible to determine whether any other students were feeling any effects of the recent news regarding the seventh grade students from a neighboring school. All students she saw said the same things—they could not believe it was being joked about, they were scared to be cornered into a fight where they had to defend themselves from someone who could potentially have a weapon with them, they just wanted the fighting to end and for their peers to realize that everyone is scared and to get along. After meeting with more students, the school counselor checked back in with the student she met with the day before. The student expressed that she was willing to talk things out with the students who were bothering her, and all the names she recited were students the school counselor has met with that day who were also grieving and expressing anger and fear.

The school counselor chose to implement a restorative circle, an intervention from restorative justice, with this group of students. Having recently been trained, and although this was the counselor's first circle, it felt as if this would be a moment for everyone to share feelings and experiences related to the fight and subsequent death of a peer within their greater school and city community. Students all took turns answering questions related to how they were feeling, what they felt when they found out, how they have coped, and what fears they continue to have. The circle started out tense, with all students not looking at each other, their body language signaling discomfort and distrust. At the end of the circle, the students were giggling, thanking each other for being part of the circle, and anxious to get back to their other peers, as if there was a group they could return to when things started to feel heavy again. Until the end of the school year, that group of students was inseparable. They asked the school counselor if they would be in all the same classes again the following year, and always stopped by to let her know of any other students who would benefit from a circle.

DISCUSSION QUESTIONS

1. Beyond the actions described by the school counselor, what else could you have done?
2. What cultural identities or systems of oppression should be considered?
3. What is your role in getting restorative justice integrated systemically?

PRACTICAL APPLICATION

- After greeting students in the morning, check emails, messages, and voice mail for urgency and respond to those before starting the day.
- Spend the end of the day answering (and deleting) nonemergency emails, voice mails, and messages.
- Set boundaries with your availability outside of the school day.
- Create a Doodle poll, virtual office hours, or SignUpGenius for teachers to schedule times and appointments.

KEY REFERENCES

Only key references appear in the print edition. The full reference list appears in the digital product on Springer Publishing Connect: connect.springerpub.com/content/book/978-0-8261-8753-6/part/part01/chapter/ch03

American School Counselor Association. (2016). *ASCA ethical standards for school counselors*. https://www.schoolcounselor.org/getmedia/f041cbd0-7004-47a5-ba01-3a5d657c6743/Ethical-Standards.pdf

American School Counselor Association. (2019b). *ASCA national model: A framework for school counseling programs* (4th ed.).

American School Counselor Association. (2021). *The school counselor and anti-racist practices*. https://www.schoolcounselor.org/Standards-Positions/Position-Statements/ASCA-Position-Statements/The-School-Counselor-and-Anti-Racist-Practices

Erford, B. T. (2019). Becoming a professional school counselor: Current perspectives, historical roots, and future challenges. In B. T. Erford (Ed.), *Transforming the school counseling profession* (5th ed., pp. 1–25). Pearson.

Flattau, P. E., Bracken, J., Atta, R. V., Bandeh-Ahmadi, A., Cruz, R. D., & Sullivan, K. (2006). *The National Defense Education Act of 1958: Selected outcomes*. Institute for Defense Analyses Science and Technology Policy Institute. https://www.ida.org/-/media/feature/publications/t/th/the-national-defense-education-act-of-1958-selected-outcomes/d-3306.ashx

Gysbers, N. C. (n.d.-a). *Embrace the past, welcome the future: A brief history of school counseling*. American School Counselor Association. https://www.schoolcounselor.org/getmedia/52aaab9f-39ae-4fd0-8387-1d9c10b9ccb8/History-of-School-Counseling.pdf

Mason, E., Robertson, A., Gay, J., Clarke, N., & Holcomb-McCoy, C. (2021). Antiracist school counselor preparation: Expanding on the five tenets of the transforming school counseling initiative. *Teaching and Supervision in Counseling*, 3(2). https://doi.org/10.7290/tsc030202

Zyromski, B., Hudson, T. B., Baker, E., & Granello, D. H. (2019). Guidance counselors or school counselors: How the name of the profession influences perceptions of competence. *Professional School Counseling*, 22(1), 1–10. https://doi.org/10.1177/2156759X19855654

PART II

Differentiating Aspirational From Actuality: The Impact of the American School Counselor Association on the School Counseling Profession

CHAPTER 4

The ASCA National Model

EVA M. GIBSON, CONSTANCE B. CERTION, AND LATRACI D. ALDRIDGE

LEARNING OBJECTIVES

After reading this chapter, students will be able to:

- Identify the process to define, manage, deliver, and assess a comprehensive school counseling program.
- Select strategies for virtual settings.
- Apply ASCA National Model to practice.
- Employ advocacy and social justice considerations into practice.

STUDENT VOICE

Student "S.T." provided the following testimonial about her experience with a school counselor:

"The greatest impact that a school counselor had on me was during my sophomore year of high school. I didn't realize the impact it would have on me at the time. I was scrolling on Facebook when I saw a post by my stepsister's mom saying that she was missing. I remember being so afraid but also so upset that this was something I found out on social media. I had a lot of emotions, but I didn't really know what to do or say about them. My mom reached out to my counselor hoping that she would give me the skills to cope and someone to talk to. In the moment I didn't really feel the need to talk, but I'm glad that my mom made that decision for me. When I think back to that time of my life, I still feel a sense of dread and worry, so I cannot imagine how much worse it would be if I never took the time to talk to the counselor and process how I was feeling. I never expected that a school counselor could have such an impact on me because I had never reached out before. I was considered a high-achieving student and didn't necessarily feel the need to seek outside support prior to this experience. Now I can look back at that experience and recognize that talking to my counselor was the thing that sparked my interest in working in the mental health field as a psychiatrist."

INTRODUCTION

School counseling programs have dramatically expanded since Jesse Davis's development of a guidance program in the early 1900s (Studer, 2015). Since then, the formation of the American School Counselor Association (ASCA) in the 1950s further supported the school counseling profession. Although the organization provided more resources for practitioners, role ambiguity was quite common within the field. Gysbers and Moore are credited with the development of the first theoretical framework and national model in 1981, which served to guide the profession and school counseling services (Gysbers, 2010). Program components included guidance curriculum, individual planning, responsive services, and system support. The ASCA National Model (2019a) has been updated four times since then; the most recent edition includes revised components: (a) define, (b) manage, (c) deliver, and (d) assess.

Define

The first component, *define*, identifies the student and professional standards that characterize comprehensive school counseling programs. The student standards, *ASCA Mindsets & Behaviors for Student Success: K–12 College-, Career-, and Life-Readiness Standards for Every Student*, are research-based standards that outline desired student outcomes demonstrated by knowledge, skills, and attitudes (ASCA, 2021). The standards should be used to create programming, guide services, and evaluate student development and can be applied to the following domains: (a) academic development, (b) career development, and (c) social/emotional development. The 35 standards are organized into two broad categories, mindsets and behaviors, then into smaller subcategories. The six mindset standards relate to the beliefs or attitudes students exhibit. The 30 behavior standards are visible indicators organized into the following groups: (a) learning strategies, (b) self-management skills, and (c) social skills. Table 4.1 provides a brief illustration of the student standards.

The professional standards include the *ASCA Ethical Standards for School Counselors* and the *ASCA School Counselor Professional Standards & Competencies*. The ethical standards were created to clarify the norms, values, and beliefs of the school counseling profession and present expected practices (ASCA, 2016). The ethical standards address the following responsibilities for school counselors: (a) students, (b) parents/guardians, school, and self, (c) school counselor administrators/supervisors, (d) school counseling intern site supervisors, (e) maintenance of standards, and (f) ethical decision-making. Adherence to these ethical standards helps protect students and counselors. The *ASCA School Counselor Professional Standards & Competencies* parallel the student standards in that they outline the mindsets and behaviors school counselors need (ASCA, 2019b). Similar to the student standards, these professional competencies

TABLE 4.1 Student Standards Overview

CATEGORY	DESCRIPTION
Mindset Standards (6)	Includes student perceptions, attitudes, and beliefs
Behavior Standards	Learning Strategies (10): illustrates the demonstration of student cognitive processes
	Self-management Skills (10): illustrates the demonstration of student self-regulation
	Social Skills (10): illustrates the demonstration of appropriate student interpersonal skills

TABLE 4.2   Professional Standards and Competencies Overview

CATEGORY	DESCRIPTION
Mindset Standards (7)	Includes school counselor perceptions, attitudes, and beliefs about student success
Behavior Standards	Professional Foundation (9): illustrates the required skills of professional orientation
	Direct and Indirect Student Services (6): details appropriate interactions with students and stakeholders
	Planning and Evaluation (9): illustrates required activities to successfully design, implement, and assess comprehensive school counseling programs

may be used to guide and evaluate services to support student academic, career, and social/emotional development. The 31 standards are organized into two broad categories, mindsets and behaviors, then into smaller subcategories. The seven mindset standards refer to the beliefs counselors hold regarding student success. The 24 behavior standards are visible indicators organized into the following groups: (a) professional foundation, (b) direct and indirect student services, and (c) planning and evaluation. Table 4.2 provides a brief illustration of the professional standards and competencies.

Manage

The second component, manage, provides tools that school counselors can use to design and implement effective comprehensive school counseling programs that meet the needs of all students (ASCA, 2019a). This component includes a program focus section as well as a program planning sections. The program focus section addresses identification of counselor beliefs and development of program vision and mission statements. Counselor introspection is important in this process as personal beliefs impact the delivery of student services. Engaging in cultural humility allows school counselors the opportunity to reflect on personal privilege, bias, and intersecting identities while also considering the cultural context, clients, and system. Upon the conclusion of this reflection, school counselors develop a program vision statement illustrating a desired future of student outcomes along with a mission statement that clearly aligns with the school's mission (ASCA, 2019a).

The program planning section includes tools and resources for school counselors to use as they create and maintain comprehensive programs. This subcategory addresses the following considerations: (a) data, (b) annual student outcome goals, (c) school data summary, (d) action plans, (e) program results data, (f) lesson plans, (g) calendars, (h) advisory council, and (i) annual administrative conference. Table 4.3 provides a brief overview of the manage component.

Deliver

The third component, deliver, identifies the means by which school counselors provide services to students and stakeholders (ASCA, 2019a). Direct student services are provided to students, and indirect student services are provided to other stakeholders (i.e., administrators, teachers, parents, school staff, and community stakeholders) on behalf of students. Direct student services include instruction, appraisal/advisement, and counseling. Instruction can be provided in classroom settings (e.g., social-emotional learning lessons), small-group settings (e.g., study skills group), or individual settings (individual instruction to support a student conducting research on postsecondary options). During the appraisal process, school counselors help students identify their abilities, interests,

TABLE 4.3   Manage Component Overview

CATEGORY	DESCRIPTION
Program Focus	Beliefs: School counselors should reflect on personal beliefs as they assess the impact on service delivery.
	Vision statement: School counselors should develop a vision of student outcomes based on counselor beliefs as well as the school and district vision.
	Mission statement: School counselors should create a mission statement that operationalizes the path to the vision and allows for equitable access and opportunities.
Program Planning	Data: School counselors should track and analyze participation, mndsets and behaviors, and outcome data to assess program effectiveness.
	Annual student outcome goals: School counselors should develop measurable goals based on needs determined by analysis of achievement, attendance, and discipline data.
	School data summary: School counselors should analyze school achievement, attendance, and discipline data, as well as supporting information, in an effort to identify strengths and opportunities for growth.
	Action plans: School counselors should develop classroom/group and closing-the-gap action plans to define the scope, focus, and timing of instruction. The ASCA provides templates that school counselors can use.
	Program results data: School counselors should reflect on the previously mentioned action plans and assess the effectiveness of interventions. This data informs future services and should be reported to stakeholders in a concise document.
	Lesson plans: School counselors should create lesson plans that are intentional, data informed, and tied to student standards. The ASCA provides a template that school counselors can use.
	Calendars: School counselors should create and share annual and weekly calendars that communicate program priorities to stakeholders.
	Advisory council: School counselors should form program advisory councils made up of a diverse group of stakeholders to solicit feedback and recommendations. The ASCA provides webinars and additional resources for advisory council development.
	Annual administrative conference: School counselors may use the ASCA's template to create this counselor role agreement. After drafting a proposed agreement, school counselors should meet with school administrators to discuss goals and responsibilities for the upcoming school year.

and skills. This may be achieved through analysis of student data from tests or interest inventories. Based on this information, school counselors offer advisement and make recommendations for students as they develop goals and plans. School counselors also offer short-term theory-based counseling to students in need. School counselors collaborate with families and other professionals to make external counseling referrals for students in need of long-term counseling services.

Indirect student services include consultation, collaboration, and referrals (ASCA, 2019a). Through consultation, school counselors provide (or solicit) information and recommendations to support student needs. Based on the individual situation and school district, school counselors may be sought for advice as an expert, or they may seek advice

TABLE 4.4 Deliver Component Overview

CATEGORY	DESCRIPTION	
Direct Student Services (provided to students)	Instruction: provided in classroom, small-group, or individual settings	
	Appraisal: used to help students identify their abilities, interests, and skills	
	Advisement: recommendations for students as they develop goals and plans	
	Counseling: short-term, theory-based sessions	
Indirect Student Services (provided on behalf of students)	Consultation: means by which school counselors provide (or solicit) information and expert recommendations to support student needs	
	Collaboration: engaging in shared work to achieve a common goal; may be accomplished through teaming/partnering, school/district committees, parent workshops, community partnerships, and crisis response	
	Referrals: provided when student needs are beyond the scope of counselor practice; may encompass academic, career, or social/emotional supports	

from another professional. Through collaboration, school counselors work alongside others to achieve a common goal. School counselors may collaborate through teaming/partnering, serving on school/district committees, facilitating parent workshops, participating in community partnerships, and assisting with crisis response efforts. School counselors make referrals when student needs are beyond their scope of practice. Referrals may encompass academic supports (e.g., tutoring, special education referrals, etc.), career supports (e.g., employment training), or social/emotional supports (e.g., external counseling from community agencies, resources for food scarcity, etc.). Table 4.4 provides a brief overview of the deliver component.

Assess

The fourth component, assess, offers tools and resources for school counselors to evaluate the effectiveness of their program and services (ASCA, 2019a). This component includes a program assessment section as well as a school counselor assessment and appraisal section. The program assessment section provides a school counseling program assessment as well as practical information on annual results reports. The ASCA supplies a template for the school counseling program assessment that school counselors can use to evaluate the implementation of their program. This tool may identify program strengths and opportunities for improvement. School counselors can then use this information to create actionable plans for program improvement. Annual results reports include an analysis of the *Classroom and Group Mindsets & Behaviors Results Reports* as well as the *Closing-the-Gap Results Report* noted in the manage component. This data review allows for a clear focus on student participation, student standards, and outcome data and demonstrates how students are impacted by the counseling program. Results of this analysis should inform and guide future programming. This information should be reported to stakeholders (i.e., student, administrators, teachers, parents, school staff, and community members) to educate the public and advocate for comprehensive school counseling programs. Program results can be shared on websites, in infographics, through presentations, via one-page handouts, at school board meetings, and in school/district data materials. School counselors should also conduct needs assessments several times a year. The initial needs

TABLE 4.5   Assess Component Overview

CATEGORY	DESCRIPTION
Program Assessment	School counseling program assessment: evaluates effectiveness of program implementation; identifies program strengths and opportunities for improvement; ASCA provides a template that school counselors can use
	Annual results reports: analysis of classroom/group mindsets and behaviors results reports and closing-the-gap results report; reviews student participation, mindsets and behaviors, and outcome data
School Counselor Assessment and Appraisal	ASCA School Counselor Professional Standards & Competencies Assessment: allows school counselors to self-assess mindsets and behaviors
	School Counselor Performance Appraisal Template: sample evaluation for administrators and supervisors

assessment in the beginning of the year will provide foundational information regarding programming needed. Ideally, needs assessments should be given to all school stakeholders, including students and parents.

The school counselor assessment and appraisal section provide the following resources: the *ASCA School Counselor Professional Standards & Competencies Assessment* and the *School Counselor Performance Appraisal Template* (ASCA, 2019a). The *ASCA School Counselor Professional Standards & Competencies Assessment* is a self-report instrument in which school counselors rate their mindsets and behaviors as referenced in the manage component. Results of this self-assessment can be used to create personal goals and development plans. The *School Counselor Performance Appraisal Template* is a sample evaluation that administrators and supervisors can use to provide feedback to school counselors. Table 4.5 provides a brief overview of the assess component.

THE ASCA NATIONAL MODEL FOR THE VIRTUAL SCHOOL COUNSELOR

Despite the growth of virtual school counseling, there has been minimal research about this type of school counseling. Of the available research, most has explored how school counselors use technology as a component in their programs (Osborn et al., 2015; Steele et al., 2014). Although these studies can help to describe how society has moved to virtual education in the PK–12 sector, they do not address the roles, functions, and expectations for virtual school counseling programs. While training for virtual counseling may be helpful for graduate students, there is limited information readily available. The sections below outline comprehensive program considerations for virtual school counselors.

Define in Virtual School Counseling

ASCA's define component includes student and professional standards. School counselors working in virtual settings must reimagine what these standards look like in an online format. Notably, ASCA (2017) adopted a position statement, that indicated that virtual school counselors should uphold the same expectations yet recognize and address the challenges of the online environment. Additionally, recent updates to the ASCA ethical code (2016) draw attention to digital citizenship (Section A.14) and virtual school counseling (Section A.15).

Manage in Virtual School Counseling

As previously noted, planning is a large part of the manage component. This is especially true for virtual school counseling as the setting varies from the traditional environment. It is essential that virtual school counselors create routines and procedures in a similar process. Use of a virtual office or classroom can be beneficial resources for students and families. Bitmoji and Google classrooms are free options for school counselors to use. Within these platforms, school counselors can upload information about calendars, resources, and procedures. School counselors must also consider how they will be accessible to students and families. Programs such as Remind, Bloomz, Google Voice, and Smore newsletters are viable options for communication. Two-way communication is important, but be sure to provide clear information about office hours and response times.

Deliver in Virtual School Counseling

As previously noted, direct and indirect student services are associated with the deliver component. School counselors who provide virtual services must be intentional. Every interaction should have a purpose. This is true in a traditional setting, but it is even more important in the virtual setting. Additionally, virtual school counselors must be mindful of how their actions and interactions are perceived in the virtual setting. What may be easily understood in person, may not be the case virtually. School counselors who service both in-person and virtual students must take special care to provide equitable services in both domains.

Assess in Virtual School Counseling

As school counselors assess their programs and services, they must do so in an inclusive manner and consider accessibility issues. To provide a comprehensive evaluation, all students and stakeholders must be included in the process. The use of online forms and telephone surveys can be beneficial tools to reach stakeholders who do not physically come into the building. Providing school counseling services in a virtual environment requires unique considerations, but school counselors who use intentional practices are better equipped to build a comprehensive virtual program.

Providing school counseling services in a virtual environment requires unique considerations. School counselors delivering virtual school counseling core curriculum must make lessons engaging and interactive. Most students do not want to sit passively and listen to an adult talk nonstop for a class period. Try using interactive worksheets and activities. Consider opportunities for discussion or group work. Depending on the virtual platform, there may be options to put students in breakout rooms to work together or to have small-group discussions. Be mindful about classroom management practices. Sometimes managing a virtual classroom can be more difficult than an in-person classroom. Presenting expectations to students early and consistently can contribute to a positive and productive learning environment. These are all strategies school counselors currently use in a traditional setting that can be applied virtually.

College and career readiness can also be addressed in a virtual format. For example, school counselors may first use school counseling core curriculum to help students learn about careers and colleges. Then, school counselors may implement a virtual career fair for students to learn more about specific careers in their area of interests. A virtual career fair takes advance planning, just as does an on-ground career fair; however, one of the major differences is to ensure the presenters use the same online platform the school uses. One strategy may be to hold an information session with the panelists prior to the actual career fair. This provides an opportunity for them to become familiar with the platform and test out different features. Another best practice is to have additional staff on hand the day of the career fair to assist with any unexpected tech issues. With technology, always be prepared for any issues that may arise.

THE ASCA NATIONAL MODEL AND THE INTEGRATION OF SOCIAL JUSTICE ADVOCACY

School counselors who engage in social justice advocacy adopt a courageous approach to dismantling systemic oppression and barriers within the school (Sandifer et al., 2021). This work requires continuous intentional and proactive efforts on behalf of the school counselor. An initial task for school counselors committed to social justice is a comprehensive exploration of student needs and strengths from a cultural, historical, ecological, psychosocial, and sociopolitical lens. As school counselors develop programs, they must focus on creating spaces of equity and justice for historically marginalized students. School counselors are the "keepers of school culture" and should engage in culturally sustaining practices and social justice advocacy (Atkins & Oglesby, 2019, p. 55). The following sections will revisit the ASCA National Model with a social justice lens.

Define With a Social Justice Lens

As previously mentioned, the define component identifies the student and professional standards that characterize comprehensive school counseling programs (ASCA, 2019a). School counselors must be conscious and critical as they navigate this component. While the *ASCA Mindsets & Behaviors for Student Success: K-12 College-, Career-, and Life-Readiness Standards for Every Student* is research based, it is important to note that standards often reflect the norms and assumptions of the group that holds the most power, and other subgroup norms are viewed as deficient (Grothaus et al., 2020). Additionally, although the ASCA provides student standards, school counselors develop competencies that define how students demonstrate proficiency. School counselors must consider the following: (a) What values are embedded and what groups align with (and benefit from) these values? (b) What contextual factors are considered during criterion interpretation? (c) Do the student expectations overlook the values of historically marginalized groups? (d) How can biases impact the evaluation of demonstrated behaviors? As school counselors often integrate standards into curriculum for classroom and small-group lessons, it is important that programming is culturally relevant and reflects a commitment to diversity in delivery and assessment.

As previously noted, the professional standards (i.e., *ASCA Ethical Standards for School Counselors* and the *ASCA School Counselor Professional Standards & Competencies*) were created to guide school counselor behaviors and present expected practices (ASCA, 2019a). As these standards have been updated over the years, it is important that school counselors remain up to date on most recent changes. For example, the most recent version of the ethical codes added topics on sexual orientation, gender identity/expression, counselor bias, and underserved and at-risk populations (ASCA, 2016). ASCA ethical standards were created and updated to clarify the values of the profession, but Grothaus et al. (2020) presented some additional ethical models for consideration. These approaches include that of Luke et al. (2013; as cited in Grothaus et al., 2020), intercultural model of ethical decision-making for school counselors; Garcia et al. (2003; as cited in Grothaus et al, 2020), transcultural integrative model; and Frame and Williams (2005; as cited in Grothaus et al., 2020), multicultural ethical decision-making model (as cited in Grothaus et al., 2020). As school counselors adhere to *ASCA's School Counselor Professional Standards & Competencies*, they should intentionally integrate a culturally affirming approach.

Manage With a Social Justice Lens

As previously mentioned, the manage section provides program focus and program planning tools for the design and implementation of comprehensive school counseling programs (ASCA, 2019a). As school counselors focus on culturally affirming program development, they identify beliefs and create a vision and mission statement. Grothaus et al. (2020) provided some sentence stems that school counselors can use as they explore their beliefs. They include self-reflection on areas of how you feel regarding equity for all, roles as advocates, teaching strategies and curriculum development, culturally relevant discipline, and family engagement. School counselor beliefs and practices should demonstrate a commitment to an equitable and inclusive program centered around social justice.

The program vision statement illustrates the school counselor's hopes for the students and articulates how students are impacted by the counseling program (ASCA, 2019c). The vision statement should be aligned with that of the school and district and is enhanced by stakeholder input. Culturally diverse contributions from various stakeholders allow for a more inclusive statement that reflects expanded worldviews. School counselors must be intentional and actively invite others to participate in this process, especially those in historically marginalized groups. The following hypothetical example may be helpful as school counselors create their own vision statement:

> The students of Sankofa Middle School are lifelong learners, independent thinkers, respectful individuals, and responsible citizens. They celebrate diversity and advocate for the needs of others. Students from our school excel in their academics, careers, and social/emotional relationships. As respectful, responsible, and engaged citizens, our students continue to maximize their strengths and seek opportunities to grow.

The program mission statement, aligned with that of the school and district, illustrates how the school counseling program will achieve the vision (ASCA, 2019c). This statement conveys actions that support the development of a culturally affirming program centered around student success. The following hypothetical example may be helpful as school counselors create their own mission statement:

> The mission of the Sankofa Middle School Counseling Center is to provide all students with a counseling program to help meet their potential. We strive to provide culturally affirming educational programs and material to students, parents, and staff and to enhance communication and inclusion between all three entities. As advocates for equitable access and opportunities, we also engage in the development of students' academic, career, and social/emotional arenas to empower them to become successful in the school and when they depart.

As school counselors develop plans for culturally affirming programs, they must use a social justice lens when considering data, annual student outcome goals, the school data summary, action plans, program results data, lesson plans, calendars, advisory councils, and the annual administrative conference. The following questions may serve as a resource during this planning process:

- What gaps are evident between groups as we review achievement, attendance, and discipline data?
- Are we discussing culturally relevant factors as we create student outcome goals?
- Do our goals serve to reduce barriers?
- Are we integrating culturally relevant perception data in our planning process?

- Do we plan lessons that celebrate diversity and various cultures?
- Are we creating culturally inviting climates?
- Do our calendars include cultural considerations such as diverse events, holidays, and programs? Are they in languages other than English?
- Do we use our annual administrative conference as an opportunity to advocate?
- Does our advisory council reflect a variety of cultural groups?

Exploration of these questions may provide school counselors with a sound foundation as they continue to build a program that focuses on social justice and advocacy.

Deliver With a Social Justice Lens

As previously mentioned, the deliver section identifies the means by which school counselors provide direct and indirect services to students and stakeholders (ASCA, 2019a). In response to a rash of public displays of racial injustice, the ASCA released the *Eliminating racism and bias in schools Standards in Practice* (2020), *which* explicitly outlines responsibilities for school counselors as advocates within the deliver component. This document describes specific actions that promote social justice within school counseling programs. As instruction can be provided in classroom, small-group, or individual settings, school counselors have the opportunity and responsibility to integrate culturally affirming practices in a variety of methods. Scholars note that the use of culturally affirming teaching strategies supports the development of all students and fosters positive relationships (Gibson, 2020). The ASCA (2020) recommends that school counselors deliver lessons that facilitate cultural awareness, create a sense of belonging, address racism and bias, introduce advocacy skills, examine bias, and explore strategies to navigate oppressive and unjust systems. Additionally, school counselors should use culturally inclusive materials and elevate the voices of diverse guest speakers. During the delivery of lessons, it is critically important that school counselors reject punitive and oppressive approaches to classroom management and adopt restorative approaches instead. While the ASCA website offers instructional resources for social justice– oriented counselors, *Learning for Justice* (https://www.learningforjustice.org/) also provides free tools, trainings, and lessons for educators.

During appraisal and advisement, it is crucial for school counselors to approach this process with awareness and cultural sensitivity. Unfortunately, research indicates that, although school counselors are tasked with the responsibility to support all students, eligible students of color are provided fewer opportunities for advanced placement classes and gifted programs (Davis et al., 2013; Francis et al., 2019; Wright et al., 2017), but are overidentified for special education programs and retention (Sandifer & Gibson, 2020; Sandifer et al., 2021). School counselors committed to social justice should deliver and interpret assessments with a culturally affirming lens. Use of a strength-based approach allows for an exploration of best fit and embraces student potential.

School counselors can also use individual and small-group counseling to lean into social justice work. Counseling approaches that center sociocultural understandings of students, such as narrative, social constructivism, strength-based approaches, ecological frameworks, and critical theories (e.g., African American male theory, critical race theory, feminist theory, relational cultural theory, queer theory, etc.) are relevant frameworks that school counselors can apply to student sessions (Sandifer et al., 2021). It is also important that school counselors validate the feelings of students who verbalize oppressive experiences and help students navigate barriers. Additionally, school counselors must also support and educate students who engage in harmful behaviors against others (ASCA, 2020). School counselors may teach offending students' skills and strategies to repair the harm they have inflicted.

Consultation is a flexible process in that at times the school counselor may be sought as an expert consultant and other times the school counselor may seek out consultation. When providing consultation services, Grothaus et al. (2020) recommends applying a culturally affirming, multitiered approach. At Tier 1, consultation may look like the provision of professional development for school staff based on identified needs (e.g., facilitating trainings on working with Latino families). At Tier 2, after further disaggregation of data (e.g., examining discipline referral rates by classroom), consultation may look like working with small groups of teachers who need additional support with classroom management and culturally appropriate responses to behavior. At Tier 3, consultation may look like targeted classroom observations with follow-up individual teacher sessions to cocreate an action plan that considers culture and context of student behavior. At times, school counselors may need to seek out cultural consultation services to better inform their work with students. School counselors should develop relationships with cultural brokers that they can lean into for support. Cultural brokers are defined as individuals from diverse cultural backgrounds who may help bridge the gap between the professional and the target population (Bryan et al., 2020). Intentionally creating and fostering these relationships strengthens the connection between school counselors and stakeholders.

Collaboration varies from consultation in that it is a shared process with communal responsibilities (ASCA, 2019a). As previously noted, school counselors may collaborate through teaming/partnering, serving on school/district committees, facilitating parent workshops, participating in community partnerships, and assisting with crisis response efforts. Using a collaborative, assets-based approach provides more opportunities for diverse perspectives, which may result in more inclusive culturally affirming programs and practices. It is also important to note that individuals from marginalized groups may not be included in decision-making and planning processes. As such, school counselors are tasked with the responsibility to invite diverse members, elevate their voices, and bring up cultural considerations if these voices are not represented.

As stated earlier, school counselors make referrals when student needs are beyond the scope of their practice. A culturally affirming approach to referrals entails the use of community asset mapping. This process is defined as informal research into community capital to help students and families become aware of local resources (Griffin & Farris, 2010). Community asset mapping may be used to identify systems of support within the area to include individual assets (e.g., clinical mental health counselors), community groups (e.g., mentoring programs), and official support organizations (e.g., translation services, local Social Security office, etc.). Additionally, school counselors should also refer students who have experienced racism and bias to school or community resources that offer support and encourage healing. ASCA (2020) also urges school counselors to refer perpetrators of racism to appropriate resources for follow-up. For example, while school counselors are not disciplinarians, they can support responsible parties by teaching appropriate skills, soliciting the assistance of school administrators, and providing resources for parents/caregivers.

Assess With a Social Justice Lens

As previously mentioned, the assess component provides guidance and tools for program and service evaluation (ASCA, 2019a). Assessment data can be used to advocate and support students, or if used haphazardly, it can prove harmful. School counselors must be mindful of equitable data usage practices and consider how bias may impact the process of gathering and collecting data (Grothaus et al., 2020). School counselors committed to social justice engage in comprehensive critiques to identify what data is missing and develop an evaluation plan that targets equity efforts while centering culturally affirming practices. When conducting program evaluations, the following questions may be helpful starting points:

- Do we lead (or initiate) equity-related trainings for faculty and staff?
- Do we engage in efforts to bolster school climate?
- Are we soliciting feedback from diverse groups?
- Is our programming accessible?
- Do we use cultural brokers and engage in community asset mapping?
- Are we promoting positive behavior support and restorative practices in classroom management?
- What policies/practices do we have in place that are oppressive?
- What are we doing to disrupt systemic barriers?

School counselors should consider these questions and others as they evaluate their program and services through an equity lens.

VOICES FROM THE FIELD

Name: Constance B. Certion, EdD (she/her)

Where You Practice: Shelby County Schools, Memphis, Tennessee

Professional Job Title: School Counselor; Counseling Service Manager

Bio: Constance is a Counseling Service Manager and advocate for students in the Shelby County School District.

While the daily work of a practicing school counselor can be rewarding in many ways, at times it can be unpredictable, fast-paced, and overwhelming if great care isn't taken to prepare for potentially stress-inducing moments such as schoolwide or individual crisis situations with students, ethical dilemmas, and irate parents to name a few. ASCA's National Model (2019a) provides a blueprint that can be implemented practically while providing school counselors with the flexibility to develop a program that is unique and specific to their counseling style as well as the needs of the school population that they serve.

Managing a school counseling program can be intimidating to a new school counselor due to the emphasis on defining the focus of the program and mapping out a plan to execute this effectively. As a practicing school counselor, I found that it was helpful to use all resources that were available to me, including various sources of data, the invaluable perspectives of stakeholders, and consultative conversations with school leaders. Data such as quarterly and annual attendance reports, disciplinary action reports, standardized test scores, pretest/posttest scores, American College Testing (ACT) scores, and college acceptance rates can be disaggregated and examined to help identify potential areas of focus. The formation of a knowledgeable and diverse advisory council can also strengthen a counselor's ability to see beyond the numbers. It has been my experience that our school's leadership team, composed of department chairs, Parent/Teacher/Student Association executive board members, and a wide sampling of current students, are the most accessible stakeholders to include on the council. Using this model to form an advisory council has usually yielded insightful ideas and feedback that are often a reflection of the larger body of stakeholders.

Once the focus is narrowed, the action steps are easier to define. Counselors within my district are keen on developing a calendar at the start of the school year that provides an overview for counseling services that will be provided for the year. The contents of the calendar for an elementary school counselor may look entirely different from that of a high school counselor. For example, an elementary school counselor's calendar may contain the scheduled outline of topics for social-emotional learning lessons conducted with classes throughout the year, whereas the high school counselor's calendar might be filled with dates to conduct specific events such as a college/career fair, ACT boot camps, Free Application for Federal Student Aid (FAFSA) Nights for parents, Armed Services Vocational Aptitude Battery (ASVAB) testing, and individual student course planning meetings. However, at the heart of the activities on either calendar should be the reverberation of the outlined focus of the counseling program.

It would be considered unwise to begin constructing a house without a blueprint; similarly, comprehensive school counseling programs must be developed with an end goal or vision in mind. These goals are often shaped and driven by the needs of a particular school. Perhaps the goal for a school with dismal attendance rates or spikes in disciplinary issues would be to improve those areas by a certain percentage. A high school with a low rate of students matriculating to 2- or 4-year colleges might establish a focus on fostering a college-going and college-ready culture with a focus on access. School counseling is not a one-size-fits-all approach, and for this reason, it is highly beneficial to conduct needs assessments to determine what the specific needs of the school might be. It is often desirable to obtain multiple perspectives from key stakeholders, such as students, teachers, parents, and administrators. Needs assessments can also be conducted with smaller groups or on an individual basis to guide the services provided by the counselor. Within my current district, we survey parents at the district level and often include specific questions in the needs assessment that speak to the areas that counselors would typically be involved in overseeing, such as social-emotional learning, mental health, and college/career readiness. If it is not standard practice for your district to conduct this type of survey with students or parents, do not let that deter you from getting the information that you need. There is a multitude of services available to administer online surveys, such as Survey Monkey, Qualtrics, and Google Form. The results are typically provided in a clear manner that makes the analysis of the data simple and easy to understand.

It is imperative that school counselors not only develop a system for examining the needs of the populations they serve but also create a tool to assess the quality and effectiveness of their programs and services. One example of when this could occur would be if a counselor desired to gauge how successful interventions were with a student or a group of students. Another example of this might be the evaluation of a program following a specific event, such as a parent workshop or guest speaker for students. This information would be useful in shaping future events and determining how to strengthen them and enhance participation or engagement in the future. The same online resources used for needs assessments could be utilized or some counselors may prefer the more traditional paper-and-pencil evaluations of their program(s). Regardless of the method, the value of this piece of information cannot be underestimated as it will allow counselors to measure the quality and effectiveness of individuals as well as comprehensive school counseling programs.

SUMMARY AND CONCLUSION

The field of school counseling has evolved over the years from the early days of "guidance counseling" to the current expectations of comprehensive school counseling programs. School counselors are uniquely trained to address the academic, career, and social/emotional needs of all students. Effective programs are inclusive and well-planned. This chapter presents practical applications for school counselors to adequately define, manage, deliver, and assess their on-ground or virtual programs. Additionally, this chapter addresses culturally affirming practices as school counselors implement programming. While this chapter lays a foundation for effective practice, school counselors must commit to ongoing professional development in an effort to maintain competency and to best support students.

CASE STUDY

Shontia is a second-year counselor who is excited about her job but is still acclimating to the profession and her school. She has been working on developing relationships with stakeholders to best meet the needs of her students. Her efforts have produced positive results, and school administrators are beginning to see her as a collaborative partner and welcome her professional contributions. Recently, school administrators called a meeting in the auditorium for all the students with excessive discipline points. The purpose of the meeting is to encourage the students to make better choices to avoid further negative consequences. They invite Shontia to be present as well. During the meeting, she looks around the auditorium and realizes that the majority of the students are African American males. Shontia recently reviewed her school data and remembers that African Americans make up only 38% of the student body, yet, as she looks around, she notices that they are the overwhelming majority of the students receiving discipline referrals. What should Shontia do about this disparity?

Shontia created a 6-week group for African American male students with excessive discipline referrals. She used a strengths-based approach and created lessons based on success skills, relevant cultural issues, and the ASCA Mindsets & Behavior Standards. She informed administration and teachers about group meeting times and topics. She also invited African American male guest speakers to participate in the process. Shontia presented the data on school discipline disparities during a faculty meeting and discussed implicit bias. She also started integrating cultural topics and relevant resources into her monthly newsletter that she sent to faculty and staff. She remained connected to the families of participants and sent relevant opportunities and resources to them as well. During the implementation period, Shontia collected participant preperception/postperception data, weekly discipline data, and weekly academic data. Upon the conclusion of the group, participants demonstrated a 73.68% decrease in overall group average rate of discipline referrals earned during the marking period. Although the sessions focused on behaviors rather than academics, student grades improved. Additionally, participants expressed a sense of belonging, and teachers initiated more frequent collaboration when concerns arose regarding these students. Outcome and perception data indicated that this intervention was successful. Although Shontia was pleased with the results, she also knows that continued work is needed to champion equity and student success.

DISCUSSION QUESTIONS

1. Beyond the courses I am taking in my graduate program, how can I prepare for the field? What resources can I begin to collect to support my work with students? How can I develop mentors within the field?
2. How do I begin to plan a comprehensive program that is equitable and inclusive? What actionable tasks and relevant timelines do I need to establish?
3. When I start working at a school, how can I develop positive relationships with students? Administration? Faculty/staff? Families? Community stakeholders?
4. How will I hold myself accountable?

PRACTICAL APPLICATION

- Develop an ASCA National Model checklist for integrating the framework for both in-person and virtual settings.
- Offer a professional development for the whole school on the ASCA National Model and its importance.
- Use an electronic newsletter to solicit feedback and share program data. If your school already has a newsletter, consider having a section dedicated to school counselor communication where you share information and reiterate the lessons for the week or month.
- Ensure that your school—brick and mortar or virtual—has protocols for dealing with assessing crisis situations and for crisis response. Be familiar with the school's policies to determine how to respond to situations such as these from a virtual platform.

KEY REFERENCES

Only key references appear in the print edition. The full reference list appears in the digital product on Springer Publishing Connect: connect.springerpub.com/content/book/978-0-8261-8753-6/part/part02/chapter/ch04

American School Counselor Association. (2016). *ASCA ethical standards for school counselors.*

American School Counselor Association. (2019a). *The ASCA National Model: A framework for school counseling programs* (4th ed.).

American School Counselor Association. (2019b). *ASCA school counselor professional standards & competencies.*

American School Counselor Association. (2019c). *The ASCA National Model implementation guide: Manage & assess* (2nd ed.).

American School Counselor Association. (2020). *Eliminating racism and bias in schools.* https://www.schoolcounselor.org/getmedia/542b085a-7eda-48ba-906e-24cd3f08a03f/SIP-Racism-Bias.pdf

American School Counselor Association. (2021). *Mindsets and behaviors for student success: K–12 college-, career-, and life-readiness standards for every student.*

Atkins, R., & Oglesby, A. (2019). *Interrupting racism: Equity and social justice in school counseling.* Routledge.

Grothaus, T., Johnson, K. F., & Edirmanasinghe, N. (2020). *Culturally sustaining school counseling: Implementing diverse, equitable, inclusive programs*. The American School Counseling Association.

Sandifer, M. C., Gibson, E. M., & Brant-Rajahn, S. N. (2021). WOKE: Advocacy for African American students. In M. A. Rausch & L. L Gallo (Eds.), *Strengthening school counselor advocacy and practice for important populations and difficult topics* (pp. 19–40). IGI Global. http://doi:10.4018/978-1-7998-7319-8.ch002

CHAPTER 5

Mindsets and Behaviors for Students and Professional School Counselors

NANCY CHAE, ANGELA I. SHEELY-MOORE, AND CONSTANCE JOHNSON

LEARNING OBJECTIVES

After reading this chapter, students will be able to:

- Define student standards to support students' academic, social and emotional, and college and career development as well as to enhance professional school counseling practice.
- Explain the development of the ASCA student standards to inform how school counselors develop professional competence to promote student success.
- Apply relevant student standards when developing school counseling core curriculum in addition to small-group and individual counseling interventions.
- Assess limitations of the ASCA Student Standards and supplement gaps with other tools to support students' academic, social and emotional, and postsecondary development, as well as employ social justice advocacy with school counseling practice.

STUDENT VOICE

Ms. Bookman, an elementary school counselor, used the behavior standard, B-SMS 7, Demonstrate effective coping skills when faced with a problem, to teach students to identify and cope with their emotions. Using the Zones of Regulation (Kuypers, 2011), a research-informed curriculum to teach emotional regulation, students learned to categorize their feelings into four colored zones: (1) blue identified slow-moving emotions, like sad and tired; (2) green referred to being calm and alert; (3) yellow referred to elevated emotions, such as stress, excitement, and nervousness; and (4) red described intensified emotional states, such as being out of control with elation, anger, or frustration. The zones provided a common language for students and staff to describe feelings. Ms. Bookman not only taught these zones to students, but she also trained teachers to use the zones in their classrooms and during their daily morning meetings. One day, during a family event at the school,

Mrs. Cruz, the mother of a third-grade student named Katrina, stopped to talk to Ms. Bookman about her daughter. Mrs. Cruz remarked that Katrina began telling her family members which zones they were in and ways to calm themselves. "At first, I kept wondering why Katrina was saying that I was in yellow and on my way to red. It was annoying me! However, now that I understand the zones, we're using it to talk about feelings at home too!" Mrs. Cruz shared. Ms. Bookman was excited to hear that Katrina taught and shared the zones with her family, which also supported improved family communication and strengthened connections.

INTRODUCTION

According to the American School Counselor Association (ASCA), mindset standards are beliefs and psychosocial attitudes of school counselors and students that translate into actions, and behavior standards consist of measurable skills and competencies. Mindsets and behaviors comprise the ASCA Student Standards, which convey the knowledge, attitudes, and skills that school counselors develop and possess to deliver a comprehensive school counseling program (ASCA, 2019b). The standards ensure that comprehensive school counseling programs serve the needs of all students in these key areas. The student standards are also the knowledge, attitudes, and skills recommended by the ASCA to promote students' academic achievement, college and career planning, and social/emotional development (ASCA, 2014). Hence, the ASCA uses the language of mindsets and behaviors to define standards for students (i.e., the ASCA Student Standards: Mindsets & Behaviors for Student Success: K-12 College-, Career-, and Life-Readiness Standards for Every Student) and professional practice (i.e., ASCA School Counselor Professional Standards and Competencies). Both documents can be found on the ASCA website at www .schoolcounselor.org.

Within the "Define" component of the ASCA National Model (ASCA, 2019a), the ASCA Mindsets & Behaviors for Student Success: K-12 College-, Career-, and Life-Readiness Standards for Every Student (ASCA, 2014) and the ASCA School Counselor Professional Standards and Competencies (ASCA, 2019b) are two of three documents of school counseling standards that define the school counseling profession (the third document being the ASCA Ethical Standards for School Counselors; ASCA, 2016a). This chapter (a) delves into the ASCA Student Standards: Mindsets & Behaviors for Student Success: K-12 College-, Career-, and Life-Readiness Standards for Every Student, which discusses applications to classroom lessons and small-group and individual counseling, and noted limitations; (b) explores the ASCA School Counselor Professional Standards and Competencies to support school counselor professional development and practice; and (c) presents social justice advocacy and virtual school counseling issues and their connections to applying the ASCA Student Standards.

ASCA STUDENT STANDARDS: MINDSETS AND BEHAVIORS FOR STUDENT SUCCESS

Historical Background

In 1997, on behalf of the ASCA, Campbell and Dahir published The National Standards for School Counseling Programs, which was followed by an implementation guide, Vision into Action: Implementing the National Standards for School Counseling Programs (Dahir et al., 1998). These seminal publications served to clarify the roles of school counselors, improve school counselor training opportunities, and provide a structure for a comprehensive and developmentally focused school counseling programming

(Campbell & Dahir, 1997). The ASCA eventually adapted Campbell and Dahir's work and retitled it as the ASCA National Standards for Students (ASCA, 2004) to promote a vision for comprehensive school counseling programs as a means for school counselors to equitably support and advocate for all students' academic, social and emotional, and postsecondary needs.

The National Standards for School Counseling Programs (Campbell & Dahir, 1997) and the ASCA National Standards for Students (2004) outlined nine standards across three student developmental domains: academic, career, and personal/social. Each standard included specific competencies (i.e., student expectations for each content standard) and indicators (i.e., students' demonstration of having met the competency), totaling 16 competencies and 122 indicators overall (ASCA, 2005). School counselors then identify and focus on specific standards and competencies that align with the school's and school counseling program's mission statements, as well as plan, design, implement, and evaluate classroom lessons, small-group curriculum, and individual counseling sessions in the areas of academic, career, and personal/social development (ASCA, 2005). Altogether, school counselors use these standards to measure student growth and development, guide program activities, and promote a comprehensive program to support students in achieving their highest potential.

The Next Iterations of Student Standards

The ASCA released the next generation of the ASCA National Standards for Students in 2014, entitled The ASCA Mindsets & Behaviors for Student Success: K-12 College-, Career-, and Life-Readiness Standards for Every Student. Streamlined from the vast number of indicators in former iterations, the ASCA Mindsets and Behaviors delineated 35 mindset and behavior standards, that reflect specific knowledge, skills, and attitudes across the academic, college and career, and social/emotional developmental domains that students should be able to demonstrate as a result of participating in a comprehensive school counseling program. In 2021, ASCA released the newest iteration, *ASCA Student Standards: Mindsets & Behaviors for Student Success: K–12 College-, Career-, and Life-Readiness Standards for Every Student* (ASCA, 2021a). Updates within this latest version include (a) one additional social skills standard (B-SS 10, Cultural awareness, sensitivity, and responsiveness), for a total of 36 standards; (b) updated language about acceptance, respect, inclusion, and diversity, with inspiration from Learning for Justice's Social Justice Standards (Teaching Tolerance, 2018); and (c) modified language of competencies to reflect grade-level learning objectives. The University of Chicago Consortium on Chicago School Research's (2012) *Teaching Adolescents to Become Learners* proposed five categories of noncognitive factors (i.e., academic behaviors, academic perseverance, academic mindsets, learning strategies, and social skills) that serve as the primary framework to inform the development of both iterations.

The ASCA Student Standards include two categories of standards: mindset standards and behavior standards. Mindset standards consist of six mindsets related to students' beliefs and attitudes about themselves in relation to their academics, social/emotional wellness, and postsecondary endeavors across the lifespan. The behavior standards include 30 behaviors associated with student success and are grouped into three subcategories: (a) learning strategies, (b) self-management skills, and (c) social skills (ASCA, 2021a). Furthermore, ASCA created the ASCA Student Standards Database (https://www.schoolcounselor.org/), which includes sample learning objectives to help school counselors meet students' developmental needs and align with academic content. Ultimately, school counselors operationalize these mindset and behavior standards by identifying learning objectives when planning and implementing core curriculum lessons, small groups, and other activities related to addressing student developmental needs.

RESEARCH ABOUT THE ASCA STUDENT STANDARDS

Although the development of the ASCA Student Standards is based on a combination of theory, research, and practices, there are no empirical studies to date that substantiate the effectiveness of using the ASCA Student Standards (Chae, 2020). Practitioners have, however, led research studies that support using these student standards to inform, target, and measure outcomes of selected noncognitive areas related to academic and social success for elementary-aged students (Abel et al., 2016; Mariani et al., 2016). Mariani et al. (2016) developed a college and career-readiness unit for fifth-grade students called Operation Occupation, which was aligned with identified mindsets and behaviors standards and Kentucky's Common Core Standards, and reported increases in students' knowledge and awareness of college and career-readiness standards as a result of the intervention. Similarly, Abel et al. (2016) evaluated the Student Success Skills (SSS) program using teacher-reported ratings of five student learning behaviors in the ASCA Student Standards (i.e., self-motivation/self-direction, self-discipline/self-control, coping skills, listening skills, and positive/supportive relationships), and found that teachers reported increased observations of the five learning behaviors, albeit with small effect sizes (Abel et al., 2016). Researchers have also used the ASCA Mindsets and Behaviors as a framework for studies in an international context (e.g., Karaman et al., 2019; Yavuz, 2019).

Other researchers have suggested the application of ASCA Mindsets and Behaviors within multitiered systems of support (MTSS), which is a tiered system of support to proactively and responsively provide a continuum of evidence-based practices that promote students' academic, behavioral, social, and emotional outcomes (Sugai et al., 2019). Mindsets and behaviors can be used when planning and delivering interventions across all tiers. For example, by integrating Tier 1 interventions (e.g., core curriculum lessons, schoolwide activities) with the mindsets and behaviors, school counselors can facilitate systemic change as well as promote student resilience and strengths (Mason & Lopez-Perry, 2019; Sink, 2019). School counselors focus on implementing the mindsets and behaviors during MTSS-based interventions, while reflecting on ways to assess mindsets and behaviors to show evidence that students are, in fact, demonstrating the identified standards (Sink, 2019).

Implementation of the ASCA Student Standards

School counselors use the ASCA Student Standards to identify specific knowledge, attitudes, and skills that students are expected to demonstrate. ASCA Student Standards must be developmentally appropriate and executed systemically and sequentially, starting from kindergarten, so that students can make connections between academics, college and career readiness, and social/emotional development (Erford, 2019). These standards are delivered across the elementary and secondary grade levels, although each standard may not be necessary, required, or practical to be addressed at every grade level. The ASCA provided the *ASCA Mindsets and Behaviors: Program Planning Tool* (ASCA, 2003) and the *Classroom and Group Mindsets & Behaviors Action Plan* (ASCA, n.d.-a) for school counselors to identify mindsets and behaviors of focus for each school year, articulate which classroom and group activities will address the standards, and assess potential gaps within specific grade levels or developmental domains. ASCA provided a 10-step implementation guide for the ASCA Student Standards (Table 5.1). For detailed instructions of implementing the ASCA Student Standards, see pp. 4 and 5 in the *ASCA Student Standards* (ASCA, 2021a). For additional suggestions of Do's and Don'ts when using the ASCA Mindsets and Behaviors, see p. 59 of the *ASCA National Model Implementation Guide*.

TABLE 5.1   Ten Steps to Implement the ASCA Student Standards

Step 1: Identify need.
Step 2: Collect supplemental data.
Step 3: Select student standard.
Step 4: Write learning objectives aligned with the student standard.
Step 5: Create preassessment/postassessment.
Step 6: Select or develop strategies.
Step 7: Administer pretest.
Step 8: Deliver selected or designed strategies.
Step 9: Administer posttest.
Step 10: Reflect for improvement of practice.

Source: Adapted from American School Counselor Association. (2021a). ASCA student standards; mindsets and behaviors for student success. https://www.schoolcounselor.org/getmedia/7428a787-a452-4abb-afec-d78ec77870cd/Mindsets-Behaviors.pdf

VIGNETTE

The following example illustrates the aforementioned implementation steps for Mrs. McIntosh, a first-year high school counselor at Apple High School (AHS). AHS is a large high school of 1,500 students, a majority of whom receive free and reduced lunch and identify as Black/African American and Hispanic/Latinx. In the past few years, the school data showed a lower rate of passing scores for the PSAT/NMSQT (Preliminary SAT/National Merit Scholarship Qualifying Test), particularly for 10th-grade students at AHS, compared to the state's passing rate. Based on a needs assessment with 10th-grade students, students reported unfamiliarity with the expectations of the PSAT exam and needed test-taking strategies to improve their performance and confidence.

In alignment with AHS's School Improvement Plan (SIP) goal to improve Preliminary Scholastic Aptitude Test (PSAT) scores and the school counseling program goal to develop student academic learning strategies with college readiness assessments, including the PSAT, Mrs. McIntosh developed a classroom lesson for all ninthth- and 10th-grade students. This lesson plan included sharing specific content areas and sample questions on the PSAT, as well as teaching test-taking strategies in preparation for the PSAT exam. Mrs. McIntosh identified one learning strategy from the behaviors standards as the focus of the lesson: B-LS 3, Use time-management, organizational, and study skills. When writing the learning objectives for the lesson, Mrs. McIntosh articulated the selected behavior standard, using Bloom's taxonomy, into two learning objectives: students will be able to (a) identify and apply at least two long-term and at least two short-term PSAT test preparation strategies, and (b) describe the three key content areas of the PSAT exam. Mrs. McIntosh also provided follow-up lesson plans and resources for ninth and 10th-grade teachers to implement in their classrooms, tailor to their subject areas, and continue teaching general test-taking strategies. After comparing the results of the preassessments/postassessments, 75% of ninth-grade students and 84% of 10th-grade students fulfilled the learning objectives. The following year's AHS testing data reported an 8% increase in PSAT scores for 10th-graders.

ASCA Student Standards and the Recognized ASCA Model Program

The Recognized ASCA Model Program (RAMP) is a designation from ASCA that a PK–12 school counseling program adheres to the ASCA National Model and implements and measures outcomes through data-driven practices (ASCA, 2021b; Mullen et al., 2019). School counselors seeking RAMP status for their building must include selected ASCA

TABLE 5.2   Guidance for Utilizing the ASCA Student Standards for RAMP Applications

- Utilize the ASCA Mindsets & Behaviors Planning tool.
- Specify which grade levels will address specific mindset and behavior standards.
- Articulate how selected mindset and behavior standards impact student outcomes related to program goals.
- Describe how and why mindsets and behavior standards were selected for classroom lessons, small groups, closing-the-gap, and other program activities.
- Describe how mindsets and behavior standards are reviewed and revised annually to meet the changing needs of students and the school.

Source: American School Counselor Association. (2016b). *ASCA National Model implementation guide: Foundation, management, and accountability.* Author.

Student Standards for the application review. For example, one of the 10 required components for the RAMP application process, consistent with the fourth edition of the ASCA National Model, is completing the Classroom and Group Mindsets & Behaviors Action Plan (ASCA, n.d.-a). For resources, templates, and rubrics about RAMP, refer to the ASCA website. The ASCA National Model Implementation Guide: Foundation, Management, and Accountability (2016b) provided helpful guidance when including mindsets and behaviors in RAMP applications (see Table 5.2).

Limitations of the ASCA Student Standards

The ASCA Student Standards hold merit as a useful tool for school counselors to support student success. It also presents a number of strengths related to program development and supporting all students' academic, college and career, and social/emotional success. However, the Mindsets and Behaviors are not without limitations. First, although the ASCA Student Standards are based on a review of research and various college- and career-readiness documents (ASCA, 2014), it still remains unclear what exactly from this review of the literature informed each specific standard. The framework of noncognitive factors (University of Chicago Consortium on Chicago School Research, 2012) included a range of characteristics important for student success. However, the applicability and cultural relevancy of this reputable study may not necessarily connect with "success for every student," as noted by the full title of the document, ASCA Student Standards: Mindsets & Behaviors for Student Success: K-12 College-, Career-, and Life-Readiness Standards for Every Student. Chae (2020) compared the ASCA Student Standards with another research-informed model to evaluate the strengths and gaps of the Mindsets and Behaviors. Whereas the Mindsets and Behaviors intend to set high expectations, Chae (2020) found that the standards may unintentionally communicate an imbalance of exceedingly high expectations and fewer opportunities for sufficient encouragement, support, and space for all students to be successful.

Finally, it is unclear how these specific mindsets and behaviors can be objectively and equitably defined as standards for all students. More research and information are needed to substantiate how the standards are identified, defined, applied, and evaluated. School counselors will need to collaborate with colleagues and stakeholders to critically assess whether the existing standards effectively and inclusively represent the diverse cultural beliefs, values, strengths, and skill sets of all students (ASCA, 2016a; Chae, 2020). The ASCA Student Standards may present "an inequitable one-size-fits-all approach to success due to its prescriptive language, though there is flexibility in how professional school counselors select and develop competencies to address student developmental needs" (Chae, 2020, p. 14). Further research and development are needed to strengthen the efficacy of the standards as well as to enhance inclusivity to account for the diverse needs and cultural contexts of all students.

ASCA SCHOOL COUNSELOR PROFESSIONAL STANDARDS AND COMPETENCIES

To maintain longevity of the school counseling profession, it is critical to have a solid roadmap for school counselors to use to engage in, maintain, and assess their professional practice. For school counselors, this roadmap is known as the *ASCA School Counselor Professional Standards and Competencies* (ASCA, 2019b), with its origins tracing back to the *ASCA School Counselor Competencies* (ASCA, 2012b). These professional standards are embedded within the fourth edition of the ASCA National Model (2019a) and outline 31 mindsets and behaviors regarding what school counselors believe and ways to translate these beliefs into the creation, sustainability, and optimization of comprehensive school counseling programs.

These mindsets serve as the catalyst for school counselors to develop and maintain effective comprehensive school counseling programs through three areas of competencies: (a) professional foundations, (b) direct and indirect student services, and (c) planning and assessment (ASCA, 2019b). The fourth edition of the ASCA National Model (ASCA, 2019a) presented five implementation steps of the *ASCA School Counseling Professional Standards and Competencies* (see Table 5.3).

First, competencies within professional foundations category include awareness, knowledge, and skills for all school counselors when working with various stakeholders in schools (ASCA, 2019b) to optimize the roles of school counselors as leaders, advocates, and collaborators to design and maintain a flourishing comprehensive school counseling program. Second, competencies within the direct and indirect student services category can be exemplified via MTSS to deliver an array of academic, social and emotional, and college and career services to address identified needs of students (Lean & Colucci, 2013). For example, school counselors can use appropriate screening and assessment procedures to systematically implement direct and indirect services in three general ways: (a) Tier 1 interventions, such as a schoolwide antibullying curriculum; (b) Tier 2 interventions, such as small-group counseling for students who experience testing anxiety; and (c) Tier 3 interventions, such as individual support and counseling services for a student who recently lost one of their caregivers to COVID-19. Third, Planning and Assessment competencies outline how school counseling programs meet students' needs and measure program effectiveness on student outcomes in collaboration with stakeholders (ASCA, 2019b). Ultimately, through data-driven school counseling practices, school counselors answer the key question, "How are students different as a result of the school counseling program?"

TABLE 5.3 Implementation Steps of the ASCA School Counseling Professional Standards and Competencies

1. Engage in self-assessment related to school counseling professional standards and competencies.
2. Remain current with school counseling research and best practices.
3. Use personal reflection, consultation, and supervision to promote professional growth and development.
4. Develop a yearly professional development plan that reflects professional standards and competencies along with personal limitations.
5. Use district or state evaluation initiatives for planning and assessment.

Source: Adapted from American School Counselor Association. (2019a). *The ASCA National Model: A framework for school counseling programs* (4th ed., p. 15). Author.

VIGNETTE

The following example highlights the aforementioned implementation steps for a newly hired middle school counselor named Zoë. In preparation for her first year, Zoë completed a self-assessment of the *ASCA School Counselor Professional Standards and Competencies* at the start of the school year to identify her annual professional development goals. During this process, Zoë discovered her limited knowledge of the lesbian, gay, bisexual, transgender, and queer (LGBTQIA+) student populations. In fact, the only exposure Zoë recalls is one class lecture on the entire LGBTQIA+ community in her multicultural counseling course. Zoë dove into the literature to identify evidence-based practices to optimize the learning environment for the LGBTQIA+ students at her middle school. This exploration became even more relevant and necessary when Zoë uncovered The Trevor Project's (2020) national survey, which included over 40,000 LGBTQIA+ youth who resided in the United States, of whom 40% reported seriously contemplated suicide within the last 12 months.

Having obtained key articles and resources on LGBTQIA+ school-aged youth, Zoë identified and reflected on standards that would serve as a blueprint to advocate for LGBTQIA+ students to facilitate their academic success: (a) M 7. *School counseling programs promote and enhance student academic, career, and social/emotional outcomes*, and (b) B-PF 6. *Demonstrate understanding of the impact of cultural, social, and environmental influences on student success and opportunities*. With these professional standards in mind, Zoë identified next steps for her professional development and comprehensive school counseling program development. Zoë used the Annual Administrative Conference template (ASCA, n.d.-b) to meet with her administrator to share the goals of the school counseling program and her professional development goals. Using the template, she justified the priorities of the school counseling program to provide social and emotional support for LGBTQIA+ middle school students via small-group and individual counseling, which was also aligned with the districtwide goals related to promoting a safe school climate. Her proposed program also included a schedule of professional development activities (e.g., webinars, conferences, articles) specific to learning more about supporting students who self-identify within the LGBTQIA+ community. Considering that she still has a lot to learn about the LGBTQIA+ community, Zoë has exciting plans to connect with a local LGBTQIA+ advocacy organization to visit her school and provide training to teachers, administrators, caregivers, and students about how to effectively support the social and emotional needs of LGBTQIA+ middle school students.

ASCA STUDENT STANDARDS AND INTEGRATION OF SOCIAL JUSTICE ADVOCACY

Ongoing injustices in the United States have captured the public's attention through various media coverage, including the death of George Floyd by the knee of a police officer in Minneapolis, Minnesota, in 2020. Demonstrations calling for equity and a more just world included Black Lives Matter, a movement in response to the deadly violence conducted by police officers toward Black and Brown individuals (Black Lives Matter, 2013). In the same year, one of the many tragic outcomes of the COVID-19 pandemic toward marginalized groups was an increase in racist and xenophobic actions toward Asian Americans and Pacific Islanders (AAPIs). Such racial attacks on the AAPI community resulted in the deaths of six Asian American women in Atlanta, Georgia, in 2021. In addition, anti-Islamic hate crimes and discrimination have been on the rise since 1995, especially post-9/11 and after the recent enactment of policies, such as the 2001 Patriot

TABLE 5.4   Highlights of Social Justice and Advocacy-Based Standards in the
Professional Standards

- B-PF 2. a. Explain the organizational structure and governance of the American educational system as well as cultural, political, and social influences on current educational practices.
- B-PF 6. Demonstrate understanding of the impact of cultural, social, and environmental influences on student success and opportunities.
- B-SS 1. b. Assess cultural and social trends when developing and choosing curricula.
- B-SS 1. d. Demonstrate pedagogical skills, including culturally responsive classroom management strategies, lesson planning, and personalized instruction.
- B-SS 6. a. Partner with others to advocate for student achievement and educational equity and opportunities.

Source: Adapted from American School Counselor Association. (2019b). *ASCA school counselor professional standards & competencies.* Author. https://www.schoolcounselor.org/getmedia/a8d59c2c-51de-4ec3-a565-a3235f3b93c3/SC-Competencies.pdf

Act and 2017 Muslim Ban (Ramadan, 2021). Tragically, these few examples are just a few of what is broadcasted on newsfeeds and social media outlets. There are innumerable accounts of mistreatment, harassment, and violence toward marginalized populations that do not make national headlines, but that are just as deadly and traumatic.

For school counselors, this charge to eliminate barriers and inequities is paramount to students' overall well-being and success. In response, ASCA updated the ASCA Student Standards to include language related to inclusion, diversity, and cultural awareness, proficiency, and responsiveness (ASCA, 2021a). Moreover, the *ASCA School Counselor Professional Standards and Competencies* (ASCA, 2019b) includes several social justice and advocacy-based standards and competencies (see Table 5.4). A supplemental document for school counselors to identify and remedy oppressive factors within the school environment is ASCA's Eliminating Racism and Bias in Schools: The School Counselor's Role (ASCA, n.d.-c). This document provided concrete ways for school counselors to address racism and bias within the four components of the ASCA National Model (ASCA, n.d.-c). For example, school counselors can apply specific competencies within the ASCA Student Standards when delivering lessons to students at the classroom, small-group, or individual levels about racism and cultural awareness, such as self-identifying unconscious biases and assumptions (ASCA, n.d.-c). Furthermore, school counselors can initiate systemic change within schools by collecting and analyzing data to identify and address inequities of student outcomes. For easy referencing, specific standards are indicated within Eliminating Racism and Bias in Schools: The School Counselor's Role (ASCA, n.d.-c). Overall, the ASCA Student Standards for both students and school counseling professionals provide a framework to use to begin the task of identifying and addressing gaps within the school as a system that disadvantages some students to the advantage of others.

Aspirations to identify, uproot, and dismantle systemic inequities and injustices can be challenging to translate into actual practice for school counselors. Newly hired school counselors may just be beginning to understand the school culture in which they are employed, including spoken and unspoken norms of school operation. Broaching race can also be taboo in school settings, and as result, individuals may feel discouraged, both subtly and directly, from exploring race. With its origins in counseling, broaching the topic involves the process of clinicians engaging in intentional discussions about race and ethnicity with clients to better understand and respond to clients' presenting issues (Day-Vines et al., 2020). Unfortunately, disrupting the status quo for newly employed school counselors (and even seasoned school counselors) might be a risk many will choose not to take for the sake of job security, despite the charge for school counselors to enact change and address systemic racism (Bemak & Chung, 2008).

TABLE 5.5   Self-Reflection Questions for Social Justice Advocacy in School Counseling Practice

- How do you self-identify racially?
- How do you define race, racism, and microaggressions?
- What has been your personal experience with racism and with microaggressions?
- Are you familiar with different types of racial identity models? If so, which model do you ascribe to, and why?
- How does your racial identity impact your role as a professional school counselor and how you plan and deliver your school counseling program?
- How do you see power, privilege, and oppression operationalized within the school system, and in what ways does your school counseling role and program dismantle systemically racist and oppressive practices that harm students?
- Describe your level of comfort when addressing race and racism with the following stakeholders: colleagues, administrators, students, caregivers, and community members.
- What are your perceptions of individuals who do not share the same racial background as your own? Where might these perceptions stem from?
- What are your biases and assumptions related to various racial groups regarding academic and postsecondary success and social and emotional development?

With the plethora of strategies provided within the ASCA Student Standards and the School Counseling Professional Standards & Competencies, one key aspect missing is the ongoing intrapersonal work of advocacy. That is, what is the self-efficacy of school counselors to address race and racism? It is necessary for school counselors to have an honest and open exploration of their comfort level, knowledge, training, awareness, and sensitivity to this issue. It cannot be assumed that all school counselors feel adequately prepared to lead this charge given the very nature of the topic can be uncomfortable for many individuals and taboo for others. However, it is critical for school counselors and leaders within the school system to self-reflect on their cultural competencies. Another limitation of the ASCA Student Standards is the potential for these student standards to perpetuate racist and inequitable outcomes. Duarte et al. (2020) urged that school counselors must critically consider the origins of the student standards, how such standards impact historically marginalized students, explicit and implicit biases, and racist views in order to align with an antiracist stance when assessing students' academic, social and emotional, and postsecondary development. School counselors are challenged to examine their beliefs and mindsets and work toward changing systems and policies to create a more equitable learning environment for all students (Education Trust, 2020). Therefore, when integrating and applying social justice advocacy into school counseling practice, school counselors must unpack their cultural competencies and critically consider areas for continued growth (see Table 5.5). These self-reflection questions are difficult, yet essential, for school counselors to regularly explore and assess how their answers correspond to the stated beliefs and behaviors within ASCA Student Standards and the School Counseling Professional Standards & Competencies. To examine possible instances of institutional racism within schools, it is imperative for school counselors to explore the *personal* meaning and impact of race and racism on their daily professional practice and lived experiences.

Supplementing the ASCA Student Standards for Social Justice Advocacy

In addition to school counselors (and other key stakeholders) assessing their own cultural competencies, there are several practical remedies to begin addressing race and racism within comprehensive school counseling programs. First, school counselors should be knowledgeable regarding theories that directly examine oppressive factors within the environment, including schools. Critical race theory, intersectionality theory, relational cultural theory, and liberation psychology are just a few social justice theories that can be explored and applied within the context of schools (Singh et al., 2020). Second, omitting the use of a deficit-based model to characterize student difficulties solely based on their cultural backgrounds would reflect a more inclusive, socially just school climate. These students are typically labeled as "at-risk" and mistakenly blamed for their conditions (e.g., poverty, low academic performance), when, in fact, it is racist policies that construct and maintain such barriers to economic prosperity and academic success (Kendi, 2019).

One approach to envisioning the strengths of Black and Brown students is Yosso's (2005) community cultural wealth model. Grounded in the tenets of critical race theory, Yosso's (2005) community cultural wealth model honors the unrecognized assets and strengths of marginalized students of color. This model identifies six forms of capital based on cultural wealth: "aspirational, navigational, social, linguistic, familial, and resistant" (Yosso, 2005, p. 69). Using this framework, school counselors can decolonize schools by honoring and supporting cultural values that are not typically acknowledged among historically marginalized student groups.

Another approach to implement developmentally appropriate antibias education for all students is the *Social Justice Standards: The Teaching Tolerance Anti-Bias Framework* (Teaching Tolerance, 2018) developed by Learning for Justice (formerly known as Teaching Tolerance). These standards include four domains of social justice for students, including identity, diversity, justice, and action, as well as key anchor standards and grade-level outcomes within each domain to promote students' knowledge and skills in reducing prejudice and advocating for collective action among students (Teaching Tolerance, 2018). The Social Justice Standards help educators guide equitable curriculum development and engage with students in issues related to antibias, multiculturalism, and social justice (Teaching Tolerance, 2018). School counselors are encouraged to supplement the ASCA Student Standards with the Social Justice Standards when delivering schoolwide activities, classroom lessons, and small group and individual counseling to support students' racial identity development, increase awareness of diversity, recognize privileges, understand how injustices impact communities, and take action to advocate for others.

Whether with Yosso's model or the Social Justice Standards, school counselors can integrate equity-focused frameworks to address injustices in school settings when using the ASCA Student Standards. School counselors play an important role in planning, delivering, and implementing equitable and social justice–focused school counseling programming that highlights students' strengths and empowers them to be active contributors to eliminating systemic racism and inequities. In addition to identifying, examining, and dismantling systemically racist practices and policies in schools, school counselors must continue to engage in consistent and thorough critical self-reflection of their own personal and professional learning needs. As social justice advocates, school counselors uplift the voices of marginalized students and families, call out injustices that harm or prevent equitable access for students and school communities, and create systemic changes.

ASCA STUDENT STANDARDS FOR THE VIRTUAL SCHOOL COUNSELOR

States and their respective school districts provide varied opportunities for virtual, hybrid, and distance learning for students. ASCA's position statement on virtual school counseling (ASCA, 2017) indicates that school counselors working in virtual settings should abide by the same standards and ethics as those working in more traditional school settings. Despite the change of the delivery and format within virtual platforms, the quality of content and application of the ASCA Student Standards should remain unchanged. With virtual settings, school counselors are encouraged to recognize potential challenges to direct service delivery, such as limitations to confidentiality, responses to emergency situations, and counseling relationship development with students.

School counselors should remain aware of and incorporate current trends in technology in their professional development and ethical practice (ASCA, 2016a, 2019b). With equity in mind, school counselors using virtual spaces should provide activities and services that are accessible to students with varying access to technology and internet service, as well as with varied technology skills. This process may require school counselors to develop both synchronous and asynchronous activities to ensure equitable access to the school counseling program for all students. School counselors may also need to engage in intentional modification of the format, delivery, and response options. Specifically, school counselors must consider students' developmental levels and enhance inclusion of students with disabilities, students learning English as another language, and students with limited technology skills. This awareness, as well as teaching virtual learning tools and expectations, will benefit both school counselors and students.

When students' educational experiences are disrupted due to a national crisis, school counselors may need to transition from traditional to virtual school counseling settings. The COVID-19 pandemic in 2020 suddenly and unexpectedly thrust school counselors into virtual learning due to long-term school closures, many of which continued into the following school year. As students switched to online learning, school counselors were required to embrace technology to sustain their programs. Unlike school counselors who were already in virtual settings, counselors in brick-and-mortar schools needed to quickly learn and adapt to the new education landscape, while considering the health, social, and emotional impact of the ongoing COVID-19 pandemic. As a response to the pandemic, ASCA developed Planning for Virtual/Distance School Counseling During an Emergency Shutdown (ASCA, n.d.-d), which provided recommendations for school counselors to focus on specific standards that prioritized student needs in relation to the heightened stress of the pandemic (see Table 5.6). Delivering content virtually with guidance from the ASCA Student Standards can still align with the academic, social/emotional, and college and career domains of student development as well as also present important opportunities to educate students and families about safe and appropriate online conduct and use of digital literacy (ASCA, 2017).

TABLE 5.6   Highlights of Student Standards for Virtual School Counseling Contexts

▪ M 1. Belief in development of whole self, including a healthy balance of mental, social/emotional and physical well-being
▪ M 2. Self-confidence in ability to succeed
▪ B-SMS 7. Demonstrate effective coping skills when faced with a problem
▪ B-SMS 9. Demonstrate personal safety skills
▪ B-SMS 10. Demonstrate ability to manage transitions and ability to adapt to changing situations and responsibilities
▪ B-SS 9. Demonstrate social maturity and behaviors appropriate to the situation and environment

Source: Adapted from American School Counselor Association. (n.d.-d). *Planning for virtual/distance school counseling during an emergency shutdown.* https://www.schoolcounselor.org/getmedia/8e31740f-d6af-4f62-a9e3-26563c488443/emergency-shutdown.pdf

VIGNETTE

The following example features how Mr. Harris, a sixth-grade school counselor at Waves Middle School, responded to the COVID-19 pandemic. As students continued with virtual learning, Mr. Harris identified students who received Ds and Fs despite having passing grades in elementary school and found that they were logging into class inconsistently. Results from a needs assessment also revealed that students missed their social connections with the transition to middle school during the pandemic.

Mr. Harris developed and delivered a series of synchronous and asynchronous classroom lessons for all sixth-grade students using the Behavior standard B-SMS 10. Demonstrate ability to manage transitions and ability to adapt to changing situations and responsibilities and Mindset standard M 3. Sense of belonging in the school environment. The topics included stress-management skills and organization in a virtual setting, while also including technology-based social opportunities to help students connect with one another. Lesson objectives articulated that students will be able to (a) identify signs of stress and apply two stress management strategies; (b) utilize an agenda to track assignments; and (c) communicate with at least one peer about feelings. Mr. Harris also shared the lessons and tips with sixth-grade families during the virtual Coffee With the Counselors, and those unable to attend Coffee With the Counselors received a tip sheet and recording session via email. As a result of the lessons, 76% of sixth-grade students identified stress-management strategies, and 82% reported an increased level of comfort in using an agenda to track their virtual assignments. By the end of the second quarter, students' grades improved by 45% and attendance increased by 61%.

VOICES FROM THE FIELD

Name: Constance Johnson, MS

Where You Practice: Charles County Public Schools, Waldorf, Maryland

Professional Job Title: School Counselor

Bio: Constance Johnson is a school counselor at an elementary school in Maryland. She has been an elementary school counselor for 11 years.

Working as an elementary school counselor, the majority of my time is spent planning and delivering the school counseling core curriculum to 600 students. The ASCA Student Standards help me to align my work with standards for student learning. They're also a great way to show teachers and administrators that my time with students, whether in the classroom or in small groups, is intentional and aligned with specific goals. When teachers see me using the ASCA Student Standards to develop lesson objectives, they recognize me as an additional instructor to their students in the area of social and emotional learning (SEL) and college and career readiness, rather than an occasional visitor.

Each year, I use school data (e.g., academic, behavior, and attendance) and conduct a needs assessment to create a curriculum map (e.g., Classroom and Group Mindsets and Behaviors Action Plan; ASCA, n.d.-a) to ensure my time is spent teaching the most skills to the most students. The curriculum map outlines the lessons that I will teach to each grade throughout the year, as well as the aligned ASCA Mindsets and Behaviors. Some standards carry throughout all my activities. For example, Mindset standard M 3. Sense of belonging in the school environment, underscores every aspect of my efforts to build relationships and community, such as through restzrative circles and lunch bunches. Additionally, each year we host a schoolwide college and career month focused on building awareness about postsecondary pathways, which addresses the Mindset standard M 4. Understanding that postsecondary education and lifelong learning are necessary for long-term career success.

Other standards are more specific to identifying academic, behavioral, and attendance issues. In addition, I employ the student standards in developmentally appropriate ways across grade levels. For example, the Behavior standard B-SS 1. Use effective oral and written communication skills and listening skills, is applicable when I teach about whole body listening to my kindergarten to second-grade students. To promote continuity, the school counseling program builds on this skill later in the third through fifth grades by practicing active listening and respectful communication with students during conflict resolution. One school year, the behavioral indicators on the quarterly report cards showed that our second-grade students needed support in developing the learning behaviors to be successful in school. When creating classroom lessons and small group counseling sessions, I focused on five ASCA Mindsets and Behaviors Standards over the course of five classroom lessons. For a small group counseling curriculum focused on study skills, I focused on (a) M 5. Belief in using abilities to their fullest to achieve high-quality results and outcomes; (b) M 6. Positive attitude toward work and learning; (c) B-LS 3. Use time-management, organizational and study skills; (d) B-LS 7. Identify long- and short-term academic, career and social/emotional goals; and (e) B-SMS 2, Demonstrate self-discipline and self-control.

There are some limitations, however, when using the ASCA Student Standards in my everyday practice. The mindsets tend to focus more on preparation for academic and career success and less on social-emotional learning, which is problematic since our students' personal and social experiences can greatly impact their learning. While there are some standards that speak to social and emotional development, I would like to see more. I also believe that the standards could include more focus on diversity, inclusion, and relationship skills with other students as part of diverse school communities. In these cases, I lean on organizations such as the Collaborative for Academic, Social, and Emotional Learning's (CASEL) framework and competencies (CASEL, 2020), as well as on the Learning for Justice's Social Justice Standards. These additional tools supplement and expand my school counseling program in meaningful ways, while still remaining aligned with goals of the ASCA National Model (ASCA, 2019a).

SUMMARY AND CONCLUSION

The ASCA Student Standards guide school counselors' work and advocacy for and on behalf of students' academic, social and emotional, and college and career development. The Student Standards also inform school counselors' professional development and implementation of comprehensive school counseling programs to ensure that they effectively and equitably serve the needs of all students. Therefore, using and supplementing these standards with other equity- and social justice–focused tools can inform and inspire systemic change among students and within school communities. It is helpful for the school counselor to reflect on and evaluate how they may use the ASCA Standard to differentiate classroom and small group curricula for elementary, middle, and high school levels. School counselors that plan a virtual classroom lesson should consider which standards are most relevant and how to incorporate digital literacy into the lesson. It is essential for school counselors to review the Social Justice Standards (Teaching Tolerance, 2018) from Learning for Justice, asking themselves what standards and learning objectives can be incorporated with selected ASCA Student Standards to help service delivery for *all* students, specifically being mindful of marginalized communities.

CASE STUDY: AN ELEMENTARY SCHOOL COUNSELOR'S RESPONSE TO RECESS REFERRALS

Ms. Mikeal is a second-year school counselor at an elementary school with 633 students on her caseload. At the beginning of the second year, Ms. Mikeal decided to be more proactive after noticing a significant amount of time spent on "putting out fires," especially issues related to peer conflicts during recess time. Upon reviewing behavioral referral data from the previous year, Ms. Mikeal noticed that most referrals at recess involved fourth- and fifth-grade students. Specifically, of the 217 behavioral referrals for the school year, 38% of the referrals came from recess-related physical or verbal aggression, and 30% of these referrals involved fourth- and fifth-grade students. These incidents occurring among fourth- and fifth-graders included threatening language, physical and verbal aggression, exclusion, and bullying behaviors. She also invited fourth- and fifth-grade teachers, in addition to recess monitors, to complete a needs assessment about common concerns and skills related to resolving peer conflicts.

Results from the needs assessment revealed that most students had one referral related to peer conflicts, whereas other students had multiple referrals. Ms. Mikeal planned ways to address conflict resolution and peer social skills for the upcoming school year through the school counseling program. She looked into the ASCA Student Standards to determine relevant standards for fourth and fifth grades and then developed specific learning objectives (see Table 5.7).

Ms. Mikeal developed three lessons per unit for each grade level after researching and consulting with fellow school counseling colleagues in the district. One unit for fourth-grade students included topics about communication skills, empathy, and inclusion of others. The fifth-grade unit included lessons about conflict resolution and decision-making, as well as bullying prevention activities. With each lesson, Ms. Mikeal developed and implemented pre- and posttests to assess student perceptions and understandings about communication, empathy, and peer relationships. Her overarching goal was to reduce recess referrals for fourth- and fifth-grade students by 10%.

After completing the units for both grade levels, Ms. Mikeal was excited to see changes in the student perception data and schoolwide recess referral data. Out of 100 fourth-graders, 89% could write and verbalize at least one I-message statement in response to a peer conflict issue. Out of 107 fifth-graders, 92% could define bullying and 65% could articulate and describe the three Rs (i.e., Recognize, Report, and Refuse) from Second Step's bullying prevention program (Committee for Children, 2021). The number of behavioral referrals during recess time for physical or verbal aggression for fourth- and fifth-graders decreased by 9%.

TABLE 5.7   Aligning ASCA Student Standards and Learning Objectives to Address Increasing Recess Referrals

ASCA STUDENT STANDARD	LEARNING OBJECTIVE
B-SS 1. *Use effective oral and written communication skills and listening skills*	Students will be able to create I-messages to respond to select social scenarios.
B-SS 2. *Create positive and supportive relationships with other students*	Students will be able to identify ways to include other students in play at recess.
B-SS 4. *Demonstrate empathy*	Students will be able to analyze and demonstrate understanding of diverse perspectives after completing the "walking in someone's shoes" activity.

Positive takeaways also included observations from their teachers and the recess monitors of students engaging in more cooperative behaviors during recess time. Ms. Mikeal created classroom posters for the fourth- and fifth-grade classrooms as well as outdoor and indoor recess spaces reminding students to use I-messages and engage in bullying prevention steps. These visual reminders could also translate into the classroom, with teachers encouraging continued use of such language.

After a closer examination of the student perception data, Ms. Mikeal noticed how students commonly misunderstood the third R, Refuse, in the bullying prevention program. In the future, Ms. Mikeal plans to include interactive engagement in lessons, such as role play, for students to practice refusing bullying as well as supplement the lesson with other evidence-based bystander interventions. Ms. Mikeal also hopes to proactively teach these concepts earlier with the K–3 grade levels to mitigate future behavioral issues during recess play.

DISCUSSION QUESTIONS

1. In addition to the ASCA Student Standards identified, consider additional standards and learning objectives to address the needs of Ms. Mikeal's students. What might these classroom lessons entail?
2. Ms. Mikeal focused her interventions on Tier 1 classroom-level support for fourth and fifth graders. What are some potential Tier 2 and 3 interventions (e.g., small group and individual counseling) that would be appropriate for these grade levels?
3. How can Ms. Mikeal collaborate with parents/guardians/caregivers, teachers, administrators, and community members to support her efforts?

PRACTICAL APPLICATION

- Consider quality over quantity when selecting relevant ASCA Student Standards for classroom lessons and small group and individual counseling. In other words, focus on a few standards in-depth rather than more standards superficially; less is more.

- Use data to inform appropriate selections of ASCA Student Standards, and present data after implementing school counseling activities to demonstrate outcomes.

- Supplement the ASCA Student Standards with other theories and tools (e.g., CASEL's SEL framework and competencies, Learning for Justice's Social Justice Standards, Yosso's community cultural wealth model) to comprehensively address issues of diversity, inclusion, and equity in school counseling program activities.

KEY REFERENCES

Only key references appear in the print edition. The full reference list appears in the digital product on Springer Publishing Connect: connect.springerpub.com/content/book/978-0-8261-8753-6/part/part02/chapter/ch05

American School Counselor Association. (n.d.-c). *Eliminating racism and bias in schools: The school counselor's role.* https://www.schoolcounselor.org/getmedia/542b085a-7eda-48ba-906e-24cd3f08a03f/SIP-Racism-Bias.pdf

American School Counselor Association. (2019a). *The ASCA national model: A framework for school counseling programs* (4th ed.).

American School Counselor Association. (2019b). *ASCA school counselor professional standards & competencies.* https://www.schoolcounselor.org/getmedia/a8d59c2c-51de-4ec3-a565-a3235f3b93c3/SC-Competencies.pdf

American School Counselor Association. (2021a). *ASCA student standards; mindsets and behaviors for student success*. https://www.schoolcounselor.org/getmedia/7428a787-a452-4abb-afec-d78ec77870cd/Mindsets-Behaviors.pdf

Duarte, D., Edirmanasinghe, N., & Nwosu, J. (2020, October 15). *An antiracist foundation to school counseling: Students' mindsets and behaviors* [Video]. American University School of Education YouTube Channel. https://www.youtube.com/watch?app=desktop&v=E-0RWJIFDms

Education Trust. (2020). *Social, emotional, and academic development through an equity lens*. https://edtrust.org/wp-content/uploads/2014/09/Social-Emotional-and-Academic-Development-Through-an-Equity-Lens-August-6-2020.pdf

Teaching Tolerance. (2018). *Social justice standards: The teaching tolerance anti-bias framework*. https://www.learningforjustice.org/sites/default/files/2020-09/TT-Social-Justice-Standards-Anti-bias-framework-2020.pdf

CHAPTER 6

Finding Meaning in ASCA-Identified Inappropriate Duties

ADRIANA M. WISSEL, HANNAH BRINSER, AND REBECCA HRUSKA

LEARNING OBJECTIVES

After reading this chapter, students will be able to:

- Describe the context and history related to the role of the school counselor.
- Discuss the key roles of the school counselor at each level.
- Distinguish inappropriate activities that are commonly asked of school counselors.
- Discover how inappropriate duties can be reimagined to be meaningful school counseling activities.

STUDENT VOICE

Student "O," seventh-grader, provided the following testimonial about her experience with a school counselor:

"You helped me so much in such a horrible time. It was so special I could go to someone who would listen and understand what I was going through. It has almost been a year since my dad left, but I am so thankful that my parents are happy together now. Even the days where I had nothing to say and didn't need to come see you because things were better with them, I still would look forward to always seeing you during lunch and recess. It made it easier to get through the school day. So thank you so much for listening and talking and helping me."

INTRODUCTION

The school counseling profession has evolved considerably over the decades. Driven largely by historical changes, the roles prescribed to school counselors have also changed. According to the American School Counselor Association (ASCA), the 1900s brought about a vocational and service-based approach. This quickly became a person-centered approach focusing on comprehensive and result-based developments (ASCA, 2019a).

Despite these refinements to the role, a specific job description lacks consistency. For many years, there were no set guidelines for the school counselor. To remedy this, in 2003 ASCA published a national model that detailed academic, career, and social emotional development as three key areas of the school counselors' role (ASCA, 2019a). Furthermore, comprehensive school counseling programs are built on data-informed decisions that are systematic, developmentally appropriate, and focused on closing the achievement and opportunity gap for all students (ASCA, 2019a).

Due to the lack of standards for school counselors before 2003, it became common practice for these professionals to be assigned duties that did not fall under their perceived umbrella of responsibility (Chandler et al., 2017). This led to confusion that remains, to some extent, today. Presently, school counselors, staff, and administrators do not have a clear understanding of what the school counseling role should look like. Unger et al. (2021) found that 20% of school counselors did not fully comprehend their duties. The addition of the ASCA National Model and delineation of responsibilities clearly defined the appropriate and inappropriate duties of the school counselor. According to ASCA, inappropriate activities range from data entry to handling disciplinary actions. But when activities that are considered inappropriate have been omitted from school counselors' job descriptions, some have wondered whether valuable outlets for connecting with students have also been removed. There has been considerable research done regarding the appropriate and inappropriate duties of school counselors, as well as the public perception of school counselors and their job. However, little research has been conducted on the effectiveness of giving school counselors opportunities to implement activities that have traditionally been deemed inappropriate. These practices may hold more value in the profession than one may think.

To accurately assess the duties of a school counselor and the outcomes that those responsibilities may produce, it is important to understand the historical context of appropriate and inappropriate duties. To examine the roles of professional school counselors, Chandler et al. (2017) concluded that school counselors were being given activities that were more administratively focused that took them away from meaningful time that could be spent with their students. They attributed the assignment of these activities to prior historical practices and customs. In their study, they explained inappropriate activities as those that were more clerical, such as creating schedules with the goal of aiding in the overall effectiveness of the school system (Chandler et al., 2017). However, in understanding these different ends of the spectrum, it is important to consider what ASCA has identified as appropriate and inappropriate school counseling duties. To make this clear, ASCA created a graphic (available at schoolcounselor.org) of some of the appropriate activities, including academic advising for new students; interpreting achievement tests; providing counseling to students who are tardy, absent, or have disciplinary problems; and protecting student records. In contrast, inappropriate school counseling activities included assigning discipline consequences, supervising classrooms or common areas, and assisting with duties in the principal's office (ASCA, n.d.-a).

These parameters outlined by ASCA can be difficult to implement owing to the complex nature of a school system. Stone (2017) noted the challenge of developing a comprehensive school counseling program due to the duties required of the school counselor, which are often administrative and clerical in nature. These specific inappropriate duties may distract from the three key areas of ASCA: social/emotional, academic achievement, and career and college readiness needs of students.

When school counselors know how to work within their political and cultural environments and advocate for their role, they will be best equipped to make changes in the school system through student support (Stone, 2017). Though sometimes difficult, it is important for school counselors to continue to advocate for their role and clarify it with others (Stone, 2017). Even with advocacy, the needs of the school may make it difficult to be perfectly aligned to only the identified "appropriate activities." Unger et al. (2021) note that some principals believe school counselors should still help with some administrative activities, such as overseeing a classroom or aiding in disciplinary action.

School counselors may use their leadership skills to advocate for what they think will be the most effective in serving the students at their school. For instance, if asked to supervise classrooms or common areas, an inappropriate task identified by ASCA (n.d.-a), school counselors can integrate their work into this task by using the opportunity to get to know students or observe dynamics between different students. This willingness to connect the work of a school counselor to these activities can be helpful while working toward the implementation of a comprehensive school counseling program. In collaboration with school administration, school counselors can collect data on time spent completing these activities, quantify the unmet needs of students and families while conducting the inappropriate activities, and help brainstorm other, more sustainable, solutions. Fortunately, because school counselors often have some freedom to determine how to best implement a comprehensive school counseling program, they can create a program that is not overwhelmed by inappropriate duties (Stone, 2017). To this end, it is crucial that school counselors understand their role and function as defined by ASCA. Without this framework, it can be difficult to advocate for themselves to their principals and other stakeholders (Unger et al., 2021).

In the next section we will review the roles of the school counselor at each level, discuss the appropriate and inappropriate activities as defined by the ASCA (n.d.-a), and demonstrate how even inappropriate activities can be reimagined as relevant work aligned to the goal of the comprehensive school counseling program.

ROLE OF THE SCHOOL COUNSELOR AS OUTLINED BY ASCA

The role of a school counselor is vast yet purposeful. The ASCA (2019a) has identified clear and specific roles and responsibilities for certificated school counselors for their support of the entire school system and the students and stakeholders within it. At the core, the role of the school counselor is described through implementation of direct and indirect services. Direct student services are those supports that *directly* impact students. These services include both individual and small-group counseling, classroom guidance curriculum, and advisement and appraisal. Indirect services refer to the services conducted *on behalf* of the student and include consultation, collaboration, and referrals (ASCA, 2019a). It should be noted, however, that consultation may be counted as direct service hours per Council for Accreditation of Counseling and Related Education Programs (CACREP) requirements (2016).

Elementary School

Beyond the foundational roles of school counselors, students at each developmental level require different types of support. Given the different requirements, school counselors must be prepared to adjust their practice to meet the needs at each level. At the elementary level, there is often only one school counselor in the building. As such, the school counselor must actively collaborate with classroom teachers, specialists, administrators, families, and caregivers to support students (ASCA, 2019b).

Often the first to hear about concerns, challenges, or needs of students and families, elementary school counselors are frequently part of developing early interventions and initial placement processes because of their expertise on child development and social emotional learning (ASCA, 2019b). This work requires regular and strong communication with families and caregivers. Special consideration should be given to those who may benefit from translation services, alternate meeting times, or different forms of communication (school text and email). When communicating, the school counselor must work to ensure understanding of process, vocabulary, and school requirements (Trusty et al., 2008). When serving as a meeting facilitator or participant, school counselors can advocate for clear communication from the school. When necessary, school counselors at the elementary level must also be prepared to make relevant and appropriate referrals for students who require support beyond the scope of the school counselor.

At the elementary level, school counselors are uniquely positioned to team with classroom teachers (ASCA, 2019b). To this end, school counselors work to establish strong working alliances with teachers by being available, helpful, and reliable. This relationship takes time to establish and maintain, and school counselors must continue to show, through their actions, how they can contribute to the teacher's success. This relationship is key to the school counselor gaining access to the classroom. At the elementary level, the school counselor can serve all students in the building by teaching prosocial skills through classroom guidance curriculum (ASCA, 2019b). Common topics covered at this level include school readiness, conflict resolution, personal safety, bully prevention, emotional regulation, community building, empathy and kindness, respecting differences, and career exploration. School counselors collaborate with classroom teachers to identify meeting times, specific class needs, and follow-up lessons and support.

Middle School

Work at the middle level reflects much of the roles and responsibilities of the elementary school counselor, supporting the academic, social/emotional, and college- and career-readiness skills of students, with more of an emphasis on academic achievement and grades (ASCA, 2019c). Serving at the middle level is sometimes seen as challenging or intimidating by school counselors, in part due to the complex and rapid developmental changes and needs of students (Scales, 2005). While students stay in middle school for 2–3 years, depending on the district's design, they enter as elementary school students and exit needing to navigate the demands of high school and adulthood. There is a large and sometimes painful learning curve for students and their families and caregivers alike (Scales, 2005). Collaborating with families and caregivers remains a priority, though their presence often decreases at this age as students gain independence and volunteer opportunities in the school change.

The role and expectations of the middle school counselor are clearly outlined by the ASCA (2019c). School counselors are to serve all students through direct and indirect supports, including individual and small group counseling and classroom guidance curriculum. School counselors at the middle level sometimes find it difficult to do this work. With great emphasis on academic achievement, content skill development, and pressure to protect instructional seat time, school counselors are sometimes limited to small windows of time throughout the day to offer services. These moments of time include passing periods, lunch time and recess, and after school. This is challenging when trying to conduct small groups. With rolling lunch periods, differences in scheduling such as block schedules, and the desire by many students to prioritize socially with peers during these times, finding a convenient time to consistently convene a group requires collaboration, communication, and creativity.

School counselors at the middle level conduct classroom guidance curriculum, including consistent visits to grade-level classrooms to cover a number of topics and also via advisory programming where school counselors may be responsible for a specific group of students (ASCA, 2019c). While classroom guidance curriculum is under the purview of middle-school counselors, it is not always implemented. Several factors may contribute to this. Like individual and group counseling, identifying available blocks of time in the classroom can be difficult due to teachers and administrators protecting instructional time. Sometimes, however, middle school counselors choose not to advocate for time in the classroom because either they do not prefer that method of support or may not feel as skilled or comfortable in teaching content.

High School

The role of the high school counselor is often seen as heavily focused on college and career readiness and academic success (ASCA, 2019d). This work is done while navigating often large school campuses, high student enrollment, and large numbers of school faculty and staff, including multiple administrators (Mau et al., 2016). Given this context, school counselors at the high school level may require more time to develop strong working alliances with all members of the school community. The sheer size of the school can lend itself to role confusion and less relational trust, which is critical in the work of the school counselor.

According to the ASCA (2019d), the high school counselor is responsible for meeting the developmental needs of students at this level, which can include peer relationships and pressures, drug and alcohol use, and stressors related to life after high school—college entrance, career choices, and transitions to adulthood. Much like the roles at the elementary and middle levels, high school counselors do this work via individual and small-group work, classroom lessons, and schoolwide activities.

The structure of high school can make implementation of a comprehensive program difficult, though not impossible. The number of students, class periods, and teaching staff requires the school counselor to be strategic about advocating for specific services such as small-group counseling and classroom instruction (Mau et al., 2016). Additionally, given the emphasis on credit completion, the high school counselor must be collaborative and creative in scheduling experiences for students that minimize the time spent outside the classroom (ASCA, 2019d).

REFRAMING DUTIES DEEMED INAPPROPRIATE

The school counselor's success at any level is largely attributed to and impacted by the working relationships established with administration, staff and teachers, and family and caregivers (Baker et al., 2009). Without good relationships, the school counselor will face ongoing challenges and confusion about role, function, and program implementation. It can be easy for the school counselor to feel frustrated and discouraged by the ongoing work required to educate others about their role; however, it is important to understand that not all stakeholders will have an accurate understanding (Dodson, 2009; Wilder, 2018). As such, each interaction should be seen as an opportunity to educate and increase understanding. School counselors can use these occasions to model the work and demonstrate the experience of working collaboratively.

Activities and Strategies for Integration of School Counseling Inappropriate Duties

After reading the context and roles at each level, a school counselor's duties may seem less confusing. ASCA has clearly delineated the inappropriate versus appropriate duties of the school counselor (Table 6.1). It is important to note that some schools and districts are more proactive than others to protect the school counselors' time and assigned responsibilities (Dodson, 2009). The school principal also influences the day-to-day work of the school counselor. Because schools are complex systems with great needs and often insufficient resources, school counselors often continue to be asked to perform inappropriate duties (Chandler et al., 2018; Perera-Diltz & Mason, 2008). In this section, we discuss the inappropriate duties commonly asked of school counselors and offer ways to reimagine these activities into meaningful and school counselor–aligned activities.

TABLE 6.1   ASCA Defined Appropriate and Inappropriate Activities for School Counselors

APPROPRIATE ACTIVITIES FOR SCHOOL COUNSELORS	INAPPROPRIATE ACTIVITIES FOR SCHOOL COUNSELORS
Advisement and appraisal for academic planning	Building the master schedule
Orientation, coordination, and academic advising for new students	Coordinating paperwork and data entry for all new students
Interpreting cognitive, aptitude, and achievement tests	Coordinating cognitive, aptitude, and achievement testing programs
Providing counseling to students who are tardy or absent	Signing excuses for students who are tardy or absent
Providing counseling to students who have disciplinary problems	Performing disciplinary actions or assigning discipline consequences
Providing short-term individual and small group counseling services to students	Providing long-term counseling in schools to address psychological disorders
Consulting with teachers to schedule and present school counseling curriculum lessons based on developmental needs and needs identified through data	Covering classes when teachers are absent or to create teacher planning time
Interpreting student records	Maintaining student records
Analyzing grade-point averages in relation to achievement	Computing grade-point averages
Consulting with teachers about building classroom connections, effective classroom management, and the role of noncognitive factors in student success	Supervising classrooms or common areas
Protecting student records and information per state and federal regulations	Keeping clerical records
Consulting with the school principal to identify and resolve student issues, needs, and problems	Consulting with the school principal to identify and resolve student issues, needs and problems
Advocating for students at individual education plan meetings, student study teams and school attendance review boards, as necessary	Coordinating schoolwide individual education plans, 504 plans, student study teams, response to intervention plans, the Multi-Tiered System of Supports (MTSS), and school attendance review boards
Analyzing disaggregated schoolwide and school-counseling program data	Serving as a data entry clerk

Source: Reproduced with permission from the American School Counselor Association. (n.d.-a). *Appropriate and inappropriate activities for school counselors.* https://www.schoolcounselor.org/getmedia/8fe536c2-7a32-4102-8ce7-42e9b0683b3b/appropriate-activities-of-school-counselors.pdf

Lunchroom Supervision

Managing lunch time behavior, dismissing students to recess, reminding students to dump their milk in one bin and their tray in another, and encouraging students to not share food are all reasons why providing lunchroom supervision is considered an inappropriate task for a school counselor (ASCA, n.d.-a). The visual just described reflects responsibilities that are misaligned with the work. Consider, however, the slight adjustments that could be made to lunchroom supervision that could make the task more connected to the work of the school counselor.

The lunchroom is a vibrant place that allows the school counselor to see the students in their element. It creates several opportunities for meaningful connection and data collection. Imagine the social nuances that occur in the lunchroom. A school counselor could quickly read the room and the expressed and nonverbal communication present in order to come to know their students. For example, if a student is upset because they do not have any friends, the school counselor could observe what takes place during lunch and work to support students in developing their skills. The lunchroom also provides the opportunity to learn about food insecurity, disordered eating, engagement or isolation, social skills, and other prosocial skills. It can also be an opportunity to connect with kids quickly rather than require them to leave the classroom. Finally, being in the lunchroom allows the school counselor to be present, have their face be known as a trusted adult, and develop relationships with the students and other staff on duty. As mentioned previously, building strong working relationships is critical to the role of the school counselor (Baker et al., 2009). Being in the lunchroom provides a tremendous opportunity to know and be known by your community.

Classroom Coverage

Our classroom teachers experience illness, emergencies, and other instances making them unable to be in their classrooms. While having a substitute teacher work on their behalf is preferred, not all districts or schools have access to a bank of individuals prepared to substitute teach. ASCA (2016) clearly notes that standing in for a teacher in their absence is not only an inappropriate task but also is an unethical one for a school counselor, especially if expected to grade student work. While school counselors certainly do not want to become the individual responsible for providing classroom coverage for all teacher absences (Dodson, 2009; Wilder, 2018), if an opportunity emerges in your school to support your school in this way, consider how to make it a meaningful and extension of your work.

In this situation, the school counselor could use the time in the classroom to review a previous guidance lesson or provide an "extra" lesson on a topic that may benefit all students in the room. Consider which of ASCA's Behavior and Mindset Standards (n.d.-b) you are emphasizing and use the opportunity to provide more practice. If not used for an organized lesson, this time could be used to engage in meaningful dialogue with all students about real world events and challenges, or topics relevant to that age or grade (e.g., time management with ninth-grade students). If whole class work is not feasible and students have work to complete, use this time to check in with students individually. This could look like conversations at their desks or an invitation to a neutral location in the classroom where more confidential discussions could take place. This could be an opportunity to complete grade checks with students and offer resources. Providing classroom coverage, while not a preferred practice, can offer meaningful and school counseling-rich experiences.

Drop-Off and Pick-Up Duty

Who does not enjoy the bustle of a busy school parking lot? There are now memes and videos on social media that highlight the stress-filled experience of parents getting in the pick-up line early to avoid extended time waiting for their children to pack into the family vehicle. The drop-off experience reveals a different kind of stress fueled by ensuring homework is completed and safely stowed in backpacks; lunchboxes are packed; and their children have coats, shoes, and other items for their day. This experience can be even more difficult for a student who does not feel connected to the school to enjoy the learning experience and have the tools to access learning.

While drop-off duty is an investment of time, the school counselor can use drop-off and pick-up times as opportunities to make connections with students and their caregivers. During drop-off, the school counselor can glean much information from the moment they open the car door. The opportunity can be seen as an opening to the student's world. From sensing the vibe in the car (does it feel tense or joyful?), noticing family dynamic and engagement (how do the family members in the car communicate with each other?), and seeing how the student is arriving to school (do they appear sleepy, hopeful, stressed), recognizing these emotional signs can help the counselor know what the student may need that day and support the student accordingly. This may include connecting with the teacher and linking the student to other resources. The school counselor can also take this moment to check in with the other siblings in the car, which can be a chance to reconnect with previous students or an opportunity to become familiar with the younger children.

The drop-off and pick-up experience can also be an effective way for school counselors to become known by students and caregivers (McCarthy & Watson, 2018). Presenting as a friendly and helpful adult each day reinforces the school counselor's presence in the school community and helps them to be known by others. Greeting students by name can help them to feel valued and seen (e.g., "Good morning, Raquel, I'm so glad you are here today!"). This is also an opportunity to note the names of the parents and caregivers. At the end of each day, the school counselor can make an intentional point to highlight something positive the student did that day (e.g., "Mr. Martinez, Raquel was a leader today and stopped a rumor in her class."). Conversations like this help parents and caregivers to feel like their child is welcome and valued and is important as we work to develop trust. This may also encourage them to reach out to the school counselor when needed.

Finally, drop-off and pick-up can be an opportunity to engage with parents and caregivers who may be unable to meet during school hours. For example, school counselors may use this time to schedule a meeting or get important paperwork signed, such as a permission form for group participation. Recognizing that parents and caregivers may not be able to come to school when it is convenient to the school structure demonstrates a willingness to be flexible, meet parents or caregivers where there are, and removes barriers (Musheno & Talbert, 2002). For those parents who may be reluctant owing to a past negative engagement with the school, this is an opportunity to repair relationships and show them a different experience.

Front Desk Coverage

The front desk of the main office is the command station of the school. From greeting guests, answering questions, welcoming late arrivals, tending to students who feel ill, and supporting teachers, the front office staff experiences a flurry of action all day long. When front office staff are absent, the school counselor may be called upon to help cover the front desk (Perera-Diltz & Mason, 2008). While not a long-term solution for coverage, spending time at the front desk provides school counselor a glimpse into the inner workings of the school, including contact with parents and caregivers who have questions or help in regulating those with big emotions. School counselors can be the friendly and helpful person, offer support, and even educate visitors about their role. This may lead to the school counselor connecting families to resources, learning more about a student's situation (e.g., medical appointment), and developing positive connections with parents and caregivers (Musheno & Talbert, 2002). Answering the phone and responding to teacher requests can also give the school counselor not only the opportunity to better understand the system, protocols, and needs in the building but also to be seen as a part of the collective school team.

Discipline

School counselors are not disciplinarians. This is a statement that has been shared in graduate training programs, echoed throughout school buildings, and emphasized in the ASCA Ethical Standards for School Counselors (2016). Issues of discipline must be managed by the administration to allow school counselors to maintain a trusting working relationship with the student and avoid unnecessary dual relationships (2016). At times this can be challenging, particularly when the school counselor is assigned a walkie-talkie and called to remove disruptive or insubordinate students from class. And while not the professional responsibility of school counselors to assign consequences to students, they can play an important role in the disciplinary experience of our students. For example, if a student has disrupted the learning environment and is suspended by the principal, the school counselor could use the opportunity to learn more about what may be contributing to the students' challenges and underlying needs. The school counselor could have a conversation with the student when the student reenters school, asking, How would you like to reenter? What would you like to tell other students when they ask where you have been? How can I help you? What do you need? Offering the student the opportunity to have a choice in these decisions can move this from a negative and even critical space to one that is productive and supportive.

It is important for the school counselor to remember that behavior is purposeful (Wubbolding, 2011). As such, the school counselor can see this moment as a time to learn what might be impacting the student's day. Through classroom observations, individual check-ins, and during whole group instructions, the school counselor may learn both the antecedents and consequences that emerge from the behavior. These data can inform the next interventions to use with students, including connection to additional resources. Participating in the discipline process from a place of curiosity can help the school counselor better understand needs and identify ways to use their skills more intentionally.

Testing Coordination

Standardized testing is an ever-present practice in schools today. Students are assessed two and sometimes three times each year to determine progress made toward grade-level goals and standards. While teaching academic content to students is the primary role of the classroom teacher, testing coordination falls to another staff member in a school building. While considered an inappropriate task for a school counselor (ASCA, n.d.-a), this work is often assigned to the school counselor, especially at the secondary level (Perera-Diltz & Mason, 2008).

Whereas serving in the role of testing coordinator can require closing the counseling center and pausing some services, including individual counseling, advisement, and small-group counseling, the investment of time can be viewed as an opportunity. Especially at the secondary level, where school counselors are balancing large caseloads, serving as the testing coordinator may allow interactions with a greater number of students (Perera-Diltz & Mason, 2008). With less time spent providing Tier 1 services through classroom guidance curriculum, the school counselor's time is often spent supporting students individually and thus serving a smaller percentage of their caseload. Beyond simply having "eyes on" students coordinating testing, the school counselor can learn about the student's testing behavior, support a student managing stress or worry related to the test, and be seen and experienced by the student as a helpful and kind adult in the building. This experience is another opportunity to develop positive relationships with students!

Finally, observing the test-taking experience can help the school counselor better understand the impact of the testing environment and the specific challenges and needs of students as they engage with the test. This information can increase the school counselor's ability to convey empathy toward students in the testing environment and can even strengthen other areas of their comprehensive school counseling program. For example, the school counselor could integrate classroom guidance curriculum on managing stress related to testing or even study skills. This work can help us to serve even better!

VOICES FROM THE FIELD

Name: Hannah Brinser, MA, LPC, NCC (she/her)

Where You Practice: Idaho

Professional Job Title: School Counselor (K–8) and doctoral student in the Counselor Education and Supervision program at Idaho State University.

Bio: Hannah received an MA in school counseling from Gonzaga University and a BS in psychology from Western Washington University. Hannah is a Certified School Counselor (ESA-SC), Licensed Professional Counselor (LPC), and National Certified Counselor (NCC). Her research interests include leadership and advocacy in school counseling, school counselor professional identity, and cultivating trauma-informed schools.

As a beginning school counselor, I was hesitant to participate in lunch, recess, and drop-off duties. I did not want to set the standard that this was an appropriate role for a school counselor or something I would do all the time. However, it did not take long for this work to become my favorite part of the day. Although lunch, recess, and drop-off duty initially felt like I was supervising common areas by ensuring students were safe and respectful, I realized my presence alone in these areas accomplished this. I now had space to be more intentional with this time rather than simply providing supervision. This ultimately became a time to connect with students in their element—through play, welcoming students in the morning, and connecting with students in a different way. I was able to connect with students that I typically wouldn't see in my office or those who did not need Tier 2 or Tier 3 services. In this way, I was truly able to live the mission of serving *all* students, which previously felt impossible with such a high caseload.

Drop-off duty in the mornings seemed to make a difference in the lives of my students, myself, and the school culture as a whole. I had the opportunity to greet students first thing in the morning, setting the tone for their day. I became intentional about ensuring students knew someone was excited to see them. This work also increased my visibility within the school community; I realized just how many students I had never seen or had never seen me. I certainly did not know all their names. In the cafeteria, I was able to work proactively and identify concerns with students that I would not have known about before. Rather than using this time as "behavior watching," I was able to intervene quickly and help students resolve conflict as it was occurring in the moment. I was able to be present and readily available for all students, eventually learning each of their names. Over time, I had numerous students stopping by my office and saying, "Hi, Ms. B! How are things going?! See you at lunch!", which meant the world to me.

Through this experience, I realized how lunch, recess, and drop-off duty could undoubtedly be inappropriate activities if not used intentionally. While I do not believe lunch, recess, or drop-off duty should ever be a requirement placed on school counselors, I now see it as an opportunity to connect with students in a different way. I was able to develop relationships with students I did not have the opportunity to connect with before and deepen the relationships I had with students I already knew. This presence helped students understand I was there for them all the time, not only in difficult circumstances but also in moments of celebration and joy. It became much easier to see all the good occurring in the school community once I was able to get out of my office. Students were also more accessible, and I found myself better able to celebrate their strengths and accomplishments when I became a part of their environment.

Most importantly, finding a way to reframe these inappropriate duties has reminded me of my "why" and purpose for doing this work. It is very easy to get lost in the "checklist" that sits in my office, seeing one student after the other. It also became easier to navigate challenging situations when they came up, as I had already developed a positive relationship with the student or student(s) in a different context; they knew I was a safe person who wanted to support them. For some students, this may be one of their only interactions with the school counselor outside of classroom instruction, so it is essential we use this time well. Instead of saying, "No, this is not my role," I found that saying "Yes, and I will be using this time intentionally" made a significant difference in my ability to build relationships with teachers and administrators while ensuring I was intentional with my time and serving students directly.

I worked with a seventh-grade student, Olivia (this chapter's student voice) as she was navigating her parents' separation. For many reasons, this was an exceptionally complex and difficult time for her. We began meeting each week for about 15 minutes, working on coping skills and ensuring her needs were met at home. After a month or two, Olivia did not need to come into my office weekly anymore. While her situation was certainly improving at home, she was also gaining the skills and tools she needed to navigate it effectively. However, she was concerned about not having that weekly check-in time with me anymore. This was also a time where I no longer had the capacity or availability to meet with students weekly due to needs within the school community. I was also expected to engage in lunch and recess duty, which were previously times I used to meet with students individually, as to not pull them from class.

Because I found a way to reframe lunch, recess, and drop-off duty, Olivia and I were able to connect more (and differently) than we would if she came to my office each week. Instead of having this limitation, Olivia knew I was around during those times and available for her if she needed something. In addition, I was able to build a different relationship with her, one that existed in her element. I was able to observe her interactions with friends, eat lunch at her table, and join them outside to play foursquare. As a result, I learned more about Olivia and her friends than I could have from my office. Overall, I found a way to engage intentionally with students while also being a presence in these areas to support students differently. Having that consistency with students was essential, as they knew I wasn't just there for the difficult, tear-filled moments but also for the moments they wanted to play, laugh, or tell me stories about their lives.

SUMMARY AND CONCLUSION

School counselors have long advocated for the ability to complete appropriate and role-specific activities as defined by the ASCA. With schools often operating without important resources, however, these extra responsibilities can fall to staff, including school counselors. This situation can result in school counselors feeling confused, frustrated, and even misunderstood in their work. In this chapter, we offered history and context to the role of the school counselor and the key responsibilities at each level. We identified some of the inappropriate activities assigned to school counselors and encouraged a new way of thinking of these activities, a way that reflects our role and honors our unique skill set. This reimagining of these activities allows school counselors to get creative and intentional about linking our work, standards, and goals with those other activities. We encourage you to consider the tips and hints below as you prepare to work in your future school!

CASE STUDY

Maria is a first-year Spanish-speaking school counselor at a K–6 school with 743 students. She has worked tirelessly in the first 3 months of the school year to develop relationships with the administration, staff, and teachers. In her effort to strengthen these relationships and be seen and known as a "team player," Maria is reluctant to decline any request for her assistance. With recent staff shortages, she feels compelled to help and even agrees to several tasks, believing them to be short-term.

Maria has agreed to the following:

- Supervising both lunch periods each day.
- Carrying a walkie-talkie throughout the day.
- Making photocopies for the first-grade team of teachers.
- Covering the front desk every Wednesday morning during staff meetings.
- Providing classroom coverage for the ELD classrooms when needed.

DISCUSSION QUESTIONS

1. Which of these tasks are considered *inappropriate* by the ASCA?
2. Select two tasks and describe how each could be reframed as meaningful school counseling work.
3. As a new school counselor, how might you address administration about the tasks that do not align with your work? How will you balance being a "team player" with setting clear role expectations?

PRACTICAL APPLICATION

- Consider every task and interaction as opportunities to develop and strengthen trusting work alliances with students, families, and staff. These moments can offer the chance to come to know them and be known by them. It allows the stakeholder to experience you as helpful and dependable and increases their willingness to seek you out in the future.

- Be creative in connecting assigned inappropriate duties to your work and standards. When tasked with classroom coverage or any role that places you in the position of providing supervision, link your work to the experience! When covering a kindergarten class at the start of the day, for example, consider how you might creatively embed the ASCA Behavior and Mindset standards to that story you read to the students. How can you be intentional in the questions you ask to increase the students' ability to recognize the emotions in the story's characters? With this adjustment, providing coverage can change the experience into an opportunity that is aligned with our work.

- Be clear about what you *will* do. Even with our intentional effort to connect our work to the inappropriate roles, we do continue to advocate for our role as school counselors. Remember, this should go beyond simply showing administration the list of inappropriate versus appropriate activities. Continue to have courage in your work to advocate for the role of the school counselor. Use data to illustrate how your skills may be better used in a different way.

- Be patient and willing to educate others about your role. It is important to remember that not all staff, students, and families will understand what school counselors do. For some, you may be the first school counselor they have worked with, while others may have history that informs their perception or beliefs regarding the work you do. Be willing to answer questions, educate, and help others continue to understand the work you do.

KEY REFERENCES

Only key references appear in the print edition. The full reference list appears in the digital product on Springer Publishing Connect: connect.springerpub.com/content/book/978-0-8261-8753-6/part/part02/chapter/ch06

American School Counselor Association. (2019a). *The ASCA national model: A framework for school counseling programs* (4th ed.).

American School Counselor Association. (2019b). *The essential role of elementary school counselors.* https://www.schoolcounselor.org/getmedia/1691fcb1-2dbf-49fc-9629-278610aedeaa/Why-Elem.pdf

American School Counselor Association. (2019c). *The essential role of middle school counselors.* https://www.schoolcounselor.org/getmedia/7ed7a427-a87a-4609-a4e1-ee8e5358df29/Why-Middle.pdf

Chandler, J. W., Burnham, J. J., Kiper Riechel, M. E., Dahir, C. A., Stone, C. B., Oliver, D. F., Davis, A. P., & Bledsoe, K. G. (2017). Assessing the counseling and non-counseling roles of school counselors. *Journal of School Counseling, 16.* https://eric.ed.gov/?id=EJ1182095

Perera-Diltz, D. M., & Mason, K. L. (2008). Ideal to real: Duties performed by school counselors. *Journal of School Counseling, 6*(26). Retrieved from http://www.jsc.montana.edu/articles/v6n26.pdf

CHAPTER 7

Data-Driven Services and School Counseling Efficacy Assessment

TRISH HATCH, JULIE HARTLINE, AND CHER N. EDWARDS

LEARNING OBJECTIVES

After reading this chapter, students will be able to:

- Define data-based frameworks and school counseling service delivery.
- Analyze various types of data used in schools.
- State the role of data related to school counseling interventions and program design.
- Apply assessment results to promote systems change with a focus on culturally relevant school counseling interventions, equity, and inclusion.

STUDENT VOICE

Student "R," sixth grade, provided the following testimony:

"In the middle of sixth grade, my school counselor asked to meet with me. He told me that he was meeting with all of the sixth-graders who seemed to be having a tough time in one or more of their classes. I was embarrassed at first, but he told me that I was not alone and that sixth grade can be a tough year. He asked what I thought was causing problems. I told him that middle school felt way different from my elementary school. I was feeling overwhelmed with all of the different teachers and having to move to a different classroom for each period. I had a notebook and wrote down my assignments, but I never seemed to know where the notes were. Even though I did my homework, I couldn't find it a lot of the time. I understood the stuff that we talked about in class, but I didn't feel like I really had a good system for keeping my notes together and keeping track of assignments and homework. My counselor told me that there were other students who were feeling the same way and that some students find it helpful to meet together and talk about organization skills. He said that the group could talk about ways to organize your locker and notebook and work together to create a system to keep things organized. I felt weird being a part of the group at first, but it was super helpful. When we first met, we took a survey to share about our attitudes, knowledge, and skills related to organization. We met every week for 6 weeks, and at the

end, I had an organized locker and notebook and a tracker for each class that included a calendar to write what was due and when. I even had a separate folder for each class where I could keep my notes and homework so it would not get lost or misplaced. It felt good to know where everything was and to be able to find homework that I had completed. At the end, we took the same survey that we did at our first meeting. It was cool to see how I answered the questions differently and how much I had learned! My grades got better, and I was less stressed."

INTRODUCTION

You might be asking yourself, "Why talk about data?" Before you decide to skim over this chapter as a snoozer, keep in mind that the use of data is rooted in the ethical and professional mandates of our profession, but more importantly, it helps us do our job better and allows us to advocate well for our profession. Data guide what school counseling interventions are offered to students and families. Data demonstrate to administrators (who, ahem, are in the decision-making seat regarding discretionary funds and staffing needs) how the work that school counselors do is connected to discipline referrals, student success, and graduation rates (Taylor & Burgess, 2019). Becoming a "data master" does not need to happen overnight. Start small. Do a pretest/posttest following a small group, run the grade/discipline referral reports for students. Follow up with the students, then run the reports again later in the year. Complete a schoolwide needs assessment annually to identify big picture school needs. Over time, you'll be able to compare annual data and begin to see trends and outliers that will inform your counseling practice and demonstrate how your work impacts student outcomes.

In this chapter, we begin by providing a brief overview of the Multi-Tiered System of Supports (MTSS), followed by an examination of how school counselors can use data to drive culturally relevant school counseling curriculum and targeted interventions provided within their programs, and finally, a discussion of the school counselor's role in using data to promote systemic change to promote equity and inclusion. We provide an introduction to data-based frameworks and how the delivery of a school counseling program fits within them. Next, we explore the various types of data used in schools as well as the types of data school counselors can collect related to their prevention and intervention activities. Finally, we discuss analyzing and sharing the results of the school counseling program and will provide an example of data-driven practices from a practicing school counselor.

MULTI-TIERED SYSTEM OF SUPPORTS

Response to intervention (RTI) rose to the national forefront in education in the late 1990s and grew into a comprehensive, data-based prevention model to help students who were struggling to achieve (Kennelly & Monrad, 2007). The school counselor's role in RTI aligns with the seminal framework for the profession, the American School Counselor Association (ASCA) National Model (ASCA, 2019). According to Sabella, "once you get to know the RTI process, you realize it is highly consistent with all of the components of a comprehensive school counseling program as espoused by the ASCA National Model" (Sabella, 2012, p. 73).

Similar to RTI, positive behavior interventions and supports (PBIS) emerged as a problem-solving model, utilizing differentiated instruction and employing a continuum of proactive, positive, multi-tiered behavioral interventions. Involving all members of the school in parallel endeavors, schoolwide PBIS helps students learn positive behaviors. Research has shown significant increases in student respectfulness, motivation, and responsibility when schools implement PBIS. These changes support reduced referrals, suspensions, and tardy rates, which ultimately lead to increased attendance and connectedness as well as achievement (Brown et al., 2001; Garfat & Van Bockern, 2010; Horner et al., 2009). Both RTI and PBIS promote universal instruction in Tier 1, targeted interventions in Tier 2, and individual interventions in Tier 3.

The MTSS is an outgrowth of RTI and encompasses PBIS. MTSS is a comprehensive framework that addresses both the academic and behavioral needs of all students (Cowan et al., 2013; Hawken et al., 2008). Schools benefit from multiple evidence-based interventions of varying intensity to meet the wide range of behavioral, social/emotional, and academic needs of all students (Anderson & Borgmeier, 2010). Like RTI and PBIS, MTSS promotes universal instruction for all in Tier 1, targeted interventions in Tier 2, and individual interventions in Tier 3.

As RTI and PBIS combined into MTSS, those in the school counseling field have collaborated to align comprehensive school counseling programs with MTSS (Sink, 2016). Calling on school counselors to be leaders, facilitators, and supporters of MTSS, Ziomek-Daigle et al. (2016) explored the overlap of data, evidence-based practices, collaboration, advocacy, cultural responsiveness, and systemic change between RTI, PBIS, and school counseling programs. In *A School Counselor's Guide to Multi-Tiered Systems of Support*, Goodman-Scott et al. (2019) provide school counselors with practical resources for strengthening a comprehensive school counseling program through alignment with the three tiers of support in MTSS. Additionally, the ASCA, the national professional organization that supports school counselors, released *Making MTSS Work*, which provides a wealth of information regarding the alignment of the ASCA National Model with a school's MTSS program (Goodman-Scott et al., 2019).

Multi-Tiered, Multi-Domain System of Supports

Whereas MTSS provides a framework through which to meet the varying academic and behavioral needs of students in schools (Cowan et al., 2013; Hawken et al., 2008), and those in the school counseling field have worked to align comprehensive school counseling programs with MTSS, the Multi-Tiered, Multi-Domain System of Supports (MTMDSS) is designed specifically for school counselors to incorporate the three school counseling domains of academic, college/career, and social/emotional within the tiered services (Hatch et al., 2018, 2019).

MTMDSS is a framework (see Figure 7.1) for the delivery of a school counseling program with the objectives of (a) offering a core school counseling program of curriculum, individual student planning, and schoolwide programs and activities for all students; (b) supporting the academic, college/career, and social/emotional development of all students; (c) providing targeted interventions for students with data-driven needs; and (d) ultimately, enhancing student success and achievement (Hatch et al., 2018, 2019). It is within this framework that school counselors analyze data within their schools to determine curriculum, interventions, and systemic concerns, and school counselors also collect data regarding the activities within this framework to demonstrate the impact of their work on student success.

TYPES OF DATA IN SCHOOLS

There are many types of data collected and reported in schools. School counselors, as educators, also need ways to label, organize, describe, evaluate, and share the impact of their activities. Three types of data used within schools will be shared first: student achievement data, achievement-related data, and standards- and competency-related data. Each type of data is important to the other two, and we will begin with what many consider to be the most important type of data in schools (Dimmitt et al., 2007).

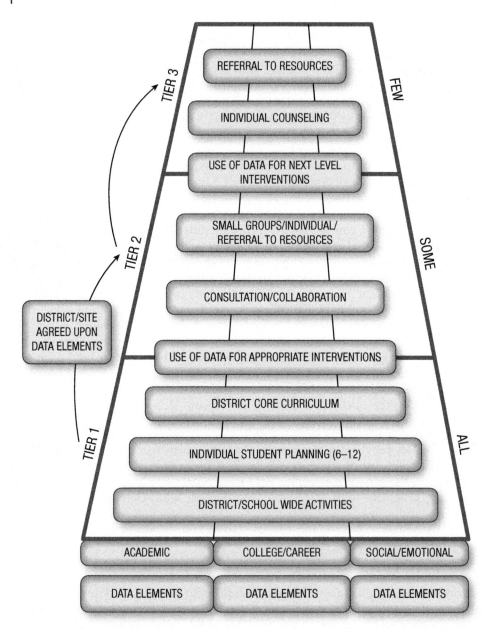

FIGURE 7.1 Multi-tiered, multi-domain system of supports graphic.

Source: Adapted from Hatch, T. (2017). Multi-tiered, multi-domain, system of supports (MTMDSS). *Hatching results blog* [Blog]. http://bit.ly/35XgYYB

Student Achievement Data

Student achievement data, often referred to as "big ticket items" (Dimmitt et al., 2007, p. 29), measure the success of schools. Families and stakeholders often look at achievement data when comparing schools; these data have been known to impact home values and drive administrative/superintendent reassignments. These data include, for example, graduation rates, college attendance rates, advanced placement (AP) test passage rates, standardized test scores, etc.

Some school counselors find it difficult to make direct correlations from their activities to specific student achievement data elements. For example, all educators work to improve standardized test scores; therefore, there is no way for counselors to show, definitively, that scores went up (or not) as a direct result of their activities, as other variables always contribute. However, while school counselors cannot take *full* credit for student improvements in achievement data, they can most certainly share how the work of the school counseling program is contributing in a meaningful way to student achievement data. Achievement data alone, however, are not enough to show the linkage between school counseling activity and results. Other data, including achievement-related data, can help to provide that linkage.

Achievement-Related Data

According to research, students' achievement-related data are the data elements that support students' achievement. Research has shown that when students behave, attend, do classwork and homework, and enroll in rigorous courses, they perform better in school (Dimmitt et al., 2007). Measuring and reporting achievement-related data can provide valuable insight regarding ways to improve achievement data. Plus, achievement-related data may be more accessible to school counselors, may appear to align more directly with their activities, and may be more closely linked to school counseling program results than are student achievement data. However, both types of data are important to collect and share. Monitoring achievement-related data provides an opportunity to demonstrate how school counselors are contributing, in part, to achievement results.

Standards- and Competency-Related Data

Standards- and competency-related data indicate whether students *learned* what they were taught. Like teachers, school counselors have standards and competencies, and just as teachers assess the impact of their lessons, so too should school counselors. Ideally, as a result of the school counselor's activity, students improve or shift their attitudes, gain more *knowledge,* or demonstrate a skill. The school counseling competencies measured often come from the ASCA Mindsets and Behaviors for Student Success: K-12 College and Career-Readiness Standards for Every Student (ASCA, 2014), but they may also come from the National Career Development Guidelines (National Career Development Association, 2013), accreditation standards and competencies, state school counseling competencies, or other standards. Careful consideration should be given to selecting and collecting data regarding indicators that are measurable, such as the percentage of students who

- *know* the required courses for graduation (knowledge);
- *believe* it is important to attend school (attitude); and,
- *demonstrate* the ability to resolve a conflict peacefully (skill).

Linking standards- and competency-related data to achievement-related data, and then to achievement data, creates the link necessary to illustrate the impact of the school counseling program. Although this link represents a correlation and not a causal relationship, school counselors can demonstrate through this linkage how they contribute in a meaningful way to the school's overall goal of academic achievement (see Figure 7.2).

SCHOOL COUNSELING PROGRAM EVALUATION DATA

The next data elements we will discuss are related to program evaluation. These data measure the impact of school counseling program activities and drive program improvements. These data show how school counselors contribute to student success. There are three different types of program evaluation data: process (participation), perception (mindsets and behaviors), and outcome.

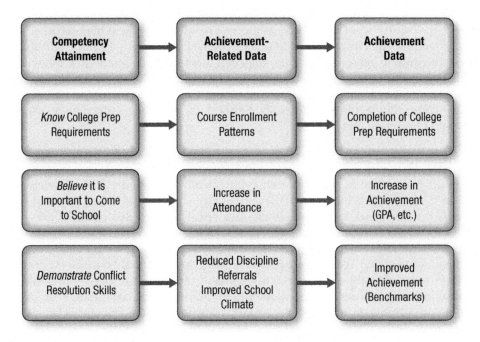

FIGURE 7.2 Linkage of competency attainment, achievement-related, and achievement data.

Source: Adapted from Hatch, 2013; Hatch, T., & Hartline, J. (2022). *The use of data in school counseling: Hatching results (and so much more) for students, programs and the profession.* Corwin.

Process (Participation) Data: What You Did for Whom

The fourth edition of the ASCA National Model renamed process data "participation data" (ASCA, 2019), but the terms are synonymous. Process, or participation, data provide evidence that an event happened. They answer the questions "What did the school counselor *do? For whom* did the counselor do it?" Process data are, in a way, "selfish" data because they communicate only what the school counselor did; they do not communicate anything about what students learned or how they are different. Process data provide the answer to the questions "who," "what," "where," "when," and "how often."

Who (received services): Which students? All students? Only a certain student group? How many?

What (did they receive): What was the activity? What need did it address? What curriculum was used? Was it implemented as prescribed or was it modified?

Where (did they receive it): Was the lesson delivered to 30 students in their classroom, 10 students in the career center, or to 300 in the multipurpose room?

When (did they receive it)/How often (was it provided): When did they receive this activity or service? All year? Once? Twice? For 30 minutes?

While some might be impressed with a school counselor's process data, others might ask, "That's great you taught this lesson, but do you know if the students learned anything? Did the activity impact the likelihood that students would attend school, behave in class, get good grades and be promoted or graduate?" Stakeholders and decision makers are generally more interested in the impact of an activity than that the activity took place. Process data tells *nothing* about whether the student is *different* as a *result* of the activity, only that the school counselor *did* the activity; these data do not indicate if there has been any change for the students. In other words, process data do not address the impact of the activity.

Perception (Mindsets and Behaviors) Data: Did You Ask?

Historically, the term *perception data* has been used to depict which *standards and competencies* students are expected to master as a result of a school counseling lesson or intervention; however, it was renamed "mindsets and behaviors" data in the fourth edition of the ASCA National Model. This type of data answers the question "What did students learn through participation in the school counseling activities?" (ASCA, 2019, p. 35). While process (or participation) data are about *what the school counselor did*, perception (or mindsets and behaviors) data address *what the students learned*. These data tell what a student thinks, knows, or can demonstrate as a result of the lesson or activity.

Why Assess?

While not required, many school counselors were teachers prior to becoming a school counselor. What do teachers do after teaching a unit to students? They assess whether students learned the content. Likewise, when school counselors teach students in the classroom or group sessions, it is appropriate for them to assess whether students learned what was taught. It answers the questions: *Was this lesson a good use of instructional learning time? Was this a valuable use of intervention time for the school counselor or students?* To determine this, assessments must be provided following the lesson or activity. Although school counselors provide counseling in their offices, they are teaching when they are in front of a group of students providing instruction. Therefore, as professional educators, it is appropriate for school counselors to assess the impact of their teaching in much the same way teachers do.

A-S-K (Ask Them What They Learned)

When assessing learning, school counselors measure the three areas called for in the ASCA *Mindsets and Behaviors* standards: attitudes, skills, and knowledge (ASK) (ASCA, 2019). The acronym ASK is a reminder for the school counselor to ASK students what they learned when they finish teaching a lesson (or series of lessons). ASK serves as a reminder to measure all three areas; however, when creating pretests/posttests, the following order of attitudes, knowledge, and skills for questions is suggested so that students build from beliefs to knowledge to skill demonstration when answering (Hatch et al., 2018).

Perception data, therefore, measure whether (a) students' attitudes or beliefs shifted; (b) students' knowledge increased; or (c) students learned the skill (attained the competency) as a result of an intervention. School counselors can show that students benefited from an activity by collecting ASK data before and after the completion of the activity. Whereas process (or participation) data measure what the counselor did, perception, (mindsets and behaviors) data indicate what students gained (Hatch et al., 2018).

Ultimately, ASK work together to influence behavior change. When school counselors design activities and lessons that address and measure all three of the ASK perception, or mindsets and behaviors, data areas, behavior change for students is more likely to occur.

Outcome Data: So What?

Outcome data measure impact on students' behaviors. It answers the question "So what?" It is the data that show application of what was learned. Outcome data serve as evidence that the school counseling activity either did or did not positively influence students' ability to utilize the learned ASK to change their behavior. For example, the counselor taught an anger management curriculum and students learned the techniques of conflict resolution, but do students now fight less? Do surveys indicate an improvement in school climate with students feeling safer in school? Outcome data provide insight as to whether students' overall behavior has changed. "Outcome data provide school counselors with the leverage to demonstrate the impact of their activities on students' ability to utilize their noncognitive abilities to improve their achievement, attendance, and discipline" (ASCA, 2019, p. 37). The three most important results school counselors can measure and report are attendance, behavior, and achievement. Research has demonstrated that better attendance improves academic achievement (NCES, 2009) and that students who behave better in school are more likely to achieve (Kremer et al., 2016; Van Horn, 2003).

Earlier, it was discussed how competency attainment can lead to improved achievement-related data, and research demonstrates that achievement-related data support student achievement data. When school counselors find improvement in student achievement–related data, it is good practice to review whether academic achievement is improving as well. While such findings do not demonstrate a causal relationship, achievement-related results often show that school counselors are contributing in a meaningful way to the overall academic achievement of students.

In summary, when school counselors collect process (or participation) data for the activities they conduct within the school counseling program, important questions about what is "being done" are answered. When they measure competency attainment data (perception, or mindsets and behaviors, data), they are collecting evidence that their objectives (improving student attitudes, knowledge, and skills) are being met. This leads to behavior change, which will be measured by achievement-related and achievement data as school counselors look for validation that the activity is contributing to overall student achievement in the school.

HATCHING RESULTS CONCEPTUAL DIAGRAM

The Hatching Results Conceptual Diagram, which was originally created by Dr. Trish Hatch in 2006, visually represents how school counseling data and activities (and ultimately, the entire school counseling program) can contribute to student achievement (see Figure 7.3). The conceptual diagram provides a practical model to guide the school counselor's use of data by visually laying out the relationship between the types of data (standards- and competency-related, achievement-related, and achievement data) and the data to evaluate (process, perception, and outcome) (Dimmitt et al., 2007; Hatch, 2005). This diagram helps to show how school counseling programs impact student achievement. Note the headings: Process Data, Perception Data, and Outcome Data. Competency attainment falls under Perception Data, and Outcome Data is an umbrella term for achievement-related data and achievement data.

Conceptual Diagram for School Counseling Curriculum

Note that Figure 7.3 reads left to right for school counseling curriculum and represents an action connecting what school counselors do (measured with process data) to the attainment of specific student competencies (measured with perception data) and behavior change, leading to an improvement in outcomes (reflected in achievement-related data and, subsequently, in achievement data). For example, when a school counselor teaches a classroom lesson on study skills, they might assess whether students acquire (a) the attitude that it is important to study, (b) the skill of organizing a study schedule, and (c) the knowledge of where and when to seek help when needed to pass their classes. In this scenario, the goal of the lesson would be to support improved classwork/homework completion (achievement related), which in turn supports improved student academic performance (achievement).

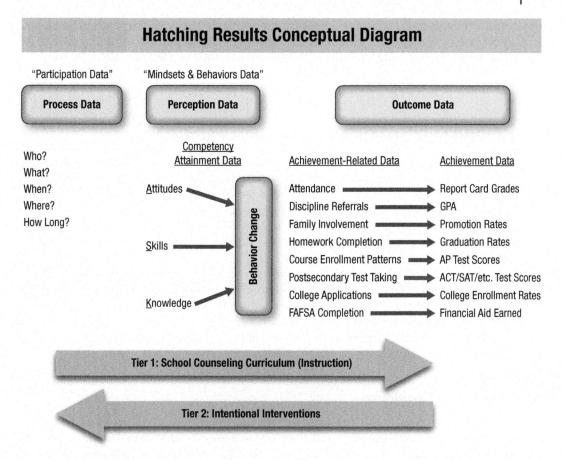

FIGURE 7.3 Hatching results' conceptual diagram.

Source: Adapted from Hatch, T. (2005, June). *Data made easy: Using data to effect change.* Paper presented at the American School Counselor Association, Orlando, Florida.

Conceptual Diagram for Intentional School Counseling

When students (or groups of students) are not performing to expectations for achievement, attendance, or behavior data elements, school counselors identify and attend to those students to provide additional support. In this case, the conceptual diagram for intentional school counseling (Figure 7.3) reads right to left. Beginning on the far right, the achievement data elements (course failure, for example) are measured and highlighted. Next, the contributing factors (achievement-related data) are identified (not completing classwork/homework).

Once the area of need (or deficiency) is identified, the next inquiry (moving left in the diagram) would be to look at the students' attitudes, skills, and knowledge (perception data) to discover what is needed (doesn't believe in doing homework; not sure how to study, etc.). Once discovered (often through surveys or individual meetings), moving left to right across the diagram again to the process data, an intervention would be implemented to target and address the specific need. Traditionally, when students struggle academically, they are given remedial courses or tutoring. However, it is important to consider that the barrier may be related to motivation. Alternatively, students may be placed in a counseling group for motivation when what they need is tutoring. Additionally, the student may not need either tutoring or counseling for motivation, but rather they may need support for coming to school regularly or for feeling unsafe/disconnected at school. All too often, the intervention is decided for students before the specific barrier is identified; determining the root cause will better align an intervention with student needs. Students, who come to school counselors from many diverse backgrounds and experiences, are often provided interventions without counselors taking the time to determine the needs arising from that student's own unique world (Lee, 2001). By using the conceptual diagram as a guide, school counselors can thoughtfully consider interventions that target actual student needs.

DATA-DRIVEN SCHOOL COUNSELING PROGRAMS

School counselors use data to ensure that every student receives instruction in three domains: academic, college/career, and social/emotional development. They use data to monitor student progress and to determine when students are in need of interventions. School counselors use data to measure the impact of their activities. They use data to share the impact and implications of their interventions with other educators. Finally, and most importantly, school counselors use data to make program improvements so that they may better serve their students.

Additionally, school counselors must also have proficiency in the analysis and interpretation of data within the context of the bigger picture for students and the school system. When data are thoroughly and thoughtfully analyzed, patterns, trends, or discrepancies may be uncovered that reveal a schoolwide need rather than a specific student need. By analyzing the larger picture, school counselors may find there is a need to advocate for systems change.

Tier 1 Curriculum Decisions

Many school counselors ask, "How do I determine what curriculum to deliver? There are only so many hours in the day, and there are so many needs." When designing school counseling curriculum to reach all students, the ASCA National Model recommends that school counselors review the *ASCA Student Standards: Mindsets & Behaviors for Student Success* (ASCA, 2021) as well as other student standards (e.g., common core, state standards) to make decisions as to which topics to deliver based on student developmental needs. School counselors use their professional wisdom (in consultation with others) to determine the number of lessons needed to address those topics for all students as well as the number of lessons that are manageable for the school counselor to deliver. Many times, school counselors find there are more lesson topics to deliver than time to deliver them. When this happens, they must prioritize lessons, and this can be done by analyzing data.

For example, in one California school district, school counselors delivered numerous lessons, including tobacco use prevention education (TUPE) lessons, to students in 10th grade. When the California Healthy Kids Survey (CHKS) data were analyzed, they discovered that very few ninth-grade students in the district smoked. In fact, the smoking rate for this district was half the state average. Since the TUPE lessons were not delivered until 10th grade, the data were not impacted by the instruction. Additionally, survey results showed that ninth graders were drinking alcohol at twice the state average, whereas seventh graders were three times as likely to use inhalants as other seventh graders in the state. Unfortunately, at that time there were no lessons being taught that addressed alcohol or inhalant use in either middle or high school. In this situation, the data served as a catalyst to focus attention on providing curriculum based on a data-driven need and resulted in additional resources needed to provide these data-driven curricula.

In an urban high school in another district, data revealed that few students were taking college entrance examinations (e.g., SAT or ACT). Despite evening presentations and posted advertisements for the tests, students were not registering for them. The school counselors at this school were able to use the data to leverage additional classroom instruction time to teach lessons about the different types of tests and the funding provided to cover the cost of exams for qualifying students. However, at a different high school in the same district, more than 90% of the students took the SAT and ACT, so teaching specific lessons about the different tests at this school was neither necessary nor an efficient use of time. Instead, school counselors briefly covered this information in the comprehensive "college knowledge" lesson for 10th graders and then disaggregated test registration data to identify students in need of additional support, encouragement, or assistance to register.

Determining Tier 2 Data Elements

It is equally important to determine and prioritize which data elements will be used to identify students in need of Tier 2 interventions because there is limited time in the day for interventions. School counselors within fully implemented programs have well-established data elements they regularly collect and analyze, and decisions regarding these data elements are often made in collaboration with data-based, decision-making teams at the school. However, for school counselors with programs that are just beginning, the recommendation is to select a few data elements that best align with school and district goals.

The school counselor can intentionally and proactively collect agreed-upon disaggregated data elements at specific time intervals throughout the school year (e.g., students who have multiple discipline referrals, who are in danger of retention, or who have missed more than 5 days in the first month of school.) Using this approach, school counselors determine students in need of additional intervention. This approach helps ensure that every student who qualifies is referred because this approach does not rely on teacher referrals but rather on when the school counselor queries data. If school counselors want to work with students who have five or more absences, would the counselors get new qualifying students every day? If so, the process might be a bit chaotic. Instead, a more efficient process might be to determine a point in time (e.g., 30 days into the school year) when the counselors collect data regarding all students with five or more absences. With this process, the school counselors are scheduling time-specific intervention points when data will be gathered. By setting a specific time to look at the students in need, the school counselors are ensuring a system is in place to manage the data and implement interventions.

With this approach, it is also important to determine the exact details defining the data element. For example, do these absences include both excused and unexcused absences? Will the element be based on a raw number or a percentage? How many referrals will trigger an intervention? Will the data element be analyzed for all grades or only certain grade levels? How often will the school counselor review the data? With whom will they review the data? How will these factors complement or align with the MTSS data elements that teachers have created for Tier 2 interventions? Finally, how will the school counselor gather the data? It is important to note that hand tallying is not a good use of school counselor time. Collaborating with the attendance staff, administration, and other existing data sources is important when assessing what data are currently being collected and how this information can be shared with the school counselor for intervention-planning purposes.

Intentional school counseling Tier 2 activities are purposeful, planned, data driven, and specific. Rather than school counselors providing primarily responsive interventions for students who are referred or refer themselves, the intentional school counseling approach requires school counselors to determine via data which students require interventions and at what intervals. School counselors then provide predetermined interventions to meet identified needs. For example, school counselors know that there will be some students in need of behavior support every year, thus they can "predetermine" the behavior intervention before identifying the students in need of the support. In this way, school counselors are preparing with intentionality, and the intervention is ready once students are identified.

Using Data to Address Systems Change

Imagine that data analysis uncovers a student who is not on track to graduate eligible for college because they are not taking any college preparatory courses, even though they have the knowledge, attitudes, and skills (awareness, desire, and ability) to enroll in those courses. The student is, in fact, not allowed to enroll in the necessary courses because the school has a policy requiring students to achieve a 3.0 or better in the required prerequisite courses, and they have not met criteria. This is an example of a systems issue for which the intervention would need to take place on a systems level, not a student level. Sometimes, interventions are required outside the students themselves, so care must be taken when considering whether the needed intervention is best focused on the student, the family, or the school.

Intentionality on the part of the school counselor is not always about addressing student issues; sometimes school counselors must be intentional in addressing systems issues, especially as it relates to the school counselor's role as a social justice advocate. Intentional school counseling involves disrupting systemic patterns of oppression by acting as an agent of change. As leaders, advocates, collaborators, and systems change agents who embody the themes of the ASCA National Model (ASCA, 2019), school counselors are social justice advocates who promote equity and access so that all students can reach their full potential. According to Holcomb-McCoy (2007, pp. 17–18), "Social justice recognizes that there are situations in which application of the same rules to unequal groups can generate unequal results. Social justice provides a framework to assess the impact of policies and practices." As social justice advocates, school counselors use their voices of privilege to uncover and address institutional oppressions and systems that have historically disenfranchised certain student groups (ASCA, 2016; Hatch, 2012; Holcomb-McCoy & Chen-Hayes, 2011).

As a social justice advocate, the school counselor must reflect on how social injustices impact the students in their school. If the school counselor fails to acknowledge disparities that exist for marginalized and at-risk students, then they are guarding the status quo of systems, policies, and practices that serve as barriers for equitable access and opportunity for these students. As social justice advocates, school counselors must recognize and acknowledge programs and systems that are failing students rather than joining those who blame students and families for the failure. The term "achievement gap" has long focused on students as the root of the issue related to lack of academic success. In response, those aware and willing to acknowledge the systemic issues that have failed certain groups of students have shifted to the term "opportunity gap" to better represent the programs' and systems' history of failure. Erford (2015) expands on this perspective by noting the negligence of school systems related to failing to protect and advocate for youth, while at the same time perpetuating issues facing these same historically disadvantaged and powerless groups. It is the educators' responsibility to create and implement school interventions and policies that promote equity and inclusion.

The Education Trust developed the program Social, Emotional, and Academic Development Through an Equity Lens to serve as a framework "to shift the focus away from 'fixing kids' and toward addressing adult beliefs and mindsets as well as school and district policies to create an equitable learning environment" (Education Trust, 2009). The Education Trust acknowledges that educators must consider the living context of their students because realities such as racism, sexism, homophobia, socioeconomic status, family dynamics, school experiences, access, and cultural background all play a role in the social/emotional and academic development of students. Rather than simply adding policies, the Education Trust suggests that schools and districts revisit existing policies to determine if they foster equitable belonging and offer the support needed by students.

Addressing Gaps Through Systemic Change

When reviewing data, school counselors may discover gaps for groups of students who are underrepresented, underserved, or underperforming academically and socially/ emotionally or who are identifiable in college/career preparation and enrollment. Intentional school counseling for systems change may require the counselor to provide deliberate activities and interventions to address the gaps in achievement or performance between or among groups of students with similar characteristics, such as race, ethnicity, nationality, home language, ability, gender identity, financial means, sexual orientation, or other such groups within the larger system. Using leadership, collaboration, and advocacy skills, intentional school counselors design opportunities for additional instruction, support, and assistance (Goodman-Scott et al., 2022).

Often, school counselors seek to close opportunity gaps by providing more purposeful Tier 1 schoolwide programs and activities. For example, an underrepresentation of students of color in college enrollment could lead school counselors to focus more efforts on promoting college during classroom lessons and registration as well as creating new schoolwide programs and activities to encourage enrollment of underrepresented students in college. While schoolwide programs and activities often tend to result in an overall improvement in the rates for all students, they can widen the gap for underrepresented students, giving even more advantage to their peers. Therefore, it is critical that the school counselor make every effort to understand which student groups are advantaged and which are disadvantaged by schoolwide programs and activities as well as to seek to close gaps through more targeted and intentional school counseling interventions for the underrepresented student groups.

However, school counselors who are acting as systems change agents must look even farther beyond the deficiencies to identify student needs. Truly closing a gap involves using school data to identify students who are missing opportunities and examining the data of various student groups to determine if gaps exist between them and their peers. Unfortunately, many school counselors do not move beyond deficiencies and therefore fail to address the needs of students who miss opportunities, such as involvement in enrichment activities or completion of postsecondary applications. Or, school counselors may not address the needs of student groups that may not be achieving at the same level as their peers, even though they have the same abilities. To truly serve as systems change agents, it is imperative that school counselors examine missed opportunities and underrepresented student groups to close achievement, opportunity, and attainment gaps for the most vulnerable student groups (Goodman-Scott et al., 2022).

Identifying and Supporting Vulnerable Student Groups

Further investigation of school data may uncover access or opportunity concerns reflecting gatekeeping policies, practices, or procedures that may also contribute to low enrollment of some student groups in a course, activity, or program (Hart & Jacobi, 1992; Hines & Lemon, 2011; Holcomb-McCoy, 2007). This is particularly essential when considering the most vulnerable groups who may not have the same access and opportunity as other students. When analyzing school data, the school counselor may realize the intervention that students need is the school counselor's advocacy to *change an existing policy or practice* that may be denying some of the most vulnerable and deserving students access to educational opportunities.

Disaggregating and analyzing access data may shed light on the ways in which the school is contributing to opportunity gaps. Access and opportunity data can be used to advocate for the right of every student to participate in programs and graduate ready for college a career (Hatch, 2012; House & Martin, 1998; Johnson, 2002; Lee & Goodnough, 2011; NWEA, n.d.). In addition to advocating for access, monitoring course enrollment and cocurricular participation opens the door for school counselors to discover why some students who have access still choose not to participate in opportunities. Conducting student and family focus groups to explore perceptions and experiences can provide rich qualitative data that may result in a call for new policies or interventions.

Ultimately, intentional school counseling for systems change calls school counselors to perform deliberate acts to guide, lead, or direct reform efforts to interrupt, revise, or eliminate policies or practices that serve as barriers to access or opportunity and that contribute to opportunity gaps for underrepresented, underserved, or underperforming students. These barriers may include social justice issues, parity issues, or issues that stir a moral imperative for school counselors to act on students' behalf (Goodman-Scott et al., 2022; Hatch, 2013; Mullen et al., 2019). In this way, the school counselor is not only a systems change agent but also a social justice advocate, striving to close achievement, opportunity, and attainment gaps.

ANALYZING AND SHARING SCHOOL COUNSELING RESULTS

An end-of-the-year school counseling results report answers the following questions: *How are students different as a result of the program/lesson/activity*? Did the program assist students in achieving competencies? Did it result in a change in students' attendance, behavior, and academic achievement?

- What standards- or competency-related data were collected? (Pretest/posttest data on attitudes, knowledge, and skills?)
- What achievement-related data were collected? (Improved classwork completion? Improved attendance? Improved quarter grades?)
- What achievement data were collected? (Increase in course completion rates? Increase in promotion/graduation rates? Improvement in grades?)

After implementing a Tier 1 schoolwide curriculum or an intentional Tier 2 school counseling intervention, school counselors look at the results and ask questions: What worked? What went well? What didn't work? What went wrong with the activity? Is there any way to improve the activity next time? What needs to be changed or shifted to get the desired results?

Sharing results with stakeholders allows school counselors to communicate the impact of their programs and services to the school community. Often, teachers and administrators are unaware of the school counseling curriculum and interventions and the impact these services provide. Taking time to share results allows teachers and other stakeholders to understand the value of the program as well as how the school counselor supports student achievement. Results are also used to market the school counseling program through the creation of advocacy tools. School counseling programs in many states are dependent on soft funds and local (site) decision-making. Unfortunately, heart-wrenching anecdotes with little evidence of success rarely garner necessary resources because policymakers fund what works, not what feels good.

Collecting and sharing results can also assist the school counselor in defining and resolving advocacy concerns (Trusty & Brown, 2005). Results can be used to help others understand and objectively assess a problem. Results can assist in focusing advocacy efforts to improve programs, policies, practices, or services to support students. For example, when results indicate that despite attempts to deliver classroom lessons to encourage all students to take honors and AP courses, certain student groups are still underrepresented. The data might lead to conversations regarding policies and procedures that serve as gatekeepers for more rigorous educational opportunities for some students. By sharing results within the context of systems, the school counseling program can offer an opportunity for school staff to discuss access, opportunity, and attainment gaps and begin the process of revising policies and procedures that may be contributing to the undesired outcomes. Addressing historically racist educational policies and systems will lead to better outcomes for all students and is an expectation of school counselors as anti-racist advocates.

The Flashlight Approach to Sharing Results

When school counselors are learning to collect and use data to share program success, it is critical that they do not try to measure everything. Although getting lost in the data can be fun at times, it can also feel very overwhelming, especially when counselors are just beginning to use data. Instead of measuring every lesson delivered or intervention conducted, it is suggested that counselors use the flashlight approach (Hatch, 2013; Lewis & Hatch, 2008) to focus on sharing the impact of one activity or intervention on one area of attendance, behavior, or achievement.

What is a flashlight? Common knowledge suggests that a real flashlight does not light up an entire room; rather, it shines a beam of light on one area or in one direction on a specific target. In the same way, rather than school counselors showing the impact of everything they do, it is suggested school counselors select one thing they have done (a school counseling curriculum or intentional intervention) and "shine the flashlight" on it.

Using the flashlight approach, the school counselor follows the counseling activity from beginning to end: standards, activity, process (or participation) data, perception (or mindsets and behaviors) data, outcome data, and implications. Flashlight slide decks and one-pagers provide a way for school counselors to share the impact of their activities with the administrators, faculty, central office, and school board members to market their programs.

VOICES FROM THE FIELD

Name: Felipe R. Zañartu (he/him)

Where You Practice: California

Professional Job Title: School Counselor

Bio: Felipe is dedicated to the field of school counseling, ensuring that counselors use comprehensive data to reach every student. Felipe is a practicing elementary school counselor and a 2019 recipient of the Recognized ASCA Model Program as a "RAMP School of Distinction," a national recognition bestowed for his comprehensive, data-driven school counseling program. Throughout 10 years of working in K–8 schools in California and Arizona, Felipe has specialized in creating and implementing data tools that demonstrate accountability and program efficacy. His specialty is in tools to make the RAMP process easy, manageable, and realistic for school counselors. For the past 5 years he has trained counselors to develop comprehensive school counseling programs. Felipe has regularly presented at state and national school counseling conferences. He currently produces the Hatching Results podcast, which broadcasts "all things school counseling" to listeners across the nation. In addition, Felipe is a part-time faculty member at San Diego State University, teaching school counseling graduate students in such areas as lesson plan development, data analysis, and results presentations.

My school counseling program is intentionally comprehensive and includes multiple tiers of service to effectively serve all students. The program works to ensure equity by implementing targeted, tiered interventions to close achievement or opportunity gaps. At Tier 1, I provide all students services via curriculum, with instruction around the attitudes, knowledge, and skills needed to be successful at school. At Tier 2, small group responsive services provide targeted support to some according to their specific needs. At Tier 3, a small number receive individualized support to help remove learning barriers (e.g., behavior) so they can be successful. I have established a service delivery model whereby all students receive the level of service that best fits their needs.

In implementing Tier 1 and Tier 2 activities, I always reflect back on the data from the previous year to determine the need. Multiple data points from one academic year suggested that second-graders needed both Tier 1 curriculum and Tier 2 interventions. By the end of their previous year as first-graders, these students had proven to be one of the most challenging groups, with 87 office referrals, the highest for the school. The largest referral category (67%) was "lack of citizenship skills," which teachers generally select when students have excessive low-level behavior issues with fellow students and/or the teacher, which tends to escalate into office referrals. Therefore, I chose to put special attention on helping these students learn the empathy skills needed to build better relationships with their peers and teachers.

I focused on creating a positive school climate with an emphasis on empathy, emotion management, and bully prevention skills, aiming to remove learning barriers to support attendance and academics. Mindsets and behaviors were analyzed in the process to ensure students were getting a healthy dose of self-management, learning strategies, and social skills to be successful. I understood that when students attend school with the attitudes, knowledge, and skills to make them successful both in and out of the classroom, they attend more often and are ready to learn.

I decided to deliver a second-grade curriculum (empathy) and an intervention for those who needed more in a similar topic area (social skills). For my curriculum, I delivered four lessons on empathy. I measured standards- and competency-related data via a six-question pretest/posttest; I asked three attitude questions, two knowledge questions, and one skill question and asked them in the suggested order so that students indicated what they believed and what they knew before they demonstrated the skill. For each of these questions, I included pictures to assist students, especially given their developmental and reading levels. For the skill question, students had to put themselves in the scenario of doing something by accident to select the appropriate answer option. I compared Work Habits and Social Skills grades on report cards, office discipline referrals, and suspensions for achievement-related outcomes. Because students being able to work with and interact effectively with their peers most certainly support improved achievement, I also compared math inventory scores.

For Tier 2 intervention, I worked with a group of second-graders who needed additional support with their work habits and social skills beyond the curriculum unit. I used several data elements to identify students for the group. Students who received multiple "Ns" (Needs Improvement) in the "work habits and social skills" section of the report card were filtered as possible group candidates; office discipline referrals were also a factor used to identify students for the group. Additionally, I reviewed the quarterly math and reading scores to see which students needed more support. For the intervention, I led an eight-session small group that met for 30 minutes each week. I used "Skits are a Hoot for Little Toots" for the sessions so that it would be engaging and interactive for the students. The curriculum is based on the Boys Town Curriculum, which breaks down social skills into three to five simple steps. Each session, students would review a skill that was an area of concern identified both by the data and teachers. They would perform a skit using a reader's theater technique and a debrief application of the skill in the session.

As with curriculum, I administered a preassessment and a postassessment. The pretest was given to students during the first session, and the posttest was given during the last session. The questions reflected the group's main objectives and included attitude questions, followed by knowledge questions, and finally a skill question. Like the curriculum, Work Habits and Social Skills grades on report cards were compared, as were office discipline referrals and suspensions, for achievement-related outcomes, as well as math inventory scores for the achievement outcome.

In evaluating results, I saw some gains in attitude, knowledge, and skill for both the Tier 1 curriculum and Tier 2 small-group intervention, and outcome data definitely supported the effectiveness of both. Over the first semester, office discipline referrals dropped by 57% and attendance improved by 1%, allowing students to spend more time in the classroom learning. By the end of the second quarter, there was a 2% growth in math scores. By the end of the school year, this grade level of students went from being the most referred group to the least referred, demonstrating a 65% decrease from one year to the next! However, through this evaluation I also learned ways that I could improve these activities in the future. I realized additional collaboration with teachers would help align skills implemented in the curriculum unit with classroom expectations, as well as to revise some questions and images on the pretests/posttests based on student developmental level for both the curriculum and small groups.

I shared the results through end-of-year presentations to staff, in counselor/administration meetings, and in my school counseling advisory council meetings. In each setting, I demonstrated the strength of the program and specifically elicited feedback in order to improve my practice and to create focused change to impact student outcomes. The program models a process of self-evaluation and self-improvement, reviewing areas of strength and areas of growth to effectively create systemic change, which leads to better outcomes for students. The process is not a quick fix but is rather a continual process of conceptualization, planning, implementation, evaluation, and reflection. This allows me to be a better school counselor every year, and to create systems change that educates and empowers students to achieve academic success, develop life skills to become lifelong learners, be creative thinkers, and become responsible community members in a diverse changing world.

SUMMARY AND CONCLUSION

As demonstrated throughout this chapter, school counselors use data within a multi-tiered delivery of services to impact student success. Whether they are delivering Tier 1 curriculum, providing Tier 2 interventions, or advocating for systems change, school counselors use data. They use data to design, implement, evaluate, market, and improve the school counseling program in alignment with the ASCA National Model (2019). Across the country, school counselors know that when budget cuts hit and financial resources are strained, difficult decisions must be made. They understand that if school counselors lack evidence of how their program activities support the mission and goals of their schools, then the counselors may be seen as more dispensable than other school-level staff (Hurwitz & Howell, 2013). Instead, these school counselors are using data and sharing results with key stakeholders to advocate for their programs and the profession so that they can continue to make a difference in the lives of their students.

CASE STUDY

Barbara is working in a brand-new elementary program. Barbara graduated from a Council for Accreditation of Counseling and Related Educational Programs (CACREP) that focused on the ASCA National Model and the importance of collecting data. Barbara has been hired to work in a higher needs school district with 550 K–5th grade students. This is the first year the school has had a full-time counselor. In the past, one elementary school counselor has been assigned two schools with 1,000 students on their caseload. Upon starting as the school counselor, Barbara noticed that most of the services were Tier 3 (putting out the fires). Barbara knew from her training that systemic prevention was needed, but where to start when she felt like her days were filled running from one crisis to another?

DISCUSSION QUESTIONS

1. Where should Barbara start?
2. What types of the following data should be collected in Barbara's school?
   - Achievement
   - Achievement-related data
   - Standards and competencies
3. What interventions could Barbara use to move services to more of a Tier 1 approach?
4. How can Barbara create a system of collaboration and buy-in?
5. What are the cultural and systemic areas that Barbara needs to consider when collecting, analyzing, and using data for services.

PRACTICAL APPLICATION

- Ensure the school counseling program consists of Tier 1, 2, and 3 services so that all students are benefiting from the school counseling program.

- Address student development in all three domains, academic, college/career, and social/emotional.

- Determine linkages between what the school counselor teaches and achievement-related and achievement data.

- Remember to ASK (attitude, knowledge, and skill) students what they learned.

- Determine which data elements to collect and at what time intervals.

- Remember that data may reveal a systems issue rather than a student issue.

- Use the data to help others understand and correct systems issues.

- Don't get lost in data.

- Remember to start by shining a light on one thing.

KEY REFERENCES

Only key references appear in the print edition. The full reference list appears in the digital product on Springer Publishing Connect: connect.springerpub.com/content/book/978-0-8261-8753-6/part/part02/chapter/ch07

Hatch, T. (2013). *The use of data in school counseling: Hatching results for students, programs, and the profession*. Corwin Press.

Hatch, T., Duarte, D., & DeGregorio, L. (2018). *Hatching results for elementary school counseling: Implementing core curriculum and other tier one activities*. Corwin.

Hatch, T., Triplett, W., Duarte, D., & Gomez, V. (2019). *Hatching results for secondary school counseling: Implementing core curriculum, individual student planning, and other tier one activities*. Corwin.

Holcomb-McCoy, C., & Chen-Hayes, S. F. (2011). Culturally competent school counselors: Affirming diversity by challenging oppression. In B. T. Erford (Ed.), *Transforming the school counseling profession* (3rd ed., pp. 90–109). Pearson.

Mullen, P. R., Newhart, S., Haskins, N. H., Shapiro, K., & Cassel, K. (2019). An examination of school counselors' leadership self-efficacy, programmatic services, and social issue advocacy. *Journal of Counselor Leadership & Advocacy, 6*(2), 160–173. https://doi.org/10.1080/2326716X.2019.1590253

PART III

Professional School Counseling
Interventions

CHAPTER 8

Individual Counseling for School Counselors

KIMBERLY J. DESMOND, STEPHANIE A. MCHUGH, AND KYLE L. BELLINGER

LEARNING OBJECTIVES

After reading this chapter, students will be able to:

- Recognize the role of individual counseling in a comprehensive school counseling program.
- Apply the basic tenets of counseling theories and apply them to the school environment.
- Apply theoretical concepts applied to a case study.
- Employ cultural considerations when providing individual counseling services in the school.

STUDENT VOICE

Student "X" provided the following testimonial about their experience with a school counselor:

"My school counselor met with me whenever I needed help and is one of the reasons I love school. He helped me identify my strengths and cope with the uncertainty I was feeling about my own abilities. If I ever need anything, he is always there for me, helping without hesitation. Thanks to my counselor, I have enjoyed learning and all the support I was given."

INTRODUCTION

Individual counseling is one service delivery method school counselors use within a comprehensive school counseling program. Although it is not realistic or feasible for school counselors to meet with all students on their caseload one-on-one, individual counseling may be the chosen intervention method in a school setting for a variety of reasons. The school counselor must consider the student's presenting problem, the most productive environment for the student, the student's comfort level, and the constraints of the school context in service delivery. School counselors also take into consideration student demographics and unique student circumstances when deciding whether individual counseling is the most appropriate delivery method.

American School Counselor Association's Position on Individual Counseling

Individual counseling has been identified by American School Counselor Association (ASCA) as an important school counseling intervention since its first national model of school counseling (ASCA, 2003). Individual counseling was recommended for use with students experiencing concerns related to interpersonal relationships, developmental tasks, and personal conflicts (Gysbers & Henderson, 2001). In 2003, the ASCA released their first national model (Gysbers, n.d.), and individual counseling was formally included as a recommended responsive service delivery method (ASCA, 2003). The most current ASCA National Model (ASCA, 2019a,b) identifies individual counseling as an appropriate responsive service as part of a comprehensive school counseling program. In the school setting, individual counseling is short-term in nature and used to support students through transition and change, during and after a crisis, at times of heightened stress, and when a specific issue interferes with students' success (ASCA, 2019a,b). Individual counseling is also used by school counselors to assist students in developing the knowledge, attitudes, and skills identified in ASCA's Mindsets & Behaviors for Student Success (ASCA, 2021). Ultimately, the purpose of individual counseling is to help students improve their achievement, attendance, and discipline. Individual counseling is beyond the scope of the school counselor when students need long-term counseling intervention and support. When this is the case, the school counselor works with the necessary stakeholders to make a referral to community resources (ASCA, 2019a,b).

The ASCA Ethical Standards for School Counselors (ASCA, 2016) and the ASCA School Counselor Professional Standards and Competencies (ASCA, 2019a) identify individual counseling as part of a school counselor's responsibility to students within a comprehensive school counseling program. Specifically, ethical standards A.1.b and A.1.h, Responsibility to Students, states that brief individual counseling is one way in which school counselors provide responsive service to students to support their academic, career, and social/emotional development (ASCA, 2016). Individual counseling is also discussed in the Deliver component of the most current edition of the ASCA National Model (ASCA, 2019b) as a proactive and responsive service to students. ASCA (2019b) recommends that school counselors spend at least 80% of their time in direct and indirect student services, with individual counseling being one direct student service. School counselors use individual counseling to assist students to develop the knowledge, attitudes, and skills outlined in the ASCA Mindsets & Behaviors for Student Success (ASCA, 2021) with the hope of improving student achievement, attendance, and discipline. Ultimately, school counselors use individual counseling with students as a short-term method of addressing life transitions and changes, during or after a crisis, at times of heightened stress, and when circumstances impede a student's ability to succeed (ASCA, 2019b).

The sections that follow will identify theoretical orientations that school counselors may use to conceptualize and work with students during individual counseling sessions. School counseling interventions should be derived from theories that are culturally and developmentally appropriate for students, supported by empirical data, and be easily measured and efficiently replicated (Lemberger-Truelove et al., 2020). For this reason, chosen theories for this chapter include solution-focused brief therapy, person-centered counseling, gestalt/expressive therapies, cognitive behavioral therapy, reality therapy, and narrative therapy. Each section will provide an overview and discussion of interventions from the theory as well as specific application to the school setting. Integrating multicultural competencies and social justice advocacy when engaging in individual counseling with students is essential to ethical practice. Multicultural competence and advocating for equity are foundational to the work of a school counselor.

MULTICULTURAL COMPETENCIES AND SOCIAL JUSTICE ADVOCACY

Schools matter! According to social reproduction theory (Adams et al., 2010), schools perpetuate or reproduce the dominant culture of society at large. What's more, there are those who believe that schools operate as microcosms of society (Adams et al., 2010). Thus, schools "have civic and public purposes" (Saltmarsh et al., 2009, p. 3). Framing the role of schools as society shapers underscores the pivotal role that effective school leadership plays in societal change. "Effective leaders are social architects who create a 'social space' that enhances or inhibits the effectiveness of an organization" (Block, 1993, p. 47). And, as directed by the ASCA National Model (2004), one of the four pillars of responsibility for school counselors is leadership.

To continue the architectural metaphor, foundational beams supporting social architecture in schools (and society) comprise inclusion, participation of both professionals and laypersons, task sharing, reciprocal behavior in solving problems, and "equality of respect for the knowledge and experience that everyone contributes to education and community building" (Saltmarsh et al., 2009, p. 6). Attention to inclusive practices through the lens of multiculturalism is critical in considering the actions of all school leaders including, and arguably especially, school counselors.

A multicultural argument can be made at a deeper level than the actions of leaders, though. Beliefs and a leader's way of being cannot help but inform that leader's actions, and "empirical work suggests that . . . leader traits do indeed increase the likelihood of a leader's effectiveness" (Spillane et al., 2004, p. 6). So, both who educators are and what they do matter: approaches and actions are equally important. Multiculturalism in leadership, school counseling, and the approaches and actions taken by all actors in their work with students would benefit from educators being "open-minded and ready to learn from others, flexible rather than dogmatic within a system of core values, persistent, resilient, and optimistic" (Spillane et al., 2004, p. 14). These core aspects of multiculturalism permeate the counseling theories and practices overviewed in this chapter.

Before we turn our attention to the theories and practices unpacked in this chapter, however, we must first attend to a macroconsideration of beliefs and actions. Although each individual counselor must make decisions throughout each day to view the application of leadership through a multicultural lens, these collective decisions made by all educators inform the climate and culture of the school setting. Our understanding of school climate and culture informs an understanding of the beliefs and experiences that can be termed *multicultural*.

Gruenert and Whitaker (2015) provide a clear delineation between school climate and school culture. School climate is akin to meteorological climate: "an upbeat, welcoming, solution-focused, no-blame, professional environment" (Portin et al., 2009, p. 59) characterizes a school climate hospitable to education. Trust is always mentioned when scholars operationalize climate. School culture, on the other hand, is "the values and rituals that provide people with continuity, tradition, identity, meaning, and significance, as well as to the norm systems that provide direction and that structure their lives" (Fiore, 2014, p. 5). Because the concepts are so closely linked, the terms *climate* and *culture* are often used interchangeably. "Culture conveys to its members what they ought to celebrate, ignore, or anticipate" so culture, therefore, "defines what it means to be normal" (Gruenert & Whitaker, 2015, pp. 13 and 14).

The core aspects of multiculturalism need to permeate the counseling theories and practices and impact the climate and culture set by the counselor. School counselors must consider how they contribute to the social and safe place in their school, one student at a time.

PERSON-CENTERED COUNSELING

Overview

Person-centered counseling (PCC) was developed by Carl Rogers in 1951 and was derived from the nondirective model of counseling. PCC, at its core, supports the belief that the role of the counselor is to be a listener who is supportive and accepting (Cepeda & Davenport, 2006). In addition, Rogers believed that all humans engage in a process called the actualizing tendency, or the belief that growth and change are innate components of the human experience (Bozarth & Bradley, 1986). Rogers considered the therapeutic relationship to be the most important aspect of the counseling process (Eager, 2010). Instead of directing the counseling process, the counselor, in partnership with the student, creates conditions that foster self-awareness and growth (Cepeda & Davenport, 2006). To this end, Rogers identified six core conditions necessary for student growth and change.

Condition 1 is *psychological contact* and refers to the belief that significant change occurs within the context of a relationship. The relationship between the counselor and student is central to the therapeutic process (Eager, 2010). Condition 2 is *student incongruence* and is frequently what brings the student to the counselor's office. Rogers (1957) defined *incongruence* as a discrepancy between the actual perceived experience of the student and the self-perception the student has of themselves. When a student perceives their incongruence, the result is a state of anxiety that can result in seeking help from a counselor (Eager, 2010). Condition 3 is *counselor congruence,* or an attitude of genuineness or wholeness. According to Tudor and Merry (2006, p. 29), congruence is a therapeutic attitude of genuineness or wholeness (Eager, 2010). Condition 4 is *unconditional positive regard* and embodies the genuine feeling of acceptance for a person, of their experiences, and of the positive and negative aspects of their personality (Tudor & Merry, 2006). Caring for a student in a way that allows for individual expression of student feelings, even if different from those of the counselor, is an important aspect of unconditional positive regard. Students experiencing unconditional positive regard from a counselor should feel open to expressing feelings and experiences without feeling judged by the counselor (Tudor & Merry, 2006). Condition 5 is *empathy* and includes the counselor's understanding of the student's experience. Rogers (1957) described empathy as comprehending the internal frame of the student and communicating that experience back to the student. The goal for the counselor is to understand the true meaning of an experience from the student's perspective (Eager, 2010). Condition 6, communication of condition achieved/perceived, is the counselor's communication of unconditional positive regard and empathy to the student. There are numerous ways the counselor can convey that these conditions are achieved/perceived, including verbal and nonverbal communication, attentive listening, and eye contact (Eager, 2010). Walker (2010) explained that understanding how a student learns, from their perspective, needs to be understood without judgment within the school environment.

PCC was developed as an antithesis to the direct interpretive nature of psychoanalysis. The use of PCC in the school environment can be beneficial not only to students, but also to the general relationship building needed in a school community. Rogers described the learning relationship in the school as one of "facilitation, not domination" (Walker, 2010, p. 120). PCC supports educational practices that fuel students' personal and social freedom. Student participation in a therapeutic alliance with the school counselor, encompassing the six conditions described above, fosters the student's ability to engage in actualized or full potential living (Lemberger & Cornelius-White, 2016). More specifically, the student's ideal self and behavioral actions are congruent.

SOLUTION-FOCUSED BRIEF THERAPY

Overview

Solution-focused brief therapy (SFBT) originated in the early 1980s from Steve De Shazer and Insoo Kim Berg out of the Brief Therapy Center in Milwaukee, Wisconsin. This approach believes the counselor is the expert on the counseling process and the student is viewed as the expert for goals and solutions. The counselor and student work in partnership to shift the focus from the problem to the solution (Moore et al., 2020). As the name indicates, the number of sessions is brief, typically no more than four to five, and concludes in student change. Three questions guide the work in SFBT: "What are your best hopes from this therapy?", "What would your day-to-day-life look like if these hopes were realized?", and "What are you already doing and have done in the past that might contribute to these hopes being realized?" (BRIEF, 2021). These questions are explored at length below.

What Are Your Best Hopes From This Therapy? This question is asking what the student would like to change or what is their preferred future. Without this question, the counselor lacks clarity on how to proceed with the student. This question clarifies how the counselor can be helpful and guide the session(s) based on the student's preferences. One technique of this approach is the *miracle question* that asks, "*Suppose that one night, while you were sleeping, there was a miracle, and the problem was solved. How would you know? What would be different?*" (De Shazer, 1988, p. 5) This question helps shift the focus from problems to possibilities. In addition, it helps the counselor and student develop clear goals for counseling (Murphy & Murphy, 2008). In summary, the student begins to develop hope for the future that their life can be different.

What Would Your Day-to-Day Life Look Like If These Hopes Were Realized? It is here that the student begins to flesh out the details of what could be different. The counselor assists the student with eliciting specifics about the change. The counselor takes a stance of curiosity and not knowing as the finer points of the realized hopes are unveiled. In doing so, the counselor is encouraging the student to engage in dialogue about change rather than problems (Gingerich & Wabeke, 2001). At this point, students are also encouraged to envision the steps for problem resolution and the behavioral changes to reach their goal. After the initial session, students are asked to pay careful attention to the situation that warrants changing and what they would like to see continue to happen (De Shazer, 1985). The student is then asked to describe, in detail, their observations during the next meeting. The purpose of this activity is to foster hope within the student that change is possible and within their control.

What Are You Already Doing and Have Done in the Past That Might Contribute to These Hopes Being Realized? It is the job of the counselor to trust that the student has the answers to guide themselves through questions as they explore possibilities (BRIEF, 2021). The student and counselor work together to identify what is already working in the given situation and what strengths the student has that could contribute to change. The student and counselor work together to uncover resources that may be undiscovered. The counselor works with the student to identify times that the problem is less prominent or influential, more specifically, identifying exceptions to the problem and increasing the frequency within which these events occur (Murphy & Murphy, 2008). The counselor provides feedback to the student about behavioral tasks that are assisting with meeting the goal. Scaling questions help the student and counselor assess progress to the goal. Students may be asked, "On a scale of 1 to 10 (least to greatest), how impactful is the current problem on your life?" Students may also be asked to rate how hopeful they are for continuing progress.

SFBT is associated with positive academic and behavioral outcomes in the school (Franklin et al., 2008). Using SFBT in the school can shift student thinking from "despair and deficiency to one of hope and potential" (Newsome, 2005). Focusing on student strengths can empower students to recognize that change is possible. With hope for change comes the identification of problems that can be addressed through the assessment of what is already working.

VIGNETTE

Melissa arrived at my door, distraught and out of breath. Her words tumbled out incoherently, and I just managed to get her seated when her equally-out-of-breath science teacher appeared in my doorway. I was surprised, and the teacher quickly explained that a neighboring teacher was watching the classroom—she wanted to ensure Melissa arrived safely. After engaging Melissa in de-escalation techniques to calm her, Melissa explained that the inciting incident occurred when she did not have the correct homework assignment completed.

Background: Melissa was diagnosed as "on the spectrum" and favored concrete, literal interpretation. Melissa frequently missed social cues and had little empathy for others. Social missteps occurred at every turn throughout her high school career. As a result, Melissa and I spent much time together each week, processing her behaviors and the reactions and consequences from others that they elicited. The "confrontation" in science class, relative to Melissa completing the incorrect homework assignment and resulting in her flight from class was due to an incongruence between Melissa's self-perception and her perception of her science class experience that day. Melissa considered herself a high academic performer and her anxiety spiked when she discovered she was unprepared for class.

Outcomes/Findings: I met with Melissa at length and helped her to reconcile the day's events with her perception of herself as an outstanding student. I used a consistent approach in accepting both her positive and negative aspects, without judgment, while prompting her to shift from the "problem" to how she could leverage her strengths toward solutions. I pressed Melissa to suspend her own judgment of herself within the frame of the day. As an expert for her own goals and solutions, Melissa applied her high-functioning capacity to understand that she could accept that she did the wrong homework for the day without approving of it. Then she could take action to move past the anxiety of the situation, changing her perception and that of her teacher's, by taking the evening to complete the correct homework.

I reminded Melissa of an earlier event between us, where she saw my complete authenticity in a moment of stress. That day, in a rare exhibition of empathy, Melissa shrugged, said, "oh, that happens to me all the time! I'll come back tomorrow!" and flounced away. When I reminded Melissa of that prior authentic moment she and I shared, I was able to underscore the imperfection in all of us. I drew a parallel between the incongruence Melissa was feeling between her self-perception and experience and her perception of me and my experience. Additionally, we focused on Melissa's best hopes for the class and school success in general, fostering continuous resiliency as a strategy.

Conclusion: After a long conversation validating Melissa's teacher's capacity to wait until the next day for the correct homework assignment, Melissa calmed down and went back to class. This situation proved helpful as a reminder to Melissa in our many future counseling sessions; it became a reference point. We worked on her understanding that we are not our actions; our actions are separate from us and our relationships with others—even and perhaps especially in times of anxious error in action—allow us to grow and learn. Our focus was always on Melissa's strengths and resources (not deficits) and her inherent power, despite her struggles with empathy. Melissa continued to be a frequent visitor, but she had a successful high school career, graduated with honors, and went on to attend college, majoring in computer science. When counseling Melissa and other students using this technique,

- Consider the lived experience and cultural context of the student.
- Be aware of the systems of oppression impacting the student.
- Address the incongruence between self-perception and world experiences to reconcile the two.
- Provide unconditional positive regard. Suspend and even challenge judgment and focus on acceptance (not approval).
- Remember that significant positive personality change does not occur in a silo but only in relationships. Healthy relationships with shared trust allow for errors and mistakes without judgment.
- Use grounding techniques to calm the student so the student can think critically.
- Use a consistent approach in accepting both positive and negative aspects, without judgment, while prompting a shift from the "problem" to how strengths may be leveraged toward solutions.
- Use authentic disclosure.
- Assume students are trustworthy and can resolve their own issues by reconciling self-perception with reality.
- Refocus students from problems to solutions to reduce anxiety.
- Shift the focus to "solution talk" with play/art and guided visualization by asking the student to imagine what life would be like without the presenting problem (the miracle question).
- Create small, achievable goals with the student using scaling questions (1–10). Discuss specific action steps that can be taken by the student to create positive changes. This can be done with visual aids.
- Adopt a two-step approach: (a) Ask the student to list three to five personal strengths and then (b) work through the articulated problem with a how-to list, applying those strengths toward solutions/goals.
- Reveal undiscovered resources to add to possible solutions.
- Focus the student on goals and solutions. Change "problem" language into an "opportunity to use personal strengths."
- Prompt students to remind themselves when and how they avoided or overcame a similar problem to tap into prior resiliency.

Scripts with utility in managing the wrap-up of a solution-focused brief session include the following:

- Let's review the plan—what will you do next?
- Ok, let's wrap up—what two or three strategies will you try in the next 24 hours? Stop in tomorrow to let me know how it goes.
- You seem to have a great plan/be feeling much better—are you ready for a pass to go back to class?
- You stated that you came in at a 9 or 10; where are you now? Ready to get back into your day? If students want to avoid/hide out, say: I want you to take a baby step, knowing you can come back if you need to. Let's give (math, science, next class) a try for now (99.9% of the time, the student gets back into the routine and doesn't return).

COGNITIVE BEHAVIORAL THERAPY

Overview

Cognitive behavioral therapy (CBT), created in the 1960s by Aaron Beck (Beck, 1963, 1970), is an evidenced-based counseling approach that has evolved into one of the most researched theories in the counseling field. It is well known that CBT has a substantial research base to justify its use, especially with individuals who experience anxiety and depression (Stone & Strunk, 2019; Strunk et al., 2017). CBT has also been found to be effective for trauma and posttraumatic stress disorder (PTSD), emotion regulation, social skills, and developmental disorders (Follette & Ruzek, 2014; Hollon & Beck, 2013; O'Donohue & Fisher, 2012).

Schemas, or organized cognitive patterns, formed in childhood are activated by events that occur in the present (O'Donohue & Fisher, 2012). At its foundation, CBT believes that individuals experience mental health issues due to activation of previous schemas in which they have inaccurate automatic negative thoughts and catastrophic interpretations. Automatic negative thoughts and catastrophic perspectives lead to distorted thinking and broad generalizations. As a result, individuals make maladaptive choices, such as avoidance or seeking validation from others (Rush & Beck, 1978; Weinrach, 1988). Ultimately, CBT believes automatic thoughts, the feelings that arise as a result (including their physiological symptoms), and subsequent behaviors are all connected (Rush & Beck, 1978).

Cognitive Behavioral Therapy Interventions

The main goal of CBT is to teach and transfer skills to the individual, and as a result, the individual can be their own counselor after termination of treatment (Rush & Beck, 1978). Because thoughts are believed to be the culprit behind mental health symptomology, interventions used in CBT focus mainly on individuals' thoughts and ways to change them. First, a CBT counselor will use psychoeducation when the counseling relationship is established to teach the expectations of counseling, build trust, and normalize thoughts and behaviors (Zayfert & Becker, 2014). As counseling progresses, Socratic questioning is used to narrow individuals' thoughts down and to assist them in drawing their own conclusions (Follette & Ruzic, 2014). Individuals will increase awareness of their irrational and distorted thought patterns as the CBT counselor asks questions that require individuals to clarify meaning, generate insight, and explore alternatives. The assumption of Socratic questioning is that individuals who reach their own conclusions about their thought patterns will benefit more than if they rely on the counselor's beliefs (Clark & Egan, 2015).

Even though thoughts are believed to be at the root of mental health issues, behavioral approaches are a necessity because individuals need to test their catastrophic interpretations in real-life situations. Individuals must learn cognitive restructuring and how to identify errors in their own logic. One way to do this is to use active scheduling, a behavioral intervention that requires individuals to choose and schedule an activity to engage in between counseling sessions. At the next counseling session, the counselor and individual discuss the previously scheduled activity and identify thoughts that surfaced as a result (Weinrach, 1988). A thought record can be suggested to track automatic negative thoughts, schemas, and cognitive distortions (Beck et al., 1979). A significant portion of cognitive restructuring relies on teaching common cognitive distortions and how to identify and challenge them. Early in CBT's development, cognitive distortions included selective abstraction, arbitrary inference, magnification and minimization, and personalization (Beck, 1963; Rush & Beck, 1978). Since then, these cognitive distortions were renamed, and others were added (Burns, 1980; Freeman & DeWolf, 1993;

Freeman & Oster, 1999). Psychoeducation continues throughout the counseling process to teach a myriad of skills, including emotion regulation, communication skills, social skills, understanding and challenging schemas, and relaxation skills for physiologic symptom reduction (O'Donohue & Fisher, 2012).

COGNITIVE BEHAVIORAL THERAPY FOR SCHOOL COUNSELORS

Evidence Based

As previously mentioned, CBT has a well-documented history of effectiveness with a variety of mental health issues, all of which affect students' ability to be productive and functional students. Specific to the school setting, CBT has been shown to be effective in reducing school refusal behaviors and significantly improving anxiety symptoms (Beidas et al., 2010; Mychailyszyn et al., 2012), improving academic performance and attendance, and decreasing discipline referrals (Michael et al., 2013). Studies have also shown that CBT is beneficial to children in individual counseling (Christner et al., 2007; Kendall et al., 2008; Miller, 2008; Sheffield et al., 2006). Schoolwide CBT curricula, such as Coping Cat and CAT Project (Kendall, 1994; Kendall & Hedtke, 2006), have been adapted for use in individual counseling in schools. These curricula have been shown to reduce anxiety symptomology and improve academics and social functioning of students.

Interventions in School

School counselors can use a CBT approach in individual counseling to benefit students (Mychailyszyn et al., 2012). It can be used to teach skills such as accurately identifying and describing feelings, self-calming and relaxation, challenging negative self-talk and cognitive distortions, social skills development, assertiveness, and cognitive restructuring (Joyce-Beaulieu & Sulkowski, 2015). While working with students, school counselors take an active role in Socratic questioning, drawing out feedback, and probing for alternative perspectives. School counselors also engage students in role playing and use modeling in individual counseling sessions (Evans et al., 2002; Thompson et al., 2013). These interventions allow students to be active participants in learning and applying CBT skills; all of which are applicable in schools and in other areas of students' lives.

From a behavioral perspective, school counselors can use behavioral exposure to help students decrease anxiety levels in anxiety-provoking situations (Joyce-Beaulieu & Sulkowski, 2015). For example, if a student is fearful of speaking in front of a class, the school counselor can first teach the student relaxation techniques to cope with the physiological symptoms of anxiety. Then, the school counselor and student can work together to identify possible scenarios that allow the student to speak in front of a group of people that seems less threatening to the student (such as a close group of friends or family). The student then continues this process with exposure to increasingly anxiety-provoking situations until he or she is able to speak in front of peers successfully. Behavioral exposure is used with students to actively help them learn that they can overcome situations that seem threatening (Beidas et al., 2010).

CBT is an adaptable therapeutic approach that can be implemented with all students at all levels. School counselors can adapt their approach by using developmentally appropriate methods and creativity in individual counseling sessions (Stone & Strunk, 2019). Where older students can be taught CBT skills and challenge their thinking through discussion, children may need more active approaches through movement, drawing, art, pictures, and stories (Joyce-Beaulieu & Sulkowski, 2015; Miller et al., 2012). Ultimately, CBT teaches students to be their own counselor (Miller et al., 2012), allowing the benefits of the approach to continue when treatment is concluded.

REALITY THERAPY

Overview

Reality therapy is centered on the principles of personal responsibility, genetically ingrained human wants and needs, choice theory, and the quality world. Individuals must accept responsibility for themselves and their choices. Reality therapy believes that all human behavior is purposeful and chosen (Glasser, 1964, 1965) to meet five basic human wants and needs, which include survival/self-preservation, love and belonging, power (also described as inner control, achievement, and accomplishment), freedom/independence, and fun/enjoyment (Wubbolding, 2015). Wubbolding (2015) added that the five basic wants and needs are universal, meaning they are applicable to all humans regardless of cultural and racial background. Furthermore, Mason and Duba (2009) stated that love and belonging is the primary need of all humans and is the most difficult to satisfy because it requires other individuals in the process of getting that need met.

Choice theory also stresses that all human behaviors are attempts to satisfy one or more perceived human wants or needs. These perceived wants and needs come together to create an individuals' quality world. Wubbolding (2000) defined the quality world as a pseudoimaginary world that consists of a file of wants and needs created in the mind shortly after birth and developed continually throughout life. The quality world is made up of possessions, situations, activities, beliefs, and people, with people being the most important component. Unfulfilled wants and needs in a human's quality world lead to dissatisfaction which in turn leads to feelings of unhappiness, loneliness, and discomfort. This mix of feelings typically motivates humans to make choices to meet the discrepancy between their perceived wants and needs and their current reality (Fuller, 2015; Glasser, 1998; Wubbolding, 2015). Glasser (1964) also emphasized the importance of focusing on the present and believed that a past focus in counseling would only reinforce past negative choices that individuals have made. For individuals to accept responsibility and move forward, counseling must focus on what can be changed—the present.

Therapeutic Conditions, Interventions, and Goals

The therapeutic environment in reality therapy must create a nonthreatening relationship between students and the counselor. To create this optimal environment, the counselor must possess the qualities of warmth, sincerity, openness, empathy, congruence, and positive regard, as well as be supportive, accepting, trusting, and respectful (Mason & Duba, 2009; Mason & Dye, 2017; Wubbolding, 2015). The reality therapy counselor also demonstrates effective counseling skills that include attending behaviors, suspension of judgment, appropriate facilitative self-disclosure, summarizing, and focusing (Wubbolding, 2000). Essentially, these characteristics and qualities put counselors in a position to be included in students' quality world (Glasser, 1998). This combination of qualities and skills set the stage for confronting and challenging students' current behaviors as a trusted and genuinely concerned person in their quality world. Change happens when students see for themselves, with challenging from the counselor, that their chosen behaviors are not effectively moving them toward meeting their wants and needs (Glasser, 1964; Mason & Duba, 2009).

Goals in reality therapy focus on students taking responsibility for their choices, increasing self-awareness to focus on current behaviors, and identifying and implementing healthier, more responsible behaviors to meet wants and needs (Can & Robey, 2021; Fuller, 2015; Mason & Dye, 2017). To move students toward these goals, reality therapy counselors use a systematic and cyclical approach using the WDEP acronym, which stands for *wants, doing, evaluate, plan* (Wubbolding, 1995, 2011, 2015). Counselors use this framework to process individuals' wants and desires and their commitment level to change (wants);

to identify choices individuals are currently making (doing); to assist and challenge individuals to self-evaluate their behaviors, wants/needs, level of commitment, and plans (evaluate); and to discuss ways individuals can meet their wants/needs (plan) (Fuller, 2015; Wubbolding, 1995, 2011). Even though reality therapy does not specify interventions in a traditional sense, Wubbolding (2017) stated, "the counseling environment serves as the basis for counseling interventions that more specifically represent reality therapy" (p. 44). Wubbolding (2017) added that individuals have unique and varied wants and needs, which leads to an endless amount of possible counseling interventions.

Reality Therapy and Individual Counseling With Students

Previous research has shown that reality therapy is effective in schools (Glasser, 1990, 1993) and in individual counseling (Wubbolding, 2000, 2004; Wubbolding & Bricknell, 1999). Responsibility and choice theory are foundational for children in schools. Children will feel successful when they meet the five basic wants and needs. Children want and need to belong and have meaningful friendships; believe they are important, recognized, and worthwhile; can engage in active means of fun, enjoyment, and learning; and have independence and autonomy. When students' wants and needs are successfully achieved, they make more appropriate choices, are better able to learn, and believe education is valuable and important to their lives (Glasser & Wubbolding, 1997). If wants and needs are unmet, children may feel unhappy, lonely, and discomfort, which can present as depression or withdrawal, acting out, negative thoughts about self and others, and physical illness (Fuller, 2015). Students identified for individual counseling have likely chosen inappropriate behaviors to meet unfulfilled wants and needs.

Building strong relationships with students is essential for school counselors. Mason and Dye (2017) recommend that school counselors build strong relationships with students by eliminating the "seven deadly habits of criticizing, blaming, complaining, threatening, punishing, nagging, and rewarding for control" (p. 50) and replacing them with the "seven caring habits of supporting, encouraging, listening, accepting, trusting, respecting, and negotiating differences" (p. 50). Can and Robey (2021) stated that reality therapy is an individual counseling approach that can be used by the school counselor since it can be implemented as a brief counseling model and provides a framework for school counselors to assist students in meeting their wants and needs in academic, career, and social-emotional domains. In individual counseling, students must be allowed to process and explore their wants and needs, and Mason and Duba (2009) stated administering the Choice Theory Career Rating Scale and the Choice Theory Needs Rating Scale can provide valuable academic, career, and social-emotional information for use in counseling. Ultimately, the goal of reality therapy is to eliminate or minimize barriers to academic performance and social-emotional development (Can & Robey, 2021).

VIGNETTE

The presenting incident occurred when a custodian left his cart outside the cafeteria, which was situated at the midway point in a main thoroughfare of the high school—one of the most highly trafficked hallways in the entire building. Upon exiting from lunch, Lori grabbed a bottle of cleaner with bleach from the cart and, as throngs of students made their way to and from lunch, popped the cap on the bottle and sprayed several students with the bleach cleanser. She ruined clothing and possessions, caused skin irritation, and even impacted students' hair. Based on this "final straw," the administration moved to expel Lori. I wasn't sure how much I could continue to lose credibility as I argued with administration that Lori was a round peg who just did not fit into our square holes.

(continued)

VIGNETTE *(continued)*

Background: Lori arrived as one of 365 entering high school freshman and, within the first week, made her presence known. She dressed in black baggy pants, scuffed black shoes, baggy black T-shirt, dyed hair, black nails, and black gummy bracelets around her wrists. She was challenging to teachers and often sent to the principal's office. She was a pretty girl with freckles; however, the constant scowl she wore made it difficult to see.

Lori had been abused by her brother—who was about 5 years older—throughout most of her childhood, culminating in his physical assault on her with a knife. She was angry at the world and had engaged in several years of self-harm and self-mutilation with multiple interventions, therapists, and hospitalizations, both for suicidal ideation and suicide attempts. Lori had multiple behavioral and discipline referrals, and I continuously argued for clemency, additional mental health support, and even psychological testing. I couldn't believe that she was not already identified as a student in need of social and emotional support! Lori would refuse the tests administered by school psychologists, and her grades were also failing.

Outcome/Findings: I advocated for an alternative school placement where I had seen significant positive impact in the past. The trick was getting Lori to agree that this was a good solution for her. Luckily, the alternative school was also attached to a career and technical education school. If I could find a program that appealed to Lori, I might be able to persuade her. Because of my counseling relationship with Lori, I knew cooking was my hook. Lori liked to cook, and the culinary program had open seats. I tried every strategy I knew with Lori. Lori soundly rejected every strategy to elicit agreement to the alternative school and culinary program placement.

I decided to switch gears and talk with Lori about how she views herself. I asked how she would describe herself as a student. She replied, "I do not consider myself a student. I don't care about school, and I am not smart enough to pass. I *should* do better but I *can't*." This was the opening I needed to explore Lori's irrational beliefs about her capabilities as a student. We challenged her beliefs of herself as a student, and I intentionally used language that created space for other ways of being. For example, replacing "I should" with "I could" language. Through this rather simplistic intervention, I modeled for Lori acceptance and the ability to believe in herself.

Conclusion: Lori didn't come around right away, but she did accept the offer to go to the alternative school and the culinary program. Within the year, she was the star of the program. Within a year and a half, she was the school's Student-of-the-Year, and by her senior year, she had the most Student-of-the-Month certificates of all the graduates. Lori invited me to attend the luncheon where she was presented with her Senior Award. I have a picture with Lori, both of us grinning, and her holding her award. That picture is one of the most prized possessions of my career. This happy ending required a dose of reality and choice: Lori's choice in how she wanted to be defined by herself and by other people. At the awards luncheon, Lori told me that was one of the most important conversations of her life. When counseling Lori and other students using these techniques, consider the following:

- Take into account the lived experience and cultural context of the student.
- Remember the systems of oppression impacting student.
- Use "straight talk" and direct language to challenge and provide choice.
- Empower students with choice and agency to self-select options with autonomy.
- Be prepared for strong emotions.
- Actively monitor self-talk and restructure the emotional to the cognitive (e.g. ask "what makes you think that?").
- Challenge irrational beliefs.

- Focus on thinking and acting rather than spiraling through the overexpression of feelings.
- Use humor.
- Identify maladaptive self-talk and substitute adaptive self-talk.
- Restructure and rescript sentences: "That was then. This is now. You have the power to rescript the play of your life."
- Squelch venting; it is not productive.
- Define and accomplish tasks that combat self-criticism and feelings of being overwhelmed and perfectionism.
- Actively challenge cognitions to produce desired changes in affect and behavior.
- Confront and challenge.
- Encourage less emotionally reactive behavior and more cognitive behavior.
- Attack shame and self-fulfilling prophecy.
- Use the ABC framework to reframe B (beliefs) by adding a "D": dispute the belief.
- Change behavior in order to change thinking: "Fake it 'til you feel it!'"
- Replace rigid "must" and "should" language with preferences to generate empowered thinking.

NARRATIVE THERAPY

Overview

Narrative therapy was developed in the 1980s by Michael White and David Epston. They believed that the student was the expert in their own life and any difficulties experienced were separate from the individual. What gives the difficulty meaning is how it is discussed or the discourse about the experience (Combs & Freedman, 2012). The counselor works in partnership with the student to identify strengths to fight against the problem and redefine the narrative. Narrative therapy pays attention to the language used to describe an experience and how it can define and maintain problems (Etchison & Kleist, 2020). Neuger (2015) explained, "The emphasis is on the one who has the story to tell rather than the one with the 'expert' knowledge to apply" (p. 16). Narrative therapy seeks to help people identify their values, and the skills and knowledge they have to live these values, so they can effectively confront whatever problems they face (Gilling, 2016, p. 80).

Curiosity

The counselor engages in a stance of curiosity about the student's life and experiences. By asking questions to better understand the difficulties faced, the student can begin to change the relationship with the problem in their life (Morgan, 2000). Learning about what steps have already been taken to reduce the impact of the problem on the student's life is necessary in narrative therapy. The counselor listens for what is important to the student, what is valued, and how events are linked together to create meaning (Dolman, 2020). This meaning is referred to as the dominant narrative.

Alternative Story

The student works with the counselor to re-author the dominant narrative into a preferred story about their life or experience. The alternative story is developed with rich descriptions and defines how the student prefers to live. Narrative therapy asserts that human beings are consistently interpreting and evaluating their experiences. Consequently, dominant and alternative stories are created that give life meaning. Through alternative stories, new possibilities for living are created, and the influence of the problem is decreased (Morgan, 2000).

Externalizing the Problem

A foundation of narrative therapy is separating the problem from the student, or externalizing. It is through this basic tenet that the student can be empowered to fight against the challenge as opposed to being defined by it (Menard et al., 2018). Externalizing encourages the student to objectify the problem and name and characterize it so that it is no longer internal to the individual (Gilling, 2016). By creating distance between the student and the dominant story through externalization, the student can begin to construct an alternative or preferred narrative.

Students make meaning of life events and experiences through stories. White and Epson (1990) explained that narrative therapy is based on the idea that problems are manufactured in social, cultural, and political contexts. As the counselor listens to a student's story, exceptions, alternatives, and counterexamples are identified that assist the student with exploring alternative stories (Combs & Freedman, 2012). Because the student is the expert in their lived experience, alternative stories are authored by the student rather than the counselor.

As White and Epson (1990) explained, "The person is not the problem. The problem is the problem." Externalizing the problem so that the student is not defined by it is a central tenet of narrative therapy. As individuals are separated from the problem, they experience more freedom and less guilt and blame (Combs & Freedman, 2012). Narrative therapy can empower students to identify strengths, values, and exceptions to dominant stories shaped by the contexts in which they live. Curiosity and asking questions for deep understanding are part of the narrative therapy process.

GESTALT AND EXPRESSIVE THERAPIES: PLAY AND ART

Gestalt therapy, expressive arts, and play methods can be combined for use in individual counseling with students. School counselors using a gestalt theoretical lens work to understand students' unique worldview while keeping in mind the entire context of the student (Blom, 2006). All students are self-regulating individuals who seek homeostasis and choose behaviors to meet their perceived needs. Students are viewed as equals in the counselor–student relationship, and the school counselor does not judge and fully accepts all students (Oaklander, 2001). To completely understand a student, the school counselor must be authentic, genuine, and fully present to join their world.

Resistance (or self-defense) that students experience impact their behaviors in school. For example, projection (when individuals place aspects of themselves they cannot or will not recognize onto others) can interfere with bonding in students' peer relationships (Oaklander, 2006). Retroflection and deflection often occur when students internalize or avoid expressing emotions. Students who engage in behaviors congruent with retroflection and deflection may present with physical symptoms (such as body aches), withdrawal (not speak to others), and turn unexpressed feelings into aggressive behaviors (such as hitting others) (Oaklander, 2006). Oaklander (2001) summed up student behavior by stating "behaviors and symptoms . . . are actually children's fierce attempts to cope and survive in this stressful world. . . ." (p. 48).

Joining with and addressing common projections in students is most effectively done by engaging them with creative interventions and play. Creative interventions and play provide students the means to communicate aspects of self that they are unable to do in traditional "talk" therapy (Swank, 2014). Play is a developmentally appropriate and purposeful way young students grow mentally, physically, and socially, while also providing a method for them to communicate without words (Oaklander, 2001). The following section provides specific creative and expressive methods to address student behaviors in a school setting.

Gestalt, Play, and Expressive Art Interventions in Schools

Gestalt, play, and expressive arts interventions are essential to the school counselor's toolbox, especially at a time when school counselors must be efficient with their time and prove they are effective in creating student change. Expressive arts and gestalt creative interventions can be used in individual counseling to work with students on meeting specific competencies in the ASCA's (2019a,b) academic, career, and social-emotional domains, some of which include self-awareness, self-confidence, communication, cooperation, problem-solving, and decision-making (Degges-White & Colon, 2014). Visual arts, music, movement and dance, writing and poetry, and drama, are creative and expressive ways to engage students regardless of their learning style. This allows students to creatively imagine their goals and future self and express their thoughts and feelings nonverbally. These methods provide creative means to assist students in outwardly expressing their inner world and communicating their thoughts, feelings, and worldview (Ray et al., 2004). Expressive and creative gestalt interventions also motivate positive change within students and are an efficient use of the time and resources of a school counselor (Degges-White & Colon, 2014). Violet Oaklander, considered the founder of gestalt play therapy (Blom, 2006), has demonstrated how gestalt play therapy can be implemented with children (see Oaklander, 1982, 1988, 1992, 1994, 1997, 2001, 2006) to effectively create change in their social-emotional functioning.

Gestalt therapy is a blend of previously existing principles for the creation of a unique modality of counseling. Gestalt therapy, expressive arts, and play can be effective and efficient interventions for the school counselor. Gestalt therapy, expressive arts, and play can be implemented successfully to conceptualize and intervene on an individual level with students of all ages.

VIGNETTE

Amy and I bonded when she was in ninth grade, and she was a frequent visitor to my office almost every day. She presented late in the spring of her junior year with news that her dad was moving into a different school district. With divorced parents, Amy had a choice to make: would she live with her mother or her father? **Background:** Amy was a student with learning difficulties in math and reading, making every course in school exceptionally challenging "kryptonite" for her. Her "superpower" was resiliency. No one worked harder than Amy. Her father was a contractor and construction worker with a separate family, including a new wife and kids. Amy saw little of her dad. Amy currently lived with her mom in our school district. Her mom struggled with addiction to alcohol and drugs. As so often happens with children whose parents battle addiction, Amy was mature far beyond her years. Though home life and the "paperwork" of school was a struggle, Amy was a masterful verbal communicator, and I've never seen a better self-advocate. Amy knew that graduating from her current affluent high school could open postsecondary doors for her that could eventually be her ticket to a better life. Understanding the benefits of our privileged school district became our go-to rescripting when Amy would come in with tears and complaints about the perceived trivial complaints of her peers. Amy's surroundings continually frustrated her as she had much deeper issues with which to contend and had to fight for her every win. Amy would present with physical symptoms, withdrawal, and anger.

(continued)

Outcomes/Findings: Amy and I engaged in several conversations about what she wanted her life to look like. I had her fold a paper into thirds identifying a column for past, present, and future. I then asked her to use words or pictures to describe each column. Through this expressive arts activity we engaged in a dialogue about how her circumstances are external to her and do not define her in the past, present, or future. She renamed her circumstances as "hurdles" and visualized herself as a track star jumping over hurdles. Ultimately, Amy decided to stay in her current district. She cited many reasons for this decision, including uncertainty about how she would fit into her dad's new family structure, abandonment guilt regarding her younger brother and his safety, and being in the "home-stretch" of her high school career. She also shared that she knew she had the ability to overcome the "hurdles."

Conclusion: Amy used her strengths to view her life circumstances as hurdles to be overcome. Due to this shift in narrative, she began increasing her confidence, thus enabling her to plan for the future. The counseling relationship allowed for a safe space to dream about a preferred future. Ultimately, Amy was able to decide that staying in her current district allowed for more opportunities and increased her ability to reach her goals. When counseling Amy or other students using GT and NT, consider the following:

- Recognize the lived experience and cultural context of the student.
- Recognize systems of oppression impacting the student.
- Move students who internalize their emotions past their own resistance, using retroflection and deflection through expression.
- Unveil that students are much more than the sum of their parts when addressed holistically. The gestalt cycle of experience (Zinker, 1977) focuses on six stages: sensation, awareness, energy, action, contact, and withdrawal.
- Put student in the "author's seat" in scripting the student's own life.
- Externalize problems and that which is out of our personal control in order to navigate solutions objectively. Externalize the problem from the person: refer to "Trouble" or "Drama" as a separate and distinct "person." When does Trouble come? How does Drama make your life better or worse?
- Focus on primary tools for success.
- Use student-first language; the problem is the problem; the person is not the problem.
- Use metaphors to understand children's stories because children are very effective metaphor-makers.
- Look for counterexamples, outliers, and exceptions: for instance, when Trouble showed up in one class, you didn't react like you did in the other.
- Use respectful curiosity, where judgment and advice are completely suspended and the student is the author of his/her/their own script, with significant others in the student's life playing a role.
- Use respectful curiosity, which allows for diversity and the distinct cultural forces at work in children's lives, bringing an opportunity for social justice.
- Support continuously the student's competence and resourcefulness.
- Use play theory; sandboxes, toys, and other manipulatives; art, role play, and dramatization; poetry, song lyrics, journaling, and other forms of creative writing to engage the student in creative expression.

VOICES FROM THE FIELD

Name: Kyle L. Bellinger, Ph.D., LPC (he/him)

Where You Practice: Troy School District, Troy, Pennsylvania

Professional Job Title: School Counselor

Bio: Kyle is a school counselor in Pennsylvania and a graduate of Indiana Universty of Pennsylvania's doctoral program in Counselor Education and Supervision.

As a school counselor in my current school district, I provide academic, career, and social-emotional services to kindergarten, first-, and second-grade students through classroom guidance lessons and in group and individual counseling sessions. I teach three classroom guidance lessons each day, as I am included in the rotation of "specials" that all students attend. Every afternoon, I am in the classroom from 12:25 p.m. until 2:40 p.m. and see all students on a 6-day rotation. During the day, I typically provide individual counseling to anywhere from three to five students. Ideally, these individual counseling sessions last from 20 to 30 minutes maximum. Typically, I also run at least one group a day that lasts between 30 and 45 minutes. If a crisis arises in my school, I am the first to respond and assess the situation. I am also the first point of contact as a crisis consultant to three other school counselors and the district social worker. If a crisis arises in other school buildings, I must be available to provide consultation. Throughout the day, I consult and collaborate with classroom teachers, the principal, and the other school counselors and district social worker as needed. I often find that students I am working with in my school are connected to students in the other schools in the district, meaning that I often collaborate with the school counselors and district social worker to provide the most comprehensive services possible. On top of these tasks, I also contact parents/guardians and community stakeholders as needed. Since I am the first school counselor at the elementary school in my district in 6 years, I often spend time developing various parts of the school counseling program. While I am thankful to have the freedom to create and implement student services that I believe are most needed in the school, it can be overwhelming to find time each day to work on these tasks and solicit feedback on current services from relevant stakeholders.

What I like most about my current position are the genuine connections and relationships with students. On days when the job gets overwhelming and I am unsure of how to tackle what seems to be an endless list of tasks, having a student ask for, or just give, a genuine hug makes all the stress worth it! It is rewarding to hear students say thank you for something that seems insignificant to me. The smallest things matter to the students!

I least like navigating challenging relationships with other professionals in the school district. While working with my district mentor last school year, we had many discussions about how to strategically work with others who did not seem to buy in to the vision of the school counseling program, which she had been doing for 10 years in the district before mentoring me. It can be difficult collaborating with professionals who have differing personalities, do not believe in the necessity of school counselors, and seem to prefer to work in isolation.

In one classroom where I consistently taught lessons, there was a student, E, who did not seem interested in any of the previous lessons I had taught throughout the year. I was hopeful that a lesson I was teaching about kindness based on the story "How Full is Your Bucket?

For Kids" by Tom Rath and Mary Reckmeyer would grab the student's attention. I taught the lesson as planned, and E did not seem any more interested in this lesson than he was in any of the others. I felt disappointed that the lesson did not seem to "hit home" with E. I moved forward hoping to find another way to catch his attention. I was shocked when I returned to his class the following week and E's classroom aide told me that he had been a completely different student in the week since I taught that lesson! The classroom aide told me that E had been reminding himself and others to "fill each other's buckets" by being kind. E also interrupted me during the next lesson and whispered in my ear, "Mr. Bellinger, you're filling my bucket." The lesson did land with E, which serves as a constant reminder to me that lessons may stick with students more than it may initially seem.

Always keep students' best interest at the forefront of everything you do. School counseling will be challenging and test your true character. At times, the most difficult parts of being a school counselor will not be related to students, and these difficulties can shift the focus away from the purpose of school counseling. I constantly remind myself that helping students is the reason I chose to become a school counselor. This mindset motivates me to be the best school counselor I can be for students and keeps me away from potentially harmful dynamics that could develop. My hope for all future school counselors is to keep a student-first mentality when the thought of wanting to give up creeps in.

SUMMARY AND CONCLUSION

Although school counselors engage in many forms of direct and indirect services, this chapter focuses on individual counseling theory and interventions. The ASCA (2019a,b) supports the use of individual counseling as an intervention when responding to student concerns. The chapter explores empirically based theories and interventions compatible with school-aged populations. School counselors can conceptualize their short-term individual counseling work from theoretical frameworks to guide students and yield positive outcomes. Regardless of theory, it is essential that attention be devoted to fostering the counseling relationship when delivering services. It is the responsibility of the school counselor to determine the appropriateness of interventions based on a student's individual needs, culture, development, and barriers (Lemberger-Truelove et al., 2020). After all, a theoretical approach is only as effective as the counselor that administers it.

CASE STUDY

Tanya, a second-grader, was a part of an F.I.T. (Families in Transition/Changing Families) Group that you offered at your school for students whose parents are in the process of divorcing or were recently divorced. At the end of the group, Tanya asked if she could meet with you to talk further about some of the topics covered, and she shared that there were some things that she felt like she needed to talk to you about. You agree to meet with her, and upon doing so, it is clear that Tanya is really struggling and that she would benefit from additional counseling support.

DISCUSSION QUESTIONS

1. Does Tanya's counseling needs exceed the scope of practice of school counselors? If so, how can the school counselor continue to support Tanya at school?

2. What types of interventions or activities might be useful if you do provide individual counseling with Tanya to build on the support received during the small group? What if Tanya were a middle school student? High school?
3. What are important considerations to be mindful of when providing individual counseling as a school counselor for Tanya? What if she were in middle school? High school?
4. How much individual counseling is appropriate for a student?

PRACTICAL APPLICATION

- Remember that school counseling interventions should have a lens addressing the three domains of school counseling—social/emotional, career/college, and academic.

- When addressing student needs through individual counseling, be mindful of how the issue is impacting the students' academic success.

- Be aware of issues outside of the scope of practice. School counselors should not be providing therapy, even if they are dual trained as a mental health counselor as well as a school counselor unless their contract specifies this specific and unique role.

- Be sure to remind students of the limits of confidentiality (abuse/neglect, threat to self or others, subpoena) as soon as possible when you meet.

- If the student is seeing an outside counselor for therapy, consider requesting a release of information so that you and the community counselor can ensure that you are on the same page regarding what each is addressing with the student and promote open communication.

- Be mindful of instructional time that the student is missing as a result of individual counseling and communicate with classroom teachers—do your best to avoid the student missing class by connecting during recess, lunch, advisory periods, or other unstructured time.

- Check with your building administrator regarding permission form requirements if you plan to meet with the student regularly. Some districts may require parent permission, depending on the age of the student.

KEY REFERENCES

Only key references appear in the print edition. The full reference list appears in the digital product on Springer Publishing Connect: connect.springerpub.com/content/book/978-0-8261-8753-6/part/part03/chapter/ch08

Franklin, C., Moore, K., & Hopson, L. (2008). Effectiveness of solution-focused brief therapy in a school setting. *Children & Schools, 30*(1), 15–26. https://doi.org/10.1093/cs/30.1.15

Gingerich, W. J., & Wabeke, T. (2001). A solution-focused approach to mental health intervention in school settings. *Children & Schools, 23*(1), 33–47. https://doi.org/10.1093/cs/23.1.33

Joyce-Beaulieu, D., & Sulkowski, M. L. (2015). *Cognitive behavioral therapy in K-12 school settings: A practitioner's toolkit*, Springer Publishing Company.

Lemberger-Truelove, M. E., Ceballos, P. L., Molina, C. E., & Dehner, J. M. (2020). Inclusion of theory for evidence-based school counseling practice and scholarship. *Professional School Counseling, 23*(1 Part 3). https://doi.org/10.1177/2156759X20903576

Mason, C. P., & Duba, J. D. (2009). Using reality therapy in schools: Its potential impact on the effectiveness of the ASCA national model. *International Journal of Reality Therapy, 29,* 5–13. http://digitalcommons .wku.edu/csa_fac_pub/33

Mason, C. P., & Dye, L. (2017). Attending to basic needs: Implementing reality therapy in school counseling programs to enhance academic achievement and career decision-making skills. *International Journal of Choice Theory and Reality Therapy, 37*(1), 46–55. http://proxy-iup.klnpa.org/login?url=https:// search.ebscohost.com/login.aspx?direct=true&db=pbh&AN=126409630&site=eds-live

Miller, L. D., Shumka, E., & Baker, H. (2012). Special applications: A review of cognitive behavioral mental health interventions for children in clinical and school-based settings. In S. A. Lee & D. M. Edget (Eds.), *Cognitive behavioral therapy: Applications, methods, and outcomes* (pp. 1–36). Nova Science Publishers.

Moore, C. P., Ohrt, J., & Packer-Williams, C. L. (2020). A solution-focused approach to student reintegration into the traditional school setting after a disciplinary alternative school placement. *Journal of Child and Adolescent Counseling, 6*(2), 83–96. https://doi.org/10.1080/23727810.2020.1719350

Swank, J. M. (2014). Incorporating play techniques in comprehensive school counseling programs. In J. R. Curry & L. J. Fazio-Griffith (Eds.), *Integrating play techniques in comprehensive school counseling programs* (pp. 1–18). Information Age Publishing.

Wubbolding, R. E. (2017). *Reality therapy and self-evaluation: The key to client change.* American Counseling Association.

CHAPTER 9

Group Counseling for School Counselors

CHER N. EDWARDS AND **SAM STEEN**

LEARNING OBJECTIVES

After reading this chapter, students will be able to:

- Recognize ASCA expectations related to group counseling interventions for school counselors.
- Use advocacy and social justice considerations in practice.
- Identify basics of group counseling practice, including logistic and application practices of running groups in PK–12 settings.
- Modify group counseling strategies based on developmental considerations of various educational levels.

STUDENT VOICE

Student "J" shared their thoughts related to their "Transition to Middle School" group experience:

"My mom signed me up for the group. I guess my school counselor told fifth-grade parents that she was running it. I really did not want to go at first but I'm glad I did. I was really nervous about going to middle school. I had heard rumors about kids who were stuffed in lockers, mean teachers, hard classes, bullies, and not being able to get your locker open. The school counselor talked about everything! We even practiced opening a combination lock until we were all good at it! During one group meeting, we even got to meet some of the eighth-graders at the middle school that a lot of us were going to. We were allowed to write questions on pieces of paper, and then the eighth-graders answered them. They knew a lot and seemed nice! I was a lot less nervous about going to middle school than some of my friends who were not in the group. During sixth grade, I kept remembering things that my school counselor talked about in group. It helped me feel more confident related to how to meet new friends, get to know people, how to talk to teachers, and of course ... open my locker!"

INTRODUCTION: GROUP COUNSELING AND PRACTITIONER APPLICATION

To say that we are huge fans of group counseling is an understatement! Group counseling allows school counselors to have authentic connections with a group of students as well as to facilitate relationships and support among the students themselves. It provides an opportunity to model skills and teach lessons that will ideally transcend the group experience and, just perhaps, create a meaningful support system that will follow the student after the group has ended.

As all school counselors will tell you, there are very few moments of boredom in the days of a school counselor. Our schedules are packed! You'll see us running from the classroom to the hallway to our office and back—again and again. We move quickly from presenting to a classroom to meeting with our administrator regarding a student of concern, followed by a few check-ins with students, and then (not enough) time to answer email and phone calls—some taking longer than planned with worried parents and caregivers. After that (Oh shoot! My stomach is growling!), more students (our favorite part), an unexpected guest (Child Protective Services? A less-than-happy parent?), and a few meetings later, it's time to prep for that after-school program.

The days are long and demanding, yet rich and fulfilling. Knowing that we are changing lives and can to advocate for students—particularly those whose voices are often unheard—is exciting. Although we end each day exhausted, there is nothing you could do to keep us from eagerly awaiting the challenges of the next day. Okay, so maybe not every day (we are human after all), but being a school counselor is exciting! So, when we tell you that there is a way to be up to 800% more effective and accomplished, wouldn't you jump at it? Of course! This chapter will focus on a school counseling intervention that allows us to intentionally focus and provide meaningful counseling to not just one, but multiple students at the same time, and accomplish more than we could through individual counseling because a group provides the added benefit of peer interaction.

AMERICAN SCHOOL COUNSELOR ASSOCIATION POSITION STATEMENT ON GROUP COUNSELING

According to the American School Counselor Association (ASCA) Position Statement on Group Counseling (ASCA, 2021), group interventions offered within school settings are useful as a component of comprehensive developmental school counseling programs. Group interventions can be used to help students mitigate common milestones and transitions, discuss academic difficulties, and explore college- and career-related material. Research continues to show that there are a number of positive effects on social/emotional learning, academic achievement, and career exploration. For example, school counselors and student interns led an 8-week small-group intervention with ninth- and 10th-grade students that resulted in improvement in their motivation, organizational skills, and time management (Berger, 2013).

In another study, Steen and colleagues (2018) focused on a school-based group counseling intervention with a high-risk population of students who recently immigrated to the United States. The purpose was to determine whether the group members' attitudes about learning, self-esteem, school adjustment, and academic performance could be improved. In this case, the school counselors were successful using a group counseling intervention to foster positive school adjustment. Results of this study showed that students in the treatment group received significantly higher scores for school adjustment and an increased grade point average after controlling for preintervention scores. Through reflections in journals, students were able to express some of their thoughts and feelings, which allowed the school counselors to better understand the students' experiences.

In another study intended to assess the efficacy of group counseling, school counselors created a group intervention that focused on the cultural strengths of students, aiming to dismantle a deficit model that is often associated with students of color. The goal was to promote a culturally appropriate group intervention that fostered a supportive environment for students who were emerging bilingual/English language learners to share their experiences at school (Montes & Ramos, 2020). This group counseling experience allowed the school counselors to build on the strengths of the students while positioning them for success following the intervention. Outcomes of the group experience included feelings of social support, improved behavior and social skills, confidence, and hope. The students reported that they gained a supportive alliance of peers and adults within their school (Montes & Ramos, 2020).

The emerging body of group counseling research continues to establish evidence demonstrating the positive impact of small groups on students' academic and personal success. This line of inquiry offers justification for school administration and school districts to support these efforts more intentionally (ASCA, 2021).

GROUP COUNSELING BASICS FOR PK–12 SETTINGS

There are several considerations related to group counseling in school settings. These include a number of considerations, including

- recruitment, assessment, and preparation,
- intervention development,
- implementation and evaluation, and
- dissemination of findings and follow-up.

Next, we provide further details about each of these important aspects that are helpful as school counselors consider facilitating groups with children and adolescents in school settings.

Recruitment, Assessment, and Preparation

School counselors using small groups as part of a comprehensive school counseling program will not create an intervention without examining an appropriate body of data collected within school settings to inform the goals and objectives of an intervention. Once this is determined, a concerted focus to collaborate with teachers, school administrators, and caretakers to identify potential participants must occur. School counselors cannot accomplish this critical feat alone. Collaborating with stakeholders will increase the likelihood that students will participate in environments that are inclusive and affirming. This is imperative because the group environment can foster spaces of healing or perpetuate oppressive encounters, even if unintentionally. Relying on a collection of constituents to help determine student members' specific needs, growth areas, and strengths will increase the likelihood that school counselors will foster environments that cultivate healing and development.

After students are identified, culturally appropriate assessments can help determine the students' goals and how they are currently experiencing life inside and outside school. Assessment information can also provide needed information to later build sessions that are directly meaningful to the participants, caretakers, and school leaders. These assessments must be examined to ensure that the language is not discriminatory or exclusive. Ideally assessments that are normed on developmentally appropriate populations and created specifically for children and adolescents can reinforce the intentional efforts at fostering inclusive spaces. In addition to determining who is selected to participate and assessing areas for growth, students' strengths can be recorded to avoid a deficit-focused process.

The next step is to preparing the students for what a small-group experience might entail. Important considerations for preparation include both formal and informal aspects of group work. Students who are unfamiliar with group counseling can more fully take advantage of the process if they have some insight into what the experience could be like. Formal aspects a school counselor must attend to include informed consent, confidentiality considerations, and group goals and objectives. Informed consent entails gaining permission from caretakers for their child to participate. This permission increases parent support and helps to reduce stress and faulty assumptions about the process.

Confidentiality and its limits will provide a security net for the school counselor. However, it must be made explicit that while confidentiality can be encouraged and stated, it cannot be guaranteed due to the nature of group counseling. Unlike individual sessions in which the counseling experience is limited to the student and school counselor, groups include other students. Effective group leaders take time during both the group member selection process and the group meetings to explain the importance of maintaining what is said in group private and confidential. It may be helpful for students to know that they are welcome to share with others about group topics and what the student shared, but not what others share. It is helpful to process with group members the relevance of this group rule or norm and agree on consequences for not following this expectation. For a group to be effective, students must feel safe to share.

As mentioned previously, clearly articulating the goal and potential objectives of the group can increase the chances of a groups' success. The overarching goal must be determined ahead of time (e.g., social skills, career exploration, etc.), while the objectives can be a bit more flexible as group sessions progress.

Additional, less formal, information that school counselors can provide the group members include insight into the counselor's group leadership style; skills that might be employed; and the importance of race, gender, and other cultural aspects of identity that may impact the group. Preparing students for what they might experience in a group setting increases the chances for the members to fully benefit from future interactions and may reduce some anxiety related to group membership.

Intervention Development

Small-group interventions offered in school settings can be highly structured or they can be more flexible and supportive in nature resembling a less formal environment (Steen et al., 2021). Group interventions that focus on academic development sometimes use a curriculum that has a specifically designed protocol and at other times may use a less rigid structure. However, in both cases, research findings in a comparative literature review reported strong favorable outcomes for both structured and less-structured group interventions facilitated by school counselors in school settings (Steen et al., 2021). That said, the following must be considered when creating a group intervention by school counselors within a school setting: any relevant school demographic data that highlight the necessity for the group; the data that can be gleaned from teachers, school administrators, caretakers, and the students themselves during the recruitment, assessment, and preparation of the participants that highlight specific areas to consider; and the school counselor's unique skill set, interests, creativity, and ability to collaborate with any number of stakeholders.

Implementation and Evaluation

Creating a small group is not a static endeavor. Specifically, small-group interventions will need to have goals and objectives, curriculum or activities, a clear number of sessions, a specific length for each session, a location to hold the group, and materials to ensure the group can be delivered. The ASCA has a generic resource called the ASCA Mindset & Behaviors (2021) that can serve as a starting point to identify goals and objectives that might be useful for structuring group sessions. It is imperative that the specific language used with the students is not oppressive, limiting, or intended to cultivate a narrow-minded way of experiencing the school and community environment. Moreover, during implementation of each session, the tentative objectives and desired focus employed may highlight additional areas to discuss that were not necessarily important during the planning stage but appear to be salient to the specific students being served in the group. Having an open mind when planning and implementing small groups will remain critical to ensure that the needs of the students are always at the forefront. Keeping students as the centerpiece of the group interventions increases the chances that students will benefit from the experience.

Small groups in schools typically last approximately six to eight sessions (Gladding, 2020). Recently, it has been suggested, and reinforced by an emerging body of literature, that small groups should last at least 12 sessions (Berger, 2013) and up to 20 sessions (Steen et al., 2021). These sessions typically need more time to see the most positive outcomes, but that may not be conducive to a school environment. Some challenges to overcome include school counselor's limited confidence and efficacy with their leadership skills (Springer, 2016), time constraints (Steen et al., 2007), student-to-school counselor ratio (ASCA, 2021), and lack of understanding and support from school stakeholders (ASCA, 2021). To overcome these challenges, it may be beneficial for school counselors to plan "basic" and "advanced" groups that build on each other to support additional learning and growth.

The evaluation of small groups can simply focus on reassessing the students to determine any growth that may have occurred, such as using a pretest, posttest format. However, if other stakeholders completed assessment forms to help decide who would participate, it may be useful to reconnect to see if their perceptions of their student had changed in any way. The recommendation that both quantitative and qualitative data be collected as often the qualitative data provide specific narratives to provide clarification on positive outcomes and areas for improvement. These findings, even when less favorable, are quite helpful for program improvement, justification for offering additional services in the future, and critical discourse on ways to continue offering a space for students to receive academic, career-related, and social-emotional interventions. The evaluation can be easily overlooked, but it is imperative that school counselors who wish to engage in evidenced-based and culturally responsive practice will use data when planning, implementing, and subsequently evaluating this important work.

MULTICULTURAL COMPETENCIES AND SOCIAL JUSTICE ADVOCACY IN GROUP COUNSELING

Being a culturally competent group-counseling leader is not a unique skillset that differs from cultural competency in other school counseling interventions. Nor does it entail specialized social justice advocacy abilities or interests. Rather, it is the intentional focus of addressing issues of diversity to promote equity, inclusion, and safe schools for all students as you plan and implement small-group interventions in your school and include culturally relevant curriculum and group practices in your work. As a privileged group, we have a responsibility to advocate for social justice (Edwards, 2012). School counselors benefit from regular assessment of their skills related to culturally competent counseling practice and address opportunities for professional development (Rodgers & Furcron, 2019).

As addressed earlier in this chapter, the first step to leading a group is not curriculum development, but rather needs assessment. It is important that school counselors are asking the right questions. What issues need to be addressed right now? Is group counseling the best intervention for that need? Being intentional about asking students about issues that are relevant to them and doing so in a way that allows them to safely respond demonstrates that you "see" them. If we do not ask questions related to students' needs, we are unlikely to receive it. It is important to ask students, parents/caregivers, and teachers about what is going on in students' lives. Ask for attendance records, grades, and discipline referrals. All of these sources are opportunities for data collection that will guide group topics and curriculum development. As school counselors, we want to care for students and to advocate for their success toward graduation and beyond. If students are experiencing issues that serve as a barrier to this success, we need to find out how best to intervene.

Aside from needs assessment, other important considerations related to advocacy and cultural competency include being thoughtful about group focus or the name of the group. For example, if you assess that students are struggling with test anxiety or anxiety in general, it is helpful to be aware that not all cultures are comfortable acknowledging what is perceived to be a mental health issue. An alternative focus or term, while still addressing the same content, might be *mindfulness* or *academic success* and be more readily received by some students and families. Consider group topics that attend to diverse student needs. It is important to incorporate topics that include opportunities to explore race, gender, culture, and to respect/appreciate differences.

Regarding permissions, ensure that the forms are sent home in a manner that is accessible to all families in terms of ability to read and comprehend the content. If need be, use district resources (not students!) for translation purposes. Placing a student in the role of translator often offsets the family hierarchy and is likely to be experienced as disrespectful. It could be embarrassing or offensive to family members to have their child explain aspects of the educational system or interventions to them. When planning group content, be mindful of emerging bilingual skills of students and activities that may prove prove to be a barrier to participation. Recognize that not all cultures are comfortable with traditional "talk therapy" and that creative interventions may be needed to encourage participation. Expressive art activities, play techniques, integration of music and movement are great alternative activities to add to your group practice. Practices that demonstrate an awareness and sensitivity to the needs, worldviews, and culture of the students that are served are important to support their academic success (Dameron et al., 2020).

DEVELOPMENTAL CONSIDERATIONS OF GROUP COUNSELING

Although the basics of group counseling as an intervention are fundamentally the same regardless of the developmental level of the participants, there are important considerations with each age group. The topics addressed, length of session, activities within the session, and even location are all important to keep in mind when planning groups at the various levels (Sink et al., 2012). In Elementary School Counseling section, we explore aspects of group work at the elementary, middle/junior high, and high school levels and the important issues to be aware of for each group of students.

Elementary School Counseling

This age group is widely considered to be a natural fit for group counseling interventions due to the interest, captive audience (they generally do not leave the school campus without permission), more flexible class schedule, and developmental stage of the students served. Elementary students benefit from the social skills learning that the group format can provide. Group provides the occasion to practice listening skills, impulse control, appropriate sharing, and appreciation for differences. These many opportunities also present important considerations. We will address some aspects of group counseling that may be especially relevant for the youngest group of the students that we serve as school counselors.

Group Topics, Format, and Best Practices

Elementary students make great academic, social, and developmental strides during the 6 years they typically remain at this level. While there are topics that span all grade levels, there are some that are important to target for specific grades. There are many transitions at this level. A group might focus on students who may find being away from home or the lack of structure of a daycare may find kindergarten overwhelming and scary (Yaffe, 2018). First grade is also a significant transition as many first-grade teachers begin to implement greater routine and increased expectations (Sink et al., 2007). As students anticipate the transition to middle school, anxiety typically rises as they are uncertain what lies ahead (Coelho et al., 2017). Attending to these milestones is important, and students benefit from groups that offer support, strategies, and the opportunity to learn that they are not alone. Therefore, groups specifically focused on transition to kindergarten, first grade, and middle school are generally well received at this level. Friendship skills, study skills, changing families, and exploring interests (precareer exploration) are all fantastic topics for this age group. As with all group planning, let the data from your needs assessment drive this intervention and guide group implementation.

Location is an important consideration for this developmental stage. The younger children may be more comfortable sitting on the floor than in chairs. Be sure to be at eye level with your students. Be thoughtful about the surroundings and what might serve as competition for attention. A group held in a room with lots of toys, books, and interesting objects may add a layer of complexity to keeping the group members focused on the group topic and each other. Integrating opportunities for movement is important at this age as the younger children are prone to lots of wiggling. Expressive art activities are usually a hit, as are snacks, but be sure to check with caregivers regarding allergies and dietary preferences.

Group length is also an important consideration due to the attention span of this age group. A half-hour group is usually a good length of time to allow for content while maintaining attention. Keep in mind that group management may be a heavy task at this stage, so keeping the group on the smaller side, such as four to six students, ensures that you are able to redirect student behavior that is not conducive to group productivity. As the group leader, you are teaching the students how to be a part of a group. You may need to employ a "talking stick" or stuffed animal that is passed around to help the students designate who should be speaking and who should be listening. When group rules or norms are created, it may be helpful to go over these rules weekly to remind students at the beginning of each group what the expectations are for being a part of the group experience (Sink et al., 2012).

Although the elementary level is somewhat more conducive to meeting during class time than other levels, meeting during lunch or recess allows the student to participate in groups without missing class. If the group does meet when students are typically in class, it is recommended that the school counselor alternate between meeting times so that the student does not miss the same content each week. After-school programs are often popular at this level as many elementary schools end the day before parents and caregivers finish their work hours. If your school allows it, and you are interested, some schools permit school counselors to offer after-school programming groups through a special contract for additional compensation.

Given the significant developmental differences that span the elementary school years, it is important to consider attending to one or two grade levels at a time for group offerings, rather than attempting to offer a group open to all grades at this level. Gender is less of a relevant consideration given that most of the topics addressed at this level benefit from diverse perspectives. Some school counselors prefer to offer gender-specific groups, such as "Girl Power" topics; however, we would encourage group leaders to be thoughtful regarding how they will integrate gender identity considerations to ensure inclusivity and access for students who would benefit from this topic.

Most importantly, have fun! This age group is generally excited to be a part of something special and outside the typical classroom experience. They are eager learners and are less likely to have been socialized to refrain from sharing. These students often talk openly (sometimes too much so!) and excitedly, and they are thrilled with the opportunity to have your, and their peers', undivided attention.

Middle/Junior High School Counseling

So many big feelings and changes! This developmental stage is sure to keep you on your toes! Although this age group often feels the need to balance their eagerness to participate with the importance of not appearing too eager, group is generally a welcome intervention. Middle school and junior high are a time of immense transition. As sixth-graders they come to us as a slightly grown-up version of an elementary student, and they leave our building just a few years later, on the verge of adulthood—taller, hairier, and definitely stinkier—or at least having the potential to be. This age group is often clumsily navigating their physical and emotional changes and benefit from support in several areas (Sink et al., 2012). Group counseling can attend to many of these topics well; however, it is important to be mindful of the unique aspects of this age group.

Group Topics, Format, and Best Practices

With all the changes that middle school/junior high students experience, a natural group topic is related to the adjustments that students are experiencing. Students at this level have big emotions and benefit from support and education related to making sense of how they are feeling and strategies for managing these experiences. This is also a fantastic time to step up the focus on career and interest exploration (Ahearn, 2021), as students often are faced with the new opportunity of selecting electives and engaging in school sports. This level may present challenges to students without organization and study skills. As such, groups specifically focusing on these topics, as well as test anxiety, may be helpful. Of course, as students approach the end of their experience in middle school and junior high, a transition to a high school group will provide additional assistance for those students who are feeling anxious regarding this next step on their PK–12 journey (Sink et al., 2012).

This age group is typically able to sit still for longer periods of time than were their former elementary selves. As such, it is common for students to participate in a group for an entire class period. Many students have advisory periods or study halls, which are great times to offer groups so that groups do not impact student classroom learning. As with elementary school, lunch periods are often a preferred time to meet in small groups. Some school counselors like to create an open group where students can come and go and where the curriculum is extremely flexible, allowing students to have lunch with the counselor and play games while talking about various topics of interest. If holding a lunch group—open, closed, structured, or unstructured—communicate with students the expectations related to eating and group start and end times. It may be possible to arrange for students to leave their class a few minutes early to be at the front of the line for school lunches to ensure that you are able to begin the group as soon as possible. If there are group members with allergies, it is important to communicate with all group members to ensure that the group time is safe for all. Students at this age may require less attention to manage; thus, larger groups of six or seven tend to work well, although smaller numbers can also be effective.

Some practitioners feel that gender-specific groups are advantageous at this level (Waters, 2017) due to the developmental milestones and associated needs typically aligned with this age group. However, rather than a blanket policy, it may be more meaningful to assess the needs and culture of the school and make decisions based on the group topic and students identified as in need of support. If gender-specific groups are implemented, it is encouraged to consider the gender identity of the students desiring additional support related to group planning and implementation. Research has noted the benefits of interaction between LGBTQA+ and straight youth to promote ally behavior and reduce bullying (Knepp, 2022).

High School Counseling

High school embodies the last leg of the PK–12 journey for students. While still navigating the many physical and emotional changes associated with puberty and development, for most this is not new territory. Academic demands are high, and many students are juggling school, activities, and possibly part-time employment or family responsibilities. High schoolers are fast approaching the culmination of, typically, 13 years of classes, homework, tests, and quizzes and will soon need to shift their focus to life beyond high school. Group-counseling interventions are less frequent at this level as high-stakes testing and academic demands tend to discourage students from missing class time. Lunch groups and advisory periods tend to be the most probable option for school counselors hoping to integrate group into their practice. Although not as common, some high schools have created "wellness" or social-emotional learning periods or a half-period for students to select from various self-care–related activities. If you are fortunate enough to work in a school with this practice, this is a fantastic opportunity for group work!

Group Topics, Format, and Best Practices

Academic success, college and career planning, life skills, healthy relationships, managing stress, and grief and loss groups are great areas of focus for this developmental stage (Sink et al., 2012). In summary, topics that prepare students for high school and beyond related to social-emotional learning, academic skills, and preparing for life after high school are the primary focus for this level (Woods & Domina, 2014). Many students experience stress and anxiety as they navigate high school and focus on postsecondary planning (Javadian & Sabet Eqlidi, 2022). The group format should be flexible and plan for potential absences as high school students have been known to forget or intentionally miss activities that they perceive as optional. For this reason, group leaders may opt to begin the group with a larger number of students, knowing that attrition or inconsistent attendance is likely. Usually between seven or eight students can work well at this level, depending on the topic. Group meetings need to be especially engaging and allow students to see a clear "value added" as a result of their group participation. Snacks are a definite plus for this age group! Most topics work well with mixed gender representation. Although not as common, when counselors are able to run groups at this level, they are usually a lot of fun. What is unique—and exciting—about this age group is their potential for independence. Unlike younger students, who may be experiencing barriers due to their family of origin and current living environment, older students will soon be autonomous and able to make decisions that allow additional opportunities and a path of their choosing. Helping students realize their own potential and explore options beyond what they may think possible is a rewarding experience!

VOICES FROM THE FIELD

Name: Kaley Mitchell, PhD (she/her)

Where You Practice: Washington

Professional Job Title: School Counselor (Middle School)

Bio: After graduating from Seattle Pacific University with a certificate in school counseling and a doctorate in counselor education, Dr. Mitchell has practiced as a middle school counselor where she works to leverage the educational attainment of adolescents from disadvantaged backgrounds.

Preferred pronouns: She/Her

You ask about school counseling groups. I love them. They are incredibly effective and a good use of my time, but I also need to be transparent about the reality of school counseling groups. In every district I have ever worked, this delivery method of the ASCA National Model simply gets swept under the rug or put on the "to do later" list, particularly at the middle school and high school level. It is why practicum and internship students constantly struggle with getting their course-mandated groups up and running. It simply is not a part of many middle school and high school counseling programs. And in my experience, it's not because school counselors don't know the ASCA National Model or that school counselors don't want to run them, but rather because there is a plethora of other responsive tasks that get in the way, and school counselors have to push them off until they never start.

When groups are ran, most school counselors love running them. It is because so much growth and learning takes place during school counseling groups. You observe the transformations occur right before you. If you have already run your first group, you have observed the power of peers learning from peers. Currently, I am running a school counseling group focused on the challenges of being a Black middle school student. As a White and privileged female school counselor, I am coleading it with a Black educator in my building. Here we are in the middle of a session, and the students are discussing an incident that occurred at school where one group member gave their White friend the "N-word pass," which caused that friend to experience serious social repercussions for using the N-word, including being canceled from the social group. I knew a lot about this situation because it caused an uproar in the social ethos of our middle school. So, who better than the members of the Black student group to reflect on it and determine what to do about it. The coleader and myself asked the students, "what do you think should be done about it?" And you know what!? Their ideas and perspective were amazing! Each person had an equal opportunity to share their perspective, and then the group came to some definite conclusions about what to do. They agreed that the group member should not be giving out the N-word pass, and then came to some ideas about how to handle the situation with the White student. I cannot possibly imagine this amazing outcome one-on-one in my office. This is why I love groups!

To get these moments, however, you will have to run groups. For me, I keep it as simple as possible. Over the past decades, I have seen so many school counselors get tripped up over the complexities of group, but it does not need to be hard. At the beginning of the school year, I know that I am going to be bombarded with extra tasks, as all educators are at the beginning of the school year. To prepare for this, I always run groups during lunch in the beginning of the school year. I keep them short, 30-minutes long, and I make them activity-based groups instead of processing groups where students need more time. My favorite one that I have run for nearly a decade is Lego Lunch, where we work on the basics of building friendships and social skills. Students are given a pass to skip the lunch line, get a to-go plate, walk to the classroom where I am hosting, and join in on Lego challenges and activities until the bell rings. It's minimal, and it accomplishes the goals of reinforcing social skills and helping students make friends. Students love it. In addition, to keep things simple, I continue to use the same curriculum over and over again, with adjustments. For groups, I recommend finding a curriculum or a format you love and are confident in and stick to it.

Another thing I do is be intentional about running groups. I calendar groups at the beginning of the school year based on a needs assessment; that way I don't just keep "putting it off." I give a simple online needs assessment to all of my students and ask if they would be interested in participating in a group related to stress/anxiety, making friends, doing better in school, and understanding their identity. It is these four categories that I shape quarterly groups out of. Then I put all of the dates on my individual calendar and on my team's calendar. Trust me, if you don't do this, you will also become victim of the "to do later."

Like me, you may be paving the way as an advocate for school counseling groups in your school, or your school may already have a culture of groups. Either way, I challenge you to keep things simple and to be intentional about planning for them in your calendaring. Just start. The rewards will amaze you.

SUMMARY AND CONCLUSION

Groups are a fantastic opportunity for school counselors to provide targeted support to specific students in a time-effective manner. Not only do school counselors benefit from having the opportunity to attend to multiple students at one time, the group experience will also provide students the opportunity to practice social skills with each other (Sink et al., 2012). Appropriate group topics include many aspects of social, career, and academic areas that students at all levels will gain from. Using needs assessment data to guide your group offerings and being mindful of specific considerations at each grade level will help set up your group counseling offerings for success!

CASE STUDY

Mx. Jones recently completed a needs assessment at the middle school where they are employed as a school counselor. Data revealed that a significant number of fifth-graders are feeling anxious about the transition to high school. They decide that a support group focusing on this topic would be of interest and decide to begin planning the curriculum attending to this topic.

DISCUSSION QUESTIONS

1. What steps would Mx. Jones need to be mindful of related to group planning?
2. What are some logistic considerations that are important for this type of group?
3. How could Mx. Jones be intentional about attending to the needs of diverse students when planning and implementing this group?
4. What topics might work well for the focus of this 6-week group?

PRACTICAL APPLICATION

- Be intentional about including group counseling in your school counseling interventions. Especially at the secondary level, groups are often underutilized.

- It is important to be thoughtful about attending to culturally relevant considerations for group planning and implementation.

- Get creative with group work! If your school culture and scheduling do not allow for formal, structured groups, meet during lunch or other unstructured time in the school day.

- Communicate well with classroom teachers related to when groups start, end, and what they can expect in terms of the general focus of the group work. Teachers can provide great data related to behavioral changes that they see in students during, and after, group participation!

- Get those permission forms out early; it is usually not a quick turnaround.

KEY REFERENCES

Only key references appear in the print edition. The full reference list appears in the digital product on Springer Publishing Connect: connect.springerpub.com/content/book/978-0-8261-8753-6/part/part03/chapter/ch09

Dameron, M. L., Camp, A., Friedmann, B., & Parikh, F. S. (2020). Multicultural education and perceived multicultural competency of school counselors. *Journal of Multicultural Counseling & Development, 48*(3), 176–190. https://doi.org/10.1002/jmcd.12176

Gladding, S. T. (2020). *Groups: A counseling specialty* (8th ed.). Pearson.

Javadian, S. R., & Sabet Eqlidi, S. (2022). The effectiveness of solution-focused group counseling on anxiety and social skills among female students. *Social Work in Mental Health, 20*(2), 174–183. https://doi.org/10.1080/15332985.2021.1995571

Sink, C., Edwards, C. N., & Eppler, C. (2012). *School-based group counseling*. Brooks/Cole Cengage Learning.

Sink, C. A., Edwards, C. N., & Weir, S. J. (2007). Helping children transition from kindergarten to first grade. *Professional School Counseling*. https://doi.org/10.1177/2156759X0701000303

Steen, S., Bauman, S., & Smith, J. (2007). Professional school counselors and the practice of group work. *Professional School Counseling, 11*(2), 72–80. https://doi.org/10.5330/PSC.n.2010-11.72

Steen, S., Shi, Q., & Melfie, J. (2021). A systematic literature review of school-counsellor-led group counselling interventions targeting academic achievement: Implications for research and practice. *Journal of School-Based Counseling Policy and Evaluation, 3*(1), 6–18. https://doi.org/https://doi.org/10.25774/sgvv-ta47

CHAPTER 10

Classroom Guidance for School Counselors

STEPHANIE EBERTS AND MARY AMANDA GRAHAM

LEARNING OBJECTIVES

After reading this chapter, students will be able to:

- Apply developmentally appropriate strategies in classroom guidance.
- Recognize the data in relationship to constructing classroom guidance lessons.
- Create developmentally appropriate guidance lessons.

STUDENT VOICE

Student "K" provided the following testimonial about her experience with a school counselor:

"I am a senior now, but remember when I was in the fourth grade, our class was having lots of problems with teasing and bullying. I think our whole school was struggling with this. Our school counselor, Mrs. G, would come in weekly to facilitate class meetings. One week she brought in a stack of cut-out paper hearts. She gave each of us a heart and told us not to do anything with it. We always listened to Mrs. G because she was the best school counselor and we loved her. Mrs. G asked us "what is this" as she held up the heart. We all answered. She then asked, "what does your heart do?" Some of us were funny and said, pump blood and keep us alive. Others said, it has love and loves others. Mrs. G said that we were going to talk about the part of our heart that loved today. She asked us to hold up our paper hearts and told us that each time she said something that sounded like teasing or hurtful to crumble the heart. She said we could smash it on our desks too. She said about five hurtful things (things we had been saying to each other). She then asked us to smooth the heart back out and get it back to the way it was when we started. We tried and smoothed and some of us taped, but we couldn't get it back to the way it was before we crumbled it. Mrs. G. explained that this is what happens when we say and hear hurtful things to one another. We can say we are sorry, but we can't take it back, and damage is done to the heart. She explained that the heart will still love but that it is changed when it gets hurt. I am a senior now, and I still have that heart. I will never forget that classroom lesson on kindness and the impact hurtful words have on a person's mind and soul. Thank you, Mrs. G, You still are the best counselor ever!"

INTRODUCTION

Over the years, terminology related to instruction in classrooms by school counselors has shifted. Emerging school counselors may hear multiple references to the delivery of large-group lessons as classroom guidance, classroom lessons, and large-group instruction. Core curriculum is often used to describe the curriculum that school counselors infuse into student learning. For the purposes of this chapter, the term *classroom guidance* will be used.

The American School Counseling Association (ASCA) strongly suggests the use of classroom guidance as a part of a comprehensive school-counseling program (ASCA, 2019a, 2019b). In the fourth edition of the ASCA Model, classroom guidance falls under the Deliver section in direct services (ASCA, 2019a, 2019b). Direct services are those activities in which counselors are in direct contact with students. Other direct services include counseling, appraisal, and advisement. ASCA recommends that school counselors spend 80% of their time in direct service to students (ASCA, 2019a, 2019b). Classroom guidance is an excellent way to deliver services directly to many students. Classroom guidance enables school counselors to have more face-to-face time with students, thus building stronger relationships. Goodman-Scott et al. (2020), speak to the importance of aligning comprehensive school-counseling programs to a multi-tiered system of supports (MTSS) framework by providing Tier 1 supports. These include interventions that are systemic and schoolwide. Classroom guidance is considered a Tier 1 intervention and is extremely important in the role of school counselor (Goodman-Scott et al., 2020).

When delivering classroom guidance, school counselors are expected to examine data to determine need and develop or access programming. School counselors play a pivotal role in student achievement and emotional wellness. Developing classroom guidance that is based on data strengthens student success. School counselors review student data on discipline, attendance, and academics. Hatch (2014) reinforces that student data are the bridge to building intentional classroom guidance that directly impacts student need. School counselors are expected to implement curriculum that is evidence based, developmentally appropriate, and culturally relevant to their students (ASCA, 2019a, 2019b). There are multiple steps to implementing effective classroom guidance.

IMPLEMENTATION OF CLASSROOM GUIDANCE

Emerging school counselors may wonder how to decide what topics to focus on during classroom guidance. First, the school counselor must understand the needs of their students and identify or develop content that meets those needs while applying the standards of both the district and the mindsets and behaviors put forth by ASCA (n.d.). Therefore, it is vital to facilitate a needs assessment. Needs assessments should be given at least two times (preferably three times) per year. Needs assessments should go out to students (primary stakeholders), all school faculty (bus drivers, paraeducators, aides, teachers, administrative assistants), and to parents and guardians (Hatch, 2014). The school counselor, while constructing their guidance lessons based on data, will need to also establish pre- and postevaluation assessments. The school counselor should always gather baseline data and evaluate the effectiveness of content shared with school stakeholders. Once need is determined, it is important for the school counselor to collaborate with teachers and find mutually agreed upon times to facilitate the classroom guidance. Ideally, the teacher collaborates with the school counselors so there is a shared knowledge and language the teacher can integrate with students throughout the week.

The ASCA (2012) recommends that school counselors spend between 15% and 45% of their time, depending on the age of their students, conducting classroom lessons. Elementary school counselors fall at the higher end of that scale, whereas high school counselors who may have more challenges finding time in the academic schedule, are in the lower range of the scale. The current model (ASCA, 2019a, 2019b) recommends that school counselors spend 80% of their time in direct service to students, including classroom guidance. Lopez and Mason (2017) assert that implementing classroom guidance is an act of leadership and advocacy. Scheduling guidance can be challenging and requires school counselors to have strong working relationships with teachers and administration. When working in the elementary setting, school counselors will often collaborate with classroom teachers to find a time in the school day to present their lessons. Some elementary school counselors are on rotations with other classes that are taught quarterly, such as art, health, music, and other topics. Middle and high school counselors can develop a curriculum that compliments core subjects such as math, science, and language arts, among others. Cross-curricular efforts have the added benefit of strengthening collegial relationships and relationships between students and teachers, and they can help students find more meaning in academic content as it relates to emotional wellness. Some middle and high school counselors find time to teach during an advisory period or other ancillary time slots.

It is certain that finding time to integrate school-counseling lessons is beneficial to all students. A large study conducted by Sink and Stroh (2003) found that schools that had comprehensive school-counseling models, which include classroom guidance, had higher student achievement than those without comprehensive models. Classroom guidance is a significant element of a comprehensive program. There are other historical studies that highlight the benefits of strong curricular interventions (Villalba & Meyers, 2008; Villares et al., 2011).

DEVELOPMENTAL CONSIDERATIONS OF CLASSROOM GUIDANCE

Emerging school counselors without prior teaching experience often feel unsure about their ability to develop effective classroom guidance lessons. Johnson (2000) suggests a five-step process: (a) the development of learning objectives, (b) introduction, (c) input, (d) activity, and (e) closure. Learning objectives should be measurable and align with the focus of the lesson. The introduction of a lesson should give students an idea framework or agenda of what is to come and create student investment in the topic. The input is the teaching portion of the lesson, whereas the activity allows students to integrate new learning. The closure allows students to review their new learning. In addition to these steps, the school counselor will evaluate learning and could include an evaluation tool such as an exit ticket (a couple of questions about student learning) to the summary portion of the class. This protocol can be applied to lessons at all developmental ages. The ASCA also provides a lesson plan template that is helpful for school counselors when constructing lessons. The template provides a framework to help school counselors identify learning objectives and align with mindsets and behaviors, best practices, data, and evaluation. The template link is located in the resources at the end of the book.

Elementary School Classroom Guidance

The developmental needs of elementary students vary greatly between prekindergarten and either fourth or fifth grade, depending on the school. Starting around age 4 years, students begin to understand symbols but remain more concrete in their thinking than students who are nearing or beyond age 7 (Berk, 2017). Piaget's theory of cognitive development suggests that children's cognitive capacity grows as they age. Vygotsky attributes social interaction as the reason for this growth in cognitive development and awareness (Berk, 2017). Understanding that children are not little adults is a cornerstone of developing material that complements their classroom learning while also keeping in mind their need for movement and their shorter attention spans.

While in elementary school, children are learning not only how to read and write, they are also learning about how to be a member of group. To assist in these efforts, school counselors can provide elementary school classroom guidance lessons on social and emotional learning at the appropriate developmental level. The elementary school counselor should think in terms of Tier 1 services, spending a large amount of their time in the classroom. Preventive topics can include respect, friendship, conflict resolution, decision-making, and building coping strategies. In addition, exposing children to post-secondary options should begin as early as in elementary school by sharing information about local careers and colleges. Remedial topics can include body respect, sharing, and self-control (Bardhosh et al., 2017). From Tier 1 services (classroom guidance), elementary school counselors can identify with teachers and parents the need for Tier 2 services (small groups) based on the same topic(s) (ASCA, 2021).

Middle School Classroom Guidance

Middle school is marked by great changes both cognitively and socially. As students begin to use metacognition, thinking about their social and emotional development at this age, school counselors can deepen their lessons to match students' new cognitive abilities. Socially, middle school students begin to value how others see them, especially their peers. Believing in the invisible audience, many middle school students believe that others are watching and evaluating their every move. These elements are essential in the development of effective classroom lessons, as students may be reluctant to share in class or possibly may want to impress their friends (Berk, 2017). Preventive topics for middle school students may include education about puberty, social justice issues, advocacy and leadership lessons, bullying prevention, and safety awareness. As relationships become more complicated, remedial lessons may focus on specific relationship issues, violence, and academic success. Students may also begin exploring areas of interest for different careers. These classes can be longer than those that younger students experience, but they should be equally relevant and engaging.

High School Classroom Guidance

Classroom guidance in high school can be meaningful, preventive, and enriching. High school is a time of great transition, both physically and emotionally. High school students need assistance regarding postsecondary education options (Bryan et al., 2015), navigating relationships, mental health, and the effects of COVID (Clemens et al., 2020). School counselors can also cover relevant topics such as cyberbullying, internet safety, violence, and grief and loss. At this stage of development, students are thinking more abstractly. Because students are thinking more abstractly, they may have existential questions about their lives. Students are also processing a great deal of information daily, thus lessons in mindfulness and managing stress and anxiety can be powerful. When considering classroom guidance in high school, the school counselor should be creative and think of ways to meet social emotional and academic goals simultaneously.

CLASSROOM MANAGEMENT STRATEGIES

Some states require that school counselors have prior teaching experience to qualify as a school counselor and some do not. Having teaching experience does not have to determine your effectiveness as a school counselor. Having classroom management strategies that are effective might. Classroom management done well provides structure, connects the school counselor and student, and supports learning outcomes. Buchanan et al. (2017) speak to the importance of school counselors being proficient in the development of curriculum, understanding the structural environment of the classroom, establishing norms with students for the lesson, and the management of the lesson from the beginning to the end. Effective classroom management also includes using proximity, accessing multiple learning styles, differentiating instruction, and focus on student engagement and pacing (Geltner et al., 2011). Goodman-Scott (2018) reinforce the idea that school counselors can manage the classroom by being proactive, being able to engage and reinforce students, and accessing a variety of appropriate discipline and redirection techniques. School counselors can be proactive by being prepared for the lesson, checking in with the classroom teacher about preestablished expectations and norms, and being visible and known to students prior to engaging in teaching. School counselors can engage students by accessing creativity (art, music, technology) and keeping students engaged in the lesson from the beginning until the end. School counselors can reinforce positive classroom behavior by using the established reward system put in place by the school and the teacher. If redirection needs to occur, the school counselor should lean on what the teacher has established and what is fair and equitable. School counselors should not take the role as disciplinarian but should redirect the classes if needed (Goodman-Scott, 2018). Above all, counselors should talk with their students during classroom guidance, not at them.

INTEGRATION OF MULTICULTURAL COMPETENCIES AND SOCIAL JUSTICE ADVOCACY

According to the American Counseling Association (ACA) Multicultural and Social Justice Competencies (2015), school counselors should be aware of their own privilege and power as well as their own experiences of bias and oppression. They must also seek to understand their students' experiences of both power and privilege as well as bias and oppression. Understanding the worldview of their students is imperative to implementing strong and relevant programming. School counselors should be mindful of pronouns, microaggressions, and other forms of oppression that can occur during teaching a class, whether it is from the school counselor to the student or student to student. Those moments, when recognized, can be used as teaching moments with the class.

The ASCA School Counseling Professional Standards and Competencies (2019b) are very specific about the mandate that states that school counselors collaborate with stakeholders to provide culturally responsive content that is focused on student learning. However, building awareness and providing culturally responsive content may not be enough to meet the needs of all students. In fact, school counselors can use classroom guidance as a means to use antiracist practices. Understanding racist policies and how they impact students, while also understanding the microaggressions that occur daily in schools and society, can impact systemic inequities. Kendi (2019) suggests that the term *microaggression* does not adequately describe the abuse that these comments and behaviors perpetuate. Author Bettina Love (2019) explains that the fight for justice in the classroom and in schools begins with the concept of mattering. Honoring the intersectionality of students by bringing about awareness of inequities coupled with the need to be seen, can enable communities to come together. School counselors can offer students a safe place to explore their multiple identities and the systemic inequities that impact their day-to-day lives. Whether school counselors are affirming gender, racial, ethnic, or sexual orientation identities, the work of building self-awareness and importance of all students can be modeled through classroom guidance. School counselors can use their school's data to uncover inequities on their campuses. For example, if students of color are not participating in advanced placement (AP) classes at the same rate as their White peers, school counselors can use their guidance time to educate the students about the AP program in school, while advocating for inclusion of all students.

Ideally, school counselors will continually engage in the process of both understanding their own identity, including any biases they may hold, while also striving to understand the lived experiences of their students. This exploration is also essential to seeking content that is applicable to students' experiences and needs.

VOICES FROM THE FIELD

Name: Alaine Williamson (she/her)

Professional Job Title: Elementary School Counselor

Bio: Alaine is a school counselor, licensed professional counselor, and registered play therapist in Louisiana. She works with third- to fourth -graders and is passionate about classroom guidance.

I am typically in classrooms about 2 days a week, and I see each grade level at least five to six times per semester. I work really hard to strike a balance in my schedule. Too few counseling visits can result in becoming disconnected from the students, but too many counseling lessons on the schedule can interfere with the opportunity to run small groups, support students individually, attend meetings with parents and teachers, and promptly respond to those surprise events that will inevitably pop up during the day. In my current role, I am fortunate to have the opportunity to make my own schedule, which allows for some much-appreciated flexibility. My administration allows me to coordinate with the religion teachers and use their instructional time to be a guest speaker. I am grateful for the ability to manage my own schedule, and the teachers welcome an extra planning period here and there. Everyone wins! I have found great success in "stacking" classroom lessons for a single grade level. For example, I might arrange my schedule so that I visit third grade for three consecutive Thursdays, where we will focus on bullying. We'll read books, play games, and practice assertiveness or conflict resolution strategies. With this strategy, I am able to really dig deep and reinforce important skills. While "stacking" may slow down my rotational speed from grade to grade, I find my visits to be more meaningful, more fruitful, and more likely to "stick."

It is important to get creative when scheduling classroom lessons. Over the years, I have come to recognize that an approach for one grade level may not be the best fit for another. For example, I've found that visiting preschoolers for a 30 minute classroom lesson is not the most effective approach. Instead, I may visit during center time and pull five to six students into the hallway for a "mini group" that lasts about 10 minutes. I'll continue to rotate students in and out until every student has had a turn. I have accomplished so much with this approach: I've provided an activity that is more appropriate for their attention span, every child is given a chance to share or participate, and the lesson is more likely to be a memorable experience. In another example, I have had a blast coordinating with the physical education teachers to deliver classroom lessons. For a single homeroom, I may send the boys to P.E. and keep the girls back for some adventure therapy and bonding exercises. The following week, the girls head to P.E. while I work with the boys. This allows me to introduce activities and games that would likely be too overwhelming in a larger group setting.

Classroom lessons are a critical component of a comprehensive school-counseling program. It supports all of the work that we do as school counselors in so many ways. I find my small groups and individual sessions with students to be more effective and efficient when we have a strong foundation to work from. We have already established strong rapport and familiarity, and I can often help students to overcome their obstacles more quickly by helping them to utilize certain skills that have already been introduced to them in the classroom. Most importantly, you do not know which student may experience significant hardship in the future. I am most grateful that classroom lessons are an integrated part of my program during the most challenging sessions: when a student has experienced sudden and traumatic loss, when I am conducting an at-risk screening for self-harm or suicide, or when abuse or neglect in the home is suspected. When rapport and trust have already been established, I am better able to support my students and meet their needs.

It is important for other stakeholders to see the work that you are doing in the classrooms so that everyone in the school community can reinforce your lessons and understand their purpose. After each classroom lesson or unit, I send a short, single page newsletter to parents and teachers with a short recap and helpful resources. I have also found success in creating short, 5-minute recap videos on websites such as "Loom." Inviting an administrator to come observe a lesson that you are proud of or setting up a hallway display are other strategies for promoting your work. First, do not let a single classroom lesson go by without learning everyone's name. I like to begin class by playing *The Name Game*: try to say each student's first name out loud, and continue until you get 100% accuracy. This will take time, but (a) you are sending a priceless message that each individual in that classroom is valued, and (b) it becomes really difficult to manage behavior when you're saying, "Hey, you over there!" Second, do not let a single classroom lesson go by without reviewing expectations. For example, how do you get your class to become silent when you have important instructions? Whether it's "Give Me Five!" or "Flat Tire!", remember that you are a visitor, and your rules and expectations need to be explicitly taught each time. If you do not have a classroom management plan, I recommend spending some time observing a teacher you admire and doing some research. I love using the interactive modeling approach when teaching expectations or when I am introducing a new game. Finally, always have a backup activity ready to go. Grab a book or have a link to a supporting video. Nothing is more daunting than idle time in a classroom full of 5-year-olds!

SUMMARY AND CONCLUSION

Classroom guidance is an essential part of a school counselor's job. It can be rewarding and meaningful work. Using vetted resources and intentional planning, school counselors can impact students' lives through classroom guidance. Classroom guidance curriculum can be purchased or accessed for free. School counselors can choose to create their own curriculum or modify existing curriculum. School counselors need to be mindful when implementing any curriculum that it is a good fit for the cultural and developmental needs of the students. Regarding curriculum used, the key thing to remember is that data drives topics and curriculum (Hatch, 2014). When facilitating classroom guidance, using methods that are appealing to students, such as interactive lessons, hands-on activities, and expressive arts, school counselors will build relationships, engage students, and impact systems. Classroom guidance is a powerful Tier 1 tool for systemic change and to reach the maximum number of students as possible.

CASE STUDY

Stephanie was a school counselor in New Orleans when Hurricane Katrina struck. Though this event is in the distant past, the lessons learned from this disaster may be useful for current school counselors. Because the school counselor had a comprehensive program that included a developmentally based guidance plan that was taught every year and could be complimented by a needs-based remedial program, classroom lessons offered students a space to process their experiences with the hurricane. The elementary curriculum was designed to build skills that were needed for autonomous learning and social growth. The topics were as follows:

First grade: Conflict Resolution

Second grade: Skills for Learning

Third grade: Decision-Making

Fourth grade: Conflict Resolution

Fifth grade: Respect

The first-grade curriculum was Kelso Choice (Lee & Clark, 2000), which offered students an understanding of how to deal with difficult situation on their own, with nine choices they could use, and when to seek the help of an adult. The second-grade curriculum was the evidence-based Student Success Skills program (Brigman & Webb, 2004). Third-grade curriculum focused on the cognitive process of making decisions. The fourth-grade curriculum revisited conflict resolution by identifying difficult situations and coming up with coping strategies that would allow them to make the best decision possible for their situation. Since many fifth-graders were experiencing puberty and friendship shifts, this unit was focused on how to treat friends, avoid bullying, and respect.

After Hurricane Katrina, the school counselor believed that she would have to implement entirely new curriculum; however, what she found was that the students were able to process their experiences during the lessons that were already in place. In fourth grade the students were asked to create a comic book for an identified challenging situation. Many of the students selected losing their home or evacuating as their challenging situation. Coming up with coping strategies to deal with such a difficult situation was an additional piece of their coping sequence. In fifth grade, students discussed how it felt to attend a new school when they were evacuated and to be treated differently by the students in their new school. Skills like coping, identifying challenges, being respectful, having focus in class, and asking for help when needed, were all prevention-focused interventions, but dealing with the aftermath of a devastating event gave students a means in which to apply their learning.

The stress and anxiety of living in a destroyed city is not something that is easily described. Sadly, people around the world are dealing with similar tragedies. It is heartening to know that when a strong comprehensive program is in place, especially one that includes classroom guidance, it offers school counselors a framework for teaching much-needed coping skills. By offering students a way to process their grief, sadness, and fears after Hurricane Katrina, the school counselor was better able to understand the needs of her students. She was better able to understand the impact that the hurricane had on her students, and she was able to tailor services to meet their needs. Classroom guidance provided that data to the school counselor.

DISCUSSION QUESTIONS

1. In reviewing the case study, what other interventions or strategies would be helpful to implement in the role of the school counselor?
2. How does the school counselor check bias and privilege and remain respectful when facilitating the above lessons for students?
3. How does the school counselor partner with community and school partners to facilitate classroom guidance in this example?
4. How do school counselors help teachers find access points in academic curriculum in order to integrate social and emotional learning?

PRACTICAL APPLICATION

- Access social media platforms and groups to share ideas with other school counselors on classroom guidance and resources.
- Partner with older students to cofacilitate guidance lessons with younger students.
- Partner with teachers to integrate concepts of guidance and social-emotional learning (SEL) into the academic curriculum.
- Attend grade-planning meetings to get an idea of access points for integrating SEL.
- Find skilled and experienced teachers and observe them managing their classroom. Observe, observe, observe to gain proficient classroom management skills.

KEY REFERENCES

Only key references appear in the print edition. The full reference list appears in the digital product on Springer Publishing Connect: connect.springerpub.com/content/book/978-0-8261-8753-6/part/part03/chapter/ch10

Bardhoshi, G., Duncan, K., & Erford, B. (2017). Effect of a specialized classroom counseling intervention on increasing self-efficacy among first-grade rural students. *Professional School Counseling, 21*(1), 12–25. https://doi.org/10.5330/1096-2409-21.1.12

Goodman-Scott, E. (2018). Enhancing student learning by "Building a caring climate": School counselors' experiences with classroom management. *Professional School Counseling, 22*(1). http://doi.org/10.1177/2156759X19852618

Goodman-Scott, E., Betters-Bubon, J. Olsen, J., & Donohue, P. (2020). *Making MTSS work.* American School Counseling Association.

Hatch, T. (2014). *The use of data in school counseling: Hatching results for students, programs, and the profession.* Corwin.

Kendi, I. X. (2019). *How to be an antiracist.* Random House Books.

CHAPTER 11

Crisis Intervention for School Counselors

**AMY HAYES SILER, ARIE GREENLEAF, AND
MARY AMANDA GRAHAM**

LEARNING OBJECTIVES

After reading this chapter, students will be able to:

- Identify students who are experiencing a crisis.
- Modify structures and procedures to assist students in crisis.
- Apply culturally sensitive and inclusive interventions to crisis prevention.
- Apply advocacy and social justice considerations to crisis planning and response.

STUDENT VOICE

Student "R" provided the following testimonial about her experience with a school counselor:

"I come from a home of practicing alcoholics and addicts. There is violence in my home, and chaos. We are low income and struggle at times to pay the bills. All of these things I kept as secrets from adults in school, as long as I could. One day my brother overdosed on heroin and died. I was a total mess for a long time and didn't tell anyone. I was trying to stay focused in class, but I couldn't focus. I was angry and sad all at the same time. I felt alone, hopeless, and lost. I was starting to feel depressed and suicidal. My teacher noticed a behavioral change and referred me to the school counselor. The school counselor saved my life! She sat with me for hours as I processed my chaotic family and the death of my brother. She validated me, was nonjudgmental, and was compassionate. I knew she really cared. She talked to me about my sadness and my thoughts of suicide. We developed a plan together to help me process the grief and hopelessness and to see that life could get better, even if my family was whacked. For the rest of the year (my senior year), she checked in on me and let me know she was there for me for anything I needed. I never felt unheard or alone again in school."

INTRODUCTION

School is not the upholder of safety it once was. The most reprehensible example of this truth is the shooting, death, and mayhem that occurs on school campuses in the United States today. Once unheard of, this devastating phenomenon has become an all too familiar and frequent scourge on modern society. Albeit still rare, this occurrence has grown exponentially since the 1980s. In the mid-20th century, the average was one school shooting per year. It took nearly 40 years to accumulate a total of 25 school shootings. Alarmingly, 25 school shootings occurred in 2013 alone. The spike in these senseless tragedies coincides with other chronic natural and man-made disasters, including tornadoes, viruses, car accidents, and suicides. Although the frequency of some of these risks remains constant over time, others seem to be trending in the wrong direction. The need for crisis intervention in schools is more pronounced than ever. However, with the onslaught of dysfunctionality and unexpected natural occurrences, schools have struggled to be prepared. Perhaps Maya Angelou has captured the most appropriate response for a school as they evaluate their crisis preparation: "Hoping for the best, prepared for the worst, and unsurprised by anything in between." The question for school administrators and faculty is how to best achieve the balance between hopeful optimism and the hard work of crisis prevention and response.

ROLE OF THE SCHOOL COUNSELOR IN CRISIS PREVENTION AND INTERVENTION

One obvious answer is that, more than ever, PK–12 students and staff need school counselors who are willing and capable to address the growing crises that are now occurring on a regular basis. Whether the crisis is limited to a single student and their family or an event that shakes the lives of everyone in the school, crisis counseling is an integral aspect of the job. In fact, of the many hats school counselors wear, the crisis response hat is among those they will wear most often.

Collectively, school counselors have been through too much at this point to be too surprised by anything that happens in school. "Expect the unexpected" could be the profession's unofficial motto. After all, in what crises haven't school counselors found themselves waist-deep at one time or another in recent years? It seems that all manner of death, disease, and disorder have shown up when the bell rings. Outside of navigating a crisis response to an extraterrestrial invasion, there are few situations that a well-seasoned school counselor hasn't had thrown at them. And like an experienced combat veteran, most school counselors face down these difficult circumstances with a quiet strength, professionalism, and commitment to the mission that would curdle weaker souls. The help-wanted sign in the school window should aptly read "The faint-hearted need not apply."

Crisis

A common explanation for an internal crisis implies the precipitating event directly caused the crisis. In other words, the crisis is the event. However, this explanation is not only simplistic in many cases, but it is also rarely accurate. The event itself is usually not the crisis, per se. This is understood intuitively due to the fact that people can respond quite differently to the same situation. An individual's response to a circumstance or event determines the extent of their internal crisis. How overwhelmed a person feels in a crisis dictates their capacity to handle a situation. The more overwhelmed, the more destabilizing an event becomes, even stretching a person beyond their ability to cope. In Caplan's terms, a crisis can create a state of "psychological disequilibrium" (1964, p. 53). It is this inability to effectively cope with a particular situation that makes the event a crisis.

Crises are often major turning points. Although crises begin with psychological and emotional turmoil that can cause impactful consequences from the incident, they also represent opportunities for dramatic growth and positive change (Wethington, 2003). Most are familiar with posttraumatic stress disorder (PTSD) and its symptoms. However, posttraumatic growth (PTG) can also occur. People don't have to endure in the shadow of the crisis event for the rest of their lives; they can change in positive ways as a result of it. Changes can be characterized by a greater appreciation of life, improved relationships, seeing new possibilities, developing personal strengths, and spiritual transformation (Collier, 2016). It is important for the school counselor to keep in mind that people who are in the middle of a crisis are not fated to a life of misery, alienation, and incompleteness. Sadly, that could potentially happen, but there is also an inherent opportunity for growth. Individuals can and do successfully resolve crises all the time. Serious crises in the context of a school setting certainly add a different dimension to consider. Because of the school's social structure and close-knit community, Johnson (2000) explained, a crisis can unleash chaos into the system, thus undermining the school's safety and stability. Students and staff alike can experience a felt sense of threat, loss, and trauma. Events causing these reactions include suicide, car accidents, school shootings, natural disasters, abuse, and medical and mental health emergencies.

Crises can be experienced at both the individual and school community levels. In either case, a substantial amount of literature documents the immediate psychological effects of these crises on those impacted. Overwhelming distress, shock, and anguish are commonly experienced following a crisis incident (Collier, 2016). Although the psychological impact is often noticeable, it can also be concealed due to stigma or a lack of mental health resources. Thus, despite the great psychological pain students and staff may be experiencing, they will suffer in silence. In these instances, a long series of problems can be initiated, including PTSD, substance abuse, depression, academic issues, and strained relationships. In other words, if people do not functionally deal with the initial trauma and achieve some measure of positive resolution early in the process, they may experience chronic stress and mental illness for years to come. Or they may act upon their stress in destructive and horrific ways.

Given the eventuality that crises will occur, how a school counselor effectively manages these situations matters. Although the variables in every crisis are unique, and thus caution should be taken when applying a one-size-fits-all approach, there are certain nuts and bolts of crisis counseling that can provide helpful guidelines. Sandoval (2013) calls for counselors to attend to safety and stability as a primary start. It is also imperative to focus on interventions, remain calm, understand the facts, reflect feelings with empathy, avoid blaming, help the student process shock and denial, avoid false reassurance, and ultimately assist in helping the student return to precrisis functioning (Sandoval, 2013).

School counselors are in a natural position to be central figures in coordinating their school's crisis response. They possess a unique skill set and knowledge among school personnel. There are, in fact, no other members of the school community that possess their breadth and depth of education on topics relevant to a crisis, including an understanding of the psychological, emotional, and social impact of a crisis on an individual, family, and community.

CRISIS PREVENTION AND INTERVENTION: A SYSTEMIC APPROACH

Systemic Prevention

School counselors work collaboratively with administrators, teachers, students, parents, and community members to develop a preventive and responsive school counseling program that addresses crises and promotes safe schools. Duties of the school counselor surrounding crises include providing individual and group counseling during and after the incident; consulting with administrators, teachers, parents, and caregivers to provide insights into students' mental health needs; and coordinating with constituents in both the school and community to acquire helpful resources.

In addition to these activities, school counselors also have a responsibility to consider the multicultural and social justice implications inherent to many crises. Students' and staff's reactions to a crisis event and their coping skills, as well as their openness to counseling services, can differ significantly because of their cultural beliefs, traditions, and economic and social status. It is imperative that school counselors be culturally competent in order to develop, plan, and deliver effective mental health services during and after a crisis.

Culturally appropriate and trauma-informed prevention and intervention activities may be organized using the Multi-Tiered Systems of Support (MTSS) framework, using a whole-systems approach.

At the Tier 1 or systemwide level of MTSS, school counseling programs focus on preventive goals. Through education, collaboration, advocay, and various programming efforts, school counselors can help prevent student crises before they occur (Belser et al., 2016). Sharing common language and understanding in the school system around mental health, self-harm, violence, and other warning signs of crisis is the foundation of prevention (Masi & Heinze, 2021; National Threat Assessment Center [NTAC], 2019). Systemwide education includes classroom instruction, schoolwide programming and initiatives, violence prevention strategies, training about mental health, and crisis response. It is imperative that all stakeholders in a school system know the warning signs of mental illness and violent behaviors and are equipped with strategies to proactively intervene with students who are at risk (Masi & Heinze, 2021; NTAC, 2019). These strategies should include active listening and support, assessing safety, and accessing the proper care (Kitchener et al., 2017). The Mental Health First Aid training, for example, from the National Council for Mental Wellbeing, can be an appropriate intervention in which the entire school and community can be trained to identify, understand, and respond to signs of mental illnesses and substance use disorders (Kitchener et al., 2017).

Educational systems need to provide clear reporting procedures that anyone can use to report threatening and concerning behaviors (Masi & Heinze, 2021; NTAC, 2019). Reporting can be done by teachers and staff within the schools or anonymously by students, families, and community members (Masi & Heinze, 2021). School counselors can work with students and stakeholders to describe the situations and behaviors that need to be reported, as well as what the process will entail after the report (Masi & Heinze, 2021; NTAC, 2019). Prevention includes having a reporting procedure and screenings in place that students and faculty are aware of and can access easily.

Trauma

School counselors also need to address trauma in a systemic way (American School Counselor Association [ASCA], 2016). Specifically, counselors need to be prepared to work with students with traumatic histories, inform school staff about trauma and its effects on students' mental health and school performance, and promote a trauma-sensitive environment at their schools (ASCA, 2016; Cole et al., 2013; Rumsey & Milsom, 2019; SAMHSA, 2014). Trauma can change a child's brain development, affecting their memory, language development, attention, peer/adult relationships, and the ability to self-regulate emotions, behavior, and attention (Cole et al., 2013; Rumsey & Milsom, 2019). A trauma-informed schoolwide approach incorporates key trauma principles into the organizational culture of the schools (SAMHSA, 2014). These include the four Rs: **R**ealization of the widespread impact of trauma and its effects; **R**ecognition of signs and symptoms; **R**esponse to trauma through policies, procedures, and practices; and a commitment to **R**esist retraumatization of students and staff that may occur through organizational practices that trigger painful memories.

Universal Screening

Universal screenings for mental health issues have gained greater acceptance in recent years as a viable way to proactively identify and address students at risk for harmful behaviors (Belser et al., 2016; Lane et al., 2010; Pincus, 2020). It helps to identify students who otherwise may go unnoticed and fall through the cracks of the system. School counselors can administer screening tools to identify and support students with mental health issues such as anxiety, depression, and substance use (Pincus et al., 2020). Early identification can prompt immediate interventions by the school counselors or referrals to the community and can save lives (Belser et al., 2016).

THE SCHOOL COUNSELOR AND CRISIS TEAM

School counselors are a vital part of the school's emergency crisis team that responds to active crises of all types. In addition, they lend unique skills when dealing with individual student threats and crises. They can advocate for responsive services and referrals to community resources, assess for safety and threat, and be a calming presence to help de-escalate a crisis (ASCA, 2019). School districts are required to have an emergency operations plan (EOP) to respond to all kinds of threats and crises, both from nature and people. Schools need to know how to respond to weather disasters such as fires, floods, tornadoes, hurricanes, and earthquakes, as well as an active shooter, violence from other means, and individual crises due to mental health. The EOP will detail the behaviors of all school personnel and students, including all policies and procedures to be followed (REMS, 2013).

School counselors could provide training to school staff on the EOP and how to respond to student crises of all types. The Mental Health First Aid program can be a helpful training source (Kitchener et al., 2017), as well as psychological first aid (Brymer et al., 2012). There are also specific suicide prevention training programs accessible to schools. As mentioned previously, it is impossible to predict the types of crisis that a school counselor will handle. This chapter highlights a few regarding mental health, suicide, and grief. Many of these strategies can be adapted to crises of all types.

MENTAL HEALTH AND WELLNESS IN SCHOOLS

The Centers for Disease Control and Prevention noted that one in five children have a mental disorder, but only about 20% of those children received care from a mental health provider (American Psychological Association, 2022). It is essential that school counselors be aware of the various mental health concerns of children and adolescents and be able to proactively and reactively address them to support students.

Students who are violent and cause crises of safety in schools are either acting willfully or are suffering from a mental health issues. Although the clear majority of people (95%–97%) with mental health problems are not violent (HHS, 2022), many students who act violently have mental health disorders. In fact, 70% of youth in the juvenile justice system have a diagnosable mental health condition (National Alliance on Mental Illness [NAMI], 2022). Other mental health issues (anxiety, depression, attention-deficit hyperactive disorder [ADHD/ADD], etc.) can cause problems at schools and significant distress for the individual. About half of lifetime mental illnesses begin by age 14 (NAMI, 2022).

The most common disorders among U.S. children aged 3 to 17 years, according to 2013 to 2019 nationwide databases (Bitsko et al., 2022), were ADHD (9.8%) and anxiety problems (9.4%), each affecting more than one in 11 children. Bitsko et al. (2022) also reported depression and suicide were a risk for teens 12 to 17 years of age. Of those teens, one in five (20.9%) had experienced a major depressive episode. Furthermore, the researchers found that in 2019 more than one in three teens (36.7%) reported feeling sad or hopeless, and nearly one in five (18.8%) seriously considered attempting suicide. In 2020, there was a 31% increase in mental health–related emergency department visits (NAMI, 2022). Regarding the negative impact that the COVID-19 pandemic has had on young people, nearly one in five (18%) reported a significant negative impact on their mental health, and about half of young people with a mental health condition reported a significant negative impact from the virus (NAMI, 2022).

Mental health challenges adversely affect a student's success in school (Cavioni et al., 2020). High school students with significant symptoms of depression are more than twice as likely to drop out compared to their peers, and students aged 6 to 17 with mental, emotional or behavioral concerns are three times more likely to repeat a grade (NAMI, 2022). As seen in classrooms, students with mental health disorders often have trouble concentrating and relating to their peers.

Dikel (2020) described how various student mental health disorders appear in schools. For example, students with ADHD have trouble concentrating and paying attention, as well as remaining seated and on task. Their impulsivity can create problems. Those with oppositional defiant disorder (ODD) will also be challenged to follow directions and comply with rules. Students on the autism spectrum will have difficulties with changes in routine, as well as socializing appropriately with their peers. For those with internalizing disorders, the crisis may be that the student cannot be around others without experiencing extreme distress. They may have panic attacks, physical complaints of stomach aches and headaches, or be highly reactive to certain sensing triggers in the environment. Some students may be depressed to the point of self-harming by cutting, self-soothing with drugs and alcohol, or considering suicide to end it all. Other disorders involve a break with reality, such as schizophrenia or bipolar mania, which involve hallucinations and delusions.

Despite the high numbers of school-aged youth experiencing mental health challenges, few receive any treatment. Lambie et al. (2019) reported approximately 70% to 80% of youth in need of mental health care do not receive services. Furthermore, they explained that this is even more pronounced among ethnic and racial minorities and youth who may be economically disadvantaged and experiencing environmental stressors such as poverty, lack of health insurance, stigma, economic instability, and family stressors. School counselors can impact this gap.

As previously discussed, school counselors can address students mental health crises through systemwide prevention activities such as education, training, and universal screening. Recognizing early warning signs of developing mental health disorders is crucial. Training provided to the school community about mental health issues could include recognition of signs and symptoms, ways to address crises, and an overview of effective treatment options.

For students experiencing mental health crises, school counselors need to provide targeted, responsive interventions. At the Tier 2 (students at risk for developing crises) and Tier 3 (students with intensive needs) levels of MTSS, counselors can offer individual and group counseling to students and seamless referrals to community mental health providers. Individual and group counseling must be trauma-informed and culturally responsive. School counselors also should be aware of their own strengths and limitations in addressing student mental health needs. Community mental health clinicians are able to provide a higher level and continuity of care to students. They can be specially trained and certified to treat certain disorders such as eating disorders, suicide, trauma and PTSD, substance abuse, and psychotic illnesses. Community providers also may include medication management, which is considered best practice in treating certain mental health conditions. Referrals should be seamless and ensure equitable access for all students, especially those from marginalized groups.

School counselors can facilitate communication between students, their families, and the community clinicians. They can check in with students on a regular basis at school and consult with the students' therapists (with appropriate permissions) to reinforce treatment strategies at school. Lapan et al. (2014) found that secondary students who felt their school counselors personally knew and responded to their concerns reported feeling safer and more connected in school.

THE SCHOOL COUNSELOR AND GRIEF

Grief can occur through the traditional loss caused by a loved one's death, as well as other kinds of loss or transitions. For example, students may experience grief when a family member, friend, or beloved pet dies. They also may experience loss that comes from adapting to a new life, such as with a recent move, divorce, family members being arrested or deported, or welcoming new family members into the student's lives. Loss may occur if a student–athlete can no longer play sports or if a student needs to adapt to a new chronic illness or disability. In each of these cases, the student must adjust to a new "normal," and sometimes they can feel lost in their grief.

The most important thing school counselors and, really, anyone can do, is to listen to the student. The student doesn't need someone to "fix" their grief, and they often do not need help from "grief experts" in the community. Grieving students need to feel safe and comfortable enough to share whatever it is they are thinking and feeling, with no right or wrong way to process their grief (Highmark Caring Foundation, 2022). Sometimes adults are reluctant to talk to students about their grief because they feel unqualified or want to avoid upsetting the child/adolescent. School counselors, however, should not be hesitant to talk about the death or loss a student has experienced, as this can be therapeutic for the student and encourage healing. In working with young children, adults should use concrete terms like "death" and "died" rather than "passed away" or "lost" to avoid confusing the child (Highmark Caring Foundation, 2022).

Contrary to the popular five stages of grief model (Kubler-Ross, 1969), each person's experience with grief will be unique and will not necessarily follow the linear path of denial, anger, bargaining, depression, and acceptance. Grief is a process, and it may include a range of emotions, as well as unpredictable ups and downs. Students may be distractible, forgetful, fearful, or have a sudden outburst of tears; sometimes the grief increases over time and turns into a more serious disorder (Highmark Caring Foundation, 2022). It can be helpful for a student to know that adults at school are there for them and are willing to listen to them talk openly about their painful feelings, as well as special memories. Sometimes students may appreciate making a memorial project to honor their loved one. Promoting self-care is extremely important during the difficult grieving process (The Jed Foundation, 2022).

Additionally, students may benefit from support groups in which they are surrounded by peers who can understand and relate to what they are going through (Samide & Stockton, 2002). Community resources can aid through education, grief counseling, and support groups. School counselors should be aware of local resources they can refer to their students and families.

Finally, it is important for school counselors to be aware of how different cultures express grief. There will be differences in how various cultures mourn and gather, what they believe about death and life, and what rituals and ceremonies they have. It is important to meet each student where they are and not to make any assumptions based on the school counselor's own cultural experiences with grief and loss.

THE SCHOOL COUNSELOR AND SUICIDE

School counselors need to have a schoolwide suicide prevention plan that addresses the mental and emotional needs of students at risk for suicide (Granello & Zyromski, 2018). The ASCA position statement, "The School Counselor and Suicide Prevention/Awareness," states that school counselors need to identify suicide risk and have effective prevention programs in place (ASCA, 2018). Counselors are to immediately notify parents of students with suicide risks, and possibly child protective services (ASCA, 2018). Additionally, school counselors can be leaders in training school personnel to identify and respond to suicide ideation in students (ASCA, 2018). Granello and Zyromski (2018) proposed different types of research-supported suicide prevention programs such as universal curricular suicide education, in-service education for gatekeepers such as counselors and teachers, schoolwide suicide screening programs, and parent education to enhance student protective factors.

As reported by the American Foundation for Suicide Prevention (AFSP, 2022a), an alarming 90% of those who died by suicide had a diagnosable mental health condition at the time of death. Additionally, in 2019, nearly 9% of youth in grades nine to 12 reported that they had made at least one suicide attempt in the past 12 months. Female students (11%) attempted suicide almost twice as often as male students (6.6%), and American Indian or Alaska Native students reported the highest rate of attempts (25.5%), with White students at 8%. Youth aged 15 to 24 had a suicide rate of 13.95 per 100,000, and suicide was reported as the second leading cause of death for individuals aged 10 to 34. Suicide was particularly high for nonheterosexual individuals, such as LGBTQIA+, in which 42% considered suicide, and 52% of LGBTQIA+ youth who identify as transgender or nonbinary had suicidal ideation (NAMI, 2022).

When assessing for suicide risk, it is important for the counselor to ask direct questions and to assume that they may be the only one doing so (AFSP, 2022b). In other words, the counselor should not trust that someone else will notice and help the individual. It is important for the counselor to take all threats seriously. Some people fear that asking about a person's intent to kill themselves will place the idea in their head. This is a myth. Dazzi et al. (2014) found that talking about suicide did not significantly increase suicidal thoughts in adults and adolescents; in fact, acknowledging and talking about suicide reduced suicidal ideation. It is important for the counselor to directly ask the individual if they are considering suicide or have thoughts about ending their life. Not all individuals with depression or other mental health issues will try to end their life, but most people who complete suicide are suffering from a mental health illness. Assessing for suicide risk in students includes questions about any plans to kill themselves, as well as assessing for lethal weapons in the home, including firearms, rope, knives, and medications. Some warning signs of suicidal ideation are previous suicide attempts and statements about wanting to die (including more subtle statements such as giving up, wanting things to end, feeling like they should never have been born, etc.). The individual also may have a sudden increase in energy, giving away prized possessions, purchasing a gun or stockpiling pills. It is important for counselors to ask these questions in a supportive, nonjudgmental way, letting the person know that the counselor cares about them but not trying to convince them that life is worth living, given that they may have already convinced themselves that it is not (Curtin & Heron, 2019).

It is essential for the counselor to stay with the at-risk student until help arrives. Some school counselors may feel confident handing the student over to their families, while others will make sure the student goes to the hospital or other mental health facility. Safety plans are a common intervention in which the student at risk signs a contract or coconstructs a plan that outlines what they plan to do the next time they think about suicide (Stanley & Brown, 2008). These steps may include calling/texting a crisis line, letting a parent know, or going to the nearest emergency room. These "no-suicide" contracts, however, have not been shown to be clinically effective (McMyler & Pryjmachuk, 2008). What they may provide the student is needed resources and the ability to speak to the counselor about their thinking.

In addition to having clear procedures in place to assess for suicide risk, school counselors also need to know what to do after a student has attempted suicide or is released from the hospital. Reintegration plans should be a part of the school's crisis plans and may require continuing assessments of the student and check-ins with the school counselor, securing student permission to consult with their community mental health provider, and regular communication with the student's family. Follow-up care after hospitalization has been shown to be critical in preventing suicides. For example, follow-up 1 week after discharge from a hospitalization can reduce the risk of suicide by half over the next 6 months (Fontanella et al., 2020). School counselors can provide this follow-up as well as help to coordinate care for students with medical and psychiatric clinicians.

The school crisis plan should also document procedures in case of a suicide completion, including how the school will respond to students, families, and the community (AFSP & Suicide Prevention Resource Center, 2018). Suicides may occur in clusters in communities around the same time, and there are guidelines for how to report the suicide and what language to use that won't encourage others. Plans should also include considerations regarding how to honor the student who died without sensationalizing the suicide and inadvertently encouraging copycat behaviors.

Given the rates of suicide ideation and completion, school counselors should be vigilant in helping students who have been identified to be at risk, with special attention given to those who have had previous attempts. Individual counseling (Tier 3) with students may take the form of cognitive behavioral therapy to challenge negative thinking, which has shown success in reducing suicidality (Brodsky et al., 2018). Other successful therapy includes behavioral strategies of emotional regulation and distress tolerance from dialectical behavior therapy (McCauley et al., 2018). It is important to keep in mind that most individuals who attempt suicide are not interested in killing themselves, but rather to just make the pain go away. School counselors can work with students to teach helpful coping skills in order to challenge and accept painful thoughts and feelings. Within the scope of all crisis counseling, prevention, and intervention, a strong emphasis must be placed on being culturally sensitive and competent.

MULTICULTURAL COMPETENCIES AND ADVOCACY

Cultural competence is defined by Clark and colleagues (1989) in their seminal work as a set of congruent behaviors, attitudes, and policies that come together in a system, agency, or among professionals that enable that system, agency, or those professions to work effectively in cross-cultural situations. The term *cultural* is used because it encompasses patterns of human behavior, including thoughts, communication style, actions, customs, beliefs, values, and institutions of a racial, ethnic, religious, or social group. The term *competence*"implies the capacity to function effectively.

Cultural competence requires an understanding of the historical, social, and political events that affect the mental health of culturally diverse groups. An emphasis in this area stems from the desire to provide effective mental health services to an increasingly ethnic and culturally diverse society. It is important to recognize that everyone impacted by a crisis fundamentally functions on three levels. First, they are an individual. They have idiosyncratic differences that reflect personal resources, strengths, weaknesses, and challenges that make sufficiently supporting them a distinct enterprise. Second, they are a member of social groups that influence their beliefs, values, traditions, and language. It is important to understand how a crisis affects the specific needs within a group because there are variances. Finally, they are part of the overall school community, composed of humans. The causes and effects of trauma usually affect people in similar ways, but it requires training to determine how best to meet varying needs. Multicultural and social justice interventions in the aftermath of a crisis, for example, consider the strengths and resources of each of these levels and work within the social frameworks to deliver mental health services that align with a group's customs, norms, and core values.

Clark et al. (1989) identify five essential elements that contribute to an institution's ability to become more culturally competent. These include the focus on diversity, self-assessment regarding cultural capacity, awareness of cultural dynamics, and knowledge of institutionalized culture and systems of oppression. It is also important for the school counselor to have examined and developed a sense of service delivery, both responsive and preventive, that reflects an understanding of cultural norms, diversity, oppression, and advocacy (Clark et al., 1989).

Based on the Multicultural and Social Justice Cultural Competencies Framework (Ratts et al., 2016), Ratts and Greenleaf (2017) proposed a school counseling leadership model that lends itself well to implementing a culturally competent crisis response. Leadership is a key aspect of coordinating successful crisis interventions. According to their framework, school counselors should be competent in navigating all levels of the ecological model, including intrapersonal, interpersonal, institutional, community, public policy, and international spheres of influence. The intrapersonal sphere of influence refers to the values, beliefs, and behaviors of individual students. Interpersonal spheres refer to the friends, family, and peers that influence students through direct interactions. Institutional spheres pertain to institutions, such as schools and workplaces, that influence students directly and indirectly through their policies and practices. The community sphere of influence refers norms, values, and customs embedded within the community that directly and indirectly influence the student. Public policy refers to the larger societal rules and laws that influence a student. The international sphere pertains to how global politics and events impact students' lives. This multilevel framework for leadership contextualizes school counselor leadership around these spheres of influence, thus providing counselors with a clearer direction for assessing situations and constructing interventions. School counselor crisis interventions will occur at the intrapersonal, institutional, and community levels. However, preemptive planning can also include the public policy sphere and a close eye on the global/international levels, the latter potentially setting the stage for crises to occur at a local level.

This framework encourages school counselors to consider crisis interventions with individual students and with the people, institutions, community norms, societal rules, and global issues influencing students' beliefs and behaviors. The ecological framework also helps school counselors focus their attention broadly, while clarifying where feasible interventions can be made or where resources may be lacking. For example, it may become apparent from an ecological perspective that interventions with individual students are made more effective by first using guidance curriculum lessons in the classroom.

The Multicultural and Social Justice Leadership Form (MSJLF), developed by Ratts and Greenleaf (2017) to help school counselors frame a multicultural–social justice concern, offers additional guidelines for a crisis response. The form provides a step-by-step guide to address multicultural and social justice issues affecting students in school. In the event of a crisis, these steps can be modified to help school counselors identify how different student groups are affected differently by a multicultural–social justice issue, and how to respond more contextually.

The following steps provide a framework for a multicultural–social justice response to a crisis situation:

1. Describe the multicultural–social justice issue: Explore how the crisis may be connected to a larger multicultural or social justice issue. Many crises, for example, take place within specific communities more frequently than others.
2. Counselor self-awareness: School counselors must be cognizant of how their values, beliefs, and biases influence their perception of the crisis and its relationship to multicultural or social justice issues.
3. Client worldview: Less encumbered by their own worldview, self-aware school counselors can more readily see the world through their students' cultural frames of reference. This requires, as well, an understanding of students' cultural values, beliefs, and biases and an awareness of the relevance of social group identities (e.g., race, gender, sexual orientation, class status).
4. Counseling relationship: Combining the school counselor's self-awareness and their less-biased understanding of the student's worldview, allows the school counselor to better understand how issues of culture, identities, and the dynamics of power and privilege influence the relationship between the school counselor and student.
5. Counseling and advocacy interventions: When school counselors understand how the counseling relationship is influenced by their self-awareness and the student's worldview, they can make more informed decisions about culturally appropriate crisis interventions.

No matter what the situation, school counselors should be mindful of social and cultural contexts within crisis prevention and intervention. School counselors can use the socioecological model to determine whether individual counseling, advocacy, or a combination of the two is needed. The socioecological model contextualizes students' problems at the intrapersonal (e.g., individual attitudes, beliefs, and attributes), interpersonal (e.g., family, friends, and colleagues), institutional (e.g., school, churches, and businesses), community (e.g., spoken and unspoken values and norms in society), public policy (e.g., rules, laws, and policies), and global/international (e.g., world affairs) levels. These socioecological systems can both directly and indirectly influence the development of a crisis.

VOICES FROM THE FIELD

Name: Taylor Meyer (they/them)

Where You Practice: Tacoma School District, Tacoma, Washington

Professional Job Title: High School Counselor

Bio: Taylor is in their 10th year as a school counselor. Taylor has worked with elementary students, alternative high school students, and traditional high school students. Taylor is passionate about supporting students and building relationships. They focus a great deal of their work on and are experts in supporting students through grief and loss.

Pronouns: they/them

I have basically spent the last 10 years working with students and communities who experience a great deal of crisis. I can think of so many times in my 10-year career that I sat in my office for hours with a student who was experiencing crisis and trauma. I have learned that it is so important to have the willingness, training, and ability to sit with trauma. School counselors are called to do many things and wear many hats; what I love about this job! You must be willing to be present and available for the students when there is a crisis. You can often feel the pressure in schools to focus particularly on systems support, or meetings, or even lunchroom duty. However, sometimes, a crisis will need to be your main, and maybe only, focus. Learning to prioritize and balance all of the competing priorities of a school counselor in order to place the crisis as the sole focus is an important skill set.

When I think of crisis prevention, I think of big systems and systemic advocacy. Prevention is SO important! This can look like anything from catching a student(s) need through needs assessments, working with the teacher providing Tier 1 services, and using early warning systems of notifications. It is important to watch for school patterns and trends and address those early on with students, parents, and teachers. I ask myself constantly how can I can work with my school partners in the school system to promote the mental/emotional health and wellness of students and staff? I think it is important for emerging school counselors, and myself, to remember that crisis prevention and intervention isn't just the counselor's job. It is the job of the whole system. Continued collaboration and professional development is vital.

My role in crisis prevention as a high school counselor can sometimes feel all encompassing. I think that currently I am at least at a 60% responsive services level. Currently, my students have a wide range of social and emotional concerns. These concerns range from depression, suicide ideation and planning, sexual assault, physical abuse, and mental health/addiction concerns. One thing I do a lot of, after sitting with the student in their crisis and trying to support them, is linking them to community resources as needed. This may include law enforcement and child protective services.

I have learned to manage vicarious trauma throughout my career. As my career has progressed, I have been able to recognize the effects and process through them more completely. School counselors need to buffer themselves in order to carry pieces of others' trauma. I do this through healthy habits, processing with friends, and therapy. Lately, I have appreciated feeling a little more tender and raw around trauma and perhaps more impacted than in the past. However, this has allowed me to support students with genuine and authentic compassion and care. It is key to find the balance between feeling engulfed in the trauma of others and becoming desensitized. Neither is what the student needs.

To the new school counselor, I would say CONSULT, CONSULT, CONSULT!!! You should not make decisions in a vacuum and put the weight the student's world on your shoulders. Remember self-care, being present, setting boundaries, and that the focus is on the student. Lean into the fact that you are the person, maybe the only person, showing up for the student.

When you are sitting with a student in crisis and they have trusted you enough to share the hardest thing they ever have to talk about, it feels like a spiritual moment. This part of the job is an honor and privilege. You may be the only person the student has ever spoken to about their crisis and trauma. You have the ability to interact with them in a compassionate and supportive way and impact their level of emotional and physical safety. There is a connectedness to the student and to the work in those moments that are indescribable. It is hard, hard work, but getting to do the work of supporting the student through crisis is powerful.

SUMMARY AND CONCLUSION

School counselors do not operate in a vacuum. They are constantly communicating with all stakeholders, bridging gaps, and ensuring that all parties are heard and valued. Consultation and collaboration in the context of crisis prevention and intervention highlights the importance of responding to students with intensive needs or who are at risk of causing harm to themselves or others. School counselors collaborate with teachers to understand behaviors observed in the classroom. They collaborate with parents to understand the student's issues at home. Most importantly, they meet with students in individual sessions to hear and understand from the student what is going on. School counselors may collaborate with community therapists and healthcare workers, with student and possibly parent permissions, to further understand and develop appropriate interventions for at-risk students.

Consultations may be necessary to inform school counselors of next steps during crisis situations. They may need to consult with supervisors and community providers for suggestions regarding how to help particular students or with experts from professional associations. Consultations are especially important when assessing safety and risk of violence. These consultations may include feedback from law enforcement and professional organizations that focus on threat assessment.

All crisis prevention and intervention efforts need to intentionally address culture and show multicultural and social justice competence. Effectiveness in doing this requires a personal awareness of the school counselor's attitudes and beliefs, understanding how culture affects beliefs and behaviors, ensuring equitable access to resources, and delivering culturally sensitive counseling. Individuals are often unaware of their own biases, so it's important for school counselors to continually assess their beliefs, to consult with others, and to complete appropriate and continuous professional development trainings. School counselors should remember they are not alone in providing crisis intervention and prevention.

CASE STUDY

Another school counselor calls you from the district where you both work to check in with you about how the summer went; school starts in a week. The other school counselor says, "Isn't that sad what happened to Samuel." Samuel was a student on your caseload the previous year. He was a second-grader and was moving into the third grade. You had developed a strong therapeutic alliance with Samuel, and he was making progress in his behaviors as they related to school in counseling. You ask the other school counselor, "What happened to Samuel?" She said, "Oh no, you don't know! He was killed in a car accident in the middle of the summer." The news shocks and saddens you.

DISCUSSION QUESTIONS

1. What is the first step?
2. Who would you address (how, why, when)?
3. What would you say?
4. What are the immediate crisis responses needed?
5. What are the long-term crisis responses needed?

PRACTICAL APPLICATION

- Be a visible, supportive presence for all in the schools.
- Develop active partnerships with community mental health providers.
- Gain competence in regularly assessing students for harm.
- Advocate for and participate in a robust crisis intervention school/community team.
- Integrate social and emotional prevention into classroom curriculum.
- Be aware of state reporting requirements for involuntary commitments.
- Practice self-care and be on guard for compassion fatigue.

KEY REFERENCES

Only key references appear in the print edition. The full reference list appears in the digital product on Springer Publishing Connect: connect.springerpub.com/content/book/978-0-8261-8753-6/part/part03/chapter/ch11

American Foundation for Suicide Prevention, & Suicide Prevention Resource Center (2018). *After a suicide: A toolkit for schools* (2nd ed.). Education Development Center. https://www.sprc.org/resources-programs/after-suicide-toolkit-schools

Lambie, G. W., Stickl Haugen, J., Borland, J. R., & Campbell, L. O. (2019). Who took "counseling" out of the role of rrofessional school counselors in the United States? *Journal of School-Based Counseling Policy and Evaluation, 1*(3), 51–61. https://doi.org/10.25774/7kjb-bt85

National Alliance on Mental Illness. (2022, February). *Mental health by the numbers.* https://www.nami.org/mhstats

Ratts, M. J., & Greenleaf, A. T. (2017). Multicultural and social justice counseling competencies. *Professional School Counseling, 21.* https://doi.org/10.1177/2156759X18773582

Ratts, M. J., Singh, A. A., Nassar-McMillan, S., Butler, S. K., & McCullough, J. R. (2016). Multicultural and social justice counseling competencies: Guidelines for the counseling profession. *Journal of Multicultural Counseling and Development, 44*(1), 28–48. https://doi.org/10.1002/jmcd.12035

PART IV

School Counselors as Leaders for Student Success

CHAPTER 12

Advocacy for Safer Schools for LGBTQ+ Students

LISA LINNEA NELSON, MELANIE BIKIS, COURTNEY CONACHAN, MICHELLE MCMILLAN, SHELBY HAWKINSON, SAM RUNCKEL, AND RAFE MCCULLOUGH

LEARNING OBJECTIVES

After reading this chapter, students will be able to:

- Recognize concerns facing LGBTQ+ students.
- Modify school practices to be more inclusive to LGBTQ+ students.
- Employ best practices that create safe spaces for all students, specifically LGBTQ+ students.

STUDENT VOICE

Student "R.J." (an eighth-grade student who identifies as a gay, White, trans male, who uses he/him pronouns) provided the following testimonial about his experiences with school counselors:

"A good experience I've had with a school counselor happened in sixth grade. When I wasn't out to the general public, I was talking to her and I remember being pretty upset about an incident that had happened. There was this room that had a themed game day each week. One day was for boys only. Even though I never explicitly said I was a girl and hadn't been dressing feminine or anything, I tried to walk in and the guy at the front door said, "No, come back on Friday when it's girl's day." When I told my school counselor about it, she asked how it made me feel, and I told her that I felt disrespected and not seen. She asked me what I identified as, and I told her, I think I'm a guy. I'm pretty sure I am a guy. So we worked together for a while to figure out how to safely express my pronouns and my identity to the people around me. That is when we started working together to come up with a plan to come out to my mother. I was nervous because she was the first adult that I successfully came out to. I tried to come out in late elementary school and say, "Hey, I'm trans," but I was really quickly shut down by the adults and volunteers in my life. So having her [school counselor] actually respect that and understand that and say, "Hey, no, it's not just a phase," I felt seen and I felt really good. My advice for school counselors who are working with LGBTQ+ students would be to not make assumptions! Even if you identify as something in the gay community, experiences are different for everyone. Ask questions where questions are needed. Always ask! You may have had one experience, but a kid that you're talking to could have a completely different experience."

INTRODUCTION: LGBTQ+ IDENTITIES AND SCHOOL CLIMATE

Deepening your knowledge base can help build rapport with LGBTQ+ youth and families and serve to develop practical skills necessary to provide culturally responsive and affirming care. Universal narratives concerning the gender binary and heteronormative culture act as an oppressive force (Lugones, 2020), threatening the well-being of LGBTQ+ youth. A blanketed assumption of cisgender or heterosexual identities diminishes sexual and gender diversity and reinforces "othering" rather than creating a safe and inclusive space for all. School counselors act as system change agents, creating environments that promote and support a full spectrum of student identity and, ultimately, student success (American School Counselor Association [ASCA], 2019). It is important to remain open to the changing cultural landscapes as they form, knowing that a sense of gender, sexuality, and identity is an unfolding development for many. These are not linear, but more circular, meaning some students may feel like they haven't yet arrived at "the end" of understanding who they truly are.

The LGBTQ+ acronym is an umbrella term used to describe a rich collection of identities. The acronym represents diverse and distinct communities of people joined by a gender and sexuality alliance. The intricacies of gender and sexuality can vastly vary from person to person. Before fully unpacking the LGBTQ+ umbrella, it is important to know the difference between gender and sexuality. School counselors should demonstrate knowledge and respect for students based on sexual orientation and gender identity (ASCA, 2019).

Gender

Gender exists along a spectrum beyond the male-female binary. *Gender identity* is a person's innermost sense of self. *Gender expression* is the outward display of gender through attributes such as hair style, adornment, voice, and personal demeanor, for instance, mannerisms and interests. Gender identity and gender expression are not interchangeable terms because the former is an internal sense, whereas the latter is an external expression. *Cisgender* is identifying with the gender matching the sex assigned at birth. *Transgender* may encompass individuals who have a gender identity that is not aligned with the sex they were assigned at birth. *Nonbinary* is an umbrella term for many identities (e.g., *genderqueer, genderfluid, androgynous, pangender, gender nonconforming*) to reflect a person who does not identify or self-express according to a gender binary. Nonbinary individuals may also identify as multiple genders or no gender.

Sexual/Affectional Orientation

Sexual and affectional orientation refer to a person's sexual, romantic, or emotional attraction to others. Like gender identity, many of these terms continue to evolve as individuals self-identify with terms that feel affirming to them. In creating safe spaces for LGBTQ+ youth, it is crucial to avoid oversexualizing identity. Some more familiar terms may include lesbian, gay, bisexual, or queer. Individuals may also identify as *questioning, asexual, aromantic, pansexual,* or *omnisexual*. The "+" is representative of the many identities not fully represented in an acronym; it acknowledges the eclectic richness of the LGBTQ+ communities. It is important to ask students how they identify and what their identity means for them so school counselors better understand how to provide affirming support.

Gender Pronouns

Gender pronouns reflect a person's gender identity. There are many sets of pronouns to be aware of such as they/them. Some pronouns, such as thon/thons/thonself and ne/nis/nir, originated in the 1800s (McGaughey, 2020). A new category of pronouns, called neopro-nouns, used in place of she, he, or they, have been recently introduced. While there is not a standard neopronoun set as of now, there are a few commonly used sets. Some examples include ze/hir and xe/xem. Outside of a dominant White cultural lens, gender in many cultures is less static and binary, and counselors may find that indigenous students, or students of other cultural groups may have a different relationship with pronouns and gender based on their unique cultural identity.

Approximately 25% of LGBTQ+ youth use pronouns outside the gender binary (The Trevor Project, 2020). A 2018 worldwide gender census indicated that 24% of respondents felt comfortable using neopronouns, especially if neopronouns were socially accepted and used properly (McGaughey, 2020). Failing to accurately use a student's pronouns can harm the counseling relationship. It is our ethical duty to contribute to a safe, respectful, and inclusive school culture demonstrating respect and civility (ASCA, 2019). If a mistake is made in using pronouns correctly, simply correct the mistake and move forward without transmitting unnecessary guilt, shame, overexplaining, or bringing more attention to the situation than is needed. Practicing affirming language and actions around pronoun use is important; it begins with modeling culturally affirming language, "I use they/them pronouns. What are your pronouns?"

Intersectional Identities

Intersectionality is a framework for understanding that shows how different identities inform different values, beliefs, and lived experiences. Identity extends beyond gender and sexuality to also include race, social class, disability, family structure, spirituality, and appearance, among many others. School counselors should not examine one aspect of identity without considering others (Crenshaw, 2017), and students must be supported through an inclusive lens that considers all their identities in multiple contexts. For instance, queer and trans students of color and disabled queer and trans students may need additional support because they have been historically marginalized in school systems along multiple aspects of their identities. Queer and trans students of color may experience racism in LGBTQ+ spaces, and disabled queer and trans students may also feel unwelcome in spaces with nondisabled students, even if they purport to be openly supportive of LGBTQ+ students. School counselors should help students recognize how multiple identities interact to create unique and complex lived experiences. Discussing what external and internal factors may be shaping students' perceptions and personal presentations can build a strong connection while offering an opportunity to explore students' unique intersectional experience and cultural influence.

A strong therapeutic relationship with students is informed by intersecting identities with dynamics of power, privilege, and oppression. Developing a keen awareness of self, students' worldview, the counseling relationship, and effective counseling interventions to implement will allow development of a deeper understanding of intersectionality and build a multicultural and social justice competence (Ratts et al., 2016). Intersectionality acknowledges the compounded impact of experiencing social oppression based on multiple marginalized identities rather than a singular marginalized identity (Nye, 2021), for example, in the case of bilingual, queer, and trans students of color with disabilities. An ethical school counselor must know and understand policies affecting students and enhance their support networks, wraparound services, and educational teams to best meet the needs of students with intersecting marginalized identities (ASCA, 2019). Counselors should be aware of and recognize traits of the dominant culture, their own culture, and other cultures, and understand how they negotiate their own identity in multiple spaces (Learning for Justice, 2022a). School counselors should reflect on their own intersecting identities and how presentation of self may impact the therapeutic climate and outcomes.

School Climate for LGBTQ+ Students

School counselors strive to develop cultural sensitivity, a set of skills enabling an understanding of the similarities and differences between others, in the delivery of counseling programs that may best support the needs of diverse groups (ASCA, 2019). To a large degree, gender and sexuality are social constructs defined and perceived through a culturally created lens. Gender is a thread interwoven with other social constructs of identity; thus, it cannot be extracted or isolated from other aspects of culture, and it is therefore considered within a broader cultural landscape. Social constructs of gender create an illusion of hierarchy, producing inequalities intersecting with a variety of other marginalizing factors such as social status, cultural inclusion, access to care, and economic advancement (World Health Organization, 2022). School counselors understand and address the impact of cultural, social, and environmental influences on student opportunity (ASCA, 2019).

On a national level, the Gay Lesbian and Straight Education Network (GLSEN) is at the forefront of school climate research and school-based interventions. Every 2 years, GLSEN conducts a nationwide school climate survey that highlights the experiences of LGBTQ+ youth in U.S. middle and high schools. GLSEN is a great resource for creating your own safe school. The survey indicates that safer and more inclusive school climates include supportive educators, LGBTQ-inclusive curriculum of both history and sex education, inclusive and supportive policies, and supportive student groups, such as Gender and Sexuality Alliances and Equity Clubs (GLSEN, 2022). Schools with comprehensive antibullying/antiharassment policies were less likely to receive negative remarks about gender expression and more likely to receive reports of staff intervening against hate speech.

In 2019, GLSEN found that the vast majority of LGBTQ+ students (86.3%) experienced harassment or assault, with many avoiding gender-segregated spaces in school such as bathrooms (42.5%) and locker rooms (43.7%), and most reported avoiding school functions (77.6%) and extracurricular activities (71.8%) because they felt unsafe or uncomfortable. Based on their gender expression, 56.9% of LGBTQ+ students experienced verbal harassment, 21.8% experienced physical harassment, and 9.5% experienced physical assault (GLSEN, 2020). Students who experienced higher levels of victimization based on their gender expression were much more likely to miss school and receive disciplinary measures, earn lower GPAs, report lower levels of self-esteem and school belonging, and have higher levels of depression (GLSEN, 2020).

Alarmingly, 36.5% of gender-diverse students reported nonattendance because they felt unsafe or uncomfortable with school policies (GLSEN, 2020). Schools with gender-affirming policies protected students' name and pronoun choices and use of bathrooms and locker rooms aligning with gender; as a result, students demonstrated increased attendance and reported feeling greater belonging at their school (GLSEN, 2020). Lewis and Sembiante warn that the presence of a policy doesn't guarantee the implementation (2019). "Although policies are present, stakeholders and administrators are seldom informed of their existence, are inadequately trained to implement these faithfully, and often fail to execute these in practice" (Lewis & Sembiante, 2019, p. 6). Actively enforcing comprehensive and inclusive policies and procedures schoolwide is especially important for queer trans youth of color and youth with disabilities.

Lewis and Sembiante state, "LGBTQ+ students in middle school face more hostility, experience more victimization, and have less access to supportive resources than peers in high school environments" (2019, p. 7). GLSEN's survey reported that transgender students experience more hostile school experiences than LGBTQ+ cisgender and nonbinary students, with nonbinary students reporting more hostile experiences than cisgender students (2020). Remember that "a hostile school climate affects students' academic success and mental health. LGBTQ+ students who experience victimization and discrimination at school have worse educational outcomes and poorer psychological well-being" (GLSEN, 2020, p. 6).

GLSEN's national survey found that 56.6% of LGBTQ+ students who were harassed or assaulted did not report the incident, mostly due to doubt that the school would reprimand or fear of abuse worsening, while 60.5% reporting students said that schools did nothing in response or directed student to ignore it (2020). These statistics highlight the need for professional development to educate staff on data and intervention strategies. Some states require districts to incorporate schoolwide antibullying training, including cyberbullying, and to create task forces for implementing antibullying/antiharassment initiatives (Oregon Department of Education, 2020). Rands (2013) states, "establishing policies that prohibit harassment, bullying, and discrimination related to gender identity and gender expression is a crucial first step. However, creating truly supportive environments requires schools to go beyond reactive steps to proactive and pervasive changes at all levels of education and across all aspects of schooling" (p. 107).

After 20 years of research, GLSEN has found many interventions and resources that schools can provide to promote a safer and more inclusive school climate. Furthermore, there was an increase in reporting victimization juxtaposed with less hate speech overall (GLSEN, 2020). GLSEN's recommendations include developing comprehensive bullying and harassment policies, providing professional development for school staff, increasing the number of supportive educators, supporting student affinity clubs, and developing LGBTQ+ inclusive curriculum. If you are interested in learning more about LGBTQ+ students, some states have independent research available. Research whether your state is gathering and tracking data, as each state is unique. A good place to begin research is your state's Department of Education website.

THE ROLE OF THE SCHOOL COUNSELOR

A school counselor's role is multifaceted, yet always student centered. The inner work of counseling grows from a development of personhood and philosophy and extends to the outer work of becoming a culturally competent leader, advocate, and provider to all LGBTQ+ students. A school counselor identifies ways to seek more knowledge and training to best serve students, leveraging their education to create pathways to educational reform, systemic change, and transformed student experiences. School counselors play both a preventative role and a responsive role in creating safe spaces for LGBTQ+ youth. School counselors nurture relationships in a way that shows students they are supported as learners and deeply cared for as people.

Counselor Personhood

An effective school counselor is genuine and authentic. Success with students does not always equate to having all skills necessary to support every student, but it does require reflection as to whether you can fully support a student's unique experiences and exercise good judgment for referrals and additional services beyond your scope of expertise (Chang et al., 2018). A school counselor creates an affirming space by strengthening their therapeutic alliance. They emphasize building therapeutic rapport and supporting students through a lens of unconditional positive regard, inspiring a curiosity to learn, stay engaged, and grow through a nurturing environment. A school counselor creates positive engagement through building relationships that affirm all aspects of a students' identity and culture.

Cultivating Resilience

Cultivating resilience is critical in supporting LGBTQ+ students. Research shows that resilient youth have at least one affirming relationship with an adult role model who positively influenced their sense of self and potential (Thomsen, 2002). School counselors shape resilient students by providing opportunities for meaningful participation, leadership, developing boundaries through community agreements, and communicating high expectations for success (Henderson & Milstein, 1996).

Cultivating resilience is empowering students to discover the seeds of resilience sprouting from every adversity. Affirming students is highlighting the strengths they possess to overcome challenges. While an awareness of oppression is inherent to resilience, school counselors focus on growing students' sense of insight, self-worth, strong community support, and hope (Singh et al., 2011). Spotlight strengths of trans students who likely experience higher rates of trauma due to cultural discrimination and identify ways to bolster their support systems (Chang et al., 2018). Emphasize students' strengths and agency and collaborate with students to understand and help them navigate challenges. Our ethical obligation is to recognize student strengths and setbacks as information guiding our course of professional action (ASCA, 2019). Highlight the beauty of LGBTQ+ communities because there are so many benefits to reclaiming identity with a sense of joy and pride!

Advocates and Change Agents

School counselors are advocates and change agents (ASCA, 2019). There is much in the way of advocacy for LGBTQ+ students that needs to be facilitated in schools. Advocacy is enabling students to learn how to increase their own ability to believe in and advocate for themselves. Advocacy is helping underserved students develop essential skills, confidence, and a sense of empowerment to make meaning of and navigate through marginalizing situations (Stone & Dahir, 2016). Advocacy assumes a critical view of systems and practices, challenging the status quo, and confronting rules and regulations that interfere with students' quality of education. School counselors are uniquely positioned within the education system to serve as a channel of information for evolving practices in pursuit of justice (Lee & Rodgers, 2009).

Comprehensive Counseling Program

Establishing a comprehensive counseling program with current best practices is essential for creating safe schools for LGBTQ+ students. A strong knowledge of the American School Counseling Association's National Model (2019) and the Learning for Justice's Social Justice Standards Model (2022b) facilitate the delivery of a comprehensive school-counseling program that provides outstanding and equitable counseling services to all students. Using the ASCA's Professional Standards and Competencies and Ethical Standards for School Counselors (2019) guides thoughtful and intentional support services. These standards and competencies summarize the mindsets and behaviors that school counselors must develop to optimally serve students. A school counselor's mindsets, ethics, and philosophies will influence their design and delivery of a culturally affirming comprehensive school-counseling program. A comprehensive schoolcounseling program includes schoolwide systems for all students and staff.

Including LGBTQ+ history in curriculum, discussing culturally affirming peer relationship practices, enforcing antibias/antibullying philosophy for education around Title 9 policies, and exploring the Learning for Justice (2022b) standards are a few examples of schoolwide systems of support that can positively change the landscape of LGBTQ+ students' academic experiences.

Learning for Justice (2022b) created the framework for Social Justice Standards, divided into the four domains of identity, diversity, justice, and action. Taken together, these domains represent a continuum of engagement in antibias, multicultural, and social justice education. The standards emphasize that knowledge and skills related to both prejudice reduction and collective action are necessary social and emotional learnings. This can serve as an anchor for your counseling philosophy and provide a framework for psychoeducation and intervention services. The goal is for the Social Justice Standards to become personal attributes that have evolved into actions developed and demonstrated throughout your comprehensive counseling program. The Social Justice Standards are verbs intended to be exercised throughout every moment in your role as a counselor.

Using technology to illustrate the impact of a comprehensive school-counseling program is a powerful skill. Collecting and analyzing needs-assessment data will enable you to serve your school community with intentionality. In collaboration and consultation with your team of educators, aim to close opportunity gaps by leveraging data in a way that results in improving school policies and programs, maximizing student benefit. Student data in combination with state and national research, offers a broader presentation of LGBTQ+ experiences and effective ways to respond. Data should always be further demographically disaggregated so that school counselors can get a clear picture of which students may need more or different support. At the school level, data-driven practices include school climate surveys completed by students and analyzing student records of attendance, grades, discipline, and so on.

Data Considerations

- How are your LGBTQ+ students' needs different?
- What impacts are your intentions having on students?
- What types of assessments are you using, and is the data being disaggregated to reflect intersections of LGBTQ+ identities?
- How are you curating and targeting specific programs and outcomes?
- Are you collecting students' response surveys on school climate and culture, sense of belonging, school systems and policies, equity and inclusion, and a culturally responsive environment?
- How do other identities within the LGBTQ+ communities interact with the collection of data (e.g., bilingual or disabled students)?
  Example Survey Questions for Students:
  - Are teachers properly using your pronouns?
  - Do you feel like your identity is respected and valued?
  - Do you see yourself reflected in the curriculum?
  - Is the school designed with you in mind?
  - What would you like us to know so that we can better support you?

Example Categories for Assessment

- Cultural awareness and action
- Diversity and inclusion
- School climate (what are perceptions of the overall social and learning climate of school?)
- School safety (what are perceptions of student physical and psychological safety at school?)
- Sense of belonging (how much do students feel that they are valued members of the school community?)
- Student engagement
- Student relationships
- Teacher–student relationships (how strong the social connection is between teachers and students and beyond the classroom?)
- Administration–student relationships (are interactions punitive or restorative?)
- Counselor–student relationships

(*Source*: Adapted from Portland Public Schools. [2020]. *PPS Successful Schools Survey*.)

As school counselors conduct surveys and needs assessments for supporting LGBTQ+ students, there are some important considerations to keep in mind. When conducting surveys, some students may not feel comfortable sharing their gender and sexual identity with staff or school administrators. Also, due to the ever-changing landscape of identity and language, many new terms are being created that can make it difficult for counselors to track and understand the data, and it becomes difficult to navigate decisions around multiple choice versus blank submissions. Using terms such as *gender diverse* or *gender expansive* offer a more inclusive option. Another consideration is that students with unsupportive families may not want to participate for fear of retribution, and students impacted by harassment may be struggling with disengagement and nonattendance. Counselors need to anticipate these barriers and plan accordingly.

Elevating Student Voice

Every student voice is a vital aspect of an inclusive school culture. A primary way to develop a student's sense of agency, value, and autonomy is through language (Hammond, 2015). Celebrate the power of student voice by integrating student voice into school design. Youth often possess a keen desire and responsibility for anchoring their expertise in their own lived experiences, offering ways to incorporate affirming practices with credible sourcing into educator training (Dennis et al., 2019). Centering student voices is equalizing, democratic, and transformational for students. When elevating student voices, school counselors should be keen observers and notice which voices are lifted and which are less likely to be heard within LGBTQ+ school communities. Historically, LGBTQ+ communities have struggled to acknowledge the intersectionality in their movements, so it is important to ensure that the voices of students of color, students with disabilities, and other multiply-marginalized students are fully represented. Let students know that their voices carry weight and that their perspective contributes to change by including them in a discussion process of how their voices will be considered (Hall, 2017).

Questions to Ask Yourself:

- How are you listening to LGBTQ+ students and elevating their voices?
- How are your school climate surveys assessing LGBTQ+ student voice and how are you responding? What about LGBTQ+ students of color? Are they feeling welcome in spaces designated as supports for LGBTQ+ students? Queer, disabled students?
- How is your school offering student leadership opportunities to LGBTQ+ students?

COUNSELING SPACE AND DESIGN

School counselors need to create warm and welcoming counseling spaces that send the message "This space was designed with *you* in mind." Too often, school spaces are seen as neutral, when they are representative of an educator's worldview of the dominant culture (Hammond, 2015). For instance, often spaces reflect a White, able-bodied, heteronormative cultural space, and many will deny the cultural perspective that is present. Students can tell when their cultural identities or life experiences are not being depicted in the space. Sometimes school counselors can tell whose culture is being reflected in the space by which students feel most comfortable accessing the counseling office.

A culturally responsive counselor shows effort to create an environment that communicates care, allyship, and belonging in ways that students recognize. A counseling space should be a visual reflection of the core values of learning and social justice principles. Place great value on the student attraction to school culture and accomplish this by creating an environment of which students desire to be a part. Some examples may include "safe space" stickers or pride flags, posters explaining appropriate usage of pronouns, posters that are reflective of diverse LGBTQ+ communities, or books about LGBTQ+ individuals, including other intersections of LGBTQ+ identity such as racial and ethnic minority individuals, disabled LGBTQ+ individuals, or LGBTQ+ individuals who are bilingual.

GENDER IDENTITY AND DEVELOPMENT

Gender identity development is a complex process that is influenced by an interweaving of nature, nurture, and culture (Sansfaçon et al., 2020). Gender identity is someone's internal sense of self, including labels such as agender, cisgender, transgender, man, woman, gender nonconforming, genderfluid, genderqueer, and more. While some children learn that there are many ways to identify, most are socialized to believe there are only two identifications: male and female.

Gender learning is a psychological and social process that takes many years, with most children developing the ability to label their own and others' genders by 2 years of age (Steensma et al., 2013). Gender identity development is internal, dynamic, and highly impacted by the youth's social environment. Children learn to understand themselves in gendered ways through interactions with others. This process of gender identity development and consolidation continues to evolve throughout life.

Erickson's psychosocial model outlines eight stages of development that a person negotiates throughout their life. The initiative versus guilt stage of development happens between the ages of 3 and 5. This is when a child learns how to do things on their own. A child who does not successfully navigate this stage may be left with feelings of guilt versus a sense of purpose (Erickson, 1980). Children at this stage may begin to express their gender identity differently. The family's acceptance or rejection of the youth's gender identity and expression are key factors in the youth's physical and mental health outcomes (Turban & Ehrensaft, 2018).

The industry versus inferiority stage of development spans young childhood through the initiation of puberty. Erickson highlighted the importance of social interactions as a child's social influences expand from the family to school and peers. Youth learn through these social interactions and develop feelings of confidence, or they may result in feelings of inadequacy. Gender-expansive children may struggle to understand and assert their gender identity. Children explore during this age and are equally impacted by their own feelings and emotional responses as well as the information and responses they receive from others (Sansfaçon et al., 2020).

Although some youth know their gender identity is different at a young age, others often develop this awareness at or after the onset of puberty. Sansfaçon and colleagues found that some youth experience distress or gender dysphoria before puberty but choose not to come out in childhood (2020). Puberty fits into Erickson's ego identity versus role confusion stage of development, which spans the ages of 12 to 18. Youth begin to negotiate their sense of identity separate from the expectations of others. Not only do youth continue to develop their gender identity, they also encounter challenges of puberty, changing environments at school, differing expectations from others, and the discovery of sexuality (Steensma et al., 2013). This can be a crucial time for youth as they develop an internal sense of gender and experiment with ways to authentically express and connect with it. Of equal importance are the interactions between the youth and their surrounding environments, which includes feedback they receive from others as they express and experiment with their gender. "Though it is common for trans youth to come out at puberty, for many this is not due to the 'late onset' of dysphoric feelings or understanding themselves as trans or nonbinary, it is the result of a long and difficult process toward accepting and understanding themselves in a social context where being trans is still a difficult reality" (Sansfaçon et al., 2020, p. 318).

It is important to note that Erickson's and others' models of development have their limitations. Some critics point out that these developmental models are rooted in Western and Eurocentric ideologies and present too linear a path of development. Recent studies and research show that gender identity development is not a linear process. It is an individual and complex experience that is highly impacted by social support, affirmation, acceptance, and rejection (Sansfaçon et al., 2020).

Supporting Trans and Nonbinary Students and Families

School counselors must develop an awareness of trans and nonbinary (TNB) student experiences to appropriately provide for TNB students and their families. Staying current with statistics regarding the experiences of TNB students enables counselors to be familiar with common hardships and be proactive in response to perpetuating traumas. Troubling statistics extend beyond a hostile school climate for TNB youth. In 2021, TNB youth reported attempts of suicide at half the rate of those who did not have their pronouns respected in their homes (The Trevor Project, n.d.). According to the *U.S. Transgender Survey*, hostile environments continue into adulthood (2015). Ten percent of transgender people reported family violence because of their gender identity. TNB people also experience higher levels of poverty, unemployment, and discrimination (James et al., 2015).

The disparities are even more disturbing for trans and nonbinary people of color experiencing higher levels of violence. This is especially true for trans women of color. School counselors' awareness, understanding, and advocacy for transgender and nonbinary students is a critical piece in ensuring students are cared for in the school community and positioned for a lifetime of success. Trans and nonbinary people who feel their identity is affirmed by their social surroundings have positive outcomes in their identity development, transition, and psychological well-being (American Psychological Association [APA], 2015).

Developing a lens of trans-affirming counseling begins with a foundational knowledge of the history of transgender people on a global scale (Singh & Dickey, 2017). Though trans and nonbinary people have a rich and colorful history in civil rights movements and various cultures around the globe, history in respect to TNB students in schools is still being made. In 2021, the U.S. Department of Education announced that discrimination based on sexual orientation and gender identity would be enforced as part of Title IX of the Education Amendments of 1972 (2021). At the time of this publication, 17 states have passed legislation prohibiting discrimination based on gender identity, yet only five states have written statutes that *specifically* address the treatment of TNB students (GLSEN, 2021). School counselors must be informed of both state and local-level legislation impacting TNB students and provide responsive care in the absence of legal and social support. If the policies in your locale are harmful or nonexistent, collaborate with local TNB-affirming organizations and implement support structures and policies to create safer schools for trans and nonbinary youth.

Supporting Students in Transition

Transitioning refers to the steps a TNB person takes to affirm their gender. They may adopt a different gender expression or presentation, use new pronouns, "come out" to friends and/or family, or change their name. Sometimes transition includes medical or surgical changes that affirm one's gender identity and expression. For older youth, medical avenues may include hormone blockers or use of hormones such as testosterone or estrogen. It is important to note that transition is a unique and personal experience for

TNB students. Some students may already be transitioning, and students often explore their gender and transition options at school. School counselors meet students where they are in their identity development without an agenda or judgment. Be cognizant of biases and preconceived expectations around what a "male" or "female" student looks like, and recognize that a student's identity may fall somewhere between or outside of the binary.

Be familiar with terms and procedures for students who are considering medical transitioning or changing their body to further affirm their gender identity. The University of California-San Francisco has an excellent guide that describes transition-related terms, hormone therapy, and different surgical options that your students may consider. If a student is interested in medical transitioning, explore options with students and families. School counselors should connect families to resources and referrals in the community.

As part of transition, and for students who identify as nonbinary, restroom and locker room use can be a big decision in discovering what feels comfortable and identity-affirming. Advocate for an all-gender student restroom option if possible, and at the very least, ensure the transgender and gender nonconforming (TGNC) student's choice in using either an adult-designated bathroom or a restroom they feel most closely aligns with their gender. Avoid making assumptions about what bathroom a student prefers, such as a trans-male student exclusively wanting to use the male restroom, because this may not be the case for a variety of reasons. As an example, a trans-male student may experience bullying using a boy's bathroom, and to avoid harassment, he may choose to use a restroom designated for females, despite the misalignment with his gender identity. Trans youth face difficult choices in spaces where individuals are separated by gender, and it is important for school counselors to understand the psychosocial ramifications. For example, trans youth may avoid using bathrooms at school by holding their urine until they can relieve themselves at home or refusing to eat or drink at school. These methods of compensation are damaging to youth's physical and mental health, and it is the school counselor's duty to respond by creating safe space solutions.

In your work as a school counselor, many students may wish to change their name and gender markers on school records. To meet these needs, many resources for schools and families are available online. For example, Gender Spectrum outlines a process for registering gender-diverse students, all of which are listed in the resources chapter. By using gender-affirming language, school counselors avoid further traumatization and create inclusive and supportive environments for LGBTQ+ youth.

TRANS-AFFIRMING COUNSELING

Becoming a trans-affirming counselor begins with a development of knowledge, attitudes, and essential skills shown to best support the specific needs of trans and nonbinary youth. Counselors with limited training and experience can unknowingly cause harm. Exploring multicultural and social justice approaches to counseling and the fundamental tenets developing multicultural counseling can benefit a therapeutic alliance with TNB students. A school counselor's ethical duty is to provide effective, culturally responsive counseling services to serve students' unique needs and to seek ongoing training and consultation to stay current with best practices as they evolve (ASCA, 2016). Counseling TNB students "may range from supportive to exploratory to deeper grief or trauma recovery work" (Chang et al., 2018, p. 72). Be open to whatever students want to discuss, whether it is related to their school experiences, family life, or social identities. A student's relationship with different aspects of their social locations may impact the trajectory of your counseling relationship and their primary needs.

Due to counselors lacking the skills and knowledge needed to work with TNB youth, families' lack of financial resources, or TNB youth living in a geographical area where mental health resources are scarce, TNB students who are struggling with mental health issues often face challenges in receiving ongoing counseling. This is especially true for TNB students who live in states or local regions where they are unsupported by local legislation or by the societal norms of that environment. Often, it is only with adult allies in a school building that students feel comfortable exploring their gender identity. School counselors must continuously strive to develop gender-affirming practices by exploring their own attitudes, beliefs, identity, and worldview (Ratts et al., 2016).

Responsive school counselors should expand their understanding and application of gender-affirming care through an exploration of how they perceive gender identity, gender expression, and gender role expectations, confronting and managing personal biases that could result in unethical and harmful counseling practices. Some negative counseling experiences that trans and nonbinary people have reported are "misunderstandings, lack of knowledge of TGNC [transgender and gender nonconforming] people, expressed personal bias, invalidations, and microaggressions"' (McCullough et al., 2017, p. 429).

It is important for school counselors to use language similar to that TNB students use for themselves. Mirroring their language helps students feel affirmed. Using affirming language also signals that you have knowledge regarding their experiences and that students can trust you as a safe person with whom to share (McCullough et al., 2017). In addition to affirming their identities, modeling how to address the student with respect to other members of the school community is essential. This signaling of support can be expressed through signage in the counseling space, sharing personal pronouns verbally or visually by wearing a pronoun pin, and respecting students and staff pronouns and names.

When working with students who express experiencing gender dysphoria, acknowledging its emotional weight will build your therapeutic alliance. You may be broaching an area of their life seldom discussed, and your response carries significant weight for a young person seeking support and understanding. Disclosures such as this occur only when there is a rich rapport and sense of safety. Gender-affirming counseling skills will be crucial in maintaining a strong relationship long-term.

TNB students thrive in environments where they can talk freely about their identity, challenges, fears, and desires. When given the opportunity to be in community with other LGBTQ+ students, TNB students have expressed feeling valued, seen, and respected. Building opportunities for connection fosters "resilience, liberation, and empowerment" (Singh, 2013, p. 698). School counselors must be knowledgeable regarding school climates experienced by TNB students, and invite TNB students to build their personal narratives of hope, resilience, and success. Sharing positive stories about TNB representation invokes a strong sense of belonging for students, who will feel empowered to pursue their own positive futures.

APPLICATION OF COUNSELING PRACTICES

It can be daunting for a new school counselor to start a schoolwide comprehensive plan that directly looks at improving the experiences of LGBTQ+ students. This section outlines elements for supporting LGBTQ+ students, including in a comprehensive school-counseling program. School counselors do not need to recreate the wheel, so be sure to check the resource chapter, which includes links, resources, and sample documents for working with LGBTQ+ youth.

Individual Counseling

School counselors should deliver counseling services based on counseling theories and techniques shown to be effective in supporting LGBTQ+ students. Counseling services should be offered during times of increased stress, change, crisis, or any situation that may interfere with a student's success (ASCA, 2019). Individual counseling can be proactive and responsive, helping students process their experiences, identify problems, and explore the causes, conditions, and consequences of their lived experiences in a way that highlights students' strengths, supports, and agency in the face of challenge. Students may seek assistance themselves, be referred by school staff, or be identified through climate surveys and other data collection methods.

As always, it is best practice to refer students who need additional long-term counseling support to outside mental health practitioners (ASCA, 2019). Remember, there are a variety of barriers with outside referrals for LGBTQ+ youth. This can be due to multiple factors, such as counseling accessibility, availability, and quality of care. A lack of accessibility and availability may be a consequence of living in rural communities without LGBTQ+ services, unsupportive families, the high cost of mental health counseling, or long waiting lists to receive care. Difficulties accessing quality care may arise from an intersection of identities that makes finding a knowledgeable and relatable practitioner challenging. As a result, it is good practice for school counselors to work regularly with LGBTQ+ students in a counseling capacity when other forms of counseling access are denied or unavailable to them.

For bilingual students, students of color, disabled students, nonbinary students, or students who hold other minoritized identities, finding a counselor who is both culturally sensitive and understands students' lived experience can be incredibly difficult. Based on the data collected from the ASCA's 2020 *State of the Profession*, less than 1% of school counselors identified as nonbinary, and approximately 77% identified racially as White (ASCA, 2021). Especially for those counselors whose gender or sexual orientation does not fall under the LGBTQ+ umbrella, counselors should seek ways to collaborate and consult with other experts in the field to build efficacy in providing affirming individual counseling services. It may also be important to partner with outside agencies or groups to be sure students have access to adults who may also be sexual and gender minorities, especially if they are queer or trans people of color.

Parental rights present another barrier in supporting LGBTQ+ students with individual counseling. Each state has a different law regarding student privacy and medical rights, which can determine their ability to find counseling without the support of an adult guardian. It is important to familiarize yourself with the rights of your students and the age of medical consent in determining their access to medical services without guardian approval. Some states allow students to solicit their own medical help starting at age 13, whereas others are set at age 18. Each state has an ever-changing political landscape surrounding these laws, and school counselors should stay current with how to safely fulfill their roles as advocates while following the legal and professional standards outlined by organizations such as ASCA and the American Counselor Association.

It is important for counselor educators to help counseling students and interns develop through counseling supervision that increases understanding of how to affirm LGBTQ+ youth using improved counseling skills, resulting in greater effectiveness and higher levels of comfort and confidence (Luke & Goodrich, 2012). Luke and Goodrich suggest an LGBTQ Responsive School Counseling Supervision (RSCS) approach for supporting school counselors in effectively addressing the unique needs of LGBTQ+ students through individual counseling (2012).

Group Counseling

Moving beyond individual support, school counselors often work with LGBTQ+ students in a group setting. There are many ways to include LGBTQ+-responsive student services into school-counseling programs. Running psychoeducation group lessons within gender and sexuality alliance (GSA) clubs, peer mentoring, or other student leadership programs may be effective ways to support students' sense of belonging and connection (Goodrich et al., 2013). Targeted group work may include teaching about LGBTQ+ history, mental health, and positive relationships. School counselors can also provide group counseling and community circles. Gathering in a circle for group sessions enhances a sense of school belonging. A circle models an environment of cohesion and togetherness, both figuratively and literally, holding power to invite the group's attention into the present moment of group work (Boyes-Watson & Pranis, 2015). The circle symbolizes a space of healing and trust. What happens in the circle, stays in the circle. Trust is essential for LGBTQ+ students to feel safe in places where they often must navigate a perpetually hostile climate. During group sessions, reflect on the power of community circling and the ways a circle builds a safe and affirming space. A good resource for creating community in schools is *Circle Forward: Building a Restorative School Community* (Boyes-Watson & Pranis, 2015), which includes a large collection of circle activities.

Student Affinity Groups

It is important to center the voices and experiences of LGBTQ+ students. This can be accomplished through student leadership opportunities, service learnings, formal classes, or asking for feedback in climate surveys. The most common route is to form a school queer–straight alliance (QSA) or GSA, which is a small group, ideally meeting weekly, to interface as a social support or space for activism. Every school should offer an affinity space for LGBTQ+ students at the elementary, middle, and high school level. It is important to remember that it is the right of students to form a QSA. Under the federal Equal Access Act of 1984, any school that permits noncurriculum-related student groups must provide equal access to all student groups (Equal Access Act, H.R.5345, 1984).

Be aware of intersections of LGBTQ+ student identities at GSAs. Queer and trans students of color do not necessarily feel welcome in spaces that are intended for "LGBTQ+" students. There also may be LGBTQ+ students with other intersecting identities who may not find support in a GSA if it is not created with intentionality for being inclusive of *all* LGBTQ+ students. Remember, students of color, first-generation youth, or disabled students, for instance, may feel the impact of those identities in school more than their queer or trans identity. As such, queer and trans students with intersecting marginalized identities may need to have options to join affirming affinity groups that support other aspects of their identities that may feel more salient. School counselors, especially those holding multiple dominant identities, should seek ongoing guidance and feedback from cultural insiders for groups they serve, but for whom they are not members.

GLSEN (2019) research shows that students who feel safe and supported at school have better educational outcomes. LGBTQ+ students who have LGBTQ-related school resources report improved school experiences and academic success (Ratts et al., 2013). QSAs, GSAs, or other affinity spaces that address LGBTQ+ issues serve multiple functions. They provide a source of support, raise awareness, educate LGBTQ+ issues, and, most importantly, provide a safer space. "GSA participation has been associated with positive outcomes for LGBTQ youth, including lower levels of harassment and greater school connectedness" (Greytak et al., 2013, p. 56).

LGBTQ+ Curriculum

Reflecting student experience, curriculum can serve as a mirror. It can also serve as a window when it introduces the perspectives and experiences of people who possess different identities (GLSEN, 2019). Lewis and Sembiante (2019) asserted the normalization of curriculum that focuses on and represents homosexual [sic] and transgender topics in the classroom allows teachers to engage in discussion and learn about gender expansiveness and inclusivity. Opening up discussion and having this type of curriculum also provides and deepens safe spaces for students who identify as transgender and allows the opportunity for trusted adult and peer relationships. Inclusive curriculum promotes a healthy self-concept for LGBTQ+ students while also increasing the awareness of all students.

Education that affirms the existence and experiences of transgender and nonbinary people should be a comprehensive, essential part of curricula for students of all gender identities (Rands, 2013). Rands proposes using mathematics projects and lessons to challenge various forms of oppression. A specific project designed for sixth- or seventh-graders uses the GLSEN National School Climate Survey. Students were asked to examine specific survey results relating to harassment while learning proportional reasoning and statistical concepts. Activities such as this encourage students to develop their own sense of justice and agency about how to identify and intervene in situations where transphobia or negative gender remarks are present and there are no adults around (Rands, 2013). This kind of project-based learning engages students in practical and interesting ways.

School Trainings to Support LGBTQ+ Students

School counselors can lead or coordinate a variety of professional development trainings on important topics, including helping teachers to design inclusive curriculum so students feel their identities are reflected in academic spaces. Seek partnerships with your local community while planning schoolwide trainings. Possible professional development topics may include (a) providing staff information on anti-LGBTQ+ bullying and interventions and reminders about policies, (b) including LGBTQ+ curriculum and doing lesson plan demonstrations, (c) creating affirming classrooms and providing "safe space" kits and posters, and (d) trainings to highlight LGBTQ+ student experiences and contributions to schools. One of this chapter's authors even collaborated with their school's GSA to have students come and train teachers and staff over several professional development training sessions. Teachers rated it as one of the best trainings they had attended.

VOICES FROM THE FIELD

Name: Aléx Bassi (they/them)

Where you Practice: Jackson Middle School, Port land, Oregon

Professional Job Title: Middle School Counselor

Bio: Aléx is a proud, multiracial person of color, nonbinary, transmasculine, bilingual, first-generation college student, self-identified "nerd," serving as a middle school counselor in southwest Portland, Oregon.

I have served as a middle school counselor and leader of a GSA since 2019. I am fully transparent about my identities, prioritize working somewhere where I felt accepted, and I model this sense of pride with my students. The thing that I enjoy the most is absolutely the students! The one-on-one connections that I get to make, seeing their trust with me grow, and being able to potentially become a trusted adult in the building.

As a leader of the GSA at Jackson Middle School, I created a casual place for LGBTQ+ students to gather where students can also feel a sense of safety in discussing social and political events impacting LGBTQ+ communities. I use counseling funds to provide pronouns pins for any student who wants one. I normalize active pronoun use by wearing pronoun pins myself, and my cisgendered counseling staff also affirms active pronoun use by wearing pronoun pins. I emphasize pronoun pins as being a "safety signal" to LGBTQ+ students.

Along with my school climate team, I have cofacilitated professional development staff trainings on the importance of pronoun use and creating safe spaces for LGBTQ+ students. Intentions of staff are great, but impact often falls flat. Most staff genuinely want what is best for students, but they are heavily impacted by a learning curve in modeling affirming language and creating safe spaces for students. I receive reports from students who also feel like staff learning is too slow and is damaging student relations and school climate. I also cofacilitate success lessons with students at the beginning of the year to review pronoun use and to build respectful and supportive learning environments for LGBTQ+ students. Part of my role as advocate and school counselor is having difficult conversations with teachers and students and labeling harmful language as what it is, "hate speech." I remind teachers and students of district policies and school community agreements of creating safe and respectful spaces for all students.

I recommend emerging school counselors to have things in their offices that show allyship and safe spaces. It is critical to know where administration stands with creating safe schools for LGBTQ+ youth and to know how to navigate conversations with staff, students, and families. Equally important is knowing your district policies and federal laws in support of LGBTQ+ youth.

As an adolescent who did not feel supported by their school community, I share how important it is to build safe spaces and bridge supportive and trusting relationships. I encourage us to all find allies in the building. Knowing who your allies are is so important because allies may form a better rapport with students, and this ultimately creates a stronger network of support for students.

Moreover, many LGBTQ+ advocacy groups offer excellent training for staff. *Gender Spectrum* (2022) offers a comprehensive training called *Foundations of Gender-Inclusive Schools* that we recommend (https://genderspectrum.org/articles/professional-development-educators). Check out the resource chapter for a list of free curriculum websites for creating affirmative schools for LGBTQ+ students.

SUMMARY AND CONCLUSION

School counselors influence and shape the safety and well-being of LGBTQ+ youth. This is accomplished through the creation and delivery of a comprehensive counseling design and building students' sense of belonging and connection with their school community. School counselors should gauge their effectiveness based on student feedback and student impact. School counselors must strive toward creating school environments that welcome and foster a student's natural way of learning and creating an educational experience where students see its relevance to their personal lives (Hammond, 2015). School counselors should facilitate and inspire critical and courageous conversations, rooted in advocacy and affirmation for all LGBTQ+ students.

Advocating for safer schools is advocating for a safer society for LGBTQ+ youth whose experiences should be fundamentally reflected in schools. We must work toward LGBTQ+-affirmative schools for all students, especially for our historically and continuously marginalized students for whom navigating the walls of schools can be an act of survival every day. LGBTQ+ youth must be able to thrive and become the creative and fabulous adults that they are meant to be. Advocating for safe schools is building LGBTQ+ youth resilience. At the center of growing resiliency is positive relationships, and the positive impact of a school counselor is immeasurable.

CASE STUDY

Mariana is a 14-year-old freshman in high school who identifies as a Latina trans girl. She has been taking puberty blockers since she was 12. She loves art and playing the guitar. Mariana attends a predominantly White school in a suburban setting. Mariana's parents have been very supportive of her and "just want her to be comfortable with herself." They have been strong advocates for her, especially when she experienced significant bullying from three students in middle school and harassment from her math teacher. Lately, you have noticed that Mariana's grades have dropped, and she seems sad. You notice that she has started spending a lot of time alone, including sitting by herself at lunch. When you speak to her in your office, she says that she hates high school and has no friends. You ask her about joining the GSA and she says that she is not comfortable there and there is no one she can talk to.

DISCUSSION QUESTIONS

1. Before answering the following questions, reflect on how you feel having just read about Mariana's situation. Identify actual feelings, and any automatic thoughts you had.
2. From an intersectional lens, what do you think could be happening for Mariana at her new high school?
3. What are some resources or assets that Mariana has, and how might you help her build on these?
4. What are some things you might need to consider before you can support Mariana?

PRACTICAL APPLICATION

- Register annually with Gender Sexuality Alliance Network (gsanetwork.org) to keep "active" status and receive resources and support from the National Network.
- Work with classroom teachers to cocreate curriculum to meet social, emotional, and academic goals and to support LGBTQ+ students.
- Apply for mini-grant money from the PTA, state funding, local nonprofits, or private foundations to fund GSA.
- Offer leadership opportunities: GSA-hosted spirit week, assemblies, digital arts and technology, fundraisers for local LGBTQ+ nonprofits, and events.

KEY REFERENCES

Only key references appear in the print edition. The full reference list appears in the digital product on Springer Publishing Connect: connect.springerpub.com/content/book/978-0-8261-8753-6/part/part04/chapter/ch12

American Library Association Gay, Lesbian, Bisexual, and Transgender Round Table. (2016). *Open to all: Serving the GLBT community in your library.* http://www.ala.org/rt/sites/ala.org.rt/files/content/professionaltools/160309-glbtrt-open-to-all-toolkit-online.pdf

Chang, S. C., Singh, A. A., & Dickey, L. M. (2018). *A clinician's guide to gender-affirming care.* New Harbingers Publications.

Duran, A. (2021). "Outsiders in a niche group": Using intersectionality to examine resilience for queer students of color. *Journal of Diversity in Higher Education, 14*(2), 217–227. https://doi.org/10.1037/dhe0000144

Gender Spectrum. (2019c). *School-based professional development.* https://genderspectrum.org/articles/professional-development-educators

McCullough, R., Dispenza, F., Parker, L. K., Viehl, C. J., Chang, C. Y., & Murphy, T. M. (2017). The counseling experiences of transgender and gender nonconforming clients. *Journal of Counseling and Development, 95*(4), 423–434. https://doi.org/10.1002/jcad.12157

CHAPTER 13

Engaging Students With Individualized Education Programs (IEPs) and 504s

TAYLOR MILNER, JACQUELINE EDDY, SAMUEL SONG, AND LASHAUN LIMBRICK

LEARNING OBJECTIVES

After reading this chapter, students will be able to:

- Describe laws and regulations related to special education and exceptional students.
- Illustrate strategies school counselors can use in support of students in special education.
- Apply the ASCA National Framework in expectations for school counselors in the special education process.

STUDENT VOICE

Student "X" provided the following testimonial about her experience with a school counselor:

"I have ADHD, and I get in trouble still. Not as much as when I was younger though. I recently got in it with a friend in my English class and that teacher hates me. We both got in trouble and had to do this restorative circle thing. I was kind of worried because I never did it before, but my school counselor really helped me out a lot by letting me know what it was and speaking to my parents for me too. I did the restorative circle with my friend, teacher, other classmates, and my school counselor. It was hard to hear the truth of how I harmed others, but it felt good to share my side of the story. I also felt that I understood my friend better that he was in a bad mood because his girlfriend had broken up with him that day. Man, I felt bad! My teacher shared some helpful information too about how disruptions stress her out because she's trying to teach all of us in the classroom. I feel a lot better because we all got to understand each other better, make a plan to make things right, and prevent things from happening again. I appreciate my school counselor for believing in me and treating me like a human rather than a bad kid."

INTRODUCTION

School counselors are leaders in supporting the academic, social-emotional needs, and career trajectory of students (American School Counselor Association [ASCA], n.d.) and serve an important role in the education system to provide students with the tools and resources necessary to form healthy goals, behaviors, and attitudes (Milsom, 2006). School counselors are also trained and encouraged to work as advocates at individual, local, and systemic levels, making them a valuable stakeholder for students with special needs (Geltner & Leibforth, 2008; Milsom, 2002). In practice, students identified with special needs are often excluded from receiving school counseling interventions, despite special education law mandates and the recommendation of the American School Counselor Association (ASCA) school counseling standards (Geddes-Hall, 2015). Research indicates that schools may underuse services provided by school counselors, especially regarding postsecondary transition planning for students with disabilities and representation on multidisciplinary teams (Geddes-Hall, 2015; Owens et al., 2011). This is a missed opportunity considering the specialized knowledge and training in group dynamics, facilitation of communication and collaboration, and awareness of community resources that school counselors may contribute when planning interventions and services for students in special education (Milsom et al., 2007).

The lack of involvement is attributed to multiple daily responsibilities, lack of sufficient time to work more collaboratively with special education students, and a lack of adequate training in special education and related matters (Studer & Quigney, 2003). Regardless, the school counseling field continues to evolve and develop to suit the demands of students requiring support through special education as a result of the enactment of various special education laws and mandates (Geddes-Hall, 2015; Geltner & Leibforth, 2008). This chapter will provide a brief overview of the school counselor's role in special education, the laws associated with special education and their implications for school counseling, perspectives from practicing school counselors, and recommendations for school counselor collaboration with special education staff to ensure adequate service delivery when working with students with special needs.

ROLE OF THE SCHOOL COUNSELOR IN SPECIAL EDUCATION

According to the ASCA, school counselors are committed to helping students realize their potential as well as meet, or exceed, in their academic benchmarks, while being mindful of both the strengths and challenges that students with disabilities and other special needs experience (ASCA, 2016). School counselors provide both direct and indirect services to students with special needs in the least restrictive environment (LRE) and in the most inclusive setting afforded by the student's Individualized Education Program (IEP). They also use student support service team (SST)/multidisciplinary team (MDT) approaches to ensure that each student's unique needs and experiences are considered regarding response to intervention. responsive positive behavioral interventions, and support (ASCA, 2021).

School counselors are dedicated to supporting students in various aspects academically, socially, and behaviorally. Some responsibilities include, but are not limited to: providing school counseling curriculum lessons, providing individual and group counseling to students with special needs, providing short- and long-term counseling goals for 504 Plans and IEPs, advocating for students in school and in the community, collaborating with other related student support services (e.g., school psychologists, occupational therapists, physical therapists, special education staff, speech and language pathologists, etc.), providing support with transition, such as academic and postsecondary plans for students with IEPs and 504s (ASCA, 2021).

One way school counselors are able to serve students with special needs is through their involvement in the IEP planning process, which provides opportunities for school counselors to gain experience working with special education personnel and students in special education programs (Owens et al., 2011). In order for an IEP team to be successful in setting realistic and relevant goals for a student, there needs to be a variety of informants that can share knowledge of the student, availability of resources, and curriculum options. School counselors provide valuable information in regard to career and lifespan development, as well as specific related services and interventions, all of which are beneficial in the development of the IEP (Milsom et al., 2007). However, because school counselors are not typically included in the IEP team planning process, it is essential that practitioners advocate for themselves and their skills when it comes to involvement in special education processes; this includes advocating at the district level for better training opportunities as well as requesting support from school administrators and special education staff to ensure that healthy working relationships are being maintained (Milsom, 2002).

Working together and collaborating is an essential part of the special education process, which requires an inherent ability to work in groups. School counselor education programs encourage their students to engage in various means of effective group work to help better prepare students to expect systematic barriers and to encourage them to advocate for more resources (Williams et al., 2013). School counselors can apply their knowledge of group work to prepare IEP team members to actively and effectively participate in team meetings, provide in-service small-group training or activities to teach educators about group dynamics, and to implement services to many students at once (Milsom et al., 2007; Wisner & Norton, 2013). This specialized training in group work is also beneficial when school counselors shift from a one-to-one direct service approach, where the student is being helped individually, to one in which the school counselor is working with groups of students. Research shows working with groups to be more effective, while also allowing school counselors the ability to reach more students in the least amount of time; they cannot impact all students in meaningful ways if they are only able to provide services to a small percentage of students individually (Studer & Quigney, 2003; Galassi et al., 2008). Group counseling is an effective and necessary component of school-based services for students considered high risk due to emotional and academic difficulties and provides increasing opportunities to deliver counseling services to a much larger population of students (Bjornestad et al., 2016; Wisner & Norton, 2013).

Another major role of the school counselor is serving as an advocate on behalf of students, especially as the number of students receiving special education services continues to increase. According to a report from the U.S. Department of Education, the number of students ages 3 to 21 receiving special education services under the Individuals With Disabilities Education Improvement Act (IDEA) from the school year 2009–2010 through 2019–2020, increased from 6.5 million students, which is 13% of public school enrollment, to 7.3 million students, which accounts for 14% of public school enrollment (Geltner & Leibforth, 2008; U.S. Department of Education, 2021). School counselors are charged with creating equitable opportunities for all students to ensure their academic success. As such, school counselors must be prepared to be an active voice during IEP meetings and advocate on behalf of students with disabilities (Owens et al., 2011). One of the primary goals of school counseling is to create equitable and accessible opportunities for all students, and in order for them to be successful, they must be willing and able to be an active voice during IEP meetings to advocate on behalf of students with disabilities (Owens et al., 2011). It is unrealistic to expect school counselors to coordinate daily with special education personnel, teachers, and parents due to their multiple responsibilities. However, school counselors can improve the overall experience of students and families who are engaged in the special education process by committing to a supportive role as an advocate and liaison. By assuming a supportive role as an advocate and facilitator, school counselors can improve the overall experience for students and families going through the special education process (Geltner & Leibforth, 2008).

School counselors should also take on the role as leaders in social justice advocacy by using a multicultural and social justice leadership approach to address issues of oppression that threaten the academic, career, and personal well-being of marginalized student populations (Ratts & Greenleaf, 2018). Marginalized student populations refer to individuals who are of low socioeconomic status and students who come from diverse linguistic and cultural backgrounds that differ from those of their White peers (Garcia & Guerra, 2004). School counselors need to be mindful of how these differences influence achievement gaps for underserved individuals and how they can effectively identify inequities and develop interventions and programs to address them (Hartline & Cobia, 2012). According to the ASCA, school counselors can act as culturally responsive change agents who can use their unique training and knowledge to help develop and implement equitable services and programs for all students (ASCA, 2012; Betters-Bubon & Schultz, 2017). This requires school counselors to be aware of the challenges some children with disabilities face in terms of receiving special education services, such as the factors associated with disproportionality in special education (Cooc & Kiru, 2018). *Disproportionality* refers to the over- or underrepresentation of student groups receiving special education services, such as students of color who are notoriously overrepresented in special education programs (Cavendish et al., 2020; Cooc & Kiru, 2018).

English language learners (ELL) are students who come from households in which English is not the primary language spoken. For this population, it is vital that school counselors ensure they practice cultural humility and develop interventions that enhance ELL students' sense of belonging within the context of their school (Shi & Watkinson, 2019). ELL students are at risk of being misidentified as needing special education support as students with a specific learning disability (Ortiz et al., 2011). Therefore, school counselors should collaborate with teachers and other school personnel, such as the school psychologist, to appropriately screen and monitor ELL students' academic achievement (Ortiz et al., 2011).

Social justice advocacy is a necessary skill that all school counselors need to possess, as they play an important part in providing the integration of multicultural competencies and social justice advocacy while serving students with disabilities (Ratts et al., 2007). According to the ASCA, school counselors have a professional and ethical responsibility to expand personal multicultural and social justice advocacy, awareness, knowledge, and skills in order to be a culturally competent school counselor. It is also crucial that school counselors continue to strive toward creating a field that is culturally sustainable by pursuing systemic change through leadership, advocacy, and collaboration within the ASCA National Model (ASCA, 2021; Geltner & Leibforth, 2008). There are many ways in which school counselors can exercise their skills and advocate for equitable student outcomes. One of these is through developing strong partnerships between schools, families, and the community (Betters-Bubon & Schultz, 2017).

Parent empowerment has been identified as a powerful tool to address academic and opportunity gaps, systematic barriers, and educational inequalities that hinder students' potential as it refers to the process by which parents gain a greater influence on their families, schools, and communities through networks, resources, and information that establish skills for facilitating more effective schooling for their children. School counselors can use their efforts to facilitate meaningful conversations in which marginalized parents have the opportunity to share the challenges and barriers that they and their children experience in the school setting and use that information to promote a healthier and more positive school climate (Hartline & Cobia, 2012; Kim et al., 2017).

These partnerships can become even more effective when school counselors also form alliances with community organizations. This allows for larger, more powerful systems to be used in transforming the lives of students and families (Betters-Bubon & Schultz, 2017).

Another way school counselors can contribute to a more positive, safer, and equitable school environment that benefits the academic, career, and social-emotional needs of all students is by using positive behavioral interventions and supports (PBIS). PBIS is widely implemented in the United States and is recommended as a tiered support. School counselors have been identified as a key stakeholders in successful implementation (Goodman-Scott et al., 2015). Schoolwide positive behavior supports (SWPBIS) can be implemented with various levels of integrity and outcomes to account for the diversity seen among student populations. SWPBIS is most effective when being applied with attention to culture and context as it has the potential to address disproportionate outcomes for marginalized students in regard to behavior management practices and references for special education services (Fallon et al., 2012). It is important for school counselors to remain culturally responsive when planning, developing, and implementing any type of PBIS program in their schools (Betters-Bubon et al., 2016).

THE LAW AND THE ROLE OF THE SCHOOL COUNSELOR

The enactment of special education laws and mandates has continued to shape the field of school counseling and its implications for supporting students receiving special education services (Geddes-Hall, 2015). School counselors strive to assist all students to reach their full potential, including students with special needs, within the scope of the school counseling program of services (ASCA, 2016). Legislative mandates advocate for the collaboration of special education personnel and school counselors when it comes to decisions on behalf of the students served (Milsom et al., 2007). For a student with a disability to receive services, they must be identified and be determined to be eligible (Council for Exceptional Children, 2002).

The Individuals With Disabilities Education Improvement Act

All children with disabilities have been entitled to a free and appropriate public education (FAPE) under the Individuals With Disabilities Education Improvement Act (IDEA) of 1975, which requires public schools to provide access to a free, appropriate education in the LRE for all students (ASCA, 2016). IDEA provides federal funding to state and local education agencies that provide service to children with disabilities, and all students within the district suspected of having a disability must be identified and evaluated (Council for Exceptional Children, 2002). IDEA's definitions of disabilities include autism, deaf-blind, developmental delay, emotional disturbance, hearing impairments (including deafness), intellectual disability (formerly mental retardation), multiple disabilities, orthopedic impairments, other health impairments, specific learning disabilities, speech or language impairments, traumatic brain injury, and visual impairments (including blindness) (ASCA, 2016).

The school counselor's involvement with students with special needs and their families continues to increase as they contribute through participation in multidisciplinary prereferral teams, IEP development, and acknowledgment of legal and ethical issues regarding the provision of special education services (Geddes-Hall, 2015; Studer & Quigney, 2003). School counselors are required to participate in the identification process for students with disabilities through their service on screening teams and assisting in evaluation where appropriate, giving them the opportunity to provide input on planning and placement for students who have been identified as having a disability (Geddes-Hall, 2015).

Family Educational Rights and Privacy Act

The Family Educational Rights and Privacy Act (FERPA) is federal law that protects the privacy of a student's educational records, including health records and special education records and any records of services provided to students under Individuals with Disabilities Education Act, which includes 504 Plans (ASCA, 2010). Parents are given certain rights in regard to their children's educational records, and these rights are transferred to the child once they turn 18 or attend school beyond the high school level, in which case they are considered "eligible students" (U.S. Department of Education, 2021). Parents or eligible students have the right to inspect and review the student's educational records, request that a school make corrections to records that they believe to be inaccurate or misleading, and give written permission prior to the school releasing any information from the student's records.

There are a few conditions in which schools can give information without consent, and that would be to school officials with legitimate educational interest; to other schools to which a student is transferring; to specified officials for audit or evaluation purposes; to appropriate parties associated with financial aid to a student; to organizations conducting certain studies for or on behalf of the school; to accrediting organizations; to comply with a judicial order or lawfully issued subpoena; to appropriate officials in cases of health and safety emergencies; and to state and local authorities, within a juvenile justice system, pursuant to specific state law. Schools are allowed to disclose directory information, which is information that is not generally considered a harmful invasion of privacy, such as a student's name, address, place of birth, telephone number, dates of attendance, etc. However, the schools must inform the parent or eligible student if any directory information was given (U.S. Department of Education, 2021).

School counselors do not necessarily handle student records directly, and not all educational records are subject to the rules and regulations under FERPA. Any records made by teachers, supervisors, school counselors, administrators, and other school personnel that are kept in the sole possession of the counselor and are not accessible or revealed to anyone besides a temporary substitute on behalf of the maker of the record are exempt from being considered education records under FERPA. For example, school counselors' case notes are considered "sole-possession records" and not educational records as long as they meet a specific criteria: they serve as a memory aid, they are not accessible or shared in either verbal or written form, they are a private note created solely by the individual possessing it, and they include only observations and professional opinions (ASCA, 2008). However, such sole-possession notes may still be subpoenaed, even though they are not part of formal educational records.

504 Plans

Students who do not meet the requirements for special education services under IDEA may be eligible for a 504 Plan and thus entitled to receive a FAPE. Section 504 of the Rehabilitation Act of 1973 protects qualified individuals with disabilities from discrimination and ensures that institutions meet their unique needs by providing reasonable accommodations (Council for Exceptional Children, 2002). To qualify for a 504 Plan, students must demonstrate they (a) have a physical or mental impairment that limits one or more major life activities, such as learning; (b) have a record of such impairment; or (c) be regarded as having such impairment (U.S. Department of Education, 2016).

According to the U.S. Department of Education (2016), under Section 504, physical and mental impairments are broadly defined as any physiological or psychological disorder or condition that is not temporary and affects one or more bodily systems. It is important to note that when evaluating students for a 504 Plan, school counselors and other school personnel should consider how the student's condition impacts any major life activity, including but not limited to learning. That is, a student may qualify for a 504 Plan even if their learning is not impacted by their condition or if they are earning above average grades. School counselors should establish a Section 504 team when assessing a student's eligibility for accommodations. The Section 504 team must review multiple sources of information, such as school records, caregiver and teacher interviews, and supporting medical documentation from a pediatrician or other qualified medical professional. One thing is certain, each disability and its manifestation is unique to the individual; therefore, the determination of limitations must be made on a case-by-case basis (U.S. Department of Education, 2016).

As with the evaluation process, selecting accommodations and related services should be done on a case-by-case basis and center around the student's needs. Examples of accommodations include, but are not limited to, extended time for assignments and tests, assistive technology, note takers, and counseling services. Regardless of the type of accommodations offered, the services must be provided to the student and their family at no cost. To ensure accommodations are properly executed, the 504 Plan should include details regarding where the services will be offered (i.e., the LRE) and who is responsible for their implementation (i.e., the general education teacher U.S. Department of Education, 2016). As with an IEP, 504 Plans must be revised annually. However, if the identified accommodations or related services are not supporting the student's needs, changes may be made at the request of any Section 504 team member.

SCHOOL COUNSELORS AS 504 CASE MANAGERS

Although school counselors shouldn't be tasked with the role of 504 case manager, many school counselors are likely to be tasked with the role. Unlike the IDEA, federal regulations do not mandate a timeline for the development and implementation of a 504 Plan. However, school counselors should strive to complete an evaluation for a 504 referral within a reasonable amount of time. For instance, between 30 and 60 school calendar days should be sufficient to evaluate a student and establish reasonable accommodations. Additionally, an evaluation for a 504 Plan does not require formal assessments such as those used for determination of special education eligibility. Therefore, school counselors may gather data from various sources, such as reviewing student records and conducting interviews with caregivers and teachers, to develop reasonable accommodations that will support the student's learning. A challenge for some school counselors when writing 504 Plans is avoiding the pitfalls of recycling accommodations that are commonly used, such as preferential seating, without considering the student's needs. School counselors should strive to ensure that developing a 504 Plan is a collaborative process with the student, their caregiver, and teachers. Thus, it is important to develop partnerships with student's caregivers and empower them to actively participate in the planning process.

Additionally, selecting accommodations for a 504 Plan should be based on the student's needs rather than popularity and convenience. For instance, a student with ADHD may benefit from extended time to complete assignments, but they may also need study and organizational skills that will support their long-term success. Moreover, when writing accommodations, it is helpful to be specific so that all stakeholders are clear on how to best assist the student. For example, for a student with anxiety, a "pressure pass" may allow them to take a break from otherwise overwhelming situations. A pressure pass is a discrete way for a student to let their teacher know they need to step away without drawing attention to themselves. Some examples of a pressure pass include tokens or small laminated pieces of paper. However, school counselors can take an additional step by identifying safe areas where the student can take their break and teaching the student grounding techniques to help them maximize their pressure pass.

INDIVIDUALIZED EDUCATION PROGRAM

An IEP is a written plan, required by federal law, put in place for students who have been identified as either having a disability or being gifted, to ensure that they are receiving the proper support throughout their academic career. Although school counselors do not attend IEP meetings, they are still required to participate in the identification of students with disabilities in other ways, such as being on screening teams and assisting in evaluations when appropriate. School counselors should still be included as a member of the IEP team because they are able to provide information related to student levels of functioning in academics and personal and social domains, which is useful in the planning and placement of identified students (Geddes-Hall, 2015). School counselors can also provide direct services, such as individual and group counseling, which can be included in the IEP, as well as indirect services, such as consulting with school personnel about the identified student's educational, behavioral, and social-emotional needs and the implementation of professional training for school personnel working with exceptional students (Geddes-Hall, 2015).

Transitional Services

According to the IDEA, transitional planning is required for students in secondary schools, which is an area in which school counselors would be able to assist considering their training in career and lifespan development (Geddes-Hall, 2015; Milsom et al., 2007). For students identified with a disability, transition services are designed to be goa oriented, consisting of a coordinated set of activities that are focused on improving the academic and function achievement of the student so that they will have a smooth transition to postschool activities (e.g., postsecondary education, integrated employment, continuing and adult education, adult services, independent living, or community participation). Transitional services are also based on the individual student's needs, taking into consideration strengths, preferences, and interests, and include instruction, related services, community experiences, the development of employment and other postschool adult-living objectives, and if applicable, the acquisition of daily living skills as well as provision of a functional vocational evaluation (U.S. Department of Education, n.d.). Transition services are considered a part of special education services if they are provided as specially designed instruction or a related service that is required to assist a student with a disability (U.S. Department of Education, n.d.). Special education teachers are often expected to bear the responsibility of transitional planning due to their specialized knowledge of special education, as well as the students they serve. However, educational transitions are an identified responsibility for school counselors, and despite their expertise in related areas, they are often excluded from the postsecondary transition planning process (Milsom, 2002; Milsom et al., 2004). School counselors should collaborate with special education personnel to provide interventions and community resources to help prepare students and their families for the transition to work, postsecondary school, or a supported living environment after high school (Milsom, 2007).

REAL-WORLD SCHOOL PRACTICE

School counselors are expertly trained with a broad skill set to support the academic and social-emotional-behavioral needs of exceptional students. However, the degree to which these skills are implemented in practice often varies from district to district. Barriers such as large caseloads and limited school resources may create challenges for school counselors to provide interventions to students receiving special education services. For some school counselors in large districts, a caseload may include over 300 students with varying needs, even though ASCA (n.d.) recommends a caseload of 250 students to one counselor.

Supporting exceptional students, those who are gifted and/or have disabilities, begins with a comprehensive evaluation. School counselors typically are not required members of their school's multidisciplinary evaluation teams, and their busy schedules may prevent them from participating in eligibility meetings. Moreover, many school counselors, especially those working in high schools, are excluded from writing behavioral and academic goals for student IEPs. In fact, some school counselors may first encounter a student's IEP when arranging their class schedule. However, this does not mean school counselors should take a backseat when it comes to special education. Rather, it is essential for the school counselor to collaborate with stakeholders such as the student's caregivers and teacher of record to gain a better understanding of the student's unique needs. One important strategy for supporting student achievement is for the school counselor to take a strengths-based approach and provide students with opportunities, through classes, extracurricular activities, or vocational training, that will contribute to their success and development. In other words, pay special attention to the areas where a student excels rather than focusing on their deficits. Additionally, in accordance with ASCA (2019) professional standards, school counselors should use existing assessment data to develop action plans that align with the student's annual IEP goals.

In addition to supporting exceptional students through IEP and 504 Plan development and implementation, school counselors are a lifeline for exceptional students struggling with social problems, emotional difficulties, and homelife challenges. With large caseloads, it may be difficult for some school counselors to provide direct services to all their students in need. Therefore, school counselors can collaborate with administrators and other school personnel to establish schoolwide programs using multitiered systems of support (MTSS). MTSS is a framework that emphasizes "quality universal instruction and preventive proactive methods, while providing increasingly strategic supports for students as their needs become more severe" (Clark & Dockweiler, 2019, p. 5). MTSS frameworks are often depicted as a three-tiered triangle, with Tier 1 representing universal or schoolwide instruction, Tier 2 targeted instruction, and Tier 3 intensive instruction. For example, at Tier 1, school counselors can lead professional development training for teachers to implement preventive social-emotional curricula. For students who require additional support, Tier 2 programs may include small-group interventions, and at Tier 3, school counselors can focus on direct one-on-one interventions. Students exist within several micro -and macrosystems that impact their development. Thus, it is vital for school counselors to consider multicultural factors when planning MTSS interventions and include community and family perspectives. Though immensely beneficial, developing MTSS programming can be an arduous process, one that requires school counselors to establish a team and engage in continuous program evaluation.

It is important to recognize that every school counselor's experiences in practice will be unique. External factors such as geographical location, population served, and access to resources may impact how school counselors implement interventions to support exceptional students. Still, one thing is certain, school counselors have the skills necessary to support students receiving special education services, and it is imperative that they follow ASCA professional standards to best support this vulnerable population (ASCA, n.d.).

VOICES FROM THE FIELD

Name: Lashaun Limbrick, PhD, NCC, NCSC (he/him)

Where You Practice: Las Vegas, Nevada

Professional Job Title: School Counselor and Department Chair

Bio: Lashaun is a fifth-year school counselor/ department chair at Desert Pines High School, located on the east side of Las Vegas, Nevada, in a largely Latinx community that has historically faced perceived challenges. He is a National Certified School Counselor (NCSC) and National Certified Counselor (NCC).

On a typical day, I assist students with social-emotional, academic, and career development. I ensure special education and general education students are working toward graduation through academic monitoring and facilitate parent-teacher conferences as needed. I also teach classroom guidance lessons relative to high schoolers and partner with local colleges and universities to assist students with postsecondary options. Depending on the time of the year, I also assist students with college applications and financial aid. As a school counselor, I also assess students that are experiencing a crisis, provide short-term counseling to students, and serve as a 504 Plan liaison.

I thoroughly enjoy helping students with tackling problems and issues in their current phases of cognitive and social development. My students are at the end of their PK–12 education, and I get to help them plan for their postsecondary futures (college and career planning). In addition, I want to be a beacon of hope to communities of color, showing them a blueprint for what is possible through hard work and education.

I wish school counselors across the nation had the ASCA-recommended 250:1 student caseload, which would allow us to spend more time helping individual students. Personally, I have a high caseload and often do not get to know each of my students.

One thing I love about being a school counselor is when former students see me out in the community, either on higher education campuses or at their place of employment, and tell me that I impacted their lives. I elected to do this amazing work to help propel the next generation, and it feels good to know I am making a significant difference in the greater Las Vegas community.

Be ready to work hard! Our public schools need supportive school counselors that are willing to fully support all students, especially Students of Color. Education has its politics and challenges, but you must remain focused on helping students. Our students are watching us and need positive educators guiding them so we can dismantle systems and structures that have historically limited access for students, especially Students of Color. On a positive note, you will thoroughly love your career as you get to work with young people that are eager to do better. They just need your support to get them to the next level.

SUMMARY AND CONCLUSION

School counselors receive large amounts of specialized and different training and have expertise that makes them valuable stakeholders in the school community. School counselors have an inherent responsibility to provide support to all students in the areas of academic, social-emotional, and behavioral functioning, which includes students identified as having special needs. It is important that counselors become actively involved throughout the special education process, including identification, planning, and implementation (Geddes-Hall, 2015). However, in order for school counselors to effectively work with both students in special education and special education personnel, they need to have a solid understanding of the laws and regulations that make up special education services, but they also must be given opportunities to be involved in collaboration, advocacy, team building, and working both directly and indirectly with students in special education programs. School counselors need to advocate for themselves to receive adequate training and experience working with students and staff in special education, as well as to encourage special education personnel to include them in the development process of IEPs and 504s to ensure that exceptional students are receiving the most effective services and support they need.

CASE STUDY

Phil is a school counselor who knows how important school counselors are for students with disabilities but has not been very involved thus far. He decides to make a change in his practice in this area and begins to form a better relationship with the school psychologist. He soon finds that Mel, the school psychologist, is not only very friendly but also has collaborated with school counselors before. They hit it off and strategize to lead the school in meeting the needs of students with disabilities and all students. Together, they colead the existing student assistance team (SAT) and decide to implement interventions in an MTSS model. The school principal was excited about this because she had been wanting to begin this at the school.

They began by providing professional development to the school faculty, staff, and families about MTSS. To screen for mental health promotion tiered supports, they analyzed data from a strength-based screening tool, teacher reports, and office discipline referrals to identify students needing more support. Next, they consulted with teachers about how best to support students' mental health and wellness in the classroom for all students and students with disabilities. They coled small groups for students needing more supports and trained other mental health professionals to colead groups. Finally, they served on multidisciplinary and IEP teams to support Tier 3 interventions. They review data at least monthly with the larger SAT to determine effectiveness and how to modify the supports being implemented.

DISCUSSION QUESTIONS

1. How can you prepare yourself now to support students with disabilities?
2. Once you start working, what are some steps you can take to get to know the school psychologist and partner with them and other professionals?
3. What type of support do you think you can offer students with disabilities?
4. Begin practical application.

PRACTICAL APPLICATION

- Collaborate, collaborate, collaborate! Although many school counselors are not required members of special education evaluations and few participate in IEP development, collaborating with multidisciplinary team members allows school counselors to gain a better understanding of the school's special education programs, which in turn provides the school counselor with more information about how to best support exceptional students. Additionally, working closely with a student's caregivers and community members ensures that the student is receiving services in each of the systems to which they belong.

- School counselors should establish special education partnerships with school psychologists to support the social-emotional needs of exceptional students. For example, the school counselor and school psychologist can use their expertise in mental health to establish school-based mental health services.

- Embrace programs that provide indirect services to students. Creating schoolwide programs can be a demanding process. However, school counselors should embrace program models, such as MTSS, that allow them to reach a broader population of students.

KEY REFERENCES

Only key references appear in the print edition. The full reference list appears in the digital product on Springer Publishing Connect: connect.springerpub.com/content/book/978-0-8261-8753-6/part/part04/chapter/ch13

American School Counselor Association. (2016). *The school counselor and student with disabilities*.

Betters-Bubon, J., & Schultz, J. W. (2017). School counselors as social justice leaders. *Professional School Counseling, 21*(1b), 2156759. https://doi.org/10.1177/2156759X18773601

Kim, J., Fletcher, K., & Bryan, J. (2017). Empowering marginalized parents. *Professional School Counseling, 21*(1b), 2156759. https://doi.org/10.1177/2156759X18773585

Milsom, A., Goodnough, G., & Akos, P. (2007). School counselor contributions to the Individualized Education Program (IEP) process. *Preventing School Failure, 52*(1), 19–24. https://doi.org/10.3200/PSFL.52.1.19-24

Ratts, M. J., & Greenleaf, A. T. (2018). Multicultural and social justice counseling competencies. *Professional School Counseling, 21*(1b), 1–9. https://doi.org/10.1177/2156759x18773582

CHAPTER 14

Home Impact on Students

**MARY AMANDA GRAHAM, ROBERT PINCUS, AND
LEE NATHAN GARDNER**

LEARNING OBJECTIVES

After reading this chapter, students will be able to:

- Recognize the impact environments outside of school have on student performance.
- Modify school practices to be more supportive of students with challenging home environments.
- Use best practices that remove barriers in schools for students facing home challenges.

STUDENT VOICE

Student "J" provided the following testimonial about their experience with a school counselor:

"When I was a senior in high school, me and my family unfortunately got into a situation where we had to leave our home and couldn't find anywhere to stay, and sadly this wasn't the first time. It really affected my schooling because I was missing my classes, missing my work, and was absent a lot. I can't tell you how many nights we were driving around in a car just trying to find a place to rest, and shower, and clean up—this was honestly a rough time. I was so embarrassed about it and to explain this situation to all my teachers was hard and I'm not very good at being vulnerable.... At some point I thought I wouldn't be able to graduate, not because of my homelessness but because even before that I was failing so that just made everything worse. Eventually we found a family shelter that accepted us, and we stayed there till we got things together. After that I really started trying and pushing myself to work harder. I got my grades up and I was officially able to walk across the stage along with my graduating class, which I couldn't have done without the help of my school counselor. Mr. Stanford (see Voices From the Field) really helped me, encouraged and supported me. I will forever be thankful for that. My advice to students who are struggling with these issues is to keep pushing—of course there's going to be times where it gets hard, maybe even worse—you're allowed to scream and you're allowed to cry, but never give up. You got this! And you'll make it because I did."

INTRODUCTION

The U.S. Census Bureau (n.d.) defines a family as a group of two people or more (one of whom is the head of household) related by birth, marriage, or adoption and residing together; all such people (including related subfamily members) are considered members of one family. Through the lens of a school counselor who is working to attain a better understanding of family structure, homes, and challenges within family structures, this definition may appear limited when considering the diversity and cultural beliefs of a community. Family is a cultural construct that should not be limited to the recognition of those with blood or legal ties but rather can be examined in relationships that students consider family (Furstenberg et al., 2020). Huang et al. (2017) point out that family support by race, ethnicity, or identification may be explained by both social structures and culture. The implication for school counselors is that we must begin to change the definitions and language when working with the diversity of families and households we serve; viewing family, household, or kin from the perspective of the dominant culture may limit our ability to understand and connect with all students and families. In a discussion concerning defining household and families in regard to indigenous populations, Tam et al. (2017) remind us that trying to define family using the monocultural lens we have relied on for so long does not allow us to "embrace the complexities of other cultures" (p. 243). For school counselors to work with a student effectively and support them in challenges they may be experiencing in their home environments, it is essential that they also understand the cultural reality that defines their family and home.

SCHOOL COUNSELOR AND THE HOME: AN ADVOCACY APPROACH

Understanding the cultural context of the student's home becomes an even more significant issue when you consider the multicultural and social justice issues that many students and families continue to face when existing in a system that does not appear to acknowledge the diversity of people and families it is serving. One does not have to look very far back in the available research to understand how limited and biased the view of households and families has been within the system of education. When discussing juvenile delinquency rates, Spohn and Kurtz (2011) described homes as intact or broken. We must move beyond these simplistic and confined definitions of families and homes and begin to expand the vocabulary and discussion concerning the reality of the lives our students and families are living. Using this lens, we can best support them. Names and labels used to describe students and families "carry great emotional and psychological weight. These labels help define what behaviors and relationships are appropriate and desirable. Families are social units defined by their boundaries—who's in, and who's not" (Cohen, 2017, p. 46). Thus, it becomes even more important for school counselors to invest themselves in developing and nurturing their understanding and skills through gaining knowledge and expertise concerning multiculturalism and social justice as they work with their students and within challenges their students and families may be facing.

Multicultural and social justice competencies can no longer be a type of professional development opportunity for school counselors. For school counselors to serve as agents of change and fully support the needs of their community and challenges students face in home environments, multiculturalism and social justice must become a foundational aspect of their skills, knowledge, and work. Dameron et al. (2020) point out that the diversity of the PK–12 population will require school counselors to enhance and maintain their understanding of multiculturism and social justice to support their students and families. Simply gaining knowledge and skills, however, is just the first step in the process of school counselor support. Action-oriented approaches to the work of supporting family and systems is the next step. Taking action in a system (schools) that we recognize has proven to display systemic bias for many years will not be easy. "Taking a social justice approach to school counseling calls for school counselors to be prepared to question authority, challenge the injustices they see in their schools, and work collaboratively" (Griffin & Stern, 2011, p. 79). There are many factors and realities that can become roadblocks for counselors who commit to a multicultural and social justice approach to their work with families. When discussing the relationship shared between African American parents and schools, Shillingford et al. (2020) point out that racial stereotypes are often supported by a teacher population that is dominated by White females. This will require school counselors to not only be advocates for their students and families, but it will also require counselors to be willing to challenge and educate peers who may not have the same level of knowledge and understanding. This means finding a way to push teachers, administrators, and staff to understand that school does not occur in a vacuum for students, and bias about home situations and challenges must be eliminated for the support and success of the student. When considering the realities of a diverse student body, it is important to remember that "targeting students' academic struggles in isolation from external factors . . . limits school in addressing all of the needs of students in a way that builds on the assets of students and their communities" (Griffin & Stern, 2011, p. 75). This will require school counselors to walk a fine line of advocating while educating and supporting their peers to best serve their students from a place of high expectations and empathy. Not taking into account how marginalized students and families have experienced and continue to experience a reality that exists within a systemically biased school systems inhibits an educator's ability to fully understand the family system and what is required to support each student. School counselors' roles have expanded to include that of social justice advocates and antiracism advocates. Finally, "the introsection and intersection of multiple cultural identities and social locations for both clients and counselors yield a multitude of individual experiences of culture and power that need to be investigated" (Hays, 2020, p. 332). This understanding is imperative as school counselors support students who have challenges in their home environments that have the potential to directly impact success in the three American School Counselor Association (ASCA) domains: personal/social, career and academics.

THE IMPACT OF SUBSTANCE ABUSE

According to the National Association for Children of Alcoholics (http://nacoa.org/), 1 in 4 children live in a home/family with a parent addicted to drugs and alcohol. Research shows that parental substance abuse is a direct indicator of children's suffering future mental health and substance abuse issues (Bröning et al., 2019; Inoura et al., 2020; Jääskeläinen et al., 2016; Raitasalo et al., 2019). Parental substance abuse is considered one of the 10 signs of adverse childhood experiences (ACEs) that can also cause mental health issues in children and adolescents (Jääskeläinen et al., 2016). Studies also found that maternal substance abuse has a greater negative effect on children's mental health than father's substance abuse (Inoura et al., 2020; Jääskeläinen et al., 2016; Raitasalo et al., 2019). Maternal substance abuse has a more profound impact on children and adolescent alcohol use due to many single-family households led by mothers (Inoura et al., 2020 Raitasalo et al., 2019). Jääskeläinen et al. (2016) noted that children living with substance-abusing mothers on social assistance are almost 6 times as likely to have a mental health illness when they hit adolescence. School counselors should note that adolescents coming from a single-family home are more likely to abuse alcohol than a student coming from a two-parent home.

Another factor that must be considered is that alcoholism can be hereditary. School counselors must consider this when working with students of parental substance abusers (Jääskeläinen et al., 2016). Inoura et al. (2020) found that parental substance abuse leads to substantial alcohol binge drinking by adolescents. Raitasalo et al. (2019) noted that children of substance abusers are rarely considered in the treatment plan of their parents or even offered personal counseling. School counselors can fill in this gap of services.

There are often other variables that students face when growing up in homes with substance abuse. These can include the involvement of child protective services and law enforcement. Substance abuse has also led families to separate or divorce (Jääskeläinen et al., 2016; Raitasalo et al., 2019). In some situations, students may be removed from their home and placed in foster care. Students who live in homes where substance abuse is present report suffering from headaches, anxiety, depression, guilt, and anger. Living in homes where substances are abused can lead to trouble academically, with student concentration and behavioral issues evident in the classroom (Gullbrå et al., 2016, p. 364).

Understanding and Advocating

Often, students who are living in homes with substance abuse are afraid to ask for help due to unknown or potential negative consequences for their parents (Gullbrå et al., 2016). Students, no matter their home environments, usually care about and are loyal to their family. In her book, *It Will Never Happen to Me,* Dr. Claudia Black highlights the unspoken rules and norms in families that struggle with substance use and addictions: don't talk, don't trust, and don't feel. This dynamic often leads to students suffering in silence. It is important to remember that students living in substance use–impacted homes face issues of shame, denial, and confusion. These homes can be unpredictable, with the roles of the student and adult shifted, leaving the student to feel responsible for the caretaking of the adult in the home. These struggles can negatively affect their academics and future relationships (Bröning et al., 2019).

Gullbrå et al. (2016) suggested that school counselors working with students from substance abuse–affected homes use a person-centered counseling or Rogerian approach. Students often need to be treated with normalcy in their lives, even if there are special accommodations needed due to their parents' issues. Often adolescents will not divulge sensitive family information in a brief counseling session. Using person-centered counseling promotes a positive school counselor–student relationship. This allows for time and space for the student to feel comfortable and safe to ask for assistance. School counselors should practice going deeper in the session by using active listening, understanding the students' worldview and lived experience, and coming from a place of compassion and understanding (Gullbrå et al., 2016). Being highly visible, authentic, and approachable to all students in schools will project the message that the school counselor is present and approachable for students dealing with any situation.

School counselors act as catalysts of hope for students. In addition to supporting the student through individual counseling and systemic advocacy, school counselors should consider the facilitation of small groups. Group counseling with children or adolescents using a combination of brief person-centered and cognitive behavior therapy can be highly effective for students facing the challenges of living in substance-affected home. Bröning et al. (2019) designed a group for children of alcoholics that included sessions on promoting self-worth, substance abuse education, understanding emotions, self-efficacy, learning, and supporting new family behaviors. The group allows students facing the same situations to understand they are not alone, while learning coping mechanisms. School counselors should note that focusing on understanding substance use disorder, self-efficacy, boundaries, and family dynamics is helpful for students facing these challenges.

Elgán et al. (2016) completed a study on telemental health using the phone and computer applications before the 2020–2021 COVID-19 pandemic. The research found that because children and adolescents place a high value on their cellular phones, interventions using technology can work well for supporting students through home environments with substance abuse. In the emerging virtual school setting, school counselors could lead secure online chat groups. This could be done during lunch or advisory periods and avoids pulling students out of virtual class. The topics for the weekly group chats are similar to the topics in the group counseling curriculum. The 9-week sessions include the following:

> (1) getting acquainted with the home situation, (2) roles in the family, (3) thoughts and feelings, (4) questions and answers about mental health problems, (5) different behavior patterns, (6) social networks, (7) leading your own life with regard to social networks, and (8) the future. The ninth session is a follow-up session. After each session, the participants are required to complete a homework assignment to be discussed at the subsequent session (Elgán et al., 2016, p. 5).

Both studies showed the effectiveness of using group counseling with students struggling with parental substance abuse (Bröning et al., 2019; Elgán et al., 2016). These groups allowed children and adolescents to feel "normal" while receiving the support needed to overcome their parental obstacles.

Another support resource to consider for students is Alateen. Alateen, is a group for teenagers of alcohol/substance-abusing parents from Alcoholics Anonymous. The group can be recommended to middle and high school-aged students (Alcoholics Anonymous, n.d.). Alateen should not be the first resort for school counselors but should be presented as an additional outside option when a student is concerned about remaining anonymous in the school yet would benefit from group support. Timko et al. (2016) suggested counselors encourage students to attend Alateen on a regular basis for at least 6 months, as a study showed continuing attendance allowed the child to "learn how to handle problems due to the drinker, and increased well-being and functioning, including reduced verbal or physical abuse victimization" (p. 441).

If facilitating a small group is not achievable, school counselors should consider facilitating classroom guidance on substance abuse prevention and intervention or sharing psychoeducational resources with homeroom teachers who often have advisory periods. Given the number of students impacted by substance use, school counselors are called to think creatively about how to disseminate information and resources regarding this topic.

Checking your bias against individuals and families who struggle with substance abuse is crucial for your work as a school counselor. It will be difficult to come from a genuine, nonjudgmental, and empathetic focus if you are operating from stereotypes and bias concerning individuals and families who struggle with substance use disorder (SUD). School counselors should operate from a prevention model (American School Counselor Association [ASCA], 2019). School counselors should integrate a systemic approach to substance use prevention and intervention. This should include psychoeducation, individual counseling, class guidance, resources, family outreach, and small groups. Substance use, abuse, and addiction are among the leading causes of adolescent death in the United States (Brannigan et al., 2004). School counselors are in the unique role of being able to provide prevention and intervention services for at-risk students and families (ASCA, 2019).

THE IMPACT OF HOMELESSNESS AND POVERTY

In January 2020, before the pandemic, The Department of Housing and Urban Development indicated that 106,000 children were homeless, including almost 11,000 children living outside. Between 20% and 25% of all adolescents under 18 experience poverty or homelessness (Havlik et al., 2018; Heberle et al., 2021). Bright (2020) reported that most lower-socioeconomic students resided in rural communities, but it is important to be mindful of students affected by poverty and homelessness in urban settings as well. Lower socioeconomic and homeless students are affected in all three domains of school counseling: academic, personal/social, and career (ASCA, 2019). From a social-emotional perspective, students without permanent housing can experience "internalizing and externalizing problems, difficult[y] forming relationships with peers, and withdrawing behaviors" (Havlik et al., 2018, p. 47). This relates to the transitional impact on students and families. Students without permanent housing can experience depression and post-traumatic stress disorder (PTSD), which in turn can lead to behavior issues and suicide ideation (Havlik et al., 2018). Students struggling with lack of shelter, food, or clothing are not preoccupied with academics, school expectations, or behaviors, but rather on survival (Begg et al., 2017).

Students moving between schools and districts have pressure to consistently adapt to new schedules, new behavioral expectations, and new school personnel. Students in transition experience larger levels of grief and loss (Begg et al., 2017). Students without permanent housing can experience academic issues, gaps in learning and instruction, and lack of educational support (Begg et al., 2017; Havlik et al., 2018). Attendance may also be problematic. School counselors should consider that students impacted by homelessness may have difficulty obtaining the credits required to graduate and be lacking in the skills to pass state-required examinations for graduation due to inconsistent school attendance. The school counselor should be aware of the intersection of issues for students they work with. Many of students face challenges with peers, difficult neighborhood atmosphere, parental drug abuse, disorganized families, family history of mental health concerns, their own mental health issues, family violence, anxiety, low socioeconomic status, and a culture of drug abuse.

Understanding and Advocating

School counselors must be aware of the definitions of homelessness according to the federally mandated McKinney-Vento Homeless Assistance Act (U.S. Department of Education, 2016). The official definitions of homelessness for children and youth according to the McKinney-Vento Act (p. 5) are as follows:

- Sharing the housing of other persons due to loss of housing, economic hardship, or a similar reason (sometimes referred to as "doubled-up")
- Living in motels, hotels, trailer parks, or camping grounds due to lack of alternative adequate accommodations
- Living in emergency or transitional shelters
- Being abandoned in hospitals
- Living in a primary nighttime residence that is a public or private place not designed for, or ordinarily used as, a regular sleeping accommodation for human beings
- Living in cars, parks, public spaces, abandoned buildings, substandard housing, bus or train stations, or similar settings
- Being migratory children because they are living in circumstances described above.

The McKinney-Vento Act requires school districts to provide services for students without permanent housing, including enrolling in any school without mandatory paperwork and information (U.S. Department of Education, 2016). School districts are required to provide transportation to students to the school they are currently attending—even if they move into another school zone in the same district—to provide continuity (Havlik et al., 2018). School counselors should be aware of their district's liaison or a specific contact person to assist with needed arrangements and resources for students and families in need.

The ASCA calls for school counselors to be advocates for students who are homeless or from lower socioeconomic backgrounds (2019). School counselors can assist students without permanent housing as well as poverty-affected students by collaborating with community organizations and resources, social workers, homeless liaisons, guardians/parents, administration, and teachers (Begg et al., 2017; Havlik et al., 2018; Heberle et al., 2021). School counselors should be aware that there might be some ACEs due to homelessness or poverty (ASCA, 2019). School counselors are often the first line of defense for students in need of services (Havlik et al., 2018). In some schools, school counselors keep a closet of donated emergency supplies, such as hygiene products, clothes, and food for students and families to access.

School counselors have the opportunity to be systemic advocates and leaders for change. They act as liaisons with teachers and administrators, while advocating on behalf of parents for community service (Monaghan et al., 2020). It is recommended that school counselors meet with teachers individually to discuss the needs of the homeless and poverty-impacted students (Heberle et al., 2021). To respect the confidentiality and autonomy of students, school counselors can work with teachers on best practices for serving these students well. School counselors can also speak with the student and gain permission to discuss their situation with their teachers or encourage them to disclose themselves for additional support. Additionally, school counselors can advocate for teachers to remove penalties for late assignments due to absences or other issues due to poverty and homeless student situations.

School counselors can support homeless students through brief individual and group counseling (Havlik et al., 2018). Providing opportunities to experience an empathic adult (school counselor or school personnel) and a peer group at school for additional support can be powerful and provide the student with nurturing and stability (Begg et al., 2017). Experiential counseling, including play, sand tray, art, and bibliotherapy activities, can also help students with topics such as stress reduction, goal setting, friendship skills, academic success, and career exploration. Motivational interviewing is also a theoretical technique school counselors can use to explore a student's readiness to make changes in aspects of their lives where they do have control. This approach can help students with goal setting and action plans to support academic growth (Pincus et al., 2018).

Systemic and schoolwide programs can assist in reducing the stigma by providing psychoeducation, community, and school resources to parents in need (Havlik et al., 2018). School counselors can facilitate these interventions through scheduled nighttime parent meetings for those who have daytime work conflicts and assemblies to provide needed information and resources. Some meetings could be held outside of the school building in community centers or shelters to provide additional access to parents without transportation. It is also worth noting that school itself could be a trigger or be associated with painful memories for families, another reason to consider off-site support. School counselors in Title I schools (Title I is a federal program that gives funds to schools in need based on student enrollment and provides the free and reduced lunch cost for each school) should be highly visible and accessible throughout the building (Monaghan et al., 2020). School counselors can deliver information through classroom guidance and resource booths during lunch and make resources available at school and community events that families attend. School counselors should try to follow the ASCA National Model to focus on direct student services to provide the best support for lower socioeconomic students (ASCA, 2019), who generally have more needs than other students (Monaghan et al., 2020).

To best assist lower socioeconomic, including homeless, students, school counselors could use the social justice and humanistic-based CARE Model (Johnson, 2017). The school counselor should *cultivate* a positive relationship with students and parents, *acknowledge* without judgment the families current financial and living situation, work toward *removing* barriers through advocacy and education, and *expand* students' strengths using culturally appropriate interventions.

THE IMPACT OF IMMIGRATION AND REFUGEE STATUS

While similar, immigrants and refugees have different definitions. Webster (2021) defined an immigrant as "a person who comes to a country to take up permanent residence." The definition of a *refugee* is "a person who flees to a foreign country or power to escape danger or persecution" (Webster 2021). The Webster definition is used as it is the most general and directive. In general, refugees are leaving their country due to negative issues (Todd et al., 2020). Whatever your political thoughts on immigration, the ASCA's (2022) Code of Ethics requires students to be treated with respect regardless of immigration status. There are approximately 11.2 million undocumented immigrants in the United States, accounting for almost 4% of the population (Crawford & Valle, 2016). For this section, we will use the term *immigrants'* for both refugees and immigrants, unless otherwise noted.

Education has so many implications for immigrants, including a way to advance socioeconomic opportunities (Crawford & Valle, 2016). The Supreme Court ruled in the 1982 case *Plyler v. Dwyer* that all students, regardless of legal status, are eligible for a free PK–12 education in the United States. Additionally, the Deferred Action for Childhood Arrivals (DACA) law allowed immigrant children to attend school without the worry of immigration officials taking them into custody. Crawford and Valle noted in 2016 that in certain cities in the United States, children from Mexico crossed the border daily to attend United States schools. School counselors must understand the hardships of their students' lives. Schools cannot require immigrants to have a state ID or drivers' license to register for classes (Todd et al., 2020). Schools are not permitted to ask about an immigrant's legal status. Studies show school counselors are best suited to assist immigrants, particularly undocumented immigrants, due to confidentiality discussed in the ASCA Code of Ethics (ASCA, 2016a, 2016b; Crawford & Valle, 2016). School counselors must advocate for immigrant children and assist them in uncertain times in a new environment.

Immigrants and refugees who are in the United States without the legally required documents are considered undocumented (Crawford & Valle, 2016). Undocumented immigrants may be living in poverty, struggling with health care due to lack of services, experiencing language barriers, be placed in lower-performing schools, and often live in fear of deportation (Crawford & Valle, 2016; Todd et al., 2020). School counselors should note the additional fear their immigrant students and families face regarding being identified by government officials (Todd et al., 2020). This fear leads many undocumented immigrants and families to purposely stay isolated. Immigrants may be suffering from PTSD after suffering trauma in their home country, during their travels to the United States, and in their current household (Marshall et al., 2016; Todd et al., 2020). School counselors should note that only 5%–10% of undocumented immigrants attend college after high school graduation (Crawford & Valle, 2016). Immigrants often live in single-parent homes or with family members other than parents to access education in U.S. education systems. The McKenny Vento Act discussed earlier in the chapter applies for undocumented immigrants (Todd et al., 2020).

Understanding and Advocating

School counselors can create resilience in immigrant children by building strong relationships and advocating for appropriate services (Crawford & Valle, 2016; Marshall et al., 2016). As discussed earlier in this chapter, when working with any marginalized population, using person-centered counseling skills allows the counselor and student to build relationships (Marshall et al., 2016). The school counselor can work with students to provide hope for their future. Marshall et al. (2016) recommend a strength-based approach to assist the students with their resiliency.

School counselors must be aware that immigrants do not always trust the school system. This dynamic may create barriers in building relationships with students and families (Crawford & Valle, 2016; Marshall et al., 2020; Todd et al., 2020). School counselors can advocate for immigrant students with school administrators, teachers, and outside community organizations (Crawford & Valle, 2016). School counselors can advocate for access to mental health counseling within schools for immigrant students as families may be more comfortable with educational services than outside counseling clinics (Hoffman et al., 2018; Marshall et al., 2016). Hoffman et al. (2018) noted that immigrants and refugees may experience higher levels of "depression, anxiety, sleep disturbance, survivor's guilt, aggression, internalization of problems, learning difficulties, and impacted academic performance" (p. 45).

Marshall et al. (2016) noted the importance of school counselors' understanding the culture of the refugee and immigrant students at their schools to best assist them in a respectful manner, as many cultures have not previously been exposed to Western counseling techniques. For example, a clients' culture might be based on a collectivist society verses individualist ideas. In some cases, cultures do not accept counseling and will stigmatize members who seek counseling support. This is a reason to offer therapeutic mental health counseling within the school by contracted outside providers (Hoffman et al., 2018; Marshall et al., 2016). These providers can address mental health issues beyond the scope of school counselors, while offering easy access within the school building. Recognizing a family-systems approach allows the schools counselor to better understand the connections, both culturally and related to family history (Marshall et al., 2016).

It is crucial that school counselors focus on family engagement when assisting with basic needs, cultural adaptation, and mental health needs that may contribute to behavioral issues (McNeely et al., 2020). School counselors should ensure visibility to parents, including greeting students in the morning, home visits, and community events. If the school counselor can build trust within the community, the families will be more likely to access school and community resources. Students and families may be more likely to access school counseling interventions if they are positioned as educational in nature—such as social/emotional learning. This avoids any stigma regarding mental health (McNeely et al., 2020). Teacher–school counselor–student partnerships are essential for the success of the student and their families as they navigate and adjust. Teachers serve as a necessary bridge between school counselors and students because they have daily contact with and are influential with families. It is beneficial for school counselors to ensure that they provide nurturing relationships and communication with classroom teachers to create opportunities for referrals of students and families that would be aided by additional school counselor support.

THE IMPACT OF DEPLOYMENT

Military personnel and their families are accustomed to both short and long periods of separation. More recently, with conflicts in the Middle East and other areas of the world, families have experienced more frequent separations and adjustments in family structures and routines (Alfano et al., 2016). When children and families are separated for any reason, there is a strain on the family system. Military service may be an individual experience, but it often feels like the family is serving alongside the deployed family member. Separation from parents or caregivers for long periods of time can increase a child's anxiety levels. Branches of the military may require one, or both parents, to deploy. Deployments can be in a training capacity or can be combat related and varies in length of time. It isn't unusual for a child to experience a parent who has deployed multiple occasions throughout their childhood (Alfano et al., 2016; Cederbaum et al., 2014). Children whose parents are deployed may experience mental health concerns, trauma, and other adjustment-related concerns. Research focusing on the impact of deployment indicates there can be increased feelings of sadness and hopelessness, as well as suicidal ideation among children. One study found that 34% of adolescents with a military parent reported feelings of sadness and hopelessness that extended for longer than 2 weeks. The study also showed that 25% of adolescents with a military parent had contemplated suicide (Cederbaum et al., 2014). The impact of a deployment on the child will depend on their age and developmental stage. Younger children may experience separation anxiety and behavioral issues. Children in other developmental stages my show signs of opposition to parental direction, substance use, physical symptoms, anger outbursts, apathy, mood swings, and problematic eating patterns (Alfano et al., 2016; Cederbaum et al., 2014; Chartrand et al., 2008). It should be noted that not all children face these challenges when family members are deployed.

Family Reintegration

The return of a family member that has been deployed is often a joyous occasion. The process of a family member returning from deployment to the family routine, structure, and roles is called *family reintegration*. Even though it is generally a time to rejoice, family reintegration can also pose challenges and be a stressful occasion (Messecar, 2017). Members of the family of the returning soldier are unlikely to be privy to all or any events that happened during deployment. In turn, the deployed soldier may not be aware of changes that occurred in the family while away. These could include family changes, problems with the children at home or in school, or changes to routines. Military personnel returning from deployment may be suffering from the effects of stress. Often, after the excitement of reintegration ends, problems become evident. Some of these may include the need for control, substance abuse, high levels of irritability, and PTSD (Messecar, 2017). Taft et al., (2011) note that 1 in 3 returning military personnel are impacted by depression, PTSD, or mild traumatic brain injury. Issues that arise and are left untreated in the returned military person can put their family system at higher risk for substance abuse, inability to handle stressful situations, and family violence (Messecar, 2017). Boundaries may also pose a challenge during the reintegration period. Boundary ambiguity (Faber et al., 2008) occurs when family members are uncertain of roles and tasks to be completed within the family. Returning military personnel who have experienced the greatest impact of boundary ambiguity are those returning to systems that have had significant changes. Those returning military personnel who have also experienced a heightened and consistent level of stress during deployment may have difficulty with reentry (Faber et al., 2008). Research has shown that military families have indicated several areas that contribute to reintegration challenges. These include preparation for deployment, length of deployment, type of deployment, ability to communicate with family during deployment, and education around how deployment impacts the family system (Messecar, 2017).

Understanding and Advocating

Students are typically in school for 180 days per year, and issues facing deployment and reintegration within the family system will be present and could be problematic in school settings. School counselors are in the position to advocate and support students whose parents are deploying, deployed, or reentering family systems. Awareness of the need for support in this area will help school counselors build effective and comprehensive programming. Communication is essential between the school counselor and the family. Advocacy in the role of school counselor can include schoolwide knowledge of deployment and impact, classroom guidance, and professional development for the teachers. School counselors can provide students with individual and small-group counseling. A framework of serving students and families who are deployed, facing deployment, or reintegrating can be helpful for the school counselors providing needed support. The framework consists of preparation, length of deployment, communication, and impact (Messecar, 2017). How a family prepares for deployment, the length of deployment, and how much communication occurs during deployment, all have impact on the family system, and that knowledge is essential for a school counselor (Messecar, 2017):

- **Preparation:** The school counselor should be mindful of the demographics of their schools. Some schools are in communities with a high military concentration, while others are not. In schools that serve a significant number of military families, partnering with the military family liaison (if there is one) will be essential. Regardless of the number of military families served, the school counselor should be prepared to provide services. Communication with all families is important. Let families know that it is important to inform the school counselor of any deployments or returns of military family members. This allows the school counselor the opportunity to work with the student on preparing emotionally for the departure or return of their parent.

- **Length of deployment:** School counselors can partner with families to communicate about specific student needs during deployment and the length of deployment. The school counselor should mentally and physically note current or upcoming dates to facilitate intentional check-ins with impacted students. This gives the message that the school counselor is always available to students and lets the student know that they are not alone. When the deployment is nearing the end, the school counselor should check in with the family and inquire about needs of the family and check in with the student to help process emotions that come with a returning family member. The work does not stop there. The school counselor should be checking in with the student for several months past reintegration.

- **Communication during deployment:** The school counselor can offer their support as a liaison for communication with the student and the deployed family member. The school counselor can provide materials for letter writing and card making and help brainstorm care packages. The school counselor and the student(s) (if willing) can elicit help from the whole school in letter-writing and card-making campaigns. School counselors should note special holidays and birthdays of the deployed family member. The student will not only want to communicate in some way with the family on these special occasions but also may need extra support from the school counselor.

■ **Impact on the family system:** This is a good opportunity for the school counselor to facilitate psychoeducation with the student individually, through classroom guidance (if there are several military families in the community), and in small groups. An understanding of what could happen in family systems before, during, and after deployment is important. This information can demystify the deployment process, gives a space to process, and alleviates any guilt a student may feel for altered behavior from the family member or the family system during reintegration.

Both individual counseling and small-group interventions are recommended to support students whose parents are deployed (Cole, 2016). The ASCA (2021) has developed a group curriculum that addresses many issues that students are facing with the deployment of their parents. When researching appropriate curriculum, some may seem focused on younger students; however, topics can be developmentally adjusted for all students and used in a group setting.

Resilience to Stress

Most families have the skills to cope with deployment, but some are unable to handle the stress without negative consequences (Chandra et al., 2010; McNulty, 2005). Individuals that have learned to be resilient draw on their internal resources and the support in their environment to endure hardship (Weiss et al., 2010). Children learn these coping skills through the development of cognitive thinking, regulation of behavior, and interactions with caregivers and the environment (Masten, 2001). Young children in stressed families may not adequately learn these coping behaviors and, therefore, risk long-term physical and mental health problems caused by the effects of stress on the developing body and brain (NSCDC, 2008). As military families are faced with continued stressors from deployment and redeployment, they may seek assistance from mental health professionals. Counselors providing service to these family members must be informed about military life. This includes understanding the distinct ethics, codes of conduct, and strict hierarchical roles of the culture. Counselors must become equipped with knowledge and interventions (Weiss et al., 2010) suited for all family members, including those under the age of 6 years.

THE IMPACT OF INCARCERATION

Being a child of a family member who is incarcerated can have a substantial impact on a student's emotional, physical, and academic success. The literature notes that family members and children of incarcerated parents can be identified as hidden victims (Raeder, 2012). This means the family members of the incarcerated individuals are often unacknowledged, unheard, and receive minimal or no support (Raeder, 2012). It is estimated that approximately 2.3 million individuals are incarcerated today (Martin, 2017). The increase in incarceration started in the 1970s with the war on drugs (Martin, 2017). The authors of this chapter also refer to the war on drugs as the war on poverty and people of color, as the war on drugs (poverty and people of color) was related to the severe and inequitable penalties targeting marginalized communities. It is unclear how many children have an incarcerated parent. One estimate is between 1.7 and 2.7 million children have had a parent incarcerated once during their childhood (Martin, 2017). In the past two decades the increase of parents being arrested and placed in jail is at the highest it has been in the history of the United States (Austin et al., 2021). A report presented by the United States Government Accountability Office (2018) indicates students of color are more likely to have a parent who is incarcerated. The report also states that students of color are more likely to be disciplined by teachers for the same behaviors White students do without consequences. It is understandable that students with an absent parent may be more prone to acting out behaviors (Shlafer et al., 2017). It is important to note that the judicial system is marred by and continues to be marred by systemic racism.

The impact of adult incarceration may vary among children impacted. Children of incarcerated parents are more susceptible to exhibiting antisocial behaviors that could include criminal acts and dishonesty (Murray et al., 2012). The long-term impacts of incarceration of a parent on a childhood experience is well documented (Shlafer et al., 2017). Having an incarcerated parent is considered an ACE. Historical and current research supports that individuals with increased ACE scores are more likely to experience long-term physical and emotional challenges (Chang et al., 2019; Felitti, 1998). It is important to note that the witnessing of a parent's arrest is also cause of increased stress, confusion, and trauma. The witnessing of a parents' arrest and the loss the child faces could have an impact on a child's emotional, social, and academic development (Pehlmann-Tynan et al., 2021).

Research is somewhat limited related to the understanding of the direct impact of incarceration on a child's wellness (Martin, 2017). There are many factors, as discussed throughout this chapter, that impact a child. Families may face incarceration, economic challenges, substance abuse, and more. What is known is that any disruptions in the child's life can cause concerns in social, emotional, and academic well-being and can impact their career trajectory. Other risk factors that students face may be escalated if the incarcerated parent is a strong support in the child's life (Austin et al., 2021).

Understanding and Advocating

Confidentiality and privacy of the student and families are imperative. Some may fear being judged or ridiculed by the school system if they disclose a family member's incarceration. Students whose parents are incarcerated are often subjected to stereotypes and bias (Dallaire et al., 2010). The school counselor can have great impact on the support and advocacy of these students by modeling and teaching inclusivity and equity. The focus does not have to be solely on incarcerated parents but can also focus on schoolwide inclusivity as it relates to all families experiencing challenges. The role of a school counselor should include challenging and demystifying these biases in school systems. Teachers or school personnel who make assumptions about a student's ability or behavior based on their family situation should be reeducated and reminded that these practices are harmful and biased (Dallaire et al., 2010). School counselors can work with teachers to provide strength-based, supportive interventions that promote student emotional wellness, sense of connection, and feelings of security. The school counselor can train school personnel, partner with community agencies for support, create resources for students, teachers, and families regarding incarceration and interventions, and offer individual support and small-group counseling. Shlafer et al. (2017) encourage school professionals to identify risk and protective factors for students when developing services, programs, and interventions. Facilitating assessments is an important opportunity to identify school community needs. Some of these could include teacher and student checklists and needs assessments implemented schoolwide with students, school personnel, and families. Results data can inform needed interventions to build responsive, inclusive, and trauma-informed services for students who parents are incarcerated.

VOICES FROM THE FIELD

Name: Marwan Stanford (he/him)

Where You Practice: Clear Water High School

Professional Job Title: School Counselor and Department Chair

Bio: Marwan Stanford received his bachelor's degree at SUNY at Buffalo and his masters in counselor education at Canisius College. He has spent the past 16 years as a school counselor at the high school level in Tampa Bay. He enjoys coaching basketball, as well as serving at his local church.

Working as a professional school counselor is one of the most rewarding jobs to have. The ability to support and strengthen students in their pursuit of wellness, academic success, and in their college and career trajectory is a privilege. Understanding that students face many barriers outside of my control is an important part of being a professional school counselor. Although we wish that we could regulate all barriers in the student's environment, we cannot. What we can do is be the best advocate and supporter in the students' life during the time we have them. Losing the steady protection and comfort of a home can rock a student down to their core. It can break their spirit while forcing them to lose their focus on their future and goals. As a school counselor I can help build a support system to help the student succeed during the chaos. Keeping the lines of communication open is important. Finding a reliable phone or internet source can be challenging. I've had to intercede for the family to receive and deliver pertinent information such as assignments. Teachers are usually accommodating if they know the situation. Informing other members of your school's support services is another important step. Collaborating and consulting with your school psychologist and school social worker are important. Also as important is communication with your building principal and leadership team. They have the ability to problem solve on a broader level and may have access to resources you do not have as a professional school counselor. What is most important is keeping the faith that your students will succeed. As professional school counselors, we must continue to give positive reinforcement and encourage the student to "weather the storm."

SUMMARY AND CONCLUSION

It is necessary for future school counselors to devote themselves to the task of acquiring and using the skills necessary to become the proponent that diverse students and families have needed for far too long. "Developing and maintaining multicultural and social justice competence is a continuous, lifelong process that informs the way counselors engage in advocacy, conduct and interpret research, and educate and supervise future counselors" (Ratts et al., 2016). To be successful in this pursuit of supporting students and families, this means more than attending trainings and conferences. School counselors must truly invest in accepting and investigating their own biases and deficits in skills and knowledge as it relates to working with families and challenges their students face within the home environment (Ratts et al., 2016).

Lorelle et al. (2021) indicate that counselors who are engaged in both multicultural and social justice issues are willing to seek and integrate various theories and identity development models to best serve students and families. Counselors who aspire to serve all their students and become true agents of change within schools will look for opportunities to advocate while being willing to challenge any roadblocks that are presented.

School counselors will need to be prepared to challenge peers and staff who show an unwillingness or who perpetuate bias against families who face challenges. Shillingford et al. (2020) note that educators can do this by focusing on student achievement and school supportive relationships and by developing community partnerships that are strength focused. Only counselors who have fully integrated multiculturalism and social justice ideals and beliefs into their practice and work will be able to most effectively serve and support families who are facing the barriers addressed in this chapter (and the many more that are not addressed). Challenges facing families can adversely impact a student's academics, personal and social wellness, and career trajectory. School counselors are not only called to have specific and specialized training areas related to these challenges but also are called to have empathy, compassion, cultural humility, and humanness. Open, equitable, and inclusive communication is the foundation of supporting all students and families facing any challenges. If the school counselor is accessible and open to family partnership, it is more likely that the family will share pertinent and important information with them. The focus should always be on what we can do to support the student and their families.

CASE STUDY

You are the school counselor and have been working with Brad for the past several years. He is a sophomore in high school. Recently Brad has been showing lack of motivation in the classroom, disengaging from his assignments, and isolating from his friends. In touching base with Brad, you find out that his mother has just been deployed with the military and will be gone for the next 18 months. Although this is not her first deployment, Brad shared that this time it feels different. He reports being extremely worried and preoccupied with his mother's safety and fears that she will not return home.

DISCUSSION QUESTIONS

1. What approach will you take to support Brad?
2. What will be helpful information to have about Brad and his mother?
3. How will you advocate for Brad in your role as his school counselor?
4. What support does Brad need from you and the school?

PRACTICAL APPLICATION

- Have open lines and multiple opportunities to communicate with families so that information about the student is shared mutually and consistently.

- Consider the families' basic needs (transportation, access to food, healthcare, and other important resources) and partner with community agencies and the school social worker. Help establish transportation, if needed.

- Establish a current resource list; update and check the list every 3 months as resources in the community can change rapidly.

- Offer brief counseling. Providing a safe space for processing home and outside environmental influences is important. Students want to be heard and understood, even if there is not an immediate solution to the problem.

- School counselors should discuss future college and career opportunities with students to reduce the stereotypes of poverty in the family.

KEY REFERENCES

Only key references appear in the print edition. The full reference list appears in the digital product on Springer Publishing Connect: connect.springerpub.com/content/book/978-0-8261-8753-6/part/part04/chapter/ch14

American School Counseling Association. (1989–90/1993, 1999, 2004, 2011, 2017). *The school counselor and identification, prevention, and intervention of behaviors that are harmful and place students at risk.* https://schoolcounselor.org/Standards-Positions/Position-Statements/ASCA-Position-Statements/The-School-Counselor-and-the-Identification,-Preve

Chang, X., Jiang, X., Mkandarwire, T., & Shen, M. (2019). Associations between adverse childhood experiences and health outcomes in adults aged 18–59 years. *PLoS One, 14*(2), e0211850. https://doi.org/10.1371/journal.pone.0211850

Faber, A. J., Willerton, E., Clymer, S. R., MacDermid, S. M., & Weiss, H. M. (2008). Ambiguous absence, ambiguous presence: A qualitative study of military reserve families in wartime. *Journal of Family Psychology, 22*(2), 222–230. https://doi.org/10.1037/0893-3200.22.2.222

Hays, D. G. (2020). Multicultural and social justice counseling competency research: Opportunities for innovation. *Journal of Counseling & Development, 98*(3), 331–344. https://doi.org/10.1002/jcad.12327

Ratts, M. J., Singh, A. A., Nassar-McMillan, S., Butler, S. K., & McCullough, J. R. (2016). Multicultural and social justice counseling competencies: Guidelines for the counseling profession. *Journal of Multicultural Counseling and Development, 44*(1), 28–48. https://doi.org/10.1002/jmcd.12035

CHAPTER 15

Mandatory Reporting: Recognizing Abuse and Neglect

KATHY MCDONALD AND LAURA I. HODGES

LEARNING OBJECTIVES

After reading this chapter, students will be able to:

- Recall the historical evolution of federal laws related to child abuse and neglect, as well as their professional responsibility to become knowledgeable regarding their unique state-related laws and mandates.
- Recognize their ethical obligation as a mandated reporter as outlined by the American Counseling Association (ACA) and the American School Counselor Association (ASCA).
- Recognize the legal duty of a mandated reporter and the changes in definition from state to state.
- Identify and discuss the boundaries of confidentiality and the ethical and cultural considerations related to suspected child abuse and neglect reporting.

STUDENT VOICE

Student "R" provided the following testimonial:

The young lady introduced herself as Rebecca and asked me what I did for a living. When I replied that I was a school counselor, she exclaimed, "A school counselor saved my life!" Rebecca had my full attention. At age 14, she had been in a sexual relationship with a married man who was a decade older. The two were "in love" and life was good, until her middle school counselor found out. Rebecca was horrified when the counselor explained that she was a mandated reporter, required by law to make a CPS report. No amount of crying and pleading would change the counselor's mind. Rebecca escalated to cursing and screaming. "I hate you," were the last words she spoke as she ran out of the room. "I meant it," she told me. "I really hated her." Rebecca was relieved when her family moved to a different city. She would never have to see this counselor again. Rebecca concluded her story by telling me, "But now I get it. She didn't ruin my life. She saved it. I wish I could tell her that."

INTRODUCTION

Seldom do school counselors know the impact they have on the lives of students, especially the ones at the center of child welfare investigations. Regardless, dedicated school counselors are much more than mandated reporters. They are advocates for the welfare of students. The intent of this chapter is to prepare counseling students for outcries of abuse or neglect, to face the unimaginable realities of mistreated children, and to act without hesitation on their behalf. The primary obligation of school counselors, as outlined in the American School Counseling Association (ASCA) Ethical Standards (2022), Section A.1.a., is their responsibility to students. Of all the roles that counselors have, none is more important than fulfilling our high standard of responsibility to students. Both the ASCA Ethical Standards (2022) and the ACA Code of Ethics (2014) direct us toward professional conduct as we work to protect students from harm. Professional conduct includes complying with current federal and state laws written to safeguard children from mistreatment. Counselors, as advocates, are knowledgeable about both federal and state law as it pertains to mandated reporting. They familiarize themselves with the indicators of abuse and neglect, and they closely attend to their professional codes of ethics.

HISTORY OF CHILD PROTECTION IN THE UNITED STATES

The early evolution of child abuse laws in the United States demonstrated a slow and inauspicious start to protecting America's children (Myers, 2008). In the United States, animal protection laws existed before child protection laws. Until 1874, no law allowed for an individual to intervene on behalf of a maltreated child (Myers, 2008). The first laws related to the prevention of child maltreatment have origins in those of the American Society for the Prevention of Cruelty to Animals (ASPCA) (Eide, 1990; Myers, 2008). In this same year, the New York Society for the Prevention of Cruelty to Children (NYSPCC) was created (Eide, 1990) and dedicated to the protection of children (Myers, 2008). In NYSPCC's very first year, more than 300 cases of child abuse were investigated (Eide, 1990). Despite significant societal resistance, official legislation was passed in New York in 1876 (Eide, 1990). The NYSPCC-sponsored law, "An Act to Prevent and Punish Wrongs to Children," was the cornerstone to their advocacy for children, including future legislation related to child laborers (Eide, 1990).

Mandated Reporters

In the state of New York, child abuse and neglect could now be reported; however, laws did not exist that mandated anyone to report abuse. Kalichman (1999) wrote that "mandatory reporting of child abuse by professionals . . . did not become law until the early 1960s" (p. 13). In the 1960s, the original list of mandated reporters consisted only of physicians, but by the 1970s, the list of mandated reporters had expanded (Kalichman, 1999).

Kenny et al. (2018) reported that each state except New Jersey had enacted laws defining and detailing which professions are designated as mandated reporters. The Child Welfare Information Gateway (2019a) provided this update, "Approximately 47 States . . . designate professions whose members are mandated by law to report child maltreatment" (p. 2). The Child Welfare Information Gateway (2019a) notes that state laws are often amended. At the time of the 2019 report, three states did not specify professions as mandated reporters but rather required all persons to report.

Due to the enactment of the Child Abuse Prevention and Treatment Act of 1974 (CAPTA; Pub.L.No. 93–247), a federal definition of child abuse and neglect was created that became the foundation for state mandatory reporting laws (Kalichman, 1999). As identified in the federal definition:

Any recent act or failure to act on the part of a parent or caretaker which results in death, serious physical or emotional harm, sexual abuse or exploitation; or an act or failure to act, which presents an imminent risk of serious harm. (U.S. Department of Health & Human Services [USDHHS], 2019, pp. 102–103)

The following statement cannot be stressed enough: school counselors must familiarize themselves with their state-specific definition of child abuse and neglect and be aware of the differences and similarities in comparison to federal definitions. Each state has the authority to create its own definitions and specific requirements that surround reporting. States also set a time frame by which a report must be made after the suspicion or outcry. For example, Texas allows up to 48 hours, in contrast to Alabama's requirement to report immediately. The Child Welfare Information Gateway website provides the reader with the reporting requirements per state. Mandated reporting and mandated investigations have the potential to save lives.

The legal obligation is to report "a reasonable suspicion," rather than a certainty of abuse or neglect (Child Welfare Information Gateway, 2019b, p. 11). The mandated reporter needs to be well trained to recognize signs and symptoms of the various forms of abuse (Kesner & Robinson, 2002). Four types of abuse that are regularly covered in training include physical abuse, sexual abuse, emotional abuse, and neglect. ASCA (2021) added medical neglect and sex trafficking to the list and encouraged counselors to be aware of any other forms of abuse included in state law. Knowledge of the legal mandate is a necessary start, followed by thorough training. However, knowledge and training are not enough. Action is warranted to protect children. Mandated reporters must be observant and aware of the signs of abuse and neglect and willing to take the initiative to reach out to the student if a suspicion of abuse arises.

One hundred thirty-three student volunteers in an online school-counseling program were administered an anonymous survey on their personal child abuse histories. Participants were asked if they had been subjected to a form of abuse in childhood, and if so, what type of abuse or neglect they had suffered. Out of 133 participants, a third said they had suffered abuse, with half of the abused respondents reporting that they had been sexually assaulted in childhood. When asked who had intervened on their behalf, one respondent answered that she had told a teacher, but the teacher ignored her. All other respondents said they kept their abuse secret (McDonald, 2020). Children are often resistant to sharing information about abuse and neglect. Knowing the indicators of the different types of abuse and neglect is necessary if the protection of students is the goal.

VIGNETTE

Janet was one of our school moms, a lovely lady and a devoted mother who was active in the lives of her children. Janet stopped by my office one afternoon, and although I don't recall the initial reason for the conversation, I recall the shocking turn it took. Janet had been horribly abused as a child, she explained. She was allowed to go to school, but otherwise was banished to the basement. She was not allowed to eat dinner with the family but was called upstairs to clean the kitchen when dinner was over. "The dogs were fed before I could eat," she added. And when it was night, her stepfather would come down to the basement and sexually assault her. When I asked if any teacher had called child welfare to help her, she said no, no one knew. She had closely guarded her secret. On the day she graduated from high school, she had her suitcase packed. She left home and never looked back. If only someone had recognized the signs and reached out, Janet's suffering would have ended much sooner.

TRENDS

Counselors also remain current on abuse and neglect statistics, both state and national, that inform a mandated reporter's awareness of trends in maltreatment. Statistics reveal the type of harm that is most prevalent; abuse statistics relative to age, gender, ethnicity, and economic level; plus the risk factors that influence perpetrator behavior. The Children's Bureau collects state data that is submitted to the National Child Abuse and Neglect Data System (NCANDS), and after evaluating the data, publishes an annual report, *Child Maltreatment*, which has become an excellent source of state and national trends.

American youth are victimized at an average rate of nine out of 1,000 children, according to data collected by NCANDS and published in the annual report, USDHHS (2019). A further breakdown of the NCANDS 2019 data demonstrates the vulnerability of very young children who have not reached school age. Children ages 0 to 3 have a reported average of 15 abused children out of a total of 1,000. Although these averages are high, the number of identified victims is lower than the number of actual victims (Kesner & Robinson, 2002).

Reluctant to Report

Educators make the largest number of reports to Child Protective Services (CPS), accounting for 21% of all reports made (USDHHS, 2019). Despite the large number of reports, educators seriously underreport (Alvarez et al., 2004; Kenny & McEachern, 2002; Kesner & Robinson, 2002; Krase, 2013; Tillman et al., 2015). According to Webster et al. (2005), an astounding 85% of abuse cases in schools go unreported, with staff at small rural schools more likely to underreport cases of child maltreatment. In a survey of 133 educators enrolled in a school counseling program, 30% had never made a report of abuse or neglect (McDonald, 2020). When surveyed, educators who admitted the reluctance to report, stated that they were not comfortable making a report unless they could be certain that maltreatment had occurred. Teachers in another study cited their fear of being wrong, the lack of support from administration, and not seeing any clear signs of abuse (Kenny, 2001). Kenny (2004) determined that teachers often lack the knowledge of the signs and symptoms of abuse and lack understanding of district reporting procedures. Kenny concluded that regularly offered standardized training that includes district guidelines for reporting is essential for teachers to overcome their reluctance to report.

THE ROLE OF SCHOOL COUNSELOR: TRAINING AND SUPPORTING STAFF

Counselors have a unique place in the chain of reporting. Counselors who actively promote the welfare of students strive to be knowledgeable about state laws and district policies related to abuse and neglect. In addition, they seek further training in the recognition of the signs and indicators of child maltreatment (ASCA Ethical Standards, 2016, 2022, Section A.11.d., Section A.12.b.). With an in-depth knowledge about federal and state law, district policy surrounding the procedures for reporting, and the signs of child maltreatment, counselors can guide staff who must make reports.

Counselors, in turn, advocate for staff to have thorough training in all aspects of reporting (ASCA Ethical Standards, 2016, 2022, Section A.11.d., Section A.12.b.). In McDonald's (2020) survey of 133 counselors-in-training, 58% of respondents said their district training in mandated reporting was inadequate, a concern supported by other studies as researched by Krase (2013). Some states or districts offer mandated reporter training through annual professional development, but in some instances, counselors may have to advocate for high-quality training to be offered to staff routinely. Staff will learn during in-depth training that legal penalties may exist for failing to report suspicions of maltreatment, but legal protection is afforded to good-faith reporters. Legal penalties exist in 29 states for those who intentionally make false reports (Child Welfare Information Gateway, 2019c).

VIGNETTE

The mom appeared in my office with her daughter and demanded that I call CPS. She explained loudly that her ex-husband, who had custody, was physically abusing their daughter. The girl looked at her mom wide-eyed and anxious, but she bore no signs of physical abuse. The mom's voice rose to a shriek as she insisted that I report her abusive ex-husband to CPS. Standing firm, I said that if she had information to report she was welcome to use my phone. She shouted, "I CAN'T! The judge told me if I make one more false report to CPS he would put me in jail."

In McDonald's 2020 survey, 73% of the respondents said they would value more training in the appropriate way to speak with victims during an outcry. These respondents explained that they were fearful of eliciting any information from the student for fear of overstepping their authority. When they are well-trained, mandated reporters are less anxious and less reluctant to report (Bryant & Baldwin, 2009; Levi & Brown, 2005; Table 15.1).

VIGNETTE

"I'm scared when I go see my daddy." The tiny first grader held on to the stuffed rabbit and stared down at her feet. My heart sank. I needed to choose my words wisely and responded with, "Tell me about that." Then, I listened intently.

TABLE 15.1   Responding to Student Disclosures

Find a private place to allow the student to talk. When students share their stories before you can remind them of the limits to confidentiality, then let them know the action you will take at the end.	"This is a safe, quiet place to talk." "Remember that what you say in here is usually private, but if someone is hurting you, I will contact CPS to help."
The mandated reporter is a supportive, good listener, and does not interrupt.	"I will sit here and listen while you talk." "It is okay to tell me whatever you want to share."
Use of open-ended questions or probing statements that will allow students to share as much as they want to share.	"Tell me about that." "Tell me more." "And then what happened?" "Is there anything else you want to tell me?"
The student trusted you. Close the meeting with a thank you.	"Thank you for sharing this with me."
DO NOT...	Fill in details ("Your daddy did this to you, didn't he?") Dig for details. A trained interviewer will get the needed details. ("Was he drunk again?") Make judgmental statements about the parent or guardian, even if the parent is the perpetrator. ("That is awful! He is a bad person!") Use nonverbal language that indicates your personal distress, anger, or disgust.

(continued)

TABLE 15.1 Responding to Student Disclosures *(continued)*

Make mental or physical notes to include in the report to CPS:	Notice the child's hygiene, appearance, and behavior. Notice the location, sizes, and shape of marks or injuries (involve/consult with school nurse) Do physical injuries or marks match up with the student's story? Remember or document the student's exact words, phrases, or statements to use in your report.
If needed at the end:	*"Since someone is hurting you, I am going to call CPS to get their help."* *"You may go back to class. If another student or teacher asks about your visit, answer in a nice tone that it was a private conversation."*
When a student cries during an outcry:	Have a mirror available so they can see themselves and decide if they look ready to return to class. They may want to wash their face before returning to class.

Professional Standards

School counselors are mandated reporters, but they are also child advocates with broader ethical and moral interests. The ASCA Ethical Standards (2022) begin with a preamble that designates school counselors as advocates and then defines an advocate as someone who "acts to promote the well-being of students" (Glossary of Terms, n.p.). A word search within the ASCA Ethical Standards (2022) reveals that the word *advocate* is used 30 times, and the word *advocacy* is used 2 times, further emphasizing the scope of a school counselor's duty to act in the best interest of children.

School counselors refer to their ethical standards for guidance in ethical practice and professional behavior. Not only do school counselors practice within the boundaries of the ACA Code of Ethics and ASCA Ethical Standards, but counselors-in-training are equally responsible and should review the standards frequently. The first section of the ASCA Ethical Standards (2022), Section A, addresses the school counselor's responsibility to students. Section A., titled "Responsibility to Students," has 16 subsections, the most subsections in the document, underscoring the breadth of responsibility that counselors owe students. The standards listed in Section A.12., "Child Abuse," apply to the protection of children from maltreatment. Standards Sections A.11.a.–e., stress the school counselor's role regarding child maltreatment specific to abuse and neglect. In 2021, ASCA issued a position statement titled, "The School Counselor and Child Abuse and Neglect Prevention," which dovetails with the ASCA Ethical Standards (2022) and further defines the school counselor's role in reporting child abuse and neglect. Through their professional ethical standards, counselors are guided to consult when unsure about the proper response to an ethical dilemma (ASCA Ethical Standards, 2022, Section F.d.). Counselors are reminded to maintain confidentiality concerning a family's privacy (ASCA Ethical Standards, 2022, Section A.11.c.) and are charged with explaining the limits of confidentiality to students in developmentally appropriate terms (ASCA Ethical Standards, 2022, Section A.2.e.). The ASCA Ethical Standards (2022) are regularly revised and should be regularly reviewed by school counselors as part of their responsibility to remain current in the field. Despite revisions, the responsibility to act in a student's interest remains a fundamental duty.

Consultation

Identifying child maltreatment is frequently a difficult and emotional task. School counselors seek consultation with another mandated reporter when questions or doubts arise about reporting. The ASCA definition of consultation is "a professional relationship in which individuals meet to seek advice, information, and/or deliberation to address a student's need" (ASCA Ethical Standards, 2022, Glossary). When faced with a student concern, the school counselor consults with others whose area of expertise is helpful, such as a teacher or the school nurse. When uncertain about whether a student's situation should be reported, the law informs the mandated reporter that it is the suspicion of abuse or neglect that is reported, not the certainty of it. The submitted report then allows a child welfare employee to complete an investigation and determine the appropriate level of action. Counselors are not immune to the emotional impact of abuse and might be reluctant to make a report. Counselors consult with respected colleagues in the counseling profession to achieve clarity (ASCA Ethical Standards, 2022, Section B.3.h.) and then make the report. Additionally, the ACA Code of Ethics (2014), Section C, Professional Responsibility, Subsection C.2.e., Consultations on Ethical Obligations, contains guidance and promotes consultation with other professionals. Document the names and dates of those providing consultation, as well as their professional opinions (Herlihy & Corey, 2015).

VIGNETTE

Carol was the counselor who worked with the youngest students on our school campus. She understood the importance of parent involvement to student success and made it a priority to develop an inviting atmosphere at school for parents and guardians. One kindergarten mother remained hesitant to come to school events or to interact with her daughter's teacher. Carol worked to develop a relationship with this mother and was pleased to see her become more open and involved.

This morning, as the little kindergartner played in Carol's office, she saw a red mark on the child's lower back. With dread, she walked the little girl to the nurse's office and waited while the nurse inspected the marks. "What happened here?" Carol asked. The child simply replied that mom had been mad. The nurse documented the shape and length of the marks and the child's comment, then handed a copy of her documentation to Carol. Per district policy, Carol would add the nurse's notes to her own documentation.

Carol sent the child to class, entered my office, and sank into a chair to share her story. She asked, "What do I do?" The question surprised me because Carol knew the law. "You know what you have to do," I said. She sighed, nodded, and headed back to her office to make a report of physical abuse.

All counselors, even seasoned ones, consult with professionals who are more knowledgeable in specific areas, such as the school nurse. Counselors also consult with professionals when they are overcome with emotion or doubt. Carol needed support from another school counselor, someone who understood the dread she felt but would hold her accountable as a mandated reporter. It is what we do for each other.

Confidentialty and Minor Consent

Confidentiality is an expectation inherent to the counseling field and foundational to the student–counselor relationship (Carlson, 2017). Confidentiality is a fine line that counselors walk between the parent's legal rights and the counselor's ethical obligation to keep the student's privacy. School counselors learn the applicable laws surrounding confidentiality, informed consent as it applies to students, and the legal rights of parents versus minors (Stone & Dahir, 2016). ASCA Ethical Standards, 2022, Section A.2.a. in-structs counselors to make all stakeholders aware of the educator's legal mandate to re-port abuse and neglect. School counselors can then educate parents, students, and other stakeholders about the law and limits of confidentiality (Isaacs & Stone, 1999). Parents can be informed of the limits to confidentiality through newsletters, the website, during parent meetings, in the student handbook, and on consent forms.

School counselors also inform students that confidentiality will be breached and that the proper authorities will be contacted before a student discloses harm. Autonomy, one of five principles on which the ASCA Professional Ethical Standards (2016) are based, is the right of an individual to determine the direction of their life (ACA Code of Ethics, 2014, Preamble; ASCA Ethical Standards, 2022, Section F.e.). To uphold this principle, stu-dents are to be informed that the law requires counselors to breach confidentiality (ASCA Ethical Standards, 2022, Section A.2.d.).

Students can be informed early in the school year during classroom curriculum les-sons of the limits to confidentially, but it is wise to repeat the limits of confidentiality frequently, such as before a counseling session starts (Stone & Dahir, 2016). Limits to confidentiality should be explained to students in appropriate developmental terms to assist their understanding. Some counselors use an eye-catching poster on the office door or wall that provides examples of situations in which confidentiality would be breached. The principle of autonomy is upheld, and the relationship with the counselor more likely to remain intact, if the student is made aware of the limits to confidently before an outcry.

VIGNETTE

Every day during lunch, Colleen, a 14-year-old ninth-grader, appeared at my office door to visit. I was learning more about her through our frequent talks. She was often at home alone, which concerned me, but in some states, a 14-year-old is considered old enough to stay at home alone. In my state, CPS would not consider Colleen to be a neglected child.

On this particular day, Colleen came to my door looking frantic, exhausted, and di-sheveled. After inviting her into my office, I began sharing, once again, the limits of con-fidentiality. Colleen interrupted me. "I remember all of that—and that's why I'm here. I need your help. I need to go home for about 30 minutes. My younger brothers and sisters have not had anything to eat since I fed them breakfast this morning, and their diapers have not been changed. Can you write me a pass?" "Colleen, I will need to contact CPS about the little ones being at home alone," I explained. She hung her head and said, "I know that, but I need your help." I gathered information on the names and ages of the younger children before making my call. The little ones were at greater risk of harm, and CPS would quickly respond to this concern. By filing a report on behalf of her younger siblings, I was also drawing attention to Colleen.

Confidentialty and Need to Know

Counselors are judicious advocates of a student's privacy. Regarding a student's private information with campus personnel, only the few staff members who have an educa-tional need to know should be informed (Carlson, 2017). Even then, information is not shared in detail. Counselors understand that inquisitive people may be deeply concerned about the student and need assurance more than details. In some cases, the student's teacher will be aware of the situation. The teacher can be a source of support for the student with the counselor's guidance. Counselors remind those who have information about a report that respecting a student's privacy is not only respectful of the student and family but that it is also a legal issue (U.S. Department of Education, 1974). On occasion, a staff member will assume that because they know the student or family, that they should be told why the student visited the counselor. School counselors become adept at politely declining to answer questions.

"Thank you for your concern. I appreciate that you care about Kylie. I do, too, and I will take care of her."

Reporters are wise to document all contact with CPS, but in the spirit of confidentiality, CPS documentation is kept in a locked drawer or cabinet. District protocol might determine what is documented, the manner of documentation, and which individuals have access to this highly sensitive information. In some cases, district policy might require that mandated reporters inform an administrator before contacting CPS or to share documentation with an employee who does not have a clear need to know. When such polices conflict with the ASCA Ethical Standards, counselors advocate for revising district policy. They work with district administration to further protect the privacy of students and families.

PARENTS-CARETAKERS AS ALLEGED PERPETRATORS

According to USDHHS (2019), 91.4% of children are abused or neglected by one or both parents. If a student discloses abuse or neglect perpetrated by a parent, this information is included in the CPS report. CPS will then oversee contacting the parents. Once a report is made, the case belongs to CPS, and the counselor's job is not to contact parents, but to monitor the child's attendance and welfare.

Students will be anxious about a report being made on their behalf. The counselor can offer support that alleviates some of the anxiety. Students are often worried, uncertain of the action that the agency will take. The student cannot be assured that he or she will remain in the home. However, CPS personnel prefer to keep the family intact when there are no immediate safety concerns for the child. Another student concern is the reaction of the parent or guardian who is at the center of the report. The student needs permission from the counselor to deny any knowledge that a report was made if the situation at home seems dangerous. Students might tell parents who made the report, but parents might also guess correctly. A student's job is to protect themselves, not the one who reported.

Mandated reporters have their own concerns about how parents will react when contacted by CPS. A team plan for greeting angry parents should be initiated before a report is even made. Such a team could include the counselors, campus administrators, and employees at the school's front desk. Those at the front desk do not need details or confidential information, only the name of the staff member to contact if an angry parent comes to school. In the absence of an administrator, a cocounselor or staff member who was not involved with making the report can facilitate the parent meeting with a greater level of comfort and plausible denial. Regardless of who facilitates the meeting, the parent can be reminded that everyone on campus is mandated by law to report. The conversation might sound similar to the following:

> *Mr. Miller, I understand you want to speak with the person who made a CPS report, but as you might know, everyone on this campus is a mandated reporter. If someone here made a report, it is because our staff abides by the law. Regardless of who might have filed a report, whether it is a staff member or someone outside of the school, your questions are best answered by the assigned CPS caseworker.*

Keep in mind that most angry parents are anxious parents. Regardless, it is wise to err on the side of safety; never meet with an angry individual behind closed doors. As a precaution, the front desk can arrange for security to be nearby in case the parent escalates.

MISINTERPRETING STATE LAW

Depending on the district's reporting protocol, the school counselor might be the designated point of contact to make all mandated reporting calls (Hodges & McDonald, 2019; Tuttle et al., 2019), often due to a misinterpretation of the language in state law. A common phrase used in state law is "report or cause a report to be made." Such phrasing is often misinterpreted to mean that the outcry witness is allowed to pass information on to a designated individual who then makes the formal report to CPS. The phrasing of the law, "cause to report," does not free the outcry witness from the legal responsibility to report. The outcry witness is generally considered the first person with whom a child shares their narrative of abuse or neglect. As reported by Kenny et al. (2018), the initial outcry witness must make the mandated report, otherwise the report may be considered unsubstantiated. The information provided by the outcry witness is more credible than second-hand information reported by a designee. Some states assess fines and take other legal actions against an outcry witness who does not make a mandated report. Counselors who are appointed as the designee to handle all reports, should work with district administration to advocate for educators to fulfill their legal role as mandated reporters.

In the case of an outcry witness who is hesitant to report, the school counselor should advocate for the student by supporting the outcry witness through the mandated reporting process (Hodges & McDonald, 2019).

VIGNETTE

The counselor was greeted in the front office by Mrs. Jones, a classroom teacher. "Suzie is in the waiting area and needs to speak with you about her older brother touching her in inappropriate ways," said Mrs. Jones. The counselor guided the teacher into her office to continue the conversation in private. She gently reminded Mrs. Jones that as the outcry witness, she was legally responsible to make the report. A nervous Mrs. Jones replied, "I don't have the time right now to make a call, and, really, I don't want to get involved." The counselor nodded in understanding, but added, "Mrs. Jones, you are already involved. Suzie trusted you enough to share this information with you first, and that means you are responsible for making the report to CPS. I would like to help you make the call, though. I will gather the demographic information that CPS requires, and if you will come back to my office during your conference period, we can make the call together."

Counselors are sensitive to staff who might feel unsupported or anxious when reporting and offer them guidance and emotional support (Bryant & Baldwin, 2009; Hodges & McDonald, 2019; Levi & Brown, 2005; Sikes et al., 2010). In McDonald's (2020) survey of counselors-in-training ($n = 133$), only 26% of participants said that support from a counselor or administrator was provided to those who are first-time reporters. One participant commented:

> The administrator led me into her office, gave me the number of CPS, and then left, "the teacher explained." She just left me there, not knowing what to do. I was shaking so hard I could barely talk. The lady on the other end of the call was nice and walked me through it. After I hung up, I sat there and cried.

THE SCHOOL COUNSELOR'S ROLE IN SUPPORTING PARENTS

Counselors provide guidance and emotional support to staff who make reports, but after a report is made, the counselor's focus is on the injured party who suffered the abuse or neglect. The student is provided with individual counseling through the school's counseling program, or if the parents request, they are provided with information for counseling sources outside of the school (ASCA Ethical Standards, 2016, Section A.1.e.). Therapist recommendations are handled with care. Directly referring a student for outside counseling might place the district in the position of being financially liable for these services. The counselor should be aware of the district policy regarding referrals, as well as the ethical standard that directs the counselor to provide the parent with several referred sources. The counselor guides parents to interview the sources in order for parents to determine the best fit for their child (ASCA Ethical Standards, 2022, Section A.6.e.). The ethical principle of autonomy, Section F.g., is our reminder that counselors never make choices for the family or the student, including the family's choice of therapist or agency.

Another consideration for referring families to outside resources is when the counselor recognizes that risk factors exist within the family. Risk factors such as unemployment and poverty might lead to the abuse or neglect of the children (Sedlak et al., 2010). Stress that results from numerous risk factors can be mitigated through interventions offered by behavioral health counselors or through community-based resources that assist struggling families. School counselors, as child advocates, prevent abuse if possible, rather than simply reporting it after it happens.

VIGNETTE

Jack was suspended. Again. I remained in the room with him while waiting on his mother to pick him up. Our behavior team had intervened with this third-grader in the past, but he still wore the defiant expression I had come to expect. Defiance suddenly changed to frozen fright the second his dad walked in. His dad had never come to the school before, and even though I was surprised, I noticed that Jack appeared terrified. Recovering from his shock, he plastered his back to the wall and slid to a point in the room, far from his visibly angry father. I made a mental note to check on Jack's welfare when he returned to school. Then, in a moment of clarity, I realized that my plan was to wait and see if Jack returned abused. How could I take such a risk with Jack's welfare? I was ethically and morally obligated to prevent harm when possible. I followed the two to the exit door, and as Jack scurried out to the car, I took the opportunity to speak with his dad. "Sir, you know what I will do if Jack comes back harmed or makes a statement that he has been mistreated." The man's eyes met mine. In a calm voice he replied, "I won't hurt him, and yes, I know what you would do."

Even though Jack's behavior improved after this incident, his teacher and I closely monitored his welfare throughout the school year. He never made an outcry and the teacher never suspected abuse. In thinking it over, I believe that Jack's difficult classroom behavior was his effort at communicating that something was not going well at home. I wish I had listened.

Collaboration

Another area of advocacy for school counselors is developing a collaborative working relationship between CPS and school staff. Teachers who distrust CPS assume their reports are ignored and that no investigation takes place (Kesner & Robinson, 2002). Seldom does mandated reporter training include an explanation of the process used by CPS to screen in or screen out reports. Teachers, wanting to protect their students, are understandably frustrated when they are not apprised of the results of an investigation (Tuttle et al., 2019). School counselors are aware that maintaining student confidentiality and the privacy of families is a legal responsibility shared by CPS professionals and counselors. Teachers and staff members who grasp the legal and ethical obligation of confidentiality and understand the CPS decision-making process will likely be less offended by a school counselor or a CPS caseworker maintaining boundaries that afford privacy to the student and the family. Appendix D of USDHHS (2019) addresses each state's systematic approach to CPS reports.

MULTICULTURAL COMPETENCE AND SOCIAL JUSTICE ADVOCACY

Besharov (1986) expressed concern that the mandated reporter laws, particularly the inclusion of the phrase 'the suspicion of abuse or neglect,' had led to the increase in unfounded, or unsubstantiated, allegations. According to Feely and Bosk (2021), 50% of children in the United States will have been involved with child welfare by age 18. Unfortunately, a close look at this astounding percentage reveals a disproportionate number of children of color who are reported and then investigated by CPS (Sedlak et al., 2010). Tuttle et al. (2019) reported racial disproportionality, as seen in the child welfare system, is composed of two parts: the overrepresentation and the underrepresentation of racial populations. Children of color are overrepresented in reports to CPS. Teachers, when compared to other mandated professionals, report a greater number of children of color to CPS (Kesner & Robinson, 2002). The reporting data have been analyzed in relation to risk factors. But even when accounting for all risk factors, children of color remain more likely to be involved in the child welfare system, even though they represent a smaller number relative to the general population. In addition to reporting data, the CPS decision-making structure has been analyzed to determine whether an inherent bias exists (Feely & Bosk, 2021). School counselors are cautioned by their ethical standards to respect student diversity (ASCA Ethical Standards, 2022, Section A.6.e. and Section B.3.j.) and to never impose their personal values or biases on others. However, after careful thought, if a suspicion of abuse or neglect remains, the law mandates that the suspicion be reported to CPS.

SCHOOL COUNSELOR PRACTICAL APPLICATION

The student needing assistance arrives at the school counselor's office often in the following ways: (1) the student personally requests to see the school counselor, (2) a student will bring or provide information about another student who needs support, or (3) a teacher or other school staff member brings the student to the school counselor's office. During the outcry, counselors are sensitive and emotionally strong for the victim.

With the student in the school counselor's office or other private meeting space, the counselor begins by reminding them of the limits to confidentiality in a developmentally appropriate way. When they have confirmed their understanding of these limits, the counselor might ask a generic open-ended question that invites the student to share their narrative. Henderson (2013) offered these examples as questions that invite the student's story: "How did that happen?" or "I wonder where you learned that from?" (p. 299). Some students will share freely, while others will not. Counselors who need to encourage reticent students must be aware that questions phrased incorrectly might be leading questions that will result in tainted responses that destroy court cases. Some counselors hesitate to elicit any information, fearing that they will overstep (Henderson, 2013). Open-ended questions, however, encourage students to share using their own words.

Use of the Data Collection Tool for Suspected Child Abuse and Neglect (DCT4SCAN) created by Hodges and McDonald (2019) has proven helpful to school counselors as an organizational and documentation tool when one is not provided by the district. Notes can be written on the back of this tool when collecting and documenting the student's statement. A credible report will include direct quotes from the student, if possible, and the reporter's observations of the student's demeanor and behavior. Counselors should only record the facts, never the counselor's opinion. Once the student has completed the outcry and the information is noted, the front of the tool will guide in gathering important demographic information that will be requested by CPS. All information applicable to the outcry is noted on one document which is helpful in organizing the information. Whether reporters use the DCT4SCAN for documentation, or whether they create their own, they are encouraged to use a preformatted document to collect the data surrounding an outcry. While documenting the information prior to making the report, the reporter's thoughts become more organized, and the resulting report is clear and easy to comprehend.

Successful teamwork between mandated reporters and CPS personnel depends on fulfilling two distinct roles related to reports. The mandated reporter reports. Child welfare employees investigate. Well-intentioned counselors who step into the role of investigator create barriers for the very people whose job it is to protect the child and might even destroy a CPS court case against the perpetrator.

Child welfare workers, like other groups of professionals, are made up of individuals. Although the majority are diligent, mistakes do occur, and some situations are outside the control of CPS. Reporters must be cautious about accusing agency personnel of inaction, keeping in mind that CPS officials do not update reporters on cases. But, when it is evident that a youth in the child welfare system is not being protected, school counselors have options for turning the situation around. Police departments and school resource officers can quickly check on a child's welfare. A caseworker assigned to the student is the first contact for a follow-up call when the situation is not one of imminent danger. Even if district policy restricts educators from documenting CPS reports in detail, the contact information of caseworkers is essential to note. In addition, caseworkers have local supervisors who are another point of contact when a caseworker cannot be reached. Documentation can be used, if needed, to protect the child, but it is also evidence that the educator has fulfilled their duty as a mandated reporter.

VIGNETTE

By age seven, Will had lost one parent to suicide and the other to illness. Instead of foster care, he went to live with an extended family member in a kinship placement approved by CPS. He was quiet and withdrawn, but I developed a relationship with him and checked on him frequently. One morning on his way to class, Will stopped by my office. He whispered in my ear that James, the guardian's boyfriend, was touching him inappropriately. CPS moved quickly after I made my report and arranged to interview Will at the headquarters. Following the interview, a CPS official came by my office to inform me that they believed that Will was being sexually abused. She wanted me to understand, however, that the prosecutor would not press charges against James. Because Will was young, painfully shy, and reluctant to talk, the prosecutor did not think he could get a conviction. Instead of prosecuting James, Will's guardian was given a choice: permanently remove the boyfriend from the home or give up guardianship. She chose Will.

Will was one of many students who would stop each morning to speak with me before heading to class. One day, I noticed a deep gash on his head. He explained that James had been playing too rough and knocked him into the counter. My heart stopped. James was back in the home. Will left for class, and I retrieved my CPS file from the locked cabinet. I located the contact information of Will's case worker and called her, certain that she would act on his behalf. Once she heard my concern though, she stated firmly that Will was not telling the truth. She had called the guardian two days earlier and had been assured that, per the agreement, James was not in the home. Undeterred, I asked her to please drop by the home unannounced, just to be sure. She declined. There was a time

I would have felt defeated, but I believed Will's story. If I could not get the caseworker to help him, I would call her supervisor in the local office. After leaving two messages two days in a row, the supervisor had not returned my call. I was not willing to leave Will in the home any longer with his abuser. I decided to call the CPS state hotline, the number used for initial reports. The intake worker who answered interrupted to explain that I should be calling the caseworker. I pressed on. I had documented Will's statement verbatim and read it to her. I included the date and time that I reported James's presence to the caseworker and her exact words in reply. I noted the dates and times that I left messages for the caseworker's local supervisor. I ended by stating that I needed a caseworker to go to the home to check on James's presence. After a second of shocked silence, the intake worker said she would talk to her supervisor immediately. In 15 minutes, my phone rang. It was a CPS official calling with the name of a newly appointed caseworker. This employee shared my concern and immediately went, unannounced, to the guardian's home. Yes, James was there. Will was placed in a safe home that very day. The system had faltered, but others stepped up. I remain forever grateful to everyone at CPS who protected Will.

Compassion Fatigue

Hupe and Stevenson (2019) explored the problem of compassion fatigue in teachers related to mandated reporting. In their study of 299 teachers, as compassion fatigue increased, negative attitudes toward reporting also increased. School counselors influence mandated reporters to practice self-care strategies. Each person must find the best path to psychological and emotional recovery, but they can start with a list of useful ideas provided by the counselor.

VIGNETTE

The little boy in my office had been sexually assaulted. My counselor intern sat at the table and we both watched the child as he demonstrated his awful experience through art. The story was raw and hard to hear from the lips of a first grader. When we finished our session, we played for a few minutes until he started laughing at my silliness. When I saw the smile, I knew he was ready to go back to class. As I cleaned up the art supplies, I looked over at the intern, still sitting at the table, looking stricken. "Now, I need to take care of the intern," I thought. A knock at the door pulled me back to immediate events and I completely lost focus on the intern. The next morning the intern walked in, and I launched into a discussion of self-care. "Go for a run, take a hot bath, or pick up the phone and call a trusted professional who will listen as you talk about your feelings." The intern smiled and said that my guidance came too late. She had gone home and continued with her normal routine. That evening she watched TV, as usual, holding the cat in her lap. "Suddenly, I was crying and didn't know why," she said. "I just held the cat and cried. I didn't know what was wrong with me." I sincerely apologized for not taking care of her after we had listened to the difficult outcry. Her experience with compassion fatigue was like that of many counselors. We live busy lives and forget to process what we experienced when hearing the outcries of students. As a result, we too frequently forgo self-care. Stress builds, and we may find ourselves to be unhappy with CPS, with our jobs, with our colleagues, or with life itself. We don't even recognize what is wrong.

VOICES FROM THE FIELD

Name: Anonymous, LPC-S, NCC

Title of Current Position: School Counselor

Where You Practice: Texas

Professional Job Title: School Counselor

Describe your first experience contacting Child Protective Services (CPS).

I was a first-year school counselor, and even though 20 years have passed, I still remember this event as if it only happened yesterday. During the second week of school, while greeting the students arriving at school, a friendly little kindergarten student approached me to say she wanted to show me something. I got eye-level with her, eager to see what she would show me. She lifted the side of her uniform shorts, exposing red welts on the upper side of her leg. This was not what I was expecting. I worked hard to maintain my normal facial expression and not reveal the shock and anger I was feeling inside. There was no question in my mind about what I had to do. First, I alerted the teacher that the little 5-year-old was with me, and then she and I settled at a table in my office with crayons and paper. While we were both coloring, I asked an open-ended question, "Tell me about the marks on your leg." Nonchalantly, she replied, "My Daddy whipped me with his belt." Not wanting her to feel interrogated, we drew a bit longer before I asked a closed-ended question. "When did your daddy whip you with his belt?" Without looking up from her paper, she replied, "Last night." I had one more question to ask. "How do you feel about going home today?" The kindergartner looked a bit puzzled and said, "Fine." She didn't seem worried or scared. After she finished her drawing, she proudly presented it to me as a gift, so that I would "remember her." As I walked her to her classroom, I thanked her for spending time with me and for the gift of the beautiful drawing.

I headed to the room where records were kept to collect demographic information for CPS. An office worker located the student's file for me, but then asked out of curiosity why I needed information on the student. I thought quickly and said that the information was being requested by the district office. The office worker did not have an educational need to know why I was gathering this information, and I wanted to safeguard the privacy of this student and her family. Back in my office I called CPS, made my report, documented the date and time of the call, and the case identification number. Once finished, all documentation went into a locked file drawer in my office, per district policy.

I still have this sweet child's drawing. I will never forget her.

SUMMARY AND CONCLUSION

School counselors and other education professionals are mandated by law to report child maltreatment, including the *suspicion* of abuse or neglect. Educators are the professionals known to make the majority of reports to CPS, yet they are suspected of seriously underreporting. Many aspects of reporting create anxiety. Educators mention the lack of administrative support, the fear of being wrong, and the lack of training to feel confident in recognizing indicators of abuse. School counselors are leaders who can emotionally support staff as they make their first report and thereby ease the anxiety felt by most reporters. School counselors, as advocates, encourage quality training for campus personnel and guide reporters in adhering to district reporting procedures. Counselors are confidential but explain the limits of confidentiality to students in age-appropriate terms. When emotionally overwhelmed or struggling with a decision, counselors consult with other professionals who are knowledgeable regarding the federal and state laws and the ethical codes and then hold one another accountable. In caring for others, counselors can become emotionally depleted unless they are actively involved in self-care. Mandated reporters rarely know the outcome of an investigation or an investigation's impact on a student's future. We act, not only because it is the law, but because we are child advocates who are committed to the welfare of our students.

CASE STUDY

Anne was a very smart and responsible 16-year-old high school student and athlete. One afternoon she was participating in cross-country practice, and as the group ran past the teachers' parking lot, Anne noticed that her favorite teacher's car was still there. She broke off from the running group and headed to her teacher's classroom.

The teacher welcomed Ann, but even though Anne had initiated the visit, she seemed reluctant to talk. The teacher watched patiently as Anne struggled in turmoil. Finally, Anne found her voice. "There's something I have to tell someone. It's about my aunt's boyfriend." Anne explained that she was the after-school babysitter for her aunt's children, but sometimes the aunt's boyfriend would be in the house when she arrived. Yesterday, he was there. Anne went about her usual routine and started dinner while the kids played outside. The boyfriend walked up behind her and put his arms around her in an embrace.

Anne's words came in a rush. "I spun around to get away, but he cornered me and kissed me. I didn't know what to do! I just froze. After a minute, he walked away. I haven't been able to think all day because I am worried about the children. What if he tries something like that with them?" Anne burst into tears. "I can't tell my parents because my dad would kill him. I mean, KILL him. I needed to tell someone. Thank you for listening to me."

DISCUSSION QUESTIONS

1. Who is the victim or potential victim(s) in this case study?
2. Who is the outcry witness in this case study and why?
3. The outcry witness has had no training on mandated reporting. What steps should the outcry witness take in this immediate situation?
4. What individuals should be made aware of this situation, if any?
5. Should a report be made to CPS/DHR?

PRACTICAL APPLICATION

■ Use the following tools in your work:

DCT4SCAN Tool—located in the article by Hodges & McDonald, 2019, listed in References.

Child Welfare Information Gateway

https://www.childwelfare.gov/

Do Right by Kids (New York State)

https://www.dorightbykids.org/how-to-ask-questions/

- Have a self-care and wellness accountability partner to check in with weekly.
- Don't answer emails on the weekend. Delete the email app from your phone.
- Partake in your own therapy.

KEY REFERENCES

Only key references appear in the print edition. The full reference list appears in the digital product on Springer Publishing Connect: connect.springerpub.com/content/book/978-0-8261-8753-6/part/part04/chapter/ch15

Child Welfare Information Gateway. (2019b). *Mandatory reporters of child abuse and neglect.* U.S. Department of Health and Human Services, Children's Bureau. https://www.childwelfare.gov/pubPDFs/manda.pdf

Hodges, L. I., & McDonald, K. (2019). An organized approach: Reporting child abuse. *Journal of Professional Counseling: Practice, Theory & Research, 46*(1–2), 14–26. https://doi.org/10.1080/15566382.2019.1673093

Kalichman, S. C. (1999). *Mandated reporting of suspected child abuse: Ethics, law & policy* (2nd ed.). American Psychological Association.

Kenny, M. C., Abreu, R. L., Helpingstine, C., Lopez, A., & Mathews, B. (2018). Counselors' mandated responsibility to report child maltreatment: A review of U.S. Laws. *Journal of Counseling & Development, 96*(4), 372–387. https://doi.org/10.1002/jcad.12220

Sikes, A., Remley, Jr., T. P., & Hays, D. G. (2010). Experiences of school counselors during and after making suspected child abuse reports. *Journal of School Counseling, 8*(21). http://www.jsc.montana.edu/articles/v8n21.pdf

Stone, C., & Dahir, C. (2016). *The Transformed School Counselor. Cengage.*

U.S. Department of Health & Human Services. (2019). *Child maltreatment 2017.* https://www.acf.hhs.gov/cb/report/child-maltreatment-2017

PART V

Issues for Collaborative Professional Practice

CHAPTER 16

School Counselors and Community and Family Engagement

EMILY SALLEE AND **MARY AMANDA GRAHAM**

STUDENT VOICE

Student "O.A." provided the following testimonial about her experience with a school counselor:

"Spring before my junior year, Aggie, my school counselor, had tried to engage students in a book club–type group, and I came into it in more appreciation of the community space he was creating. There are a lot of students of color at our school, and not a lot of affinity groups or places where we could hang out, so I think we still felt like the minority in many ways (even if we weren't the minority of the school itself). Those feelings of loneliness and isolation were rampant, and I thought the creation of a Latinx student leadership affinity group would allow us to come together and empower each other, possibility resulting in less loneliness in classrooms and other spaces. Even now, 3 years later, the community space and relationships and trust have continued. That really taught me and helped me see how much people can grow when you give them the right resources and when they're provided with a community to build up.

Aggie does a great job of understanding and validating people's experiences. I think most adults in school view students as one group, but there's a lot of us who share very, very different experiences than your 'typical' student. Because I felt understood by Aggie, we were able to create a relationship that set me up for success. I always return and visit whenever I can, because, you know, I have a very special place in my heart for this school."

INTRODUCTION: ROLE OF THE SCHOOL COUNSELOR WITH COMMUNITY AND FAMILY

Students do not exist within a vacuum. They enter school buildings impacted by a multitude of outside forces and influences that impact their ability to access learning within the educational setting. As such, school personnel (teachers, support staff, administrators, and school counselors) must consider what barriers might exist as a result. School counselors are at the forefront of bridging these systems through integration, advocacy, and engagement with families and surrounding communities. School counselors should imagine that, throughout the day, some of their students are carrying invisible heavy backpacks with them that are full of various stressors. A role of the school counselor is to assist these students in unpacking these issues, so students have room to grow academically, socially, and in areas of career and postsecondary education.

It is essential for the school counselor to develop strong and working relationships with family and community partners for the academic, social/emotional, and career success of students. Strong partnerships should be maintained by the school counselor at all educational levels and continue throughout the students' PK–12 journey. There should be an emphasis on school-family and community partnerships being collaborative, equal, and inclusive (Bryan & Henry, 2012). Multisystemic approaches that honor the voices of school, family, and community will ensure the success of the student. Historical research indicates that strong partnerships between schools, families, and communities counter the educational inequities faced by many marginalized communities (Bryan & Henry, 2012).

The American School Counselor Association (ASCA, 2016) maintains a strong position regarding family and community engagement expectations of school counselors. According to the ASCA (2016) position statement, school counselors work with students, their families, school staff, and community members in the implementation of comprehensive school counseling programs to establish strong systemic partnerships and success for all students. School counselors have the unique opportunity to partner with community, pursue collaboration with family, and remove barriers that have existed for school-family and community partnerships. School counselors serve as leaders in their field and serve as advocates and liaisons in their schools. These partnerships impact the success and overall well-being of the student in academic, personal/social, and career domains (ASCA, 2016).

SYSTEMS THEORY: A PRACTICAL APPLICATION FOR SCHOOL COUNSELING

Systems impact students. Students interact daily with multiple systems that can challenge or strengthen their success. These can include school faculty and staff, family/caregivers, community, neighborhoods, places of business, and clubs, activities, sports, employment, and other activities. School counselors must understand that student success is impacted by all systems, and a large part of the counselor's role is to collaborate and coordinate in the best interest of the student. Epstein and VanVoorhis (2010) describe and illustrate a method for thinking systematically about six overarching ways to involve external partners (i.e., families and community), with the idea that each approach could directly or indirectly impact specific student outcomes. These overarching ideas are consistent with trauma-informed school counseling practices. It is also important that when operating within this framework to always use the lens of equity, culture, and inclusion. Below is a model of the six types of involvement that can be used by school counselors to form strong partnerships (Epstein & VanVoorhis, 2010; Rumsey & Milson, 2019).

- **Type 1: Parenting/caregivers information:** School counselors can provide resources, including relevant workshops or caregiver nights that focus on child development, mental health, impact of trauma, or open forums for sharing concerns. This is an opportunity for the school counselor to partner with clinical mental health providers, medical doctors, and community leaders to facilitate trainings or disseminate information.

- **Type 2: Communicating:** Inclusive and frequent communication between school counselors (PK–12) and school/community partners is essential for the success of the student. Strong communication conveys the message that school counselors are committed to a team approach to student success. Access to technology, language/reading access, and modes of information delivery are important considerations for effective communication. Most communities benefit from disseminating important communication in several languages and in multiple modes of communication. When hosting in-person events, awareness of scheduled time, location, transportation, and child care are important logistical considerations. These events are opportunities for the school counselor to partner with community leaders. Potential barriers to communication and receiving information should be assessed prior to engaging with the community and families.

- **Type 3: Volunteering (parents/community mentors):** School counselors benefit from family, caregiver, and community member support and collaboration. School counselors are instrumental in creating a school environment that encourages stakeholder engagement and fosters a strong culture of mentoring and volunteerism. One of the first things to consider when creating volunteer opportunities is to assess whether community and family members perceive the building as inclusive and welcoming and as a place where their skills will be valued. Whether guest speaking about careers, helping with tutoring, or reading to students in preferred languages, school counselors can and should be creative in ways to bring family and community into their buildings.

- **Type 4: Learning at home:** The COVID has placed a large amount of stress on the education system and the home learning environment. School counselors are required to place greater emphasis on how they collaborate with school-family-community partners through virtual learning to maintain strong relationships for the continued support of students' academic and emotional wellness. Virtual learning resources have taken on a new level of importance that goes beyond checking on homework. School counselors should be cognizant on how to disseminate and support online learning through webinars, podcasts, Zoom meetings, texts, and virtual drop-in office hours for all school stakeholders.

- **Type 5: Decision-making:** Are all voices at the table? Who is missing? This should be the first question a school counselor asks when thinking about decision-making that impacts students, policies, or school systems.

- **Type 6: Collaborating with community:** Assessing community resources is an important first step toward collaboration. This provides the school counselor with an understanding of potential partners to support student and family needs. School counselors can develop a list of these resources and keep them updated. School counselors can meet with community leaders and develop partnerships and secure mentors and support for their work. If your school doesn't have a mental health provider, research the possibility of a partnership with a local mental health agency. Connect with local cultural groups and partner with them on school improvement initiatives.

FAMILY ENGAGEMENT AND THE SCHOOL COUNSELOR

During the school year, students spend more waking time at school than they do at home; however, students bring to school a multitude of family and community influences that impact their school day. It is imperative that school personnel use collaborative practices with their students' families to support each student in their academic access and growth. School counselors bring practical training and expertise to this area, and are in a unique role that allows them to bridge gaps that often arise between families and school personnel. Whether a school counselor has 250 students or 1,000 students on their caseload, they should always incorporate family engagement practices in their work for the benefit and success of all students.

Research has shown that family/caregiver involvement in their child's education is associated with higher achievement/performance, behavior, attendance, and positive interpersonal attributes. Family involvement also has been shown to decrease rates of suspension/expulsion, drug and alcohol use, and other violent and antisocial behaviors (Stevenson et al., 2010). In a society hyperfocused on graduation rates, it isn't surprising that a bulk of the related literature targets involvement and impact on academics. A recent study by Rumsey and Milsom (2019) suggested that "high school students report their families as having the great influence on their decisions around educational attainment, with 49% attributing family as the greatest influence compared to 8% identifying teachers or counselors as having the greatest influence" (p. 6). Without family/caregiver involvement, school personnel lack a significant collaborative opportunity to support student achievement. Family engagement includes identification of barriers and negative influence impacts providing data that school counselors can address by intentionally developing targeted prevention and intervention activities, while keeping inclusivity and equity at the forefront of developing these partnerships (Adams & Forsyt, 2013).

While some school-counseling graduate programs do not include a specific stand-alone course addressing family engagement, school counselors are equipped to facilitate engagement and collaboration with families. School counselors have a unique role and ability to interact systemically with all school and community stakeholders. Specifically, their training in clinical counseling skills and understanding of family systems and group dynamics provides the necessary skills to engage in school-family-community partnerships that are supportive and inclusive (Moore-Thomas & Day-Vines, 2010). As with all roles and responsibilities that constitute the school counseling profession, this is not a one-size-fits-all model, but rather is one with endless variables and individualized considerations for each student and their family. This is also not a one-sided equation, as the capacity that families/caregivers have to engage and be involved with their child(ren)'s schooling is varied.

Joyce Epstein, director of the Center on School, Family, and Community Partnerships, categorizes parent involvement into six arenas: (1) child-rearing, (2) school communication, (3) school volunteering, (4) home-based learning, (5) school decision-making, and (6) school–community collaborations (Stevenson et al., 2010). Each arena presents differently in every family based on need, cultural contexts, and resources. Of the six categories, there are clearly some more connected to the school and role of the school counselor than others. While parent involvement is beneficial across PK–12 settings, Epstein also notes that it is more prevalent in the elementary (K–5) school years, before it tends to dwindle during middle school (grades 6–8) and significantly decline during high school (grades 9–12) years (Stevenson et al., 2010). Although evidence points that parent involvement dwindles as the students' progress through school, it is up to the school counselor to create avenues for parent involvement to continue that is developmentally appropriate. Involvement does not have to dwindle. Families/caregivers do not lose interest in their students' educational experience; schools fail to engage parents in developmentally appropriate ways. A primary question to guide the upper-level school counselor in collaborative practice should begin with *how can a school counselor create access to collaboration more inviting for middle- to upper-grade parents, caregivers, and their students?* As a school counselor, continually reflect on questions such as *What families am I **not** engaged with and/or have a relationship with? What parents have I **not** spoken to and/or haven't spoken to me? Which families do I need to be more accessible to, and what does that look like?* Identify your blind spots in family engagement and address these areas with intentionality. A way to do this is to continually assess and evaluate programming around family/caregiver engagement.

Family Engagement and Educational Assessment

Family/caregiver engagement during any educational assessment process increases student engagement and achievement. "Assessment" is a loose term to include the various assessment processes typically occurring in schools, both formal and informal, used to gain information about an individual student or groups of students related to current performance and growth over time. Regardless of the instrument or tool used for data gathering, families often play a vital role in the validity and reliability of the data itself. Some families come prepared to actively participate in their student's assessments; others do not. Those families may benefit from active and intentional engagement and support with the school counselor. Disengagement (or the perception of disengagement) gives the school counselor an opportunity to reflect on the possibility that there something in the environment that is causing this family to disengage or feel excluded. One simple way to engage a family during an assessment or meeting is to start by saying, "you know your child better than we could ever hope to, and your engagement and collaboration is incredibly valuable in helping us support their growth at school." Invitations such as these not only create space for the parent voice, but they also empower parents and families to trust themselves as they enter the school space and dialogue.

Family engagement interventions in the realm of assessment include practices such as student goal setting and student-led conferences (Stevenson et al., 2010), employing a strengths-based perspective and assessments/baseline data to identify current perspectives (McCarthy & Watson, 2018), and using measures of accountability, such as exceptionalities data, academic/behavior/attendance data, and related activities, for both the students and the referring/reporting school staff. McCarthy and Watson (2018) suggest school personnel must also be mindful and assess the attitudes of both school personnel and families, being aware of differences in values, culture, and perceptions. In this way, school counselors can recognize possible barriers to family involvement, engagement, and interventions, and come from a place of inclusivity and equity. It is important for the school counselor to check their bias when assessing family engagement. Coming from a perspective that the parent doesn't care or they don't want to be involved is not helpful or appropriate for the student or the family. School counselors entering the profession should note that parents who seem disengaged or unavailable may be working multiple jobs to support the family, be in crisis themselves, or may have a history of school-related trauma.

MULTICULTURAL APPROACHES TO FAMILY ENGAGEMENT WITH IMMIGRANT FAMILIES

Equity and inclusion are foundational to work as a school counselor and engagement with families/caregivers. In this section, multicultural approaches to family collaboration will highlight working with immigrant/refugee students/families, and student/families of color. School counselors should take note that families and caregivers come in many variations and constellations. Intersectionality of families and identities should always be considered in the work of the school counselor. The question *Do all families/*

caregivers feel engaged and welcome at my school? is the primary question to begin with in your work around engagement. While the multitude of other family/caregiver constellations (LGBTQIA+, single, blended, adoptee, and grandparents) may not be reflected in this chapter on engagement, much of the related research, and many of the practical approaches, may be applicable in the work of the school counselor.

Immigration, whether or not it involves a refugee situation, is said to have a destabilizing effect on families (Sullivan & Simonson, 2016). Families, particularly the children, are expected to acclimate and even conform to the culture and expectations in their new setting. This can lead to an enhanced generation gap that presents in a contrast between the "old" and "new" cultures (parents more likely to hold to the old culture of their homeland, and children more likely to adapt to the new culture of their new environment) (Suarez-Orozco et al., 2010). Additional variables can exacerbate this polarity, including financial constraints requiring longer work hours away from home, inability to speak/read/write the native language, and feelings of homesickness for their country of origin. Refugee families have sometimes experienced other traumas as well (Sullivan & Simonson, 2016). These family dynamics and traumas can have a direct impact on emotional problems and social challenges that may impede academic performance (Suarez-Orozco et al., 2010). Additionally, educational processes, content, assessments, and structure are likely to be different in the United States. This requires a broader understanding of educational and personal/social context as it relates to the student and their families/caregivers. These lived experiences that differ from the experience of many school counselors and school personnel require an empathetic, compassionate, and collaborative family engagement and support approach. It is vital to note, even with the best school supports, "many immigrant parents may fear or experience the unfamiliar school environment as unwelcoming, threatening, or even disrespectful to them" (Suarez-Orozco et al., p. 19).

Using trauma-informed practices is beneficial to all families, but specifically to those identified as immigrant/refugee (Sullivan & Simonson, 2016). With all families, it is imperative to address potential and existing barriers. School counselors must be in close communication with admission and attendance personnel to be alerted to new families, particularly those immigrating from other countries (and, again, whether or not they are fleeing as refugees). The school counselor should communicate as soon as possible to the family, using the information provided to the school. This may require the school to access a translator. Identifying preferred communication (language and modality) and the need for a translator (in spoken and written word) is information to be shared with classroom teacher(s) and other school staff that work with the student and/or family and should be included in the electronic information system used at the school. In addition to these initial supports, Betters-Bubon and Shultz (2018) call for educators to develop culturally and linguistically inclusive spaces for families and caregivers to connect with school systems and personnel.

In communities that have large immigrant and refugee populations, the school counselor should inquire about community resources that support this population and ways to build effective partnerships. Some schools may have specific family liaisons to fill this role. Partnership with other school staff involved in supporting the family, such as an ELL (English language learner) or ESL (English as a second language) teacher will also be important. School counselors can then begin building a relationship with the family by addressing any immediate needs (e.g., school supplies, clothing, supplies for basic needs) and follow up regularly over time. Often engagement with and support of families occurs by creating venues for families to engage with each other, and this is incredibly important for immigrant and refugee families. School counselors must consider and advocate for these opportunities for immigrant and refugee families to connect with and support one another, with or without the presence of school personnel. The school counselor serves a pivotal role for families with all lived experiences and marginalized identities (ASCA, 2018).

MULTICULTURAL APPROACHES TO FAMILY ENGAGEMENT WITH FAMILIES OF COLOR

Students of color continue to experience disproportionate rates of disciplinary referrals, suspension, expulsion, special education referrals and placements, underachievement, chronic absenteeism, and school dropout. This serves as a call for ethical competence and multicultural humility for school counselors (Moore-Thomas & Day-Vines, 2010).

School-family-community partnerships may serve as a protective factor supporting educational resilience in children by reducing negative effects and sociocultural inequities that disproportionately impact people of color (Moore-Thomas & Day-Vines, 2010; Piper et al., 2021). When considering engagement with families of color, the school counselor should place importance in understanding and advocating for diverse pedagogical strategies in classrooms and the school system (Moore-Thomas & Day-Vines, 2010). School counselors should understand and advocate for trauma-informed interventions and family engagement in their schools that take into consideration current and historical racial trauma faced by their students and families (Piper et al., 2021). These approaches and this awareness can significantly improve outcomes for students and families in communities with a large percentage of students of color. This awareness cannot be ignored when a school serves primarily White students with only a few students of color dispersed throughout the school system. Changing pedagogical frameworks, interventions, and approaches to working with families using an inclusive lens should be supported by the administration and leadership who typically give guidance and support for teachers in these practices.

Parent engagement and collaboration looks different for each family, and that can be particularly true for families of color. School counselors and personnel should be aware that families of color experience racism, microaggressions, and stereotypes at the hands of their school community. It is wise for the school counselor and all school personnel to take into consideration the obstacles families face regarding engagement. Families of color (as all families) indicate a need for understanding of the economic challenges, past trauma, and mental health issues that may be barriers to school engagement (Piper et al., 2021).

Avoid the "White savior" approach to working with students and families of color. The White savior complex is a way to describe White helpers/school personnel that consider themselves brilliant helpers to their students and families, but the focus is on the educator feeling rewarded, not on the needs of the marginalized student and family's needs. Partnerships should have valuable and mutual collaborations and shared goals of supporting students' academic and overall development. All stakeholders, including students, benefit when schools intentionally and successfully partner with families of color (Bryan et al., 2020).

Knowing your school demographics is essential. You, as an ethical and reflective school counselor, need to increase knowledge and skills and self-awareness as it pertains to all students and families in your school and community. *Counselor, know thyself.* This age-old adage applies to this conversation, as it is imperative to know who you are in your work as a school counselor. The following questions will guide your reflection in working with and serving families from all backgrounds:

1. What biases both visible and hidden influence your approach to family engagement?
2. What were your experiences as a PK–12 student in the context of family engagement?
3. How will those experiences potentially influence your work with families as a school counselor?
4. What privileged identities do you hold?
5. What marginalized identities do you hold?
6. How will these identities help or hinder your work with families?

These are crucial, important, and potentially tumultuous questions for school counselors to wrestle with and to continue wrestling with over the course of their professional career. It is recommended to consult with other school counselors to continually process and talk about these questions, and many other issues, as you move through your career as a school counselor.

SOCIAL JUSTICE ADVOCACY FOR ALL FAMILIES

The ASCA National Model Standards and Competencies (2019) endorse school counselors' roles in facilitating school–family–community partnerships as coordinators of services, consultants, advocates, liaisons, and collaborators to embody the role of transformational school leader. School counselors serve as leaders in multicultural advocacy and social justice, acting as agents of change (ASCA, 2019). School counselors are in the position to advocate for best practices, inclusivity, equity, and inclusion for all students (Betters-Bubon & Schultz, 2018). In this role as culturally responsive change agents, school counselors challenge schools to address injustices and become more responsive to the needs of all families. This can look like advocacy efforts for best practices in reducing barriers, promoting family engagement, and addressing and naming historical racial trauma and systemic infrastructure concerns (Moore-Thomas & Day-Vines, 2010; Piper et al., 2021). School counselors should not fear using terms such as anti-Black racism, racism, other -isms, White supremacy, and colonization while advocating for change. School counselors as advocates and social change agents are in the position to name these barriers and historical and present traumas and bring them to the attention of the school system so that they may be addressed.

COLLABORATIVE AND SYSTEMIC FRAMEWORKS

School counselors often serve as the bridge between various school stakeholders: administration–teachers, teachers–parents, students–teachers, and school–community. Their clinical counseling skills and systems approach to this work is valuable in facilitation, mediation, collaboration, consultation, and so on. When bridging the gap, whether narrow or wide, between stakeholders, it is imperative that school counselors aid in identifying common goals, with the student as the primary focus. Often these conversations and meetings can get derailed when that overarching focus is lost. This approach is in alignment with strengths-based practices, whereas deficit-based practices tend to lead down a rabbit hole of counterproductive meetings wrought with venting, demoralization, and pointing fingers. McCarthy and Watson (2018) note that it is important to view families from a strength-based perspective, and school counselors should seek to share the expert role with students and families. This approach, consistent with a collaborative focus, often requires the school counselor to examine interventions and services to support problem solving *with* the family versus *for* the family. While this all may sound like common knowledge in best practices for working with families and communities, school counselors often find that these are not common approaches used in schools when developing partnerships. School personnel, for the sake of time or other constraints, have been known to lead with deficits and, in the role of expert, focus on missing assignments, low grades, and poor behaviors. From a partnership viewpoint, this approach almost immediately creates defensiveness and frustration with the school system and staff facilitating the conversation.

This collaborative framework ultimately serves more than one purpose (student success); a close second is that of empowering parents to advocate for their own student(s)/family (McCarthy & Watson, 2018). School personnel often assume parents have the skills and knowledge to advocate in the current educational system. The school counselor can highlight to the family that the system is much different from what it was when they were children (and they are now in a different role). The addition of various barriers impact the ability and capacity to engage in necessary advocacy. As mentioned throughout this chapter and text, advocacy is a primary responsibility for school counselors, suggesting they are in the perfect role and station to extend an olive branch to parents in need of assistance. This is to be said for parents of students receiving general education services, but it is even more important for students with exceptionalities, requiring special education services, ESL/ELL services, and/or talented and gifted (TAG) services. Educational systems are wrought with nuances, protocols, and systems that prove difficult for most parents to navigate without the necessary support from the school team. For example, many school counselors have participated in one too many IEP meetings in which the school team talked over the parents with acronyms, assessment results, and deficit-based language, leaving the parents as outside observers to a process that not only is already anxiety provoking, but also ultimately determines the educational fate of their child. Collaborative frameworks and approaches to this work require school counselors to address all stakeholders' needs and goals, while ensuring everyone also has the skills and knowledge necessary to work toward those needs and goals.

Regardless of caseload, it's crucial that school counselors remember their role in delegation and facilitation of programmatic components and family engagement and community partnerships (ASCA, 2016). Every family needs a champion and advocate. Ensuring that every student and every family feels connected with at least one school staff person is paramount. This may not be you, as the school counselor, nor should it be you for every student and family. There are various approaches to bringing families into the school setting, either physically or emotionally (Stevenson et al., 2010). Always lead with compassion and warmth, using trauma-informed and trauma-responsive approaches with all parents/families; consider the potential trauma of the education system for parents, and avoid triggering or retraumatizing them when at all possible. Moore-Thomas and Day-Vines (2010) remind school counselors to access their foundational skills when communicating with families. They note that school counselors are well positioned to build effective, sustainable, and meaningful school–family and community partners from a strength-based and compassionate perspective. Time should be allotted for developing these sustainable and equitable partnerships between the school and community (Bryan & Holcomb-McCoy, 2010). Applying the systemic lens to this work, this looks like prevention over remediation using a multitiered systems approach by working with individual students (e.g., trauma identification, social support networks, adjustment to a new form of education/schooling), families (e.g., parent outreach, collaboration, referral), school (e.g., social dynamics, teacher collaboration), and community (e.g., linking with agencies) (Suarez-Orozco et al., 2010).

McCarthy and Watson (2018) offer a family–school problem-solving meeting (FSPSM) practice to establish a more equal partnership with families for decision-making. This model is geared to a nontraditional and alternative approach that empowers the family/caregiver to create plans for student success that are collaborative and inclusive. FSPSM is centered on a strength-based approach to problem-solving. In meeting with the family, using FSPSM, the school counselor, the family, and the student can share perspectives, develop solutions, and each have a voice that is equal. The FSPSM provides a way for families to feel empowered and honors that they are the experts in their students lives. Not only is this approach empowering to both the parents and student, it also allows for a more holistic approach to supporting the student, with all parties sharing a common goal. Similarly, student-led conferences are a way to flip the script and offer control to the student/family with support of the teacher and other school personnel. In these practices, it is important for school stakeholders to consider the developmental tasks/goals for each individual student and support their individualized needs throughout all educational activities.

Best practices in parent consultation, parent education/training, and school-based family counseling (SBFC) should include unique considerations for each component of family engagement. Common to most forms of consultation include the process of (a) rapport building, (b) problem identification, (c) intervention planning, (d) implementation of intervention where strategies are tested, and (e) evaluation of the intervention and a follow-up process, which involves assessing the outcome of the consultation process (McCarthy & Watson, 2018). School counselors have the foundational knowledge of school systems and understanding of problem-solving and school-based strategies. In many cases, the school counselor is lead in this process, and this gives them the opportunity, from the beginning, to collaborate with the family (McCarthy & Watson, 2018).

School counselors can serve a similar role in parent education/training by assisting parents in improving their parenting skills and supporting their child's academic, behavioral, social, and emotional functioning. These parent education programs are typically short-term, time-limited, and task-oriented with a focus on obtaining or improving specific skills often in prevention or resolution efforts related to children's mental health issues. Goals of parent education can include support to caregivers, development of parenting strategies, and communication. The goal of SBFC and parent education should be to resolve a child's academic or behavioral difficulties by affecting and reinforcing positive change within the child's family. In this sense, the school counselor serves as a mediator, educator, and outside support, who is objective and focused on the best outcomes for the child. Benefits of SBFC include decreased misbehavior at home, improved academic performance, decrease in emotional and behavior problems, and improved relationships and school–family engagement (McCarthy & Watson, 2018). These three components, being short-term, time-limited, and task-oriented, maximize resources by using best practices in collaborative efforts and engagement opportunities.

COMMUNITY ENGAGEMENT AND THE SCHOOL COUNSELOR

Building on the valuable information about community engagement as a seamless and necessary addition during family engagement activities, here we discuss engaging with community stakeholders, including mental health resources, business owners, spiritual/faith leaders, community members with grown children, retired community members, and any other person or entity in the surrounding community that is not already reflected in the stakeholder groups of educators or parents/families. This integrated system of social supports offers opportunities for sustainable programming, in which the school counselor has various roles. School counselor roles in community engagement may include member/participant, team leader, committee or activity leader, advisor, and serving on a district advisory committee on partnerships (among others). School counselors' actions in these various roles include communicating, disseminating, coordinating, facilitating, and evaluating (Epstein & Van Voorhis, 2010).

MULTICULTURAL AND ADVOCACY APPROACHES TO COMMUNITY ENGAGEMENT

The practice of assessment in community engagement can be similar to that in family engagement. Often, this looks informal collecting observational data in areas of visibility (events/activities/sports, PTA, neighborhoods, grocery stores, and other community settings)—although it can also consist of more formalized data obtained by the county or state. Regardless of assessment type, the purpose of community assessments is to determine available resources and resources lacking in a variety of arenas: employment, mental health, physical health, and so forth. One way to approach this through a more structured lens is with resource mapping (Arriero & Griffin, 2019), an activity that requires a person (a school counselor or otherwise) to first zoom out and look at the community from a holistic perspective before zooming in and identifying both available resources and resources lacking in the various arenas. Updated community resource maps can be an incredibly valuable when connecting families to necessary resources; it can also be a great way to actively engage in the community during the process of resource mapping. This practice will be described in greater detail as a best practice in community engagement.

According to Bryan and Holcomb-McCoy (2010), partnerships with family and community are essential given the challenges that school counselors and families face (e.g., homelessness, poverty, academic failure, school alienation). When school counselors are intentional about partnerships with families and communities, they are coming from an inclusive approach that will sustain needed prevention and intervention programs for the best outcome for the student. This approach bridges cultural and promotes empowerment (McCarthy & Watson, 2018). For example, as a school counselor (Sallee) at an elementary school that neighbored two large government-subsidized housing developments, it was important to assess community resources. Many students at the school lived in these neighborhoods in which families often financially struggled. The holiday season (as they often do) offered additional struggles and stressors in terms of parents wanting to provide gifts for their children. To meet this community need, a holiday gift program benefiting our students and their families was developed. Parents would fill out an application, noting ages and needs/wants for each child 18 and under. Tags were created for each child (respecting privacy by coding each one), and they were hung in the main office with directions for sign-ups and gift purchasing. Families within the school and other community stakeholders would purchase gifts and bring them to the school counseling office, where gifts would be organized into family groups. A schedule of family pick-up or delivery was made, and parents were provided with wrapping paper, inviting them more intimately into the gift-giving merriment. Each year the program grew, ultimately providing gifts for nearly 100 children in our school and community. This activity met a specific community need, while at the same time encouraged family and community engagement within the school and with each other. School counselors should dream big about community partnerships that support families, and cast the net of collaboration widely.

When engaging in community partnerships, school counselors must consider both academic and cultural barriers: academic barriers such as low academic achievement and high dropout rates as potential symptoms of familial lack of understanding of achieving goals and accessing resources (though possibly having high educational aspirations); and cultural barriers like ignorance toward culture and language and stereotypes/discrimination/personal belief (Arriero & Griffin, 2019). For illustration of some of these barriers, see the Student Voice section of this chapter. There, a student describes school–family–community partnerships that resulted from identifying needs and barriers in collaboration with a high school counselor, then finding creative ways to address them through engagement and ongoing partnerships.

BEST PRACTICES AND MAXIMIZING RESOURCES

In addition to practices such as school-based service learning that collaboratively addresses needs of all stakeholder partners, there are endless other ways schools can engage with their community partners. These practices will look different based on the specific needs and resources of each school and community, but here we will cover some overhead of best practices with which to start and align programmatic development.

Community asset mapping (i.e., resource mapping) is a strategy for "locating, obtaining, and mapping resources from a variety of different people and settings, such as businesses, educational institutions, and individuals. School counselors can use community asset mapping to help meet the needs of their school population by finding these resources and bringing the resources into the school" (Arriero & Griffin, 2019, p. 1). This practice can be performed by a variety of school stakeholders, but it requires ongoing engagement with the changes, needs, and resources in the broader community. When school counselors engage with direct community partnerships, they are mapping resources while also developing relationships with their community stakeholders. Community asset mapping benefits all students, particularly students of color, students experiencing poverty, and other student groups that often experience marginalization in educational settings. Research has shown that it is an effective way to (a) increase sense of ethnic identity, (b) increase school attendance, (c) increase graduation rates, and (d) increase knowledge of postsecondary options (Arriero & Griffin, 2019).

Building on this practice of asset, or resource, mapping is with integration of four equity-focused principles or pillars of partnerships: democratic collaboration, empowerment, social justice, and strengths focus (Bryan et al., 2020). Bryan et al. (2020) suggest that school counselors seek partnerships with the lens of intentionality and inclusivity. They highlight the importance of the school counselor being mindful of power inequities and imbalances in the relationship between school personnel and families from marginalized communities. School counselors should also work with partners to establish partnerships that close or eliminate inequities in opportunities, networks, information, resources, and services that foster students' resilience and success (Bryan et al., 2020). Intentional partnerships within the community offer school counselors additional resources that are not available within the confines of the school setting. Best practices in community engagement maximize resources by being strategic with community outreach and forms partnerships to expand the breadth and depth of school-related services.

ADVOCACY FOR COMMUNITIES

School counselors have the capacity and ability to be leaders in enacting change in school communities, including changes on how the school staff views family and community involvement (McCarthy & Watson, 2018). As is the case with family engagement, school counselors are often the bridge between schools and communities as the first or second point of contact, and their reliance on community connections to expand school services in meeting student (and family) needs (Bryan & Holcomb-McCoy, 2010). The ASCA (2016) addresses this role and responsibility by stating that school counselors should provide "proactive leadership, which engages all stakeholders in the delivery of activities and services to help students achieve success at school." Success in this proclamation is broad in scope, including such markers as academic engagement and achievement, positive social/emotional growth and relationships, and graduation and college-going rates. These success markers all fall within the scope of a school counselor, and community engagement allows for the entire system to work toward common goals.

Advocacy for and with communities can be partnering with mental health providers to come into the school and provide services for students otherwise unable to access the resource. It can be establishing a Backpack Buddies chapter with a local faith establishment, which allows low-income students to take home extra food for the weekends. It looks like inviting retired and/or people without children in schools to be lunch buddies for students who would benefit from a mentor or just some extra positive adult attention. It looks like collaborating with dental or medical providers to offer preventative, and sometimes treatment, services at the school site (with parent permission). It looks like all these things and more, identifying and reducing barriers to students and families accessing community resources, which in turn also benefits those resources in accessing your students and families.

The most valuable sources of collaboration in school–family–community partnerships address the needs and benefit all involved stakeholders. This approach lends to more buy-in and sustainability over time. A prime example to illustrate this framework is in school-based service-learning opportunities. School-based service-learning opportunities integrate academic content with meaningful community service experiences. It should include needs assessments for and with the community, be coordinated with the school, have a sustainable outcome, be integrated into the academic curriculum, and have time built in for reflection and reevaluation of all involved partners (Smith, 2010). While the definition focuses on the students and the school side of the partnership, school-based student-learning opportunities benefit community partners by meeting various needs often related to quality of life, poverty, and other social disparities. School counselors' roles in this approach include collaboration/coordination with school and community stakeholders, provision of leadership, facilitation of communication, and so on. When successfully implemented, school-based student-learning opportunities are the perfect examples of a collaborative framework within school–family–community partnerships and have been shown to be an effective approach for increasing academic performance, civic engagement, graduation rates, active citizenship and community involvement, and individual self-confidence and sense of agency among participants (Smith, 2010).

VOICES FROM THE FIELD

Name: Roberto "Aggie" Aguilar (he/him)

Where You Practice: Milwaukie High School, Milwaukie, Oregon

Professional Job Title: High School Counselor

Bio: Roberto is a proud, native eastern Oregonian, Latinx/Chicano, "Spanglish" bilingual, first-generation college graduate, and a school counselor for the past 20 years at Milwaukie High School located in southeast Portland, Oregon.

As a school counselor at Milwaukie High School, Milwaukie Academy of the Arts, in Milwaukie, Oregon, I would describe my duties as serving as an advocate for each student so that they are empowered to achieve their dreams. I love everything about being a school counselor, EVERYTHING. I think it comes down to having the flexibility to be intentional about creating relationships with students. I also love program development and integrating career exploration with social-emotional learning lessons.

Some of the things that I like less in my role as a school counselor is the anxiety that comes with every phone call. As school counselors, we are frequently presented with problems that need to be addressed. Many of these problems are traumatic in nature, and that buildup affects me daily. I believe what helps me in terms of dealing with these problems is collaboration.

In terms of collaboration with the school and local community to promote family engagement, as well as the positive academic implications for students, I have created and facilitated two programs. The first is "Padres" and is a Spanish language parent group that meets bi-weekly, providing a safe space for families to be heard and form a welcoming environment. Its counterpart, "Ascension," is a weekly bilingual Latinx student leadership affinity club, providing a courageous space for Latinx leaders to develop and explore, while also creating events that positively portray the culture on a daily/monthly basis, allowing the greater community to learn and value it. As the recipient of the 2017 Oregon School Counselor-of-the-Year Award, a national finalist for the 2019 ASCA School Counselor-of-the-Year Award and President of the Oregon School Counselor Association (2021/22), I am a recognized leader among school counselors and school counseling students in Oregon and nationwide. In community and family engagement, I have two pieces of advice: "Dream without limit," and "Embrace the role of the school counselor being a change agent. Dedicate yourself to the area where you believe you can positively impact the school to better the students' needs. I try to embody these charges in my daily work as a high school counselor.

SUMMARY AND CONCLUSION

Parent engagement and involvement will look different depending on the family's resources and abilities and the child's needs. Parents have different strengths, and the school counselor can help parents understand that they don't have to be experts in a subject area to support their students at home. Things like creating quiet spaces or verbal encouragement and check-ins can be valuable support from parents. The school counselor can also link parents with valuable support the school offers, like tutoring and after-school programming (Stevenson et al., 2010). Meeting parents where they are and quickly establishing resources, abilities, and needs is imperative. School counselors can collaborate and integrate community resources to support schools and family partnerships. Bryan and Holcomb-McCoy (2010) highlight that school counselors may serve as a liaison with low-income students and students of color in the transition to postsecondary education but should be cautious of biases. School counselors play a pivotal role with families in the college admissions process and can either promote or hinder college access for students, particularly those in high-poverty, high-minority schools (Bryan & Holcomb-McCoy, 2010).

Students have the capacity for higher academic achievement when parents, educators, and community stakeholders recognize and embrace their shared goals and responsibilities for student learning by working together rather than alone. The theory of overlapping spheres of influence illustrates this phenomenon by describing the overlap of home, school, and community being areas of separate and combined influences of both external and internal structures that house the six distinct types of involvement: parenting, communicating, volunteering, learning at home, decision-making, and collaborative efforts with the community. School counselors are in the prime role for activating these types of involvement between and among families and community stakeholders, creating two-way and three-way communication lines that both identify challenges for each type and respond with programmatic activities that produce results in the various arenas of student attendance, student behavior, and achievement in specific subjects (Epstein & Van Voorhis, 2010).

CASE STUDY

The high school counselor is concerned with Margie and her performance in class. Recently, Margie's attendance has dropped, her focus has shifted, and she has fallen behind academically. The counselor has been unsuccessful in reaching Margie's parent/caregivers. The school counselor has attempted to call and email Margie's parents with no response. The high school counselor knows where the student's parents are employed but is hesitant to reach out to them while they are working. Parents have stated in the past they are too busy to meet with the school counselor or teachers. The high school counselor also knows that Margie's parents are first-generation Americans and speak only Spanish.

DISCUSSION QUESTIONS

1. What bias or myths may occur that need addressed by the school counselor regarding Margie's parents?
2. What are the basic considerations or questions the school counselors should make about Margie and her parents?
3. What strategies should the school counselor put in place to engage Margie's parents?
4. How can the school counselor develop a positive relationship with Margie's parents?

PRACTICAL APPLICATION

- Consider writing a grant to strengthen partnerships with the community.
- Facilitate treatment groups in schools with community mental health therapists.
- Be highly visible at arrival/dismissal, during parent/family events, and out in the community.
- Attend school and community events at least once a quarter.
- Embrace your role as change agent and systems liaison.
- Consider training on translating international transcripts to make the transition to U.S. schools for students and families less stressful.
- When creating family engagement opportunities, always consider time and day. Offer the activities on multiple days, multiple times, and through multiple access points.
- Create webinars of all family engagement sessions for access later.
- Consider having child-friendly events so that families may bring siblings.
- Host family meet and greets at the local community center; everything does not have to happen in the school building.

KEY REFERENCES

Only key references appear in the print edition. The full reference list appears in the digital product on Springer Publishing Connect: connect.springerpub.com/content/book/978-0-8261-8753-6/part/part05/chapter/ch16

American School Counselor Association. (2016). *The school counselor and school-family-community partnerships*. https://www.schoolcounselor.org/Standards-Positions/Position-Statements/ASCA-Position-Statements/The-School-Counselor-and-School-Family-Community-P

American School Counselor Association. (2018). *The school counselor and equity for all students*. https://www.schoolcounselor.org/Standards-Positions/Position-Statements/ASCA-Position-Statements/The-School-Counselor-and-Equity-for-All-Students

American School Counselor Association. (2019). *School counselor professional standards and competencies*. https://www.schoolcounselor.org/getmedia/a8d59c2c-51de-4ec3-a565-a3235f3b93c3/SC-Competencies.pdf

Bryan, J. A., Williams, J. M., & Griffin, D. (2020). Fostering educational resilience opportunities in urban schools through equity-focused school–family–community partnerships. *Professional School Counseling, 23*(1b), 1–14. https://doi.org/10.1177/2156759X19899179

Epstein, J. L., & Van Voorhis, F. L. (2010). School counselors' roles in developing partnerships with families and communities for student success. *Professional School Counseling, 14*(1), 1–14. https://www.jstor.org/stable/42732745

McCarthy, S., & Watson, D. (2018). A new typology: Four perspectives of school counselor involvement with families. *Journal of School Counseling, 16*(1), 1–41.

Rumsey, A. D., & Milsom, A. (2019). Supporting school engagement and high school completion through trauma-informed school counseling. *Professional School Counseling, 22*(1), 1–10. https://doi.org/10.1177/2156759X19867254

CHAPTER 17

School Counseling: Collaborating With School Staff

HEIDI L. MORTON AND **NITA HILL**

LEARNING OBJECTIVES

After reading this chapter, students will be able to:

- Identify a collaboration model that is used in schools.
- Explain the importance of forming effective collaborations with school staff.
- Develop effective collaboration practices with improved program and student outcomes.
- Use the concepts and apply them to their own work as school counselors.

STUDENT VOICE

Student "M," a high school student, provided the following testimonial about her experience with a school counselor:

"During my junior year in high school, I became homeless. That year was arguably the worst year of my life. I not only struggled to keep my grades up to par, but I also struggled personally. The very first time I spoke with Ms. Han, I was in need of assistance with food and hygiene products. She kindly helped me out and also helped me find places that I could live while I still pursued school. She also helped me sign up for the McKinney-Vento Program for homeless youth, which helped me tremendously. During my senior year, I still faced many daunting problems, many of which came from being homeless. I decided to pursue an option that allowed me to take college courses that also counted toward my high school diploma. Parent/guardian signatures were required, which was not possible given my situation. I approached Ms. Han for help, and she and Ms. Davidson helped me find a path forward and provided emotional support, too. The experiences that I shared with both Ms. Davidson and Ms. Han are unforgettable. They have shaped me and my life into something beautiful, astounding. For me, these experiences were life changing. Without their help, I would not be where I am today. From the very beginning, neither of them judged me or my circumstances. They welcomed me warmly and supported me throughout the remainder of my high school career. Currently, I am approaching my final year at my community college;

afterward, I plan to transfer to a 4-year college where I will apply to their nursing program. My educational journey has been difficult yet rewarding. In the process, I have built resiliency and strengthened my endurance. I truly and sincerely thank Ms. Davidson and Ms. Han for all their hard work, patience, and time. Their help, and the many ways they've supported me that I cannot begin to list, will always be the foundation for my success."

INTRODUCTION

Collaboration is a term we hear every day, yet it differs in meaning for many. Collaboration can refer to an informal discussion or work together on an everyday project; it can also refer to very formal processes, procedures, and work roles outlined through contractual agreements. We will explore how collaboration fits within the role of the school counselor and in comprehensive school-counseling programs and learn what school counselors can do to maximize collaborative outcomes.

Collaboration is an active and intentional process that involves both the assuming and sharing of power and resources on behalf of school counselors' primary clients: our students. If school counselors are to truly impact students to the extent possible, they must be willing to both (a) seek out and assume positions and have a voice "at the tables" where decisions are made and (b) invite others to play integral roles in the shaping and guiding of the comprehensive school-counseling program.

In many ways, collaboration is at the heart of the transformation of the school-counseling paradigm in the 21st century. Among other things, this paradigm involved shifting from the idea of school counseling as a *service* and toward the understanding that school counseling is a program integral to the functioning and mission of the school. With this shift also came the acknowledgment that the implementation of effective school-counseling programs was not solely up to school counselors alone but rather relies on collaboration and support across and throughout the school community. This paradigm shift has resulted in schoo-counseling programs that are collaborative, proactive, systemic, more equitable, holistic, transparent, sustainable, and—as a result—much more impactful and more just.

In the American School Counselor Association (ASCA) National Model (2019), collaboration is one of the four overarching themes, alongside leadership, advocacy, and systemic change. It is a key element of school -counseling program delivery and falls under the category of indirect services (along with consultation and referrals). Through collaboration, school counselors grow support of comprehensive school-counseling programs, forge partnerships that support the vision and mission of the school, and—most importantly—can increase student achievement, equity, and access to services. Collaborative work as a school counselor often involves partnering and teaming with colleagues and stakeholders, serving on school district committees that further the mission and goals of the school, creating and delivering workshops for parents and guardians, establishing community partnerships to better serve students and, through both direct and indirect methods, providing crisis response during and after a crisis (ASCA, 2019). This chapter focuses on the collaborative process between school counselors and other school staff and faculty.

The primary purpose of collaboration in schools is improved academic and personal outcomes for students. Collaboration can result in other positive outcomes for participants and for the school system overall. Collaborative work increases staff members' independent problem-solving skills; improves understanding of staff roles and resources; improves staff engagement, motivation, and collective commitment; reinforces a shared vision; improves outcomes for complex problems; uses available resources efficiently; encourages innovative and creative problem-solving approaches; and improves organizational flexibility. When collaboration is intentionally approached with a specific focus on equity and social justice (as should always be the case), it also invites, values, and incorporates diverse perspectives and experiences within the decision-making process; facilitates shared power and responsibility; and increases equity and opportunity.

Collaboration is firmly integrated throughout the four quadrants in the ASCA National Model (2019). Here are some examples of collaborative actions within each quadrant:

Define—increase stakeholder awareness and understanding of the standards that guide our profession and roles; increase counselor awareness of needs and resources within their school and community;

Manage—involve others in the process of establishing, reviewing, and revising the school-counseling program beliefs, mission statement, vision statement, annual calendar, and annual outcome goals;

Deliver—work together to establish effective consultation and referral processes that will be convenient and efficient for all parties; join and contribute to building and district level committees; and

Assess—share results reports, discuss "hits and misses," and explore individual, institutional, and community resources that may be used to improve future results.

School counselors can collaborate with administrators in establishing and strengthening a shared vision. Having a shared vision maximizes resources and clarifies purpose. This can lead to improved trust and understanding between all staff members and, better utilization of existing resources, and it can reduce barriers related to time (Finkelstein, 2009).

MULTICULTURAL COMPETENCIES AND SOCIAL JUSTICE ADVOCACY IN SCHOOL COLLABORATION

The four themes of the ASCA National Model—leadership, advocacy, collaboration, and systemic change—are integral to every aspect of school counseling. We have an ethical imperative to affirm and advocate for all students, tending in particular to student populations that have been historically underserved by the school system (ASCA Ethical Standards, 2016). In short, it is impossible to have a comprehensive school counseling program that does not address issues of social justice.

Professional school counselors believe that every student can learn and succeed (ASCA, 2014). Unfortunately, there are a multitude of systemic barriers that students from marginalized groups may experience that can impede their ability to achieve their potential, including intentional and unconscious biases from their peers and from staff members; stereotype threats that can impact their own beliefs about their potential; assessment and test bias; disproportionate discipline and suspension rates; unequal opportunities to participate in advanced coursework or rigorous curriculum; and unequal and biased representation within adopted textbooks, curriculum, and in visual and verbal cues throughout the school (posters, library books, performing arts, etc.).

ASCA (2019) has outlined several collaboration strategies to address racism and bias in schools and community systems, including (a) teaming and partnering with families, educators, businesses, and community organizations focused on antiracism/bias; (b) serving on school/district committees focused on antiracism/bias; (c) presenting workshops for parents on how to support and encourage appropriate student behaviors; (d) creating community partnerships focused on antiracism/bias; and (e) working with administrators, families. and community members to organize immediate and follow-up interventions in response to a crisis (ASCA School Counseling Standards in Practice, n.d.).

The Multicultural and Social Justice Counseling Competencies (Ratts et al., 2016) outline interpersonal, institutional, and public policy interventions that culturally responsive school counselors use. Interventions and examples in action from each area are provided below.

Interpersonal: Connect students with personal sources of support. Example: Create a "lunch bunch" affinity group for Native American students who may be feeling isolated to connect, affirm, and practice their culture within the school setting.

Institutional: Work with other organizations to reduce the impacts of power, privilege, and oppression on students from marginalized populations. Example: Arrange for staff professional development on equitable behavior management and discipline procedures.

Public policy: Collaborate with students to improve policies and laws. Example: Actively support students in the school's Gay-Straight Alliance (GSA) as they review and address a school board student dress code policy that stigmatizes and discriminates against transgender and gender nonbinary students.

SCHOOLWIDE ENGAGEMENT AND THE SCHOOL COUNSELOR

Walk alongside a school counselor at any point in the school day and you will see there is no shortage of opportunities for counselors to collaborate to support students and the school community: A member of the PTA expresses a desire to support a schoolwide antibullying campaign. A teacher shares that they are noticing increased student anxiety compared to years past and is hoping for tips on how they can help address it. The school psychologist mentions an increase in referrals for special education and wonders if it is connected to new staff being less aware of resources and procedures. Collaborative engagement leads to improved student outcomes. With their unique training, perspective, and role within the building, the school counselor can be a pivotal presence and force in collaborative work.

Assessment

Through collaboration with other staff, school counselors analyze data and generate plans to improve student outcomes. School counselors also collect and use data to analyze the effectiveness of their school-counseling program and share the results with stakeholders (ASCA, 2019). Assessment methods allow us to better understand student strengths, needs, interests, progress, and trends. School counselors can also use their assessment skills to better understand the needs of the larger school community. Needs assessment surveys can help shape goals and action plans for the following school year. Universal screeners can help identify students who may need additional academic, behavior, and socioemotional support. Assessments can add to our holistic understanding of the students and community we serve (ASCA, 2019). Collaborating with others during data analysis and intentionally including diverse voices in the process can lead to additional insights that might otherwise be missed.

Data from assessments can be a very powerful advocacy tool. Both authors of this chapter have used assessment data in presentations to decision makers in ways that resulted in increased funding for professional development, additional school counselors, and dedicated administrative assistant support.

Framework

Frameworks for collaboration provide guidance as we establish our own effective practices. Here, we examine common collaborative stages and practices as well as the foundations of effective collaborations. Let's first consider the similarities and differences between collaboration and consultation. Collaboration and consultation share similarities. They both involve engaging with others to brainstorm and invite input when making decisions regarding goals and next actions. Yet, there are differences as well. In collaborative work, participants collectively determine the best path forward. In consultation, however, the consultee is soliciting input and feedback from the consultant. There is also often a power differential in consultation work (Crothers et al., 2008). Too often, consultation (and often the act of simply seeking input) is mislabeled or misinterpreted as collaboration, which can result in confusion and hurt feelings. Clarifying the nature of the relationship can prevent these problems.

Principles of Collaboration

There are principles of collaboration that can improve collaborative outcomes and experiences. Some of those principles are trust, mutual respect, benevolence and commitment, and having a common goal (Siemon et al., 2019). *Trust* is a requisite for virtually any productive working relationship. Within collaborations, trust facilitates the ability to truly listen to others' ideas; it also creates an environment within which people feel safe enough to offer up ideas of their own. *Mutual respect* involves valuing each person's unique perspectives and expertise, enriching and improving the collaborative process. Mutual respect is often a prerequisite of trust. *Benevolence* involves actively committing to the shared vision and goals and seeing the work through until positive results are achieved. *Having a common goal* clarifies the work and increases motivation and commitment as everyone "rows in the same direction." Shared *values* promote cohesiveness and trust among members (Harrison et al., 1998, p. 98). At its root, collaboration involves *the mutual sharing of resources*, both tangible (such as money or supplies) and intangible (such as knowledge, ideas, opportunities, skills, time, and relationships).

Power inequities between members can impact the quality and effectiveness of the collaborative relationship (Watson & Foster-Fishman, 2013). As a school counselor, you will have a certain degree of power and privilege. Consider how you may be able to use this position to purposefully invite and include those from less privileged or underrepresented groups to have a voice within collaborative decision-making processes, leading to not only a more socially just approach to collaboration but also to better outcomes (Florin & Wandersman, 1990, as cited in Watson and Foster-Fishman, 2013). A helpful tool for facilitating shared power in a culturally responsive way is the POWER^2 acronym (Grothaus et al., 2020). We will introduce you to this acronym through the case study later in the chapter.

At the outset of collaborations, it is important to establish working agreements as to how the group will function and proceed. Part of that process may involve establishing a social contract, or an agreement between members as to their rights and responsibilities within the group. Sometimes individuals may have *unspoken boundaries* based on internalized societal norms (Watson & Foster-Fishman, 2013). These unspoken boundaries, such as assumptions about how the group will function or whether any particular individual's thoughts and participation will be authentically welcomed, can impede the open exchange of resources. Openly discussing and collaborating on setting the group's working norms and agreements can identify unspoken boundaries that may have the potential to both disempower individuals and negatively impact collaboration outcomes.

Addressing Systemic Needs

School counselors and teachers can work together to identify areas where student standards might overlap, providing opportunities to meet academic and social-emotional learning standards at the same time (Graham et al., 2022). *Classroom lessons* can then be implemented that meet the needs of both. The School Counseling Analysis, Leadership and Evaluation (SCALE) Research Center (https://scale-research.org/), developed and maintained by ASCA, provides search tools for the ASCA Student Standards Database. Users can search by academic, behavior, and mindset standards to identify aligned learning outcomes. School counselors can also contribute their own material to add to the database. The Collaborative for Academic, Social, and Emotional Learning (CASEL) is another resource that provides examples and lesson plans that align academic standards with common social-emotional learning standards (https://casel.org/sp_faq/academic-integration/).

The student's developmental process of individuation can sometimes conflict with teachers' need to create an effective classroom environment to facilitate students meeting academic performance criteria and mandates (Craft & Jeffrey, 2008). In these circumstances, teachers may reach out to consult and collaborate with school counselors for assistance with individual students' behavior. At times, teachers may overly attribute student internal factors as the causes of behavior problems when the root of the problem may lie within factors related to teaching or the school system (Tatar & Bekerman, 2009, p. 187). There has been an evolution of our understanding of human behavior, moving away from "blaming" individuals and increasingly acknowledging the myriad of possible environmental factors.

Collaborations should establish an approach to problem-solving that systematically examines environmental factors, including evaluating for the potential presence of systemic racism and bias within any part of the school system and environment. Describing this approach as a staff at the beginning of each school year can help reduce the likelihood that staff may feel defensive when exploring contextual factors that may be influencing student behavior. School counselors can support teachers by helping them consider environmental variables, including those related to their own teaching and their classroom environment. This process is facilitated when professional trust has been established in advance.

Collecting data as part of this process is invaluable. For example, a teacher may approach the school counselor regarding a student's "acting out" behavior. The school counselor might request to come into the classroom, sit in the back, and quietly observe the student on one or more occasions. The school counselor can collect quantitative and qualitative data by using of a classroom behavior observation form, noting which behaviors are occurring at preset time intervals. Comparing the student's behavior to their peers can help identify possible contributing environmental or instructional factors. During observations, note positive behaviors and strengths as well. Presenting and debriefing the results of these observations can be one way that school counselors can approach teachers and objectively discuss possible behavioral, developmental, as well as environmental contributors to behavior.

Current evaluation frameworks emphasize the importance of working collaboratively with others (Danielson, 2013; Marzano, 2017) and require professionals to document proof of collaborative work as part of their annual evaluation process. The activities above are just a few of the ways counselors and teachers engage in meaningful collaborations.

PROFESSIONAL DEVELOPMENT AND COLLABORATION

Many opportunities exist to collaborate on professional development (PD) activities with and for staff, within the building, and across the school district. School counselors can coordinate PD activities for the start of each school year. For example, one school district that both authors worked in would task school counselors with providing presentations and trainings on the following:

- the ASCA National Model and the role of the school counselor
- suicide prevention
- McKinney-Vento Homeless Act—identifying students and connecting families with services
- mandated reporting of suspected child abuse and neglect

Throughout the year, school counselors might also contribute to PD sessions on topics such as adverse childhood experiences (ACEs) and trauma-informed schools, integrating social-emotional learning curriculum and skills development, and college and career readiness. At the district level, school counselors can advocate for and coordinate PD activities that are specific to their role as school counselors. Here are a few ways that school counselors can engage in advocacy and planning for PD:

- Attend workshops, training, and conferences with a colleague or two and then form a professional learning community (PLC) to focus on further learning and implementation.
- Survey district counselors to identify areas of expertise and propose a calendar of mini sessions.
- Inquire about and pursue sources of district funding for counselor-related PD.

MAXIMIZING RESOURCES

The ASCA School Counselor Professional Mindsets and Behaviors calls for professional school counselors to identify and use collaborative best practices in service of improving student success (ASCA, 2019, Standard B-PF-2f). Similar to the role that the therapeutic alliance plays in counseling outcomes (Ardito & Rabellino, 2011), one core collaborative best practice is tending to the quality of collaborative relationships.

A relationship of utmost importance in the school setting is the principal–school counselor relationship (Dahir et al., 2010). While the ASCA annual administrative conference (ASCA, 2019) is an important part of establishing school-counseling program goals and procedures, the day-to-day quality and strength of principal–school counselor interactions strongly influences program success. Cultivating this relationship can result in many dividends: Increased ability to understand and address unique needs of students, increased likelihood of achieving school and program goals, reduced chances of school counselor burnout (Yildirim, 2008), and improved school climate (Duslak & Geier, 2016; Rock et al., 2017) are just a few.

Many of the characteristics of effective communication in school counselor–principal relationships (College Board's National Office for School Counselor Advocacy, American School Counselor Association, and National Association of Secondary School Principals, 2009) can be applied to any collaborative work. These characteristics include open communication, opportunities to share ideas and information on needs, school counselor participation on leadership teams, joint responsibility, mutual trust, a shared vision, mutual respect, and a collective commitment to equity and opportunity.

An element that has been shown to significantly impact the counselor–principal relationship is the frequency of meetings, regardless of whether these meetings are formal and scheduled or informal in nature (Duslak & Geier, 2016). In general, more frequent meetings are associated with a more positive relationship. These meetings can be a combination of formal weekly leadership or department meetings and more informal moments as opportunities arise throughout the week.

Another best practice is for school counselors to increase the school staff's understanding of the role of the school counselor (ASCA, 2019; Duslak & Geier, 2016; Finkelstein, 2009). Many staff may be unfamiliar with the shift from counseling as a service to counseling as a program. Collaborating with your administrator to arrange an annual brief staff training about the ASCA model, counseling and consultative services provided, and ways that staff can access these services, can go a long way in increasing understanding as well as increasing the likelihood that these services are used.

In group collaborations, to develop trust and improve collaborative outcomes, group members must know each individual team member's professional role and responsibilities, but must also attend to emotional and psychological influences that may impact their perspectives and contributions within the group (Siemon et al., 2019). Taking the time to get to know each other can increase a sense of team unity and shared purpose. School counselors can play a critical role in promoting group cohesion and trust.

Group collaborations can be short or long in duration. Short-term collaborations might consist of an ad hoc collaborative team to address a specific problem at a particular point in time. Long-term collaborations involve ongoing teams, such as the multi-tiered system of support (MTSS) teams, child-study teams, school improvement teams, grade-level teams, and leadership teams.

Here are a few additional practices that can help maximize results:

- Ask building, district, and even state leaders about the potential for additional resources to support school counseling programs and collaborative work. There are often resources (funding, potential allies, opportunities for time) available that are not commonly known.

- Take time to network with other school counselors across the region and state and through related groups such as those focused on school psychology, educational leadership, and educational reform. Networking increases your "human resources."

- Get a seat at the table. Decisions are made every day at the building, district, state, and national levels that impact school counselors and school-counseling programs. Counseling representation is important. Find ways to "get yourself invited." Collaborate with peers to cover multiple spaces.

Your core counseling skills will come in handy as a collaborator. Listening for meaning, reflecting feelings and content, summarizing, using "I messages," and allowing for silence models and fosters the authentic engagement so integral to effective collaborations. Normalizing the developmental stages (forming, storming, etc.) of small groups can help if and when interpersonal frictions develop.

SCHOOL COUNSELOR AS CONSULTANT

Consultation involves informing and sharing thoughts and recommendations with others who seek expert guidance regarding student needs (ASCA, 2019, p. 140). Consultation is an indirect service that involves a nonhierarchical relationship between the consultant and consultee, with the goals of (a) improving student academic, behavioral, and social-emotional functioning and (b) supporting and empowering the consultee's problem-solving skill development (Crothers et al., 2008). Consultation can be both a responsive and preventive strategy. Consultation is an important part of equity and social justice work. ASCA recommends that school counselors work with stakeholders to locate racism and bias in schools and share strategies to end such behaviors and practices (ASCA School Counseling Standards in Practice, n.d.).

Although consultation shares many things in common with counseling, it differs from counseling in important ways. First, the consultative relationship is *triadic*. There is the consultant (here, the school counselor) and the consultee, often a teacher in your building or a staff member, parent or guardian, or administrator. The third party in the triadic relationship is the client, typically a student, or a group of students, or even the issue itself. In this way, the consultant is in an indirect role, in contrast to the direct role of a counselor engaging with a client. A second difference is that the consulting role focuses on improving a work-related issue, whereas counseling focuses on helping a client resolve personal problems. Understanding these differences will help set clear expectations about the working relationship, establish appropriate boundaries, and avoid role confusion.

Some common ways that school counselors serve as consultants in schools are as leaders or participants in ongoing MTSS teams, school improvement teams, and grade-level teams. School counselors also engage in the consultation role during multidisciplinary/individualized education program (IEP) meetings. The consultant role is often frequently assumed in less formal and more short-term instances, such as impromptu conversations before or after school, or even during lunch breaks. Regardless of the location and context, it is helpful to use existing consultation models and frameworks to guide your work.

Consultation Models

Most consultation models consist of a form of the following stages (Dickinson & Parsons, 2019):

1. **Preentry**: This is the stage in which expectations and norms regarding the consultation relationship are addressed and developed. Asking your principal for some time at a staff meeting or PD training at the start of each school year to explain your role, the school-counseling program, and procedures, is one good way to get the word out about your services and how staff, students, and parents/guardians can access them.

2. **Entry**: During this stage, focus on further cultivating a relationship built on trust and mutual respect. Use a collaborative approach, rather than taking a top-down or expert stance. Ensure that the consultee feels heard and that their own unique expertise is valued. Acknowledge and trust the strengths you bring to the process; at the same time, always practice within the scope of your expertise and your role. It is far better to say, "You know, I'm not sure what approaches have been found to be successful with this type of situation, but I am happy to do some research and share what I find out," than to give unsound advice.

3. **Exploration and defining of the problem**: Give this stage the time and space it deserves. It is critical to take time to fully explore the problem rather than rush to a solution that may end up prolonging the process and causing more discouragement. Problems that reach this stage are often complex; taking time now will minimize problems later.

   - From a **cultural and social justice** perspective, consider how the client's cultural values and norms are represented and respected in the school. Is there equity in access to resources and opportunities (Grothaus et al., 2020; McMahon et al., 2014)? Are the parties involved aware of their own biases and beliefs? Keep in mind that there are differences in transcultural perceptions of what is considered a problem behavior.

   - From a **systems-ecological** perspective, consider *intrapersonal* factors such as learning style and personality. Explore *interpersonal* factors such as relationships with peers, staff, family dynamics, cultural norms, and identity. What *institutional (school and community)* factors might be impacting the situation, including food, income, or housing insecurity? Consider both strengths and challenges at each level (McMahon et al., 2014).

- From a **solution-focused** perspective, recognize that even small changes can create ripple effects and success spirals. Use scaling questions to understand the severity and impacts of the problem as well as consultee beliefs and feelings about the problem. Identify existing strengths and resources. Look for exceptions—when has it not been a problem?

- From a **cognitive-behavioral** perspective, examine antecedents to the behavior or problem. Consider behavioral consequences that might be acting as unintentional rewards, such as peer or adult attention. Are there irrational beliefs that the consultee or client hold that might be interfering with progress in some way?

4. **Establishment of outcome goals and objectives:** Many times, smaller steps/goals are created on the path toward the larger desired outcome. The goals should be based on measurable, observable, realistic behaviors. Establish an efficient and realistic method to track goals.

5. **Development and implementation of strategies:** The consultant and consultee work together to establish strategies to help the student/client toward their goals. The choice of strategies used will be determined largely by the definition of the nature of the problem, what has been tried before, and what resources are available. If the concern is behavior, consider having the student complete a survey of behavioral reinforcers, such as the one found here: https://pbisworld.com/wp-content/uploads/Forced-Choice-Reinforcement-Menu.pdf. If the problem is systemic in nature, adjusting teaching strategies, classroom configuration, homework routines, or other environmental factors may be called for. Start small and build on successes. Many resources can be helpful as you consider potential interventions. One helpful, free resource is https://www.pbisworld.com/. Other resources can include books such as the *Pre-Referral Intervention Manual* by Hawthorne Educational Services (https://www.hawthorne-ed.com/). Your school psychologist can be a great source of support and may have materials to share or loan. Draw upon the theoretical approaches you are learning in your graduate coursework.

6. **Maintenance:** As progress is made toward goals, acknowledging and celebrating early change can reinforce and maintain the changes over time. In this and the preceding step, consider what challenges might arise that could impede or undo progress and address them in advance.

For many school counselors-in-training, it can be intimidating to picture themselves in a consultant role during the first few years in their new profession; "impostor syndrome" may rear its ugly head. Keep in mind that it is not just your graduate training (and, over time, your professional experience) that will inform your work in your consultation role; you also bring with you the power of your own lived experiences. Know that most research indicates that the most successful consultation relationships are those that are collaborative and egalitarian, not hierarchical or based on the concept of "consultant as expert." Also know that the sole responsibility for coming up with solutions should never be placed solely on the counselor; you cannot be expected to wield a magic wand when it comes to solving problems. After all, this chapter highlights the importance of collaborating with others to seek solutions for challenging problems. Know that you can always seek consultation of your own as you move through this and other aspects of your job in your early years as a school counselor and throughout your career. As long as you are transparent with consultees, understand the collaborative nature of successful consultation relationships, acknowledge where you are in your own processes and your scope of practice, and continue your own PD journey as a lifelong learner, you should do just fine.

Name: Nita Hill, MEd, Certified School Counselor (she/her)

Where You Practice: Washington State, Puyallup School District

Professional Job Title: Elementary School Counselor

Bio: Nita received her master's degree from City University and has served as a school counselor since 1997. During that time, she has achieved both National Board and RAMP certifications. Additionally, she has supported the profession and school counselors through leadership in her state association and being as an adjunct instructor with City University and Seattle Pacific University.

Our district school counselor level leads (school counselors who coordinate and support school-counseling programs and fellow counselors at the elementary, middle school/junior high, and high school levels) spent several years collaborating to develop and implement school counselor–focused professional learning days. This involved collaboration among our team and with our union and district PD department to secure a commitment to dedicated time for counselor-specific training. After several years of self-driven PD, we decided that in order to really move the work forward for ourselves and with the district, an outside training group was needed to serve as an expert voice and build in some accountability for progress. After assessing our options and selecting the best partnership, we submitted a proposal to our district's director of categorical federal programs, outlining the rationale for the training and the benefit to buildings and students. The proposal was accepted, and we were able to use a significant amount of money to hire an outside consulting agency. What started as self-advocacy and collaboration for meaningful PD has expanded to include collaboration with Title I and other district personnel for a multiyear transformational change project. We had no idea that we could ask to partner with other departments and access funding to support our needs; now we are imagining all the other possible partnerships and collaborations to support our team.

SUMMARY AND CONCLUSION

Collaboration is one of the core activities and responsibilities of professional school counselors. Collaborative work can result in immediate and long-lasting positive effects, including more socially than just decision-making processes and outcomes. Contributing as a member of a collaborative team can improve staff motivation and school climate, increase team cohesion and sense of belonging, and make use of individual and collective creativity,

School counselors possess uniquely relevant expertise and a distinct vantage point within the school ecosystem that make them valued collaborative partners and consultants. Through staff collaborations, school counselors can address barriers to student growth and potential. School counselors can team with staff to tackle systemic problems and racial biases that may be present in the schools. School counselors can collaborate with building principals and other decision makers to advocate for the resources and tools needed to have an effective and flourishing school-counseling program. School counselors across the district can collaborate on larger issues, such as improving and expanding counselor PD opportunities, advocating for changes to district policies, and advocating at the state and national levels for legislative changes that enhance school counseling and student well-being.

CASE STUDY

Sam is a 14-year-old student in ninth grade who recently transferred to your high school. In middle school, Sam received multiple in-school and out-of-school suspensions for disruptive and rule-breaking behaviors (blurting in class, arriving late to class without materials, hiding in the bathroom and locker rooms, lying down in the hallway, and leaving the school without permission).

In the time that Sam has been at your school, you have observed similar disruptive behaviors. Sam's teachers have already approached you and are frustrated about the lack of respect that he shows for them in their classrooms and the disruption to the educational environment. After looking at discipline records, you realize that Sam has been suspended more than 30 days this school year.

Background information: Good attendance; history of mental health challenges in family; family has been unable to access counseling services because of transportation issues; family is living in transitional housing due to the mental illness in the family (Dad is unable to work, Mom works but also is a caregiver for Dad and their children); cognitive ability is high average.

DISCUSSION QUESTIONS

Utilizing the POWER[2] model below (Grothaus et al., 2020, pp. 95–96), think about the many opportunities for collaboration as you explore options to support Sam.

P—Pursue possible collaborators who have diverse cultural identities, especially those who are representative of the students in your school.

1. What systems exist that would provide collaborators with opportunities to support this student? Do these systems include people with diverse identities?
2. Do they support strengths-based assessment of challenges and opportunities? If not, how could you as the school counselor improve these systems?

O—Opportunity. Identify opportunities to collaborate, especially around equity issues.

3. What might be formal and informal opportunities for collaboration here? What equity issues may be present?

W—Work together to establish common goals and discuss shared interest.

4. What are some best practices related to establishing goals with clients/students? How will you ensure that student and family voices are included as part of the plan? What facilitation strategies could be used in meetings?

E—Empower collaborators by seeking and honoring expertise and cultural wisdom.

5. How will you center collaborators with related cultural expertise when working together? What system support exists, and what training might need to occur to develop this as a practice at your site? What role should you play in that?

R—Relationship building and reporting progress and results—Continue to enhance the relationship.

6. What steps would you take to ensure that all voices had the opportunity to contribute to this process?
7. With what individuals or agencies outside of school would it be important to build relationships to support this student? What barriers will there be to sharing progress and results with members outside of the school team, and how could you address or minimize those?

PRACTICAL APPLICATION

- Keep an open mind regarding ideas generated by our collaboration partners, and strive to actively pursue and be open to alternate viewpoints and ideas. Maintain a learning stance throughout the collaborative process.

Collaboration With Teachers

- Be available and visible in the school; take a proactive stance.
- Ask to attend grade-level PLC meetings to learn more about students, review data, and develop interventions.
- Ask for time at a staff meeting to express your interest in collaborating; sometimes an in-person announcement will get more response than an email.
- Remind teachers that collaborating can be counted in their evaluation frameworks.
- Negotiate for school counselor planning and collaboration time in your contract.
- Cowrite lesson plans with grade-level/subject-lead teachers.
- Use a project wall/data wall that allows staff to share ideas and interventions.

Collaboration With Principals

- Use the ASCA annual administrative conference process and template (ASCA, 2019) to clarify and advocate for your role within the larger context of the school.
- Advocate for school and district adoption and integration of the ASCA National Model.
- Establish regular, frequent times to meet. Some principals might welcome less formal times to connect as well, such as during their lunch break; others may prefer not to be interrupted.

Collaboration With Other School Staff

- Look for opportunities to collaborate and consult with your school psychologist, school social worker, school nurse, and school-based mental health professionals regarding both student and more systemic problems.
- Work with bus drivers and playground and lunchroom staff to identify effective and socially just behavior interventions and policies. When possible, include them in trainings related to social-emotional learning, trauma-informed responses, and crisis response.

KEY REFERENCES

Only key references appear in the print edition. The full reference list appears in the digital product on Springer Publishing Connect: connect.springerpub.com/content/book/978-0-8261-8753-6/part/part05/chapter/ch17

American School Counselor Association. (2019). *The ASCA National Model: A framework for school counseling programs* (4th ed.).

Dahir, C. A., Burnham, J. J., Stone, C. B., & Cobb, N. (2010). Principals as partners: Counselors as collaborators. *NASSP Bulletin, 94*(4), 286–305. https://doi.org/10.1177/0192636511399899

Dickinson, K., & Parsons, R. (2019). *The school counselor as consultant: Expanding impact from intervention to prevention.* Cognella Academic Publishing.

Ratts, M. J., Singh, A. A., Nassar-McMillan, S., Butler, S. K., & McCullough, J. R. (2016). Multicultural and social justice counseling competencies: Guidelines for the counseling profession. *Journal of Multicultural Counseling and Development, 44*(1), 28–48. https://doi.org/10.1002/jmcd.12035

Rock, W. D., Remley, T. P., & Range, L. M. (2017). Principal-counselor collaboration and school climate. *NASSP Bulletin, 101*(1), 23–35. https://doi.org/10.1177/0192636517698037

CHAPTER 18

Building a Comprehensive School Counseling Program (CSCP)

DAVID MORAN, LISA KOENECKE, MEGAN REINIKKA, JANET CONTRERAS-GUEVARA, AND ELIZABETH GALVAN

LEARNING OBJECTIVES

After reading this chapter, students will be able to:

- Define a comprehensive school counseling program (CSCP).
- Explain how a CSCP is beneficial to stakeholders.
- Design and implement a CSCP.

STUDENT VOICE

The following is a testimony from an experience a school counselor had with a student:

"He frequently got sent to the office or the 'time out' room. When he came to middle school, he had a handful of conflicts. Because of our comprehensive school counseling program, as his middle school counselor I was able to do transition work with this student by consulting with his elementary school counselor to gather information about previous coping skills for his behaviors and academic achievement. This gave me a solid base for his social-emotional and academic needs. In addition, being that our school used restorative practices, I would sit and process with him and then have a 'circle' with him and the other student so they could have a conversation to resolve conflict. He learned to 'own' his part in conflict and was eventually able to make things right with others. By the end of eighth grade, he had minimal conflicts and thanked me for his experience in middle school. He said he felt like no one liked him in elementary school as no one ever really listened to him and he was always sent out of class. He said in middle school he felt heard and valued through our restorative process, and that was so important to him. As he transitioned to high school, I worked closely with his high school counselor and teaching team to provide them the knowledge and growth this student had built, so his team could continue to

foster to help him succeed with his social-emotional and academic goals. The way I was able to work within our comprehensive school counseling program provided for his social-emotional needs to be met and addressed. During high school, his academic achievement soared, he applied to college, which he never intended to do, and has grown into a kind, giving young man."

INTRODUCTION

A major component of school counseling practice is implementing a comprehensive school counseling program (CSCP). The school counseling profession has been fortunate to have vanguards promoting and advocating for this vital work with students. As with many professional organizations, school counselors can use the American School Counselor Association (ASCA) to access research, models, and best practice considerations that strive to continue moving the profession forward. ASCA provides overviews of important issues through position statements and provides a comprehensive model that seeks to help school counselors establish a CSCP.

According to the ASCA (2019a), a CSCP should be (a) comprehensive in scope, (b) preventive in design, and (c) developmental in nature. When school counselors combine comprehensive planning and preventive practices that are also developmentally appropriate, successful transitions will occur to improve student learning and behavior (Carey & Dimmitt, 2012). Collecting and analyzing student outcome data to close opportunity gaps will guide your CSCP.

A CSCP promotes equal opportunity and access for all students, while supporting students in developing the knowledge, attitudes, and skills necessary to become competent, confident, life-long learners. The emphasis of a CSCP is on meeting students' needs through early identification, prevention, and data-informed interventions. A CSCP includes the whole student as a human being, including their life at home, their dreams, and their current reality within the school building. This concept is applicable to all students, all abilities, all identities, all grades (even if you only have a certain caseload), at all times.

This chapter will provide a step-by-step guide through the process of developing a CSCP for master's degree students and new school counselors. Scholarly support for the benefits of a CSCP is presented and practical application of the model, including the benefits of a CSCP for multiple stakeholders, is discussed. Readers will understand how CSCPs help define the role and responsibilities of school counselors nationwide, while reducing noncounseling activities performed by school counselors.

SCHOOL COUNSELOR'S ROLE WITHIN COMPREHENSIVE SCHOOL COUNSELING PROGRAMS

Though the value of the school counselor may vary depending on the state, school district, and school building counselors find themselves in, the importance of the CSCP remains consistent (ASCA, 2021a). CSCPs help define the role and responsibilities of school counselors while reducing noncounseling activities performed by school counselors. Research indicates that school counselors who used a comprehensive program had higher levels of job satisfaction and lower levels of burnout; as well, the students who were offered CSCPs had higher grades and better peer interactions (Fye et al., 2020; Pyne, 2011; Sink, 2005).

Considerations for the Planning of a Comprehensive School Counseling Program

It is important to note that school counseling has had to adapt to meet the need of students. A well thought out CSCP will focus on providing proactive direct services to all students, rather than reactive services that focus on a few select students, while using data derived from the CSCP to effect systemic changes in schools (Dixon et al., 2010). Therefore, it is prudent for school counselors to be aware of the factors that could affect the development of CSCPs. For example, the level of administrative support for the CSCP, lack of supervision of the school counselor, role ambiguity within the school, conflict of interest by placing the school counselor in punitive rather than supportive roles, the number of inappropriate job duties assigned to the school counselor, and the size of the school counselor's caseload all impact the ability a school counselor has to develop and implement a CSCP (Camelford & Ebrahim, 2017; Fye et al., 2018; Randick et al., 2019). In school buildings where administrators are aware of CSCPs, school counselors find themselves assigned to appropriate job duties that support the implementation of CSCPs (Camelford & Ebrahim, 2017). This is important to highlight as not every school building administrator will be aware of or value the positive impact CSCPs can have in enabling school counselors to fulfill their job responsibilities. In an ideal school counseling setting, ratios would be one school counselor to 250 students (ASCA, 2021a). If school counselors are expected to perform inappropriate duties, it is the student who suffers. ASCA recommends that school counselors spend at least 80% of their time working directly with or indirectly for students (ASCA, 2019a). A CSCP can help you evade the aforementioned factors affecting implementation of a CSCP. Just as an architect uses a blueprint in their planning, the school counselor uses the CSCP to advocate for systemic change.

There is no perfect way to design a CSCP. Remember to keep the words *all* students or *every* family in your comprehensive planning as CSCPs need to be inclusive of all students and their needs. CSCPs lay the foundation for school counselors to maintain healthy, safe, and inclusive learning environments for students to thrive academically, socially, and emotionally (Dahir & Stone, 2009; Moe et al., 2011). There are options to consider when you initially develop a CSCP. Some school counselors might start with goals, others might look at data, while others might start with a calendar. Other key considerations include your school's mission statement, your school counseling/student services department goals, and the district's strategic plan. For example, if the district has a literacy goal to close achievement gaps, school counselors may want to consider how they can include that goal into the comprehensive work. CSCPs can be flexible, as school counselors can add, modify, or mark goals achieved throughout the school year or from year to year. Consulting with teachers can be helpful as they can advise school counselors on how to align the ASCA (2021b) Student Standards that focus on college and career readiness into the guidance curriculum as part of the CSCP (Cook, 2015).

Furthermore, using the ASCA's (2021b) Student Standards: Mindsets & Behaviors for Student Success K–12 College-, Career-, and Life-Readiness Standards for Every Student, consider behavior and learning strategies B-LS 5: Media and technology skills to enhance learning. Collaborate with the district's information technology department or school personnel who are savvy with technology to assist a student or group of students by using media or technology to achieve the district reading goal. If you think starting with goals is a wise approach and could use examples on how to write goals, consider reviewing Recognized ASCA Model Programs (RAMP), which can be found at https://www.schoolcounselor.org/Recognition/RAMP.

Relationships with all stakeholders are vital to supporting all students and every family. School counselors provide culturally sustaining instruction, appraisal, and advisement, as well as counseling to help all students demonstrate learning skills, self-management skills, and social skills (ASCA, 2019a) to prepare them for postsecondary life. Building a positive rapport with an administrative assistant could be a great first step in a new position. This person likely knows the details to make the day run smoothly. If this person is assisting the administrator, be kind and respectful in the event you need to meet with the administrator on short notice. Never underestimate building a relationship with your custodian, your technology person, and your food service workers. These key relationships are beneficial as you may be giving a new family a tour of the school; how you interact with support staff such as these will show how much you, the school counselor, value everyone. This will indirectly help give credence to your role and your implementation of your CSCP.

As you build your CSCP, consider the following resources to support you in implementing it:

- Current edition of the ASCA National Model (ASCA, 2019a)
- Current edition of ASCA Student Standards: Mindsets & Behaviors for Student Success (ASCA, 2021b)
- Current edition of ASCA's Ethical Standards for School Counselors (ASCA, 2016)
- Current edition of ASCA School Counselor Professional Standards & Competencies (2019b)
- Current local, state, and national standards focused on academic, social/emotional, and career development
- Data sources to inform your equitable planning and decision-making (e.g., school report card, school improvement plan, surveys, local and state assessments, national assessments)
- Your district's mission, vision, calendar, and strategic plan
- Your school counseling department's mission, vision, calendar, and strategic plan if it differs from what your district has in place
- Alternative placement and transition standards to serve all students and all abilities at all locations
- Consider collaborating with other student service team members, special education staff, exceptional/talented and gifted staff, English language learner staff, therapy staff, and paraeducators
- Additional building and district resources available to support student learning, social-emotional well-being, and college and career readiness planning

Defining Your Comprehensive School Counseling Program

A CSCP could include the use of the ASCA National Model (2019a), the ASCA's Ethical Standards for School Counselors (2016), and the ASCA's Mindsets & Behaviors for Student Success (2021a). In combination, these sources can serve as a foundation for a quality CSCP. It is also important also note that how a CSCP is developed will depend on state and regional factors. For example, in Texas resources to develop a CSCP are clearly provided by the state's education agency as special considerations need to account for the sizable immigrant population within the state (Texas Education Agency, 2022). In general, states are supportive of school counselors as they provide resources for developing and maintaining CSCPs. According to the state of Wisconsin's Department of Public Instruction (n.d.), CSCPs, when implemented properly, can promote "increased student achievement, an improved graduation rate, better attendance, reduced disciplinary referrals, completed individual learning plans, and increased student participation in the community" (para. 2).

It is ideal to first define the mission, or vision, and goals of your CSCP by reviewing the school's academic mission and goals. This will help integrate the CSCP into the everyday functioning and purpose of the school. Next, it is important to recognize that student standards related to school counseling can help define a CSCP. These standards help new and experienced school counselors develop, implement, and assess their school counseling program to improve student outcomes (ASCA, 2019a). Therefore, student standards, such as the ASCA Mindsets and Behaviors for Student Success (2021), should be used to determine what the expectations are for students within the CSCP. Two critical questions to ask while defining the CSCP are How will students benefit related to their academic, college, or career, and their social/emotional development through the CSCP?, and How will the CSCP be inclusive of all students and the identities they hold? Understanding and envisioning how students will encounter support through the CSCP in these areas puts students' needs first. And last, a CSCP will have little hope for success without ethically minded and culturally responsive school counselors. A CSCP should hold school counselors accountable in their relationships with students, parents/guardians, the school, and the profession. Incorporating the ASCA Ethical Standards for School Counseling (2016) into the CSCP serves as an important component as these standards guide interactions with the aforementioned groups and entities. The CSCP should outline how school counselors will engage with students in an inclusive and unbiased manner, respect parents/guardians rights to the educational experience of their children and adolescents while honoring the benefits and limitations of confidentiality of the counseling relationship with students, advocate the equal access to school counseling programming for all students, and engage in professional development to stay current with best practices within school counseling as a profession. As we have laid a foundation for what should be included as a CSCP is developed, we will next discuss the considerations for putting the planning of the CSCP into action through the management of the CSCP.

Managing Your Comprehensive School Counseling Program

The *manage* component of the CSCP includes program focus and program planning. Some school counseling departments will adopt the school district's mission statement, vision statement, and district strategic plan as their own. Determine what works best for your students to achieve their successful outcomes. An annual plan and daily/weekly schedules provide an opportunity for transparency, collaboration, and accountability. This is also a data collection tool to monitor the amount of your time spent in each domain as well as in each component of The ASCA National Model (ASCA, 2019a) as well as the ASCA's Mindsets & Behaviors for Student Success (ASCA, 2021b). Some school districts allocate a school counselor to more than one building—meaning their full-time employment could be scaffolded between two or three buildings. If school counselors are assigned to more than one site, it is especially important to use a calendar for best practices. A year-long master calendar is imperative for planning a program. It identifies the goals/curriculum for the year and aligns with the standards/learning targets. By using effective time management, school counselors can use teamwork to strategize, organize, plan, and schedule activities proactively rather than by being on call at anytime (Dahir & Stone, 2009).

Remember to be inclusive of all students when planning your calendars (ASCA, 2018). School counselors serve all students and are leaders in the educational setting. Religious celebrations observed by the majority of your student population might not be observed by everyone. Winter break is an equitable term to replace Christmas break. If you have students or staff who observe Ramadan, it is important to note this on your calendar. Each day during Ramadan, Muslims do not eat or drink from dawn to sunset (Yaqeen Institute for Islamic Research, 2020). Some students might have accelerated courses at a different site; consider these transitions in your planning. You will have safety drills as another component of your calendar. Department meetings, professional development days, and lunch are all important considerations in your comprehensive planning.

Developing a calendar for the program allows school counselors to transform inappropriate duties to appropriate duties, manifesting in a unified and intentional CSCP. Calendars can also be a visual representation for stakeholders that the school counseling program is developmental and proactive and is designed to reach all students PK–12. Calendars also inform administrators that implementation of a CSCP requires a great deal of a school counselor's time (Lowery et al., 2018). ASCA recommends school counselors spend a minimum of 80% of their time in direct and indirect student services and 20% or less of their time in program planning and school/system support (ASCA, 2019b). School counselors and the implementation of a CSCP are intended to help each school achieve its desired mission. School administrators may be unfamiliar with the benefits of a CSCP and how it impacts the use of school counselor's time (ASCA, 2019b; Shi & Brown, 2020). Thus, school counselors should advocate for the appropriate use of their time as it is based on student needs in recognition that there are misperceptions by school administrators related to the roles and functions of a school counselor (ASCA, 2019b; Leuwerke et al., 2009).

Delivering Your Comprehensive School Counseling Program

School counselors deliver a CSCP through direct and indirect student services (ASCA, 2019b). Direct student services include instruction, appraisal and advisement, and counseling (ASCA, 2019b). Instruction includes lessons on time management, career exploration, and conflict resolution. Examples of appraisal include completion of a career survey, standardized testing performance, and skills inventories. Individual advising supports individual students to accomplish their goals. Counseling can be done individually or in small groups and should match your CSCP goals. Indirect student services include consultation, collaboration, and referrals (ASCA, 2019c; Gibbons et al., 2010). Consultation is done with educators within your school or online community and can also be done with families. Collaboration with stakeholders will assist in delivering your CSCP. Collaborating with classroom educators to deliver a lesson on career development provides an excellent opportunity to increase a sense of ownership within your school community. Referrals to community partners expand the advocacy efforts of a well-delivered CSCP.

Through direct and indirect student services, a CSCP delivers positive attitudes, knowledge, and skills for student success. As this component of a CSCP outlines what activities a school counselor is to engage in, aligning these activities to the multitiered systems of support (MTSS) enacted within the school building is crucial. MTSS is an evidence-based framework implemented in PK–12 schools that uses data-based decision-making to integrate academic and behavioral instruction and intervention at tiered intensities to improve the learning and social/emotional functioning of all students (Sink, 2016). MTSS teams are made up of several stakeholders within the school building (e.g., teachers, instructional support staff, administration), and school counselors are certainly one of them. MTSS teams use data throughout the school year to support students and provide necessary interventions to aide in their learning. The direct and indirect services provided by school counselors within CSCPs align with MTSS by implementing classroom instruction and schoolwide programming and initiatives found in Tier 1; implementing small-group and individual counseling, consultation, and collaboration with school personnel, families, and community stakeholders found in Tier 2; and providing indirect student support services through consultation, collaboration, and facilitation of referrals common to Tier 3 (Goodman-Scott et al., 2020). CSCPs provide great opportunities to work alongside a school's mission and goals to remove systemic barriers for all students and implement specific learning supports that assist in academic and behavioral success.

Assessing Your Comprehensive School Counseling Program

To sustain a CSCP, assessments of the program, as well as an assessment and appraisal of the school counselor, must also occur with fidelity. The *assess* portion of the ASCA National Model (ASCA, 2019a) provides school counselors an opportunity to determine the CSCP effectiveness, inform improvements to their school counseling program design and delivery, and show how students are different as a result of the school counseling program (ASCA, 2019b). School counselors also self-assess their own mindsets and behaviors to inform their professional development and annually participate in a school counselor performance appraisal with a qualified administrator (ASCA, 2019b).

The ASCA National Model (ASCA, 2019a) provides the following tools to guide assessment and appraisal of a CSCP:

- Program assessment
- School counseling program assessment
- Annual results reports
- School counselor assessment and appraisal
- The School Counselor Performance Appraisal Template
- ASCA School Counselor Professional Standards & Competencies Assessment

BENEFITS OF A COMPREHENSIVE SCHOOL COUNSELING PROGRAM

Your CSCP helps to create a safe climate for all your students, staff, and families. The benefits of a CSCP encompass a wide range of stakeholders. Collaborating with stakeholders, such as families, administrators, school boards, and community members, is an essential component of your CSCP. School counselors' implementation of CSCP benefits students as counselors prepare them for the challenges in their future while supporting their academic achievement, career decision-making, and social-emotional growth (Lapan, 2012). CSCPs also benefits students as the program provides school counselors with data to advocate for individual students and to ensure equal access to opportunities (Carey & Dimmitt, 2012).

The benefits of CSCPs also extend to school counselors themselves. In a study of secondary-school counselors, Pyne (2011) suggested that school counselors who implemented a CSCP, such as the ASCA National Model, experienced greater job satisfaction compared to school counselors without such programs. Specifically, school counselors exhibited greater job satisfaction when school counseling programs had administrative support, included communication among school faculty members, possessed a clear mission statement, identified clear roles of the school counselor, served all students in the school, and included time for planning and evaluation of the school counseling program and related activities (Pyne, 2011).

RECOGNIZED ASCA MODEL PROGRAM: RAMP

Another potential benefit of building a CSCP might include some national recognition for a school counselor's dedicated efforts. The RAMP designation recognizes schools that commit resources to delivering comprehensive, data-informed school counseling programs (ASCA, 2022). While financial resources and the time it takes school counselors to achieve

RAMP designation could impose barriers for some schools (Mullen et al., 2019), it may be worth the effort to demonstrate to administrators, to school board members, and to the community that school counselors are committed to delivering an exemplary comprehensive, data-driven school counseling program. Wilkerson and colleagues (2013) researched Indiana schools that had earned the RAMP designation versus non-RAMP–designated schools. Their findings indicated that schoolwide proficiency rates in English/language arts and math were significantly higher in RAMP-designated elementary schools compared to non-RAMP elementary control schools. The RAMP application process could be the culmination of the implementation of a CSCP; however, CSCPs can still be exemplary without a RAMP designation (Milsom & Morey, 2018; Mullen et al., 2019).

The benefits of a CSCP encompass a wide range of stakeholders. Students benefit by having a school counselor advocating for their individual needs. Families benefit by having a dedicated source for career planning. Other educators benefit from a CSCP by having a master's level–trained collaborative leader facilitate social and emotional skill development. The benefits of a CSCP for school counselors is a data-informed and sustainable approach to student success. Administrators benefit by having a systemic change agent by their side. A CSCP benefits the community, business and industry, and institutes of higher education by providing knowledgeable and skilled graduates prepared to contribute to society.

VOICES FROM THE FIELD

Name: Bonnie Robbins (she/her)

Where You Practice: Whittier Middle School, University of Southern Maine

Professional Job Title: School Counselor, Adjunct Instructor

Bio: Bonnie Robbins is a school counselor at Whittier Middle School in Portland, Maine, and is an adjunct professor at the University of Southern Maine. She is a leader in the school counseling profession. She has served on the Maine School Counselor Board for several years and has also served on the American School Counselor Board of Directors. Bonnie has presented at several conferences around the country on restorative practices and has trained many schools. She is an active participant with the Maine Department of Education, conducting many trainings, and she cofacilitates weekly meetings for counselors and social workers.

When thinking about the role of a school counselor, many things come to mind. I follow the ASCA Mindsets and Behaviors, which have helped our district create a CSCP and evaluation system. I regularly conduct needs assessments with staff, families, and students and continually monitor our attendance, behavior, and academic data. Through my comprehensive program, I have created a school counseling curriculum, counsel students individually and in small groups, as well as provide responsive services to students and families in need of crisis intervention. I regularly consult, collaborate, and advocate with and for staff, families, and outside resources. I always start my day greeting students to build relationships, and I believe strongly in restorative practices as it lays the groundwork for a healthy school climate.

What I enjoy most about my current position is the students! Building relationships and genuinely getting to know each student is crucial in my job. I enjoy conducting minute meetings in the fall with our incoming seventh-graders. It gives me an opportunity to have a face-to-face interaction with each student and helps me get to know them. This has proven to be extremely effective, as students have said because of this meeting, they felt comfortable coming to see me when they needed someone to talk to. One of the biggest struggles with my position would be lack of resources working in rural Maine. I work hard to find services for students and families, but we are often limited to what is available. With that said, I never give up, and I continue to advocate for the needs of our students.

The first piece of advice I give to my graduate students entering the field of school counseling is to be yourself! School counselors need to be transparent and real with their students, which helps build relationships. Every student needs a school adult that they can connect to and to feel genuinely cared about. If that school adult is not the school counselor, then it's the school counselor's duty to find a trusted adult for that particular student.

SUMMARY AND CONCLUSION

School counseling is an integral component of a successful educational system. By building a CSCP, all students have access to a rewarding future. School counselors use student and professional standards to define their program. Program focus and program planning guide the *manage* component of a good CSCP. To deliver the program, direct and indirect student services are implemented. To determine the efficacy of the CSCP, assess the data through program and school counselor assessments and a school counselor appraisal. A CSCP benefits numerous stakeholders and provides student outcomes to improve attendance, reduce discipline referrals, and increase achievement for all.

CASE STUDY

For 20 years, there has been the same elementary school counselor in the same building. A new elementary school counselor is hired. The previous school counselor was beloved by the students, the faculty, the administration, and the community. There were beautiful bulletin boards, magical puppets, and worksheets galore. Each month had a theme and a corresponding bulletin board and classroom lesson. For 20 years, this elementary school continued to use the same materials, lessons, puppets, and worksheets without results. This elementary school counselor of 20 years was never questioned about student outcome data because "everyone was happy." In reality, reading scores and math scores were declining as discipline rates increased. It wasn't until a new administrator was hired that data became a focus. This new administrator hired a new school counselor who knew how to implement a CSCP using the ASCA National Model (ASCA, 2019a). The next year, this elementary school earned awards for their academic advancements.

DISCUSSION QUESTIONS

1. From this case study, what can you learn about data and how to use it to help your students succeed?
2. How do you advocate making systemic changes?
3. How do you continue to collaborate with current faculty who had a great relationship with the former school counselor?
4. What leadership skills must you access while you build your CSCP?

PRACTICAL APPLICATION

- Remember our domains: academic, social/emotional, and career.
- Remember to collect data that informs achievement, attendance, and discipline.
- Remember to spell principal correctly.
- Remember that we help students with their attitudes, skills, and knowledge in order to succeed.
- Remember to ask for help and that relationships matter.
- Remember to become involved in your state school counseling association.
- Remember we are school counselors . . . not the "g" word. ASCA changed our name in 1990.
- Remember that National School Counseling Week is always the first full week in February.
- Remember to always use an equitable lens while supporting your community.

KEY REFERENCES

Only key references appear in the print edition. The full reference list appears in the digital product on Springer Publishing Connect: connect.springerpub.com/content/book/978-0-8261-8753-6/part/part05/chapter/ch18

American School Counselor Association. (2019a). *ASCA National Model: A framework for school counseling programs* (4th ed.).

American School Counselor Association. (2019b). *ASCA school counselor professional standards & competencies.* https://www.schoolcounselor.org/asca/media/asca/home/SCCompetencies.pdf

American School Counselor Association. (2021a). *The role of the school counselor.* https://www.schoolcounselor.org/getmedia/ee8b2e1b-d021-4575-982c-c84402cb2cd2/Role-Statement.pdf

American School Counselor Association. (2021b). *ASCA student standards: Mindsets and behaviors for student success.*

Dahir, C. A., & Stone, C. B. (2009). School counselor accountability: The path to social justice and systemic change. *Journal of Counseling and Development, 87*(1), 12–20. https://doi.org/10.1002/j.1556-6678.2009.tb00544.x

CHAPTER 19

Online Counseling Service Delivery for School Counselors

CHER N. EDWARDS, AMANDA ROSENFELD, AND JORDAN SHANNON

LEARNING OBJECTIVES

After reading this chapter, students will be able to:

- Recognize various strategies for offering online/virtual school counseling interventions.
- Compare interventions across PK–12 levels (elementary, middle, or high) and modify to meet the developmental needs of students being served.
- Choose online/virtual counseling interventions that can be used for future practical application (e.g., practicum, internship, or as a professional school counselor).

STUDENT VOICE

Student "J," a 12th-grader attending a school that moved to virtual learning during the pandemic, provided the following testimony:

"This year has been really, REALLY hard. When I started high school, I had lots of ideas and hopes about what my senior year would look like, and, well, it doesn't look anything like I thought it would. No sports, no activities, no dances, not even a real graduation ceremony. It's been pretty depressing, if I'm being honest. I didn't get to visit any colleges. I'm going to a community college because I really don't feel like I am ready to make this big decision without really having the chance to check out the campus. One thing that helped was having my school counselor check in with us. She had office hours where she was in a virtual office, and we could log on and check in with her. Sometimes other students were there, and it was cool just to hear that other students were feeling like I was. It made me feel less alone. Sometimes we'd all just sit there and watch each other eat, which was a little weird sometimes, but she usually made up some activity or game to force us to talk. She made us have our cameras on too, which to be honest, I didn't really like at first, but it actually did make me feel more connected with other students. It got really lonely this year.

She tells us about different drop-in meetings that we can attend to talk about filling out the FASFA, scholarships, what to do after high school, and groups just for connecting with other students. Not a lot of students come, but I have found it really helpful. I feel like I could reach out if I am really having a hard time."

INTRODUCTION: ROLE OF THE SCHOOL COUNSELOR IN ONLINE COUNSELING

Scholars have argued that PK–12 traditional, also referred to as brick-and-mortar, schools have been forever changed by the online accommodations provided in response to COVID-19 and our current pandemic (Bombardieri, 2021; Friedman, 2020; Huck & Zhang, 2021). Historical practices related to snow days, teacher in-service training, and school closures may be a distant memory for future generations as schools replace closing with online instruction. At the same time, public and private online PK–12 academies offering full-time online instruction are gaining in popularity for populations who typically have not experienced success in traditional schools for varying reasons or whose schedules are not a good fit for the typical PK–12 school day (Curtis & Werth, 2015). This chapter addresses adjustments to traditional training related to school-counseling intervention delivery, assessing for lethality online, collaborating in an online format/community, and ethical considerations for online counseling. A practicing online school counselor will share tips and recommendations specific to the development and delivery of an online school counseling model.

VIRTUAL ACADEMIES/ONLINE PK–12 INSTITUTIONS

Students who attend an online academy or online PK–12 school are an exceptionally diverse group. In review of the admissions applications, one will encounter Olympians whose practice and travel schedule does not allow for traditional education, child/teen actors, a teen parent whose child care and employment needs require significant flexibility, a student who feels that their faith or religious perspective is not honored within the public school system, or perhaps a student who has experienced significant bullying. As with brick-and-mortar schools, there is no one size fits all related to the student population. One constant that may be seen is a desire for a flexible schedule; and providing flexibility is where is an area in which online learning typically excels. In response to the COVID-19 pandemic, the majority of traditional school districts were forced to move academic instruction online. Virtual academies often provide instruction to staff related to the unique needs and challenges of the student population as well as the nuances of providing instruction and interventions in an online format. Educators, including school counselors, who were trained to provide school counseling services in physical buildings, did not have the luxury of this type of professional development and found themselves having to quickly adjust to attending to student needs in this new environment. Here, we highlight strategies that support school counseling intervention efficacy and success within the online framework.

Relationships are paramount. Providing services in a virtual format requires extreme intentionality. Building relationships between students and administration, teachers, staff, and other students will require a strong online presence and scheduled opportunities. Students and staff no longer have the luxury of bumping into each other in the building hallways or cafeteria. School counselors can help students navigate these relationships by educating students about proper online etiquette and expectations. Lessons can be taught on how to write an email, contact teachers, ask for help, and how to support other students online. Students attending school online often find it challenging to ask for what they need. There is often the assumption that all of the information is housed online somewhere, and it is the students' job to find it. School counselors can help students practice self-advocacy skills by role-playing and creating scenarios in which students problem-solve together during large-group guidance or small-group counseling.

To build relationships with families, communicate, communicate, communicate. Did we mention communicate? The most parents are eager to know how their students are doing in school before having an issue escalate. School counselors can create a webpage of resources related to school counseling for families and community members to access. Students learning in a virtual setting may not be able to access information during typical business/school hours. Having a website allows students, families, and school staff to access information when it is most convenient for them. A school counselor can send out newsletters and push notifications to increase their visibility in the online setting.

To build relationships with school administration and staff, it is important to reach out to allow for online chats and phone calls to promote connections and create opportunities for collaboration. It is important for a school counselor to remember that anything in writing about the student can be considered part of their student record and therefore be accessed upon request. For this reason, direct phone calls with staff members can often be the best way to protect a student's confidentiality.

DELIVERY OF ONLINE SCHOOL COUNSELING SERVICES: A PRACTICAL APPROACH

The following paragraphs will briefly highlight how some of the most readily used school counseling interventions can be adjusted to address the needs of students in a virtual setting. Recommendations related to individual counseling, small group counseling, and large group or classroom guidance is presented.

To provide individual counseling services or brief check-ins with students, school counselors can connect with students in a way similar to that of traditional practice. As with in-person counseling, it is important to inform the student as soon as possible regarding the limitations of online counseling and confidentiality (ASCA Ethics Committee, 2020). A best practice to help students gain comfort and build a strong connection is to try to create a norm of "cameras on." If a student does not want to turn their camera on, or does not have the means, the counselor should reassure the student that it is not necessary. The school counselor should be transparent and show the student their workspace. This can help to gain trust. Counselors should be intentional about their online office presence. What the student can see will say a lot about you and your values. Do you value a safe space for all students? Find a flag or sign that makes a statement and have it visible when you are on camera. Do you love riding your bike? Are you an alumnus of a local college? This is a great way to practice minimal self-disclosure and allow students to get to know something about you.

When offering small-group counseling, confidentiality is a concern due to the nature of group work as well as the online format. There are ample opportunities for a breach to occur. A school counselor should warn of confidentiality issues, and set privacy expectations before beginning each group meeting. The school counselor may want to avoid group topics that have the potential for students to overshare in a setting where confidentiality cannot be guaranteed (ASCA Ethics Committee, 2020). Examples of sensitive topics include grief, self-harm, and eating disorders. School counselors have a responsibility to protect students from extremely sensitive topics when sharing with other students (ASCA Ethics Committee, 2020). Friendship skills, study skills, college and career planning are group topics that can be provided online without much risk of discussing a triggering topic or creating an issue with confidentiality. Although it may seem obvious, it is important to set clear expectations and rules related to recording devices, such as phones, during group meetings.

Many school districts have invested in online platforms creating opportunities for engaging classroom guidance or large-group interventions. Blackboard, Connexus, Schoology, and Google Classroom are examples of commonly used school systems. The innovative school counselor can use these platforms to create a virtual counseling room. The school counselor will be able to provide lessons to the student population in a manner similar to that of the traditional delivery models (ASCA Ethics Committee, 2020). For example, a school counselor could create a grade-level team on Google Teams, providing the option to present to the entire school or hold smaller groups by grade level based on the topic and interest level. There are many programs available online that a counselor can use to make their sessions engaging, such as NearPod, Kahoot, Flip Grid, and more. While these platforms are readily changing, the spirit of the recommendation is to encourage emerging school counselors to become familiar with the various platforms and online tools that can be used to promote student learning and engagement.

THE INTEGRATION OF MULTICULTURAL COMPETENCIES AND SOCIAL JUSTICE

Whether providing virtual school counseling services to a traditional PK–12 population or to a group of students who have chosen online education, it is important to be aware of the diversity of students that are being served and provide culturally relevant instruction, support, and counseling interventions. School counselors are to approach multicultural counseling and social justice competency as a developmental process (Ratts et al., 2016). The idea is that one does not "arrive" at competency without any necessity for scaffolded learning—it is a work in progress.

Ratts et al. (2016) articulate that the counselor approaches multicultural work through four fundamental lenses: (1) understanding the complexity of diversity and multiculturalism in the counseling relationship; (2) understanding the impact of oppression on the mental health of marginalized identities; (3) knowing that individuals exist within their social environments; and (4) incorporating social justice advocacy through the wide array of counseling modalities. Everything we do as school counselors is multicultural. School counselors are operating in ways to invite students' diverse experiences, attending to multicultural needs, and understanding that the influences of privilege and oppression maintain a palpable atmosphere.

School counselors work and live in spaces where they need to consider the importance of intersecting social locations. This can be done at the individual level, within the counseling relationship, as well as at the macrolevel, examining how educational systems and policies impact students' academic, social, and emotional wellness. Counselors should aim to dismantle systems of oppression due to the deleterious effects on student well-being. It means elevating the voices of students who hold multiple marginalized identities, because counselors recognize that White cultural norms intentionally and unintentionally have largely drowned out those students' voices.

One way school counselors can consider the multicultural context is through examining students' access to resources and by considering the educational policies in the context of the current sociocultural influence. Recently, PK–12 education has experienced a shift from a traditional in-person setting to predominantly online modalities in response to a novel coronavirus disease (COVID-19) public health crisis. Barring safety precautions, COVID-19 revealed significant health and socioeconomic disparities between Black, indigenous, persons of color (BIPOC) families, and White families (Litam & Hipolito-Delgado, 2021; Ong, 2020). For example, during the fall of 2020, Black and Latinx families were found to be 1.4 times more likely to have limited access to computer and internet services compared to non-Hispanic Whites (Ong, 2020). Litam and Hipolito-Delgado (2021) highlighted how COVID-19 shed light on the economic disparities in forms of income, housing access, and healthcare access between White and BIPOC families, with Whites having greater access across all three areas. School counselors can engage in multicultural practices by exploring how these current issues are impacting the well-being of their marginalized students through areas such as data collection and needs assessments and through leadership and advocacy support.

The physical space of the school building has benefited communities that have historically been underserved due to lack of resources. These buildings provide easy access to technology, internet access, and basic needs such as food. When instruction moved from a school building to the home environment in the form of virtual learning, students were left without the support needed to flourish academically. School counselors operating from an equity lens ensure that policies are in place to support student needs.

Collaborating and Consulting in a Virtual World: A Practical Approach

The most significant challenges for online school counseling include confidentiality, accessibility, and access to outside support. These challenges can be addressed by working together as a team of stakeholders to develop creative, accessible, and effective solutions.

Maintaining a confidential setting to practice school counseling can be difficult. The nature of the environment lends itself to interruptions in both the school counselor's office and at the student's home. The school counselor must acknowledge the limitations of confidentiality prior to beginning a session with their student. Students should be encouraged to meet in a private location or with headphones if they are going to discuss something that they are not comfortable with their family overhearing. A school counselor has the responsibility to ensure that their own space is as private as possible. This includes, but is not limited to, shutting the door, using headphones, and using a sound machine.

Providing accessible services to students can be difficult when equipment, internet, electricity, and websites are not working optimally. School districts across the country found themselves scrambling to provide resources to families so all students would have a chance to learn while the buildings were closed due to the pandemic. Some communities were able to get free or reduced internet and laptops. Many families still struggled with finding the resources that their students needed to get an equitable education. School counselors are in a pivotal role to help ensure that families find and secure access to the resources that their students need.

A challenge of online counseling in a virtual academy is related to the process of linking students to community resources. Virtual schools may have students attending from all over the state, which means identifying local resources can present a challenge. One way to help the student and their families is by connecting them to their local school district's website. Often, these websites will have local resources listed. Other resource lists can be found on city or county websites. Local libraries will also often have resources available for students to access for free.

The benefits of virtual school counseling interventions are plentiful. Virtual school counselors can provide online resources that are accessible to a wide array of students and their families. Information can be given during virtual meetings that the families can either access live or as a recording to listen to when they have the time in their schedules. Scheduling meetings and appointments allows for a greater chance of meeting the needs of the families who may not work a traditional 9-to-5 schedule. This can help to create a greater partnership between the families and the school. As school counselors, it is important to apply a strengths-based lens to the opportunity to serve an online or virtual community.

A SYSTEMIC APPROACH TO ONLINE/VIRTUAL SCHOOL COUNSELING SERVICES

A systemic approach to school counseling acknowledges that serving students alone is not enough. To be effective as a change agent and advocate for student success, the school counselor's reach must extend to parents, caregivers, and the school and building community (Todd et al., 2020). The following paragraphs briefly explore the opportunity for intentional outreach and collaboration with the various education stakeholders.

Parents/Caregivers

Students' parents and caregivers serve an important role regarding academic success. Studies show that family involvement significantly impacts the student's educational experience and outcomes (Gaxiola Romero et al., 2022; Henderson et al., 2007; Rickert & Skinner, 2022). Virtual and online school counseling provides unique opportunities to connect with parents in ways that a traditional brick-and-mortar format does not allow. The school building itself may represent pain for some historically marginalized groups and may present as a barrier to parent engagement. Online meetings, office hours, presentations, and resources allow parents to engage with the school in their own comfortable surroundings. For folks with transportation challenges, hectic work schedules, or childcare needs, virtual meetings allow for increased participation as well. The opportunity for recording meetings that can be viewed later or where transcriptions can be translated into other languages is also useful for family engagement. For families with receptive language differences, the opportunity for closed captioning is reported as helpful. Chat rooms allow for emerging bilingual families and those with expressive language differences the opportunity to engage to a greater capacity.

With the onset of mainstream online school counseling services, many counseling departments have created or expanded their online resources. Links to career and college information, mental health awareness and support, and academic success content can be accessible to both parents (as well as students and school staff) who may prefer to explore the topics on their own in lieu of reaching out to the school counselor. Some school counseling teams have also included videos that serve as "mini trainings" or presentations on important topics such as helping your student with organization or study skills, identifying suicidal risk or substance use, and other useful topics that are based on school needs assessment.

While several advantages to virtual school counseling have been identified, it is also important to recognize that this platform does invite challenges as well. Parents may not have a space for private conversations with the school counselor, depending on the home environment. For families who are unhoused, have economic hardships, have limited technical skills, or lack reliable internet access, isolation is inevitable as options outside of email and online meetings are minimal. Home environment privacy is also a concern. Depending on the type and space available in the homes of your students, parents may have little or no privacy due to their student being online. Providing information to students and families as to how to create a virtual background to avoid having the room/space or other individuals in the background while students are learning is important.

Although challenges do exist, the opportunities are noteworthy! Being aware of the potential benefits and challenges can help the school counselor plan accordingly and ensure that they are supporting the families that they serve well.

School Staff, Teachers, and Building Administrators

In addition to serving families, school counselors are called to collaborate with school staff (Atici, 2014). The benefits are many; collaborating provides the school counselor with the opportunity to share the work that they are doing with their students, as well as outcome data, and to demonstrate school counseling intervention efficacy. Collaboration also provides opportunities to create norms related to confidentiality and consultation for classroom teachers, support staff, and building administrators. Since school counselors are not able to see every student on their caseload daily, school staff can serve as important referral sources and help identify students who may need Tier 2 or 3 services (see information related to multiered systems of support [MTSS] for more information).

Opportunities to refer, collaborate, and consult often occur organically—in the hallway between classes, staff lunchroom (reminder, take a lunch, even a short one, as self-care is important, and it often provides the opportunity to connect with staff you don't usually spend time with), or during meeting breaks. When schools are online, these times to connect require additional intentionality. School administrators may need to interpret policies related to online school-counseling services. This is an important opportunity to advocate for services and may require school counselors to lean into their knowledge of building needs, counseling ethics, and best practice recommendations. School counselors may benefit from a new system to encourage teachers and school staff to refer students who have not been logging in, are experiencing academic difficulties, or who they sense may be struggling personally or academically.

Just as school counselors are typically not trained to provide online services during their counseling training program, most administrators, teachers, and support staff are often figuring out their respective professions' new delivery model along the way. It is likely that many are feeling overwhelmed and that they have a reduced bandwidth. As such, adding tasks to their plate is unlikely to be well received. Being creative about ways to lighten their load, while serving students and creating space for connections, may result in a more successful outcome. Volunteering to provide virtual classroom guidance or staff training is a great way to create space for connecting with your colleagues while providing direct and indirect services to support students.

Although purely biased, in our experience, most of the work of a school counselor is exciting, hope producing, and generally a lot of fun. There is, however, a less illustrious side of our role. Due to the nature of our work, we are both legally and ethically mandated to protect students from abuse, neglect, and harm to self or others. This next section addresses the unique considerations of serving as a mandated reporter and providing suicide prevention services in an online environment.

Assessing for Risk Online: A Practical Approach

Mandated Reporting of Child Abuse and Neglect

School counselors, whether online or in person, are mandated reporters (Hodges & McDonald, 2019). It is important to make the distinction that we are not mandated *investigators*, but *reporters*, meaning that if there is a suspicion of child abuse, there is a responsibility to report concerns to the proper authorities. It can be difficult to perceive abuse when the student's camera is off. When meeting with a student in person, a counselor has the benefit of seeing body language and observing injuries firsthand. An online counselor must often rely on written or verbal indications of abuse. A counselor may have a staff member, a student's friend, or the student themselves report the abuse. It is of utmost importance to protect the student. This may mean calling CPS with your concerns so they can investigate further. The school counselor must be aware of their local guidelines for reporting abuse. Many states have specific guidelines related to the timeframe in which a mandated reporter is required to make a report once a suspicion of abuse or neglect occurs. While making the report can feel uncomfortable or intimidating at times, it is important to do so as soon as possible in an attempt to ensure the student's safety to the extent possible. Some school counselors find it helpful to practice making a CPS referral by role-playing a call. Know that the intent of the investigative agencies is to protect students, and that their primary goal, when possible, is to maintain the child in the home or reunify the family as soon as possible.

Suicide Prevention

For legal and ethical reasons, school counselors must help assess students for suicidal ideation (Ellington, 2022). Prior to COVID-19, finding a screening tool intended for online use was difficult, and some virtual school counselors were left scrambling for a screening process. Best practice at the time was to adapt telehealth suicide screeners to fit the needs of an online school. Just as when to assessing risk of suicidality in person, the online school counselor is compelled to ensure the safety of the student until the parents/guardians and/or the appropriate authorities can be notified (Ellington, 2022). Since the student is not physically with the counselor, this means that the counselor needs to know where the student is, if there is anyone with them, and how to reach the student if the call or video is disconnected. The counselor must take swift action to report their concerns to the parents/guardians while maintaining contact with the student, as long as the parent/guardian is not a triggering factor for the suicidal ideation (Ellington, 2022). School counselors providing services virtually benefit from planning and preparation regarding meeting the needs of students who are at risk of suicide.

VOICES FROM THE FIELD

Name: Nicole Dock (she/her)

Where You Practice: Washington

Professional Job Title: School Counselor

Bio: Nicole Dock is a school counselor within Washington state. She received her MSW degree from North Carolina State University and her School Counseling Certification from Seattle Pacific University. She now serves students in grades six to twelve, focusing on students who are neurodiverse or are diagnosed on the autism spectrum disorder and with students with credit retrieval needs.

During the 2020 to 2021 school year, our school counseling department had to rethink the way we delivered services and what a virtual comprehensive school counseling program looked like during the pandemic. We had to quickly shift our program goals to ensure we were meeting the fast-changing needs of our students and community.

Through our schoolwide needs assessment, we knew our students were dealing with a lot of stress, anxiety, depression, and grief, but we did not have the bandwidth to virtually visit every classroom or check in with every student. The need for student support was high, according to the needs assessment data, teacher feedback, and families seeking support for their student. However, students were not reaching out for the support we knew they needed. We held daily drop-in hours and made ourselves accessible through various channels of communication, but we noticed a sharp decline in students seeking our support. As a result, we had to continue reexamining and trying new ways of meeting the needs of our students.

In order to support our students, we knew we had to go to them and meet them where they were. To respond to the changing needs of our students, we turned our classroom guidance lessons into a multimedia program design. This enabled us to quickly deliver schoolwide social and emotional leaning (SEL) content that directly supported our students and staff.

As a counseling team, we reviewed our needs assessment data and selected five topics based on student feedback. Next, we developed a library of virtual videos that covered topics based on students' needs. We created engaging preventative videos that were 7 to 15 minutes each to be shared with students during their advisory period. Topics included stress management (what is stress, how it manifests in our bodies, effective coping strategies, etc.), executive functioning skills (study skills, time management, goal setting, asking for help, etc.), and postsecondary planning. By providing prerecorded content, students were able to engage while staying connected with their classroom community. This was important as we were constantly looking for ways to foster community and peer engagement. In addition, we made it available via a streaming platform that enabled students to engage independently with content outside of the school day.

To be responsive to our students' needs, we attempted holding virtual groups, but we had to change how we thought about and structured groups to be effective to the needs of students while preventing harm. It was important that we created a safe space for students to explore more about the content area they learned during advisory class, but we had to take into consideration students' home environment and the risks involved with engaging online. It was difficult to ensure confidentiality within a virtual environment, inside or outside of school. Students could negatively be impacted as other group members could record or take screenshots and post what had been shared on social media. Moreover, we did not know if students had a private space where they felt safe to share.

In response to this unique challenge and the needs of our students, we set up a psycho-educational group that used an open group design. This allowed new students to join weekly, based on a topic they were interested in learning more about. Students could share personal anecdotes if desired, but the goal of the group was to delve deeper into the guidance lesson. During the group, students were given the opportunity to ask questions, discuss with each other, and learn and practice new skills. It also enabled counselors to connect with students by providing a platform for informal check-ins, which allowed us to reach more of our community.

The classroom guidance lessons delivered that year were not the planned topics we put together at the start of the school year. We had to constantly modify our plans to reflect the revolving needs of our community. It was also a deviation from how we planned on delivering our classroom guidance lessons. However, our commitment to our community allowed us to remain flexible and innovative to meet the needs of our students at a time they needed us the most.

SUMMARY AND CONCLUSION

Whether you have intentionally chosen to work at a virtual academy or online PK–12 school or you've found yourself providing online school counseling services through your work at a traditional brick-and-mortar school, it is important to be savvy regarding the distinctive needs of online communities. This chapter serves as an introduction to online school counseling and provides ideas and guidance as to how to best serve the needs of students and families virtually.

CASE STUDY

You are employed as a middle school counselor at a brick-and-mortar school in a large, urban school district. Your school provides online instruction to a small cohort through a grant that the district received to target historically underserved populations that experience barriers related to school attendance. Although your district does have a dedicated school counselor for this cohort, other district counselors rotate to provide additional assistance. While providing scheduling guidance to a student during your virtual counseling rotation, the student discloses that they are pregnant and that the father is a 24-year-old man who is a family friend.

DISCUSSION QUESTIONS

1. Does this disclosure require mandated reporting?
2. What steps would you take to consider and implement the best course of action?
3. How does serving this student virtually impact your legal and ethical responsibilities?
4. What school counseling services would this student likely benefit from?

PRACTICAL APPLICATION

- Be creative with your approach to serving students, families, and your school community. Providing school counseling services virtually is not always a direct translation from how face-to-face interventions are taught in most school-counseling preparation programs.

- Take time to research games, polling, voting, and activities that can be used online with students during virtual individual and group counseling as well as classroom guidance and trainings.

- Remember that this is a great opportunity to build on your traditional training and services—consider expanding your school's online resources to create a school counseling website with access to hotlines, relevant websites, brief video trainings, and additional tools to support all stakeholders in students success!

- Know that it is possible to develop and sustain a comprehensive school counseling program virtually.

- Acknowledge that there is fatigue associated with a substantial online presence. Be intentional about your self-care. Take breaks from your screen for the benefit of your eyes, mind, body, and spirit.

KEY REFERENCES

Only key references appear in the print edition. The full reference list appears in the digital product on Springer Publishing Connect: connect.springerpub.com/content/book/978-0-8261-8753-6/part/part05/chapter/ch19

ASCA Ethics Committee. (2020, September 1). *School counseling during a pandemic*. https://www.schoolcounselor.org/Magazines/September-October-2020/School-Counseling-During-A-Pandemic

Curtis, H., & Werth, L. (2015). Fostering student success and engagement in a K–12 online school. *Journal of Online Learning Research, 1*(2), 163–190. Association for the Advancement of Computing in Education (AACE). Retrieved September 19, 2022 from https://www.learntechlib.org/primary/p/150962/

Ellington, B. (2022). Warning signs of threats to student safety: Recommendations for virtual school counseling. *Professional School Counseling*. https://doi.org/10.1177/2156759X211067964

Hodges, L. I., & McDonald, K. (2019). An organized approach: Reporting child abuse. *Journal of Professional Counseling: Practice, Theory & Research, 46*(1/2), 14–26. https://doi.org/10.1080/15566382.2019.1673093

Huck, C., & Zhang, J. (2021). Effects of the COVID-19 pandemic on K-12 education: A systematic literature review. *New Waves-Educational Research and Development Journal, 24*(1), 53–84. https://search-ebscohost-com.ezproxy.spu.edu/login.aspx?direct=true&AuthType=ip&db=eric&AN=EJ1308731&site=ehost-live

Litam, S. D. A., & Hipolito-Delgado, C. P. (2021). When being "essential" illuminates disparities: Counseling clients affected by COVID-19. *Journal of Counseling & Development, 99*(1), 3–10. https://doi.org/10.1002/jcad.12349

Ong, P. M. (2020). *COVID-19 and the digital divide in virtual learning, fall 2020*. UCLA Center for Neighborhood Knowledge.

Ratts, M. J., Singh, A. A., Nassar-McMillan, S., Butler, S. K., & McCullough, J. R. (2016). Multicultural and social justice counseling competencies: Guidelines for the counseling profession. *Journal of Multicultural Counseling and Development, 44*(1), 28–48. https://doi.org/10.1002/jmcd.12035

Appendix: School Counseling Resources

MARY AMANDA GRAHAM

CHAPTER 1: SCHOOL COUNSELORS AS ANTIRACIST AND SOCIAL JUSTICE ADVOCATES

Note: There are many resources available to strengthen your work as an anti-racist and social justice advocate in schools. Here are a few recommended by the coeditors of this book.

Websites

American School Counseling Association (ASCA)—The School Counselor and Anti-Racist Practices
https://www.schoolcounselor.org/Standards-Positions/Position-Statements/ASCA
-Position-Statements/The-School-Counselor-and-Anti-Racist-Practices

ASCA—Anti-Racism Resources
https://www.schoolcounselor.org/Publications-Research/Publications/Free-ASCA
-Resources/Anti-Racism-Resources

Therapists of Color Network
https://nqttcn.com/en/

ASCA—Racial Justice Starts at School
https://www.schoolcounselor.org/Magazines/March-April-2021/Racial-Justice
-Starts-at-School

Edutopia—A Guide to Equity and AntiRacism
https://www.edutopia.org/article/guide-equity-and-antiracism-educators

PBS—You Have an Anti-Racist Book List, Now What?
https://www.pbs.org/education/blog/you-have-an-anti-racist-book-list-now-what

Harvard Kennedy School—Racial Justice, Racial Equity and Anti-Racism Reading List
https://www.hks.harvard.edu/faculty-research/library-knowledge-services/
collections/diversity-inclusion-belonging/anti-racist

Webinars

ASCA—Ignite Change for Equity and Inclusion-Create K–12 antibias lesson plans.
https://videos.schoolcounselor.org/ignite-change-for-equity-and-inclusion

Proactive School Counseling: Managing the Aftermath of Major Racial Incidents
https://www.youtube.com/watch?v=b444S0dHr0w

Anti-racism school counseling: A Call to Action Webinar
https://www.youtube.com/watch?v=JEjNaB2L3Vc

Abolitionist Teaching and the Future of our Schools
https://www.youtube.com/watch?v=uJZ3RPJ2rNc

Articles/Books

Delpit, L. (2006). *Other people's children: Cultural conflict in the classroom.* New Press.

Kendi, I. (2019). *How to be an anti-racist.* One World.

Love, B. (2019). *We want to do more than survive: Abolitionist teaching and the pursuit of educational freedom.* Beacon Press.

Morris, M. W. (2016). Pushout: The criminalization of Black girls in schools. The New Press.

CHAPTER 2: STRENGTH-BASED PRACTICE FOR SCHOOL COUNSELORS

Websites

Positive Psychology—Strength Based Activities and Overview
https://positivepsychology.com/strength-based-skills-activities/

Therapist Aid–Strength Based Activities
https://www.therapistaid.com/therapy-guide/strengths-based-therapy

Webinars

Cultivating Growth Mindset
https://www.youtube.com/watch?v=-8eO_kbZ-Bk

Articles/Books

Galassi, J. P., Griffin, D., & Akos, P. (2008). Strength-based school counseling and the ASCA National Model. *Professional School Counseling, 12*(2), 176–181. https://doi.org/10.1177/2156759X0801200207

Greene, R. W. (2008). *Lost at school: Why our kids with behavioral challenges are falling through the cracks and how we can help them.* Scribner.

CHAPTER 3: HISTORY OF THE PROFESSION AND FUTURE TRENDS

Websites

ASCA
https://www.schoolcounselor.org/About-School-Counseling/ASCA-National-Model-for-School-Counseling-Programs

ASCA—App
https://www.schoolcounselor.org/About-School-Counseling/ASCA-National-Model-for-School-Counseling-Programs/ASCA-National-Model-App

Webinars

ASCA 4th Edition Changes
https://videos.schoolcounselor.org/asca-national-model-fourth-edition-changes-assess

Articles/Books

ASCA 4th Edition—Executive Summary
https://www.schoolcounselor.org/getmedia/bd376246-0b4f-413f-b3e0-1b9938f36e68/ANM-executive-summary-4th-ed.pdf

ASCA—Empirical Research Studies Supporting the Value of School Counseling
https://www.schoolcounselor.org/getmedia/7d00dcff-40a6-4316-ab6c-8f3ffd7941c2/Effectiveness.pdf

Articles/Books

ASCA—Brief History of School Counseling
https://www.schoolcounselor.org/getmedia/52aaab9f-39ae-4fd0-8387-1d9c10b9ccb8/History-of-School-Counseling.pdf

CHAPTER 4: THE ASCA NATIONAL MODEL

Websites

ASCA
https://www.schoolcounselor.org/

Articles/Books

ASCA—History of School Counseling,(Gysbers)
https://www.schoolcounselor.org/getmedia/52aaab9f-39ae-4fd0-8387-1d9c10b9ccb8/History-of-School-Counseling.pdf

CHAPTER 5: MINDSETS AND BEHAVIORS FOR STUDENTS AND PROFESSIONAL SCHOOL COUNSELORS

Articles/Books

ASCA—Student Standards: Mindset & Behaviors for Student Success
https://www.schoolcounselor.org/getmedia/7428a787-a452-4abb-afec-d78ec77870cd/Mindsets-Behaviors.pdf

ASCA—Summary of the 2020–21 Revision Process of the ASCA Mindsets & Behaviors Mindset and Behaviors Update 2021
https://www.schoolcounselor.org/getmedia/aaa85b20-de6b-4a7d-8ab0-74ccf9733168/summary-of-changes-21.pdf

Springer—ASCA Mindsets & Behaviors for Student Success
https://connect.springerpub.com/content/book/978-0-8261-3615-2/back-matter/bmatter4#copy_link

CHAPTER 6: FINDING MEANING IN ASCA-IDENTIFIED INAPPROPRIATE DUTIES

Websites

Edutopia—School Administrators Guide to Supporting the Role of School Counselor
https://www.edutopia.org/blog/admin-guide-to-school-counselors-kimberlee-ratliff

Books/Articles

Education Week—7 things you need to know about recess
https://www.edweek.org/leadership/7-things-to-know-about-school-recess/2018/07

GCSCORED—The use of school counselor lunch duty to increase student contact
https://everypiecematters.com/jget/volume02-issue01/the-use-of-school-counselor-lunch-duty-to-increase-student-contact.html

CHAPTER 7: DATA-DRIVEN SERVICES AND SCHOOL COUNSELING EFFICACY ASSESSMENT

Websites

Hatching Results
https://www.hatchingresults.com/

Hatching Results–Data-Driven School Counseling and MTSS
https://www.hatchingresults.com/videos/2020/5/webinar-data-driven-school-counseling-in-a-multi-tiered-system-of-supports-mtss

American School Counseling Association Webinars on Data–Members Only
https://videos.schoolcounselor.org/?s=data

Articles/Books

ASCA—Types of Data to Measure School Counseling Program Success
https://www.schoolcounselor.org/newsletters/october-2018/types-of-data-to
-measure-school-counseling-program

Astramovich, R. L. (2016). Program evaluation interest and skills of school counselors. *Professional School Counseling, 20*, 54–64. https://doi.org/10.5330/1096-2409-20.1.54

Savitz-Romer, M. S., Nicola, T. P., Jensen, A., Hill, N. E., Liang, B., & Perella, J. (2018). Data-driven school counseling: The role of the research–practice partnership. *Professional School Counseling*. https://doi.org/10.1177/2156759X18824269

CHAPTER 8: INDIVIDUAL COUNSELING FOR SCHOOL COUNSELORS

Websites

ASCA—The School Counselor and Mental Health
https://www.schoolcounselor.org/Standards-Positions/Position-Statements/ASCA
-Position-Statements/The-School-Counselor-and-Student-Mental-Health

NAMI—Mental Health by Numbers
https://www.nami.org/mhstats

NAMI—Mental Health Kids, Teens, and- Young Adults
https://www.nami.org/Your-Journey/Kids-Teens-and-Young-Adults/Kids

Webinars

Play Therapy
https://podcasts.apple.com/us/podcast/play-therapy-community/
id1072002470?mt=2\

Using Art in Play Therapy
https://www.playtherapypodcast.org/podcast/7-art

Teens Talk to Teens About Therapy
https://podcasts.apple.com/us/podcast/teenager-therapy/id1437039510

Articles/Books:
Counseling Today—Solution Focused School Counseling in a Pandemic
https://ct.counseling.org/2020/09/solution-focused-tools-to-help-school-counselors
-in-a-pandemic/

CHAPTER 9: GROUP COUNSELING FOR SCHOOL COUNSELORS

Websites

ASCA—The School Counselor and Group Counseling
https://www.schoolcounselor.org/Standards-Positions/Position-Statements/ASCA
-Position-Statements/The-School-Counselor-and-Group-Counseling

Webinars

American School Counseling Association—Members Only
https://videos.schoolcounselor.org/?s=group

Articles/Books

ASCA—Dealing with Deployment Group
https://www.schoolcounselor.org/getmedia/b1347a4d-fcfd-4c93-b7c6-38c1548ecc69/
Dealing-with-Deployment.pdf

CHAPTER 10: CLASSROOM GUIDANCE FOR SCHOOL COUNSELORS

Websites

UMass Amherst
https://www.cscoreumass.org/sc-resources

Classroom Guidance
https://counselors.collegeboard.org/professional-learning/webinars

Nearpod—Interactive Programs for Guidance
https://nearpod.com/

Kahoot—Interactive Programs for Guidance
Kahoot.com

ASCA—Lesson Plan Template
https://www.schoolcounselor.org/About-School-Counseling/
ASCA-National-Model-for-School-Counseling-Programs/Templates-Resources

Elementary Guidance Lesson
https://www.leaderinme.org/family-resources/#section5

Webinars

Counselor Keri-SEL Videos
https://www.youtube.com/channel/UCjr80SolNTdhIFEYauXcKqg/videos

Articles/Books

Dack, H., & Merlin-Knoblich, C. (2019). Improving classroom guidance curriculum with understanding by design. *The Professional Counselor, 9*(2), 80–99. https://doi.org/10.15241/hd.9.2.80

Runyan, H., Grothaus, T., & Michel, R. E. (2018). Classroom management competencies for school counselors: A delphi study. *Professional School Counseling.* 2018. https://doi.org/10.1177/2156759X19834293

CHAPTER 11: CRISIS INTERVENTION FOR SCHOOL COUNSELORS

Websites

ASCA—The School Counselor and Safe Schools and Crisis Response Position Statement
https://www.schoolcounselor.org/Standards-Positions/Position-Statements/
ASCA-Position-Statements/The-School-Counselor-and-Safe-Schools-and-Crisis-R

ASCA—The School Counselor and Trauma-Informed Practice, Position Statement
https://www.schoolcounselor.org/Standards-Positions/Position-Statements/
ASCA-Position-Statements/The-School-Counselor-and-Trauma-Informed-Practice

ASCA—The School Counselor and Prevention of Drug-Related School Violence, Position Statement
https://www.schoolcounselor.org/Standards-Positions/Position-Statements/
ASCA-Position-Statements/The-School-Counselor-and-Prevention-of-School-Rela

Crisis Prevention Institute—Trauma-Informed Care For Educators, Free Resource
https://institute.crisisprevention.com/EDTraumaInformedCare.html?src=PPC&utm_
source=google&utm_medium=cpc&utm_campaign=bts-2021&utm_content=tofu_ed_
search&gclid=EAIaIQobChMI7fbVk6zV9gIVqxatBh3KrgJZEAMYASAAEgJYSPD_BwE

Articles/Books

Liou, Y. H. (2015). School crisis management: A model of dynamic responsiveness to crisis life cycle. *Educational Administration Quarterly, 51*(2), 247–289. https://doi.org/10.1177/0013161X14532467

Lowe, S. R., & Galea, S. (2015). The mental health consequences of mass shootings. *Trauma, Violence, & Abuse, 18*(1), 62–82. https://doi.org/10.1177/1524838015591572

Webinars

ASCA—Crisis and Trauma, Free Webinars
https://www.schoolcounselor.org/Publications-Research/Publications/Free-ASCA
-Resources/Crisis-Trauma-Resources

CHAPTER 12: ADVOCACY FOR SAFER SCHOOLS FOR LGBTQIA+ STUDENTS

Websites

APA—Toolbox to Promote Healthy LGBTQ Youth
https://www.apa.org/pi/lgbt/programs/safe-supportive/training/toolbox

ASCA—The School Counselor and LGBTQ Youth Position Statement
https://www.schoolcounselor.org/Standards-Positions/Position-Statements/ASCA
-Position-Statements/The-School-Counselor-and-LGBTQ-Youth

Gender Sexuality Alliance Resources
https://gsanetwork.org/

Oregon Safe Schools and Communities Coalition
https://www.oregonsafeschools.org/gsa-support

Trevor Project
https://www.thetrevorproject.org/

Affirmative Couch
https://affirmativecouch.com/

Gender Spectrum
https://genderspectrum.org/

Lambda Legal
https://www.lambdalegal.org/

Article/Books

Virtual GSAs in Action: Digital Organizing Toolkit
https://gsanetwork.org/wp-content/uploads/2020/10/GSA-Virtual-Toolkit-2020.pdf

Counseling Today—Promoting LGBTQ Students Well-Being in Schools
https://ct.counseling.org/2018/10/promoting-lgbtq-students-well-being-in-schools/

Human Rights Campaign-Suggestions From an LGBTQ Young Person: How School Counselors Can Support LGBTQ Youth.
https://www.hrc.org/news/how-school-counselors-can-support-lgbtq-youth

Human Rights Campaign—Active Listening and Allyship: How School Counselors Can Uplift Their LGBTQ Students
https://www.hrc.org/news/active-listening-allyship-how-school-counselors-can-uplift-their-lgbtq-students

Webinars

GLEN—Source for supporting LGBTQ students in schools
https://www.glsen.org/resources/webinars-and-workshops

CHAPTER 13: ENGAGING STUDENTS WITH INDIVIDUALIZED EDUCATION PROGRAMS (IEPs) AND 504s

Websites

ASCA—The School Counselor and Students with Disabilities Position Statement
https://schoolcounselor.org/Standards-Positions/Position-Statements/ASCA-Position-Statements/The-School-Counselor-and-Students-with-Disabilitie

Webinars

Education Week: Special Education and Support
https://www.edweek.org/events/webinars-on-special-education

Articles/Books

Barrow, J., & Mamlin, N. (2016). Collaboration between professional school counselors and special education teachers. *Ideas and research you can use: Vistas*. https://www.counseling.org/knowledge-center/vistas

Goodman-Scott, E. C., Bobzien, J., & Milsom, A. (2018). Preparing preservice school counselors to serve students with disabilities: A case study. *Professional School Counseling, 22.* https://doi.org/10.1177/2156759X19867338

CHAPTER 14: HOME IMPACT ON STUDENTS

Websites

ASCA—Working with students experiencing issues surrounding undocumented status position statement
https://schoolcounselor.org/Standards-Positions/Position-Statements/ASCA-Position-Statements/The-School-Counselor-and-Working-with-Students-Exp

SAMHSA—Alcohol and drug addiction happens in the best of families
https://store.samhsa.gov/sites/default/files/SAMHSA_Digital_Download/phd1112.pdf

SAMSHA—It is not your fault
https://nacoa.org/wp-content/uploads/2018/04/Its-Not-Your-Fault-NACoA.pdf

Articles

Vista—School counselors working with undocumented students
https://www.counseling.org/docs/default-source/vistas/article_4383fd25f1611
6603abcacff0000bee5e7.pdf?sfvrsn=4#:~:text=School%20counselors%20are%20
critical%20in,undocumented%20immigrant%20families%20and%20children

Cole, R. F. (2016). Supporting students in military families during times of transition: A call for awareness and action. *School Counseling, 20*(1), 36–43.
https://www.jstor.org/stable/90014833

ASCA—Imprisoned parents, challenge children
https://www.ascaschoolcounselor-digital.org/ascaschoolcounselor/january_
february_2018/MobilePagedArticle.action?articleId=1329904#articleId1329904

CHAPTER 15: MANDATORY REPORTING: RECOGNIZING ABUSE AND NEGLECT

Websites

ASCA—The School Counselor and Child Abuse and Neglect Position Statements
https://www.schoolcounselor.org/Standards-Positions/Position-Statements/
ASCA-Position-Statements/The-School-Counselor-and-Child-Abuse-and-Neglect
-P#:~:text=School%20counselors%20are%20among%20those,detection%20and%20
recognition%20of%20abuse

Articles/Books

Kenny, M., Abreu, R., Helpingstine, C., Lopez, A., & Mathews, B. (2018). Counselors' mandated responsibility to report child maltreatment: A review of U.S. laws. *Journal of Counseling & Development, 96*(4), 372–387. https://doi.org/10.1002/jcad.12220

Tuttle, M., Ricks, L., & Taylor, M. (2019). A child abuse reporting framework for early career school counselors. *The Professional Counselor, 9*(3), 238–251. https://doi.org/10.15241/mt.9.3.238

CHAPTER 16: SCHOOL COUNSELORS AND COMMUNITY AND FAMILY ENGAGEMENT

Websites

ASCA—School-Family-Community Partnership Position Statement
https://schoolcounselor.org/Standards-Positions/Position-Statements/
ASCA-Position-Statements/The-School-Counselor-and-School-Family-Community-P

Youth.Gov—System Level: Engaging Families as Partners in System Improvement
https://youth.gov/youth-topics/system-level-engaging-families-partners-system
-improvement

Webinars

ASCA—Maximizing School-Family-Community Partnerships
https://videos.schoolcounselor.org/maximize-your-impact-through-school-family
-community-partnerships

Articles/Books

Biag, M., & Castrechini, S. (2016). Strategies to help the whole child: Examining the contributions of full-service community schools. *Journal of Education for Students Placed at Risk, 21*(3), 157–173. https://doi.org/10.1080/10824669.2016.1172231

CHAPTER 17: SCHOOL COUNSELING: COLLABORATING WITH SCHOOL STAFF

Articles/Books

Jess Lewis—Choose Love Movement
https://chooselovemovement.org/wp-content/uploads/2020/04/Teacher
-Counselor-Collaboration.pdf

Edutopia—5 Ways to Partner With Your School Counselor
https://www.edutopia.org/blog/5-ways-partner-your-school-counselor-common-core-
anne-obrien

Webinars

ASCA—Members Only
https://videos.schoolcounselor.org/?s=school+collaboration

CHAPTER 18: BUILDING A COMPREHENSIVE SCHOOL COUNSELING PROGRAM (CSCP)

Website

ASCA—The School Counselor and School Counseling Programs
https://schoolcounselor.org/Standards-Positions/Position-Statements/ASCA
-Position-Statements/The-School-Counselor-and-School-Counseling-Program

Article/Book

VISTA—An Overview of Comprehensive School Counseling Program Assessment
Instruments to Inform Future Research
https://www.counseling.org/docs/default-source/vistas/article_65915a22f1611
6603abcacff0000bee5e7.pdf?sfvrsn=f4c422c_4

CHAPTER 19: ONLINE COUNSELING SERVICE DELIVERY FOR SCHOOL COUNSELORS

Webinars

Southern Regional Education Board: School Counseling at a Distance
https://www.sreb.org/webinar/webinar-follow-school-counseling-distance

ASCA—School Counseling in an Online World
https://videos.schoolcounselor.org/school-counseling-in-an-online-world

Index